D1616960

Outside the Law

THE JOHNS HOPKINS SERIES IN CONSTITUTIONAL THOUGHT

Sanford Levinson and Jeffrey K. Tulis, *Series Editors*

Outside the Law

Emergency and Executive Power

Clement Fatovic

The Johns Hopkins University Press

Baltimore

© 2009 The Johns Hopkins University Press
All rights reserved. Published 2009
Printed in the United States of America on acid-free paper
9 8 7 6 5 4 3 2 1

The Johns Hopkins University Press
2715 North Charles Street
Baltimore, Maryland 21218-4363
www.press.jhu.edu

Library of Congress Cataloging-in-Publication Data

Fatovic, Clement, 1973–
Outside the law : emergency and executive power / Clement Fatovic.
  p.   cm.—(The Johns Hopkins series in constitutional thought)
Includes bibliographical references and index.
ISBN-13: 978-0-8018-9362-9 (hardcover : alk. paper)
ISBN-10: 0-8018-9362-3 (hardcover : alk. paper)
1. War and emergency powers—United States—History.
2. Constitutional history—United States.   3. Political science—United
States—History.   4. United States—History—Constitutional period,
1789–1809.   I. Title.
JK339.F37 2009
352.23′501—dc22   2008055996

A catalog record for this book is available from the British Library.

*Special discounts are available for bulk purchases of this book. For more
information, please contact Special Sales at 410-516-6936 or specialsales@press
.jhu.edu.*

The Johns Hopkins University Press uses environmentally friendly book
materials, including recycled text paper that is composed of at least 30
percent post-consumer waste, whenever possible. All of our book papers are
acid-free, and our jackets and covers are printed on paper with recycled
content.

Contents

Acknowledgments

This book deals with the disruptive and destructive contingencies that roil politics, but it is itself the product of very favorable contingencies. I had the good fortune to begin working on this project in the Government Department at Cornell University, which provided an intellectual environment that fostered interesting, adventurous, and even idiosyncratic work. The examples set there by those with whom I worked and studied created the conditions that made this book possible.

My first and most important debt is to those who encouraged me to write on a dissertation topic that seemed somewhat esoteric and happily irrelevant at the time. Isaac Kramnick taught me much of what I know about political philosophy and kindled my interest in American political thought. His encyclopedic knowledge and sage advice have rescued me from more errors than I would care to admit. Nancy Hirschmann was always a model of clarity and rigor. Her trenchant but eye-opening critiques encouraged me to sharpen and refine what were all-too-often inchoate ideas. Jeremy Rabkin and I spent countless hours discussing this project in our frequent strolls around campus. He always pushed me to think through my arguments and never let me get away with hackneyed or banal points. Ted Lowi exerted a powerful influence on my work and was gracious enough to review the entire project. I was also fortunate to receive generous financial and institutional support at Cornell University from the Sage Foundation, the Olin Foundation, and the Mellon Foundation.

I would also like to acknowledge all of the friends, colleagues, and former students who discussed these ideas and helped me develop them over the years: Rique Alonso, Jeremy Bailey, Ross Corbett, Craig Ewasiuk, Kate Gordy, Ken Kersch, Ben Kleinerman, Gil Osorio, Kim Scheppele, and Daniel Schwarz. Len Kern also deserves thanks for his resourceful and timely research assistance and for the conversations we have had about this and related subjects. My colleagues in the Department of Politics and International Relations at Florida International University provided unstinting support, encouragement, and advice—especially when I was tempted to keep tinkering with this project. In particular, I would like to thank Ron Cox, Brian Nelson, Rich Olson, Nicol Rae, Becky Salokar, John Stack, and Judith Stiehm. A summer research grant from Florida International University enabled me to begin the process of revising the manuscript in earnest.

Several individuals deserve special thanks for their invaluable feedback. Jeff Tulis and Sandy Levinson read the entire manuscript with care and offered many suggestions that greatly improved the overall argument and helped me to clarify several key points. Craig Ewasiuk read parts of the manuscript with his usual acumen and made valuable substantive and stylistic suggestions that I eagerly incorporated. Nathan Tarcov and Chris Way each provided detailed and insightful comments on the chapter on Locke. Ken Kersch kindly commented on the whole manuscript with his characteristic intelligence, perspicacity, and wit. Beginning with Henry Tom, who showed great faith and patience in this book, the entire editorial staff at the Johns Hopkins University Press provided expert assistance. Martin Schneider was a diligent copyeditor whose suggestions often went beyond matters of style and syntax.

The deepest gratitude goes to my family. My brother Anthony indulged my occasional need for distractions and provided constant moral support. My parents, Jerolim and Milka, have always been there for me and encouraged all of my endeavors. This book is dedicated to them with love.

Outside the Law

Introduction

Order is essential to the very idea of law. The aim of law is to create order where it does not exist and to stabilize it where it does exist. Law pursues many other, sometimes conflicting, aims—justice, equality, the protection of individual rights, the expression of communal values, the preservation (or transformation) of the status quo, the consolidation (or dispersion) of power—but no other aim is as basic as order. The specific kind of order that law produces or preserves is defined largely by its substantive aims, but the establishment of order as such is independent of any particular set of substantive aims. The law accomplishes this aim primarily by specifying rules that minimize the variability and arbitrariness associated with discretionary action, both inside and outside government.

But the problem for any legal order is that law aims at fixity in a world beset by flux. The greatest challenge to legally established order comes not from the resistance of particular groups or individuals who object to any of its substantive aims but from the unruliness of the world itself. The stability, predictability, and regularity sought by law eventually runs up against the unavoidable instability, unpredictability, and irregularity of the world. Events constantly threaten to disrupt and destabilize the artificial order established by law. Emergencies—sudden and extreme occurrences such as the devastating terrorist attacks of September 11, an overwhelming natural disaster like Hurricane Katrina, a pandemic outbreak of avian flu, a catastrophic economic collapse, or a severe food shortage, to name just a few—dramatize the limitations of the law in dealing with unexpected and incalculable contingencies. Designed for the ordinary and the normal, law cannot always provide for such extraordinary occurrences in spite of its aspiration to comprehensiveness. When such events arise, the responsibility for formulating a response usually falls to the executive.

The executive has a unique relationship to the law and the order that it seeks, especially in a liberal constitutional system committed to the rule of law. Not only is the executive the authority most directly responsible for enforcing the law and maintaining order in ordinary circumstances, it is also the authority most immediately responsible for restoring order in extraordinary circumstances. But while the executive is expected to uphold and follow the law in normal times, emergencies sometimes compel the executive to exceed the strict letter of the law. Given the unique and irrepressible nature of emergencies, the law often provides little effective guidance, leaving executives to their own devices. Executives possess special resources and characteristics that enable them to formulate responses more rapidly, flexibly, and decisively than can legislatures, courts, and bureaucracies. Even where the law seeks to anticipate and provide for emergencies by specifying the kinds of actions that public officials are permitted or required to take, emergencies create unique opportunities for the executive to exercise an extraordinary degree of discretion. And when the law seems to be inadequate to the situation at hand, executives often claim that it necessary to go beyond its dictates by consolidating those powers ordinarily exercised by other branches of government or even by expanding the range of powers ordinarily permitted. But in seeking to bring order to the chaos that emergencies instigate, executives who take such action also bring attention to the deficiencies of the law in maintaining order, often with serious consequences for the rule of law.

The kind of extralegal action that executives are frequently called upon to take in response to emergencies is deeply problematic for liberal constitutionalism, which gives pride of place to the rule of law, both in its self-definition and in its standard mode of operation. If emergencies test the limits of those general and prospective rules that are designed to make governmental action limited and predictable, that is because emergencies are largely unpredictable and potentially limitless.[1] Yet the rule of law, which has enjoyed a distinguished position in constitutional thought going back to Aristotle, has always sought to place limits on what government may do by substituting the arbitrariness and unpredictability of extemporary decrees with the impartiality and regularity of impersonal rules promulgated in advance. The protection of individual freedom within liberal constitutionalism has come to be unimaginable where government does not operate according to general and determinate rules.[2] The rule of law has achieved primacy within liberal constitutionalism because it is considered vital to the protection of individual freedom. As Max Weber famously explained of the modern bureaucratic state, legitimacy in the liberal state is not based on habitual obedience to traditions or customs sanctified by time or on personal devotion to a charismatic individual endowed with superhuman gifts but on belief in the legality of a state that is functionally competent in administering highly impersonal but "rational rules."[3] In fact, its entire history and aim can be summed up as an attempt to curtail the kind of discretionary action associated with the arbitrary "rule of men"—by making government itself subject to the law.

The apparent primacy of law in liberal constitutionalism has led some critics to question its capacity to deal with emergencies. Foremost among these critics is German political and constitutional theorist Carl Schmitt, who concluded that liberalism is incapable of dealing with the "exception" or "a case of extreme peril" that poses "a danger to the existence of the state" without resorting to measures that contradict and undermine its commitments to the rule of law, the separation of powers, the preservation of civil liberties, and other core values.[4] In Schmitt's view, liberalism is wedded to a "normativistic" approach that seeks to regulate life according to strictly codified legal and moral rules that not only obscure the "decisionistic" basis of all law but also deny the role of personal decision-making in the interpretation, enforcement, and application of law.[5] Because legitimacy in a liberal constitutional order is based largely on adherence to formal legal procedures that restrict the kinds of actions governments are permitted to take, actions that have not been specified or authorized in advance are simply ruled out. According to Schmitt, the liberal demand that governmental action always be controllable is based on the naive belief that the world is thoroughly calculable.[6] If it expects regularity and predictability in government, it is because it understands the world in those terms, making it oblivious to the problems of contingency. Not only does this belief that the world is subject to a rational and predictable order make it difficult for liberalism to justify actions that stand outside that order, it also makes it difficult for liberalism even to acknowledge emergencies when they do arise. But Schmitt's critique goes even further than this. When liberal constitutionalism does acknowledge the exception, its commitment to the rule of law forces it to choose between potential suicide if it adheres strictly to its legalistic ideals and undeniable hypocrisy if ignores those ideals.[7] Either way, the argument goes, emergencies expose the inherent shortcomings and weaknesses of liberalism.

It is undeniable that the rule of law occupies a privileged position within liberal constitutionalism, but it is a mistake to identify liberal constitutionalism with an excessively legalistic orientation that renders it incapable of dealing effectively with emergencies. Schmitt is correct in pointing out that liberal normativism seeks to render government action as impersonal and predictable as possible in normal circumstances, but the history of liberal constitutional thought leading up to the American Founding reveals that its main proponents recognized the need to supplement the rule of law with a personal element in cases of emergency. The political writings of John Locke, David Hume, William Blackstone, and those Founders who advocated a strong presidency indicate that many early liberal constitutionalists were highly attuned to the limitations of law in dealing with events that disrupt the regular order. They were well aware that rigid adherence to the formalities of law, both in responding to emergencies and in constraining the official who formulates the response, could undermine important substantive aims and values, thereby sacrificing the ends for the means.

Their reflections on the chronic instability and irregularity of politics reveal an appreciation for the inescapable—albeit temporary—need for the sort of discretionary action that the law ordinarily seeks to circumscribe. As Locke explained in his classic formulation, that "it is impossible to foresee, and so by laws to provide for, all Accidents and Necessities, that may concern the publick" means that the formal powers of the executive specified in law must be supplemented with "prerogative," the "Power to act according to discretion, for the publick good, without the prescription of the Law, and sometimes even against it."[8] Unlike the powers of the Hobbesian sovereign, which are effectively absolute and unlimited, the exercise of prerogative is, in principle, limited in scope and duration to cases of emergency. The power to act outside and even against the law does not mean that the executive is "above the law"—

morally or politically unaccountable—but it does mean that *executive power is ultimately irreducible to law.*

The problem that early liberals from Locke to Hamilton set out to resolve was to find a way to prevent abuses of executive power in those instances in which the laws do not fully apply. There was an understanding that emergencies have the potential to create such great disruptions in the legal order that it might not be possible or desirable to subject the executive to those rules that are designed to serve as checks in ordinary circumstances. The limitations of the law made it necessary to look beyond the law for the preservation of those values that law is designed to serve within liberalism: predictability, security, and, above all, liberty. As Locke famously argued in his *Second Treatise of Government,* the possibility of "ex post control" in the form of an armed uprising against a tyrannical executive was always an option for the people, but the costs of exercising this mechanism of control after a crisis has passed are often too high and too uncertain, so it was necessary to discover "interim controls" that would keep the executive in check during the emergency itself.[9] Their understanding that emergencies have the potential to unsettle temporarily the entire system of institutional and procedural checks and balances led them to contemplate an entirely different set of mechanisms to keep the executive in check.

When everything else is uncertain and unreliable, liberals such as Locke, Blackstone, Hume, Madison, and Hamilton looked to the personal character of the executive as a stable and dependable source of certainty and reliability against the abuse of power. In the battle to preserve liberty, the virtue of the executive was the shield that would offer protection against the sword of prerogative.

As the rest of this book demonstrates, early liberal constitutionalists believed that executives who embody certain public virtues could safely be trusted with extraordinary, even extralegal, powers in situations in which events outstrip the capacity of law to keep the executive or anyone else in check. Evidence of genuine virtue was thought to provide a reasonable sense of certainty and security that the executive could exercise extraordinary powers in an emergency without abusing them for private interest or undermining the foundations of a free state. The character of the executive would thus supplement those institutional devices that ordinarily serve as checks on executive power in liberal constitutionalism. Virtue in the executive could compensate for some of the deficiencies in the rule of law by serving as an internalized check that keeps the executive from violating fundamental moral norms and principles even when it is necessary to violate important legal and institutional norms. Far from being opposed to one another, character and constitutionalism were closely linked in the political writings of many eighteenth-century liberals, who believed that the formal strictures of the rule of law were insufficient to prevent executive power from mutating into tyranny in times of emergency.[10]

There is now a general tendency on the part of courts and legislatures in the United States and elsewhere to show enormous deference to the executive in cases where an emergency has been declared, but early liberals such as Locke and Madison did not believe that all executives were equally entitled to the same degree of deference.[11] There was a fear, grounded in both theory and experience, that explicit grants of formal power open it up to corruption and abuse by executives who lack virtue. Only those executives with reputations for public virtue could be trusted to exercise emergency powers in a manner consistent with the aims of a free government. There were certain inherent powers that all executives would enjoy, but those executives with a reputation for public virtue would enjoy additional leeway to act beyond and even against the strict letter of the law in cases of emergency. The fixity of character was expected to provide some measure of confidence that a virtuous executive would not exploit the opportunities to abuse power during an emergency, when the ordinary system of legal and institutional checks and balances tends to get destabilized. Virtue in the executive was expected to mitigate the inherent dangers of discretionary action irreducible to law by providing a degree of predictability and reliability to a situation otherwise fraught with uncertainty and risk. Ideally, the virtue of the executive would serve as a calm island of stability, safeguarding the liberty of the people in the middle of a violent tempest that threatens to overpower and destroy the established order.

These ideas are still relevant today, not only because these writers had a profound impact on early American understandings of executive power and its role in the constitutional order, but also because questions concerning presidential character and emergency powers have become so much more important since September 11, 2001. In many respects, concerns about the character and emergency powers of the executive became deeply intertwined during the so-called war on terror. Unprecedented assertions of executive power by President George W. Bush and others in his administration prompted searing questions about the personal and political motives of the president.[12] From allegations that President Bush valued and demanded personal loyalty above professional competence when it came to hiring, firing, and promoting officials to reports that sensitive information had been classified and declassified for partisan and electoral advantage; from accusations that government contracts had been awarded in a partisan and self-interested manner to stories that nepotism and favoritism had been behind the distribution of federal aid and emergency relief in the aftermath of Hurricane Katrina; from intellectually serious criticisms that the escalating use of presidential signing statements and other controversial assertions of executive power were based on a theory of the unitary executive that conflicts with constitutional norms to wild psycho-dramatic speculation about the president's Oedipal motivations in starting the war in Iraq, there was a growing sense that, to put it mildly, the virtues of the executive play a significant role in determining exactly how the president exercises certain powers—even as all parties debate whether the public and the other branches of government ought to allow it.[13]

The link between character and executive powers is also implicit in the campaign rhetoric of recent presidential elections. The facile charge that a presidential candidate "flip-flops" on the issues is often made to suggest that the candidate is an opportunistic and untrustworthy office-seeker driven by crass electoral ambitions rather than a selfless concern for the best interests of the country. The prominence of patriotism as a central theme of the 2008 presidential election campaign was a sign of heightened sensitivity to the relationship between character and power. While questions about the patriotism of Democratic presidential candidate Barack Obama were ignited by internet rumors that the Illinois senator's background and faith might inhibit his ability to pursue the best interests of the nation, Republican nominee John McCain used his record as a war hero and his reputation as a straight-talking maverick to bolster confidence that he would continue to place the public good before more parochial concerns. McCain made repeated references to a lifelong career of public service not only to highlight his extensive political experience but also to spotlight his virtue in an effort to convince voters that he "will always, always put our country first . . . before any personal or partisan interest."[14]

Contemporary understandings of the link between presidential character and executive power do not always correspond to the understandings of seventeenth- and eighteenth-century liberals, but they do suggest that there is a need to revisit received notions about the role of personality in defining the scope and limits of power in liberal constitutionalism. Ever since the publication of Richard Neustadt's enormously influential *Presidential Power* in 1960, presidential scholars have debated the interplay between those formal institutional powers derived from constitutional authority and statutory delegations, on the one hand, and those informal powers resting on the president's rhetorical skills, popular mandate, and psychological traits, on the other.[15] According to Kenneth Mayer, the main divide among presidential scholars prior to September 11 separated those who believed that a legal or institutional approach best explained the scope and limitations of presidential power, and those who argued that a behavioral approach that looked to the personal qualities of the president, among other things, offered the best explanation for what a president could and could not do.[16] But with the exception of some historians and (not surprisingly) many biographers, presidential scholars have generally downplayed the role of individual personality and focused instead on the structural, institutional, and historical forces beyond the control of hapless presidents.[17] The studies of presidential character that have been produced tend to diverge greatly. As Jeffrey Tulis observes, "The range of issues that have been conflated into the concept of 'character'" in presidential studies has made it difficult to figure out which qualities voters should look for in their presidents.[18]

This book contributes to the debate on the sources and scope of presidential power by examining the role that early liberal constitutionalists expected public virtue to play in justifying extraordinary and even extralegal action in emergencies. What the writings of liberals from Locke to the American Founders suggest is that the powers of the executive should vary according to the character of the person exercising that authority. Contrary to the lament that the institutional "machinery" of constitutional democracy leaves little scope for transformative leadership in the world today, their writings serve as a sobering reminder that the opportunities for extraordinary action—good and bad—are everpresent.[19]

Perhaps even more important, the link between virtue and emergency powers suggests that it may be necessary to reassess the role of legal rules and formal institutions in liberal constitutionalism. There is an overwhelming tendency on the part of academics, politicians, judges, and the lay public to equate constitutionalism with the judicial opinions compiled in casebooks. Whenever a constitutional question about presidential power—or anything else, for that matter—arises, the first instinct of nearly everyone, regardless of the position taken, is to seek a definitive judicial resolution that bypasses the elective branches of government.[20] In many respects, this reflects an implicit belief in a supposed distinction between the uncomfortable uncertainties of politics and the reassuring determinacy of law that was not necessarily shared by early liberals.

This open-ended conception of constitutionalism clashes with the views of those who believe that the U.S. Constitution imposes strict legal constraints that limit the president to the exercise of expressly enumerated powers as well as those who believe that it grants the president far-reaching powers inherent in the very idea of executive power. In addition to supporting statutory limitations on the president's powers to deploy military forces, enter international agreements, control the bureaucracy, and respond to emergencies, many critics, often following the framework developed by Justice Robert Jackson in his famous concurrence in the Steel Seizure Case, contend that the Constitution already restricts the ability of the president to take certain actions without the approval of Congress.[21] However, the common impulse to identify American constitutionalism with the juridical limits on power enshrined in the Bill of Rights tends to obscure the extent to which the framers of the Constitution deliberately designed a flexible instrument of government that enables the exercise of discretionary powers irreducible to law—though never above the law. Nowhere is this more evident than in the vesting clause of Article II of the Constitution, which stipulates that "the executive Power shall be vested in a President of the United States of America" but never specifies the precise meaning of "executive Power." This and other examples of indeterminacy and open-endedness create numerous opportunities for the misuse and abuse of power, but they also reflect an awareness that more careful definitions and detailed specifications of power could leave the government incapable of dealing with unforeseeable contingencies.

The views of those who advocate an expansive conception of executive power tend to be just as formalistic and dogmatic in asserting that the "executive Power" vested in the president has a precise and unambiguous meaning in a system based on the separation of powers. Proponents of the "unitary theory of the executive" also seek a kind of legal closure that would curtail political debates about the limits of presidential power.[22] Their contention that Article II gives the president exclusive control over the executive branch ignores the extent to which the functional powers of government are shared among the three branches. What is often forgotten or ignored is that the only explicit constitutional grant of emergency power to the president involves Congress as well. It states that the president "may, on extraordinary Occasions, convene both Houses, or either of them." But in seeking to prevent encroachments on the powers of the presidency, the "unitary theory of the executive" frequently relies on a highly formalistic interpretation of the separation of powers that ends up weakening the powers of Congress and the judiciary and foreclosing public deliberation on appropriate responses to crises.[23] As Jack Goldsmith has argued, an excessively legalistic insistence that the president already possesses as a matter of constitutional right all the powers necessary to deal with a threat like terrorism can provoke a backlash that ultimately impairs the ability of government to deal with emergencies.[24]

The indeterminacy of the U.S. Constitution has been a source of great controversy and consternation, but that indeterminacy was a deliberate feature of liberal constitutionalism in the seventeenth and eighteenth centuries. As this book aims to demonstrate, this is because the problem of contingency was never far from the minds of those who developed the Anglo-American tradition of liberal constitutionalism. Their goal was to design a system of government that would be safe and effective both during periods of normalcy and in moments of crisis. Toward that end they looked beyond those devices and practices typically associated with the rule of law to the character of the executive.

The following chapters examine these ideas on the emergency powers of the executive in the writings of Locke, Hume, Blackstone, and those involved in the struggle over ratification of the U.S. Constitution. Though there are undeniable and even significant differences among these writers, their discussions of executive power have two things in common. One is an openness to exercises of extralegal prerogative in cases of emergency. The other is a belief in the continuing need for virtue in the executive to inhibit abuses of prerogative. Both ideas rest on an acknowledgment that contingency is the inescapable condition of politics. Before exploring these conceptions of executive power in detail, it is first necessary to consider their understandings of contingency. To do that, the following discussion will begin with what is perhaps the most provocative presentation of the problem of contingency, which appears in the writings of Machiavelli.

CHAPTER ONE

"So Many Unexpected Things"

Contingency and Character in Modern Political Thought

> If how human affairs proceed is considered well, it will be seen that often things arise and accidents come about that the heavens have not altogether wished to be provided against.   NICCOLÒ MACHIAVELLI

Machiavelli and the Problem of Contingency

Niccolò Machiavelli's insight that contingency is the single constant in politics forms the backdrop for any serious investigation of executive power in modern political and constitutional thought—if not for the study of politics as such. Any theory that supports energy and flexibility in the executive must take as its starting point a Machiavellian understanding of how easily and suddenly unexpected occurrences can interrupt established routines. The Florentine's provocative contention that *fortuna* "is the arbiter of half of our actions" suggests that even the best-laid plans and most scrupulously designed institutions will occasionally experience serious and unsettling disruptions.[1] Variously identified with the destructive force of a raging river, the supposed fickleness of women, the good luck of providential success, an unfortunate turn of events, and a momentary condition that could change in an instant, the elusive concept of *fortuna* is used to refer generally to the unsettling haphazardness of politics. The major implication of this idea is that humans can never fully control or permanently master events because unforeseen and uncontainable accidents are bound to arise. Machiavelli's frequent use of the term *accidenti* in his *Discourses on Livy* to refer to various irregular (if not unpredictable) occurrences that threaten to destabilize the political order accentuates his preoccupation with the problem of contingency.[2] If there is a single idea that Machiavelli stressed in his two most important political works, it is the idea that "often things arise and accidents come about that the heavens have not altogether wished to be provided against."[3] This applies to domestic no less than to foreign affairs—if it is even possible to maintain such clear-cut distinctions in an environment where change can come so rapidly and unexpectedly.

The inescapable fact that nothing is permanent, that no order is completely stable, that no condition is ever fixed for long, means that extraordinary acts of intervention will always be necessary to try to set things right, if only for the moment. Machiavelli's understanding of politics as a realm of arbitrary and irrational occurrences led him to conclude that princes should not be bound by rules and prescriptions that might hamper their ability to deal with sudden events that themselves obey no rules and follow no prescriptions.[4] Though he often insisted in the *Discourses* that emergency powers ought to be constitutionally prescribed in advance to avoid setting precedents that allow institutions to be broken, he recognized that a thin veneer of legality could— and would often have to—suffice. Modern political thinkers (and citizens) have had to contend with the implications of the idea that executive power is irreducible to law ever since Machiavelli liberated the prince from those strictures that would restrain rulers and ruled alike from committing deeds that flout legal, religious, and moral conventions.[5]

Given his dynamic conception of politics as a realm where "so many unexpected things can happen," it is not at all surprising that Machiavelli would make considerations of expediency and necessity a prince's highest priority.[6] But in describing *how* rulers should act and *what* qualities they should possess, he redefined what it meant to be a "good" ruler. Machiavelli did this in two ways, both of which underscored the autonomy of politics. One way he did this was by using the classical rhetorical strategy of *paradiastole* to re-describe traditional moral virtues as (political) vices and traditional moral vices as (political) virtues, as in his recommendation of swift and decisive acts of targeted cruelty as evidence of a merciful disposition toward the people and his denunciation of extravagant generosity as a prelude to burdensome and tightfisted meanness.[7] The other, and perhaps more significant, way that he did this was by emptying the concept of moral content altogether to redefine the "virtues" of a "good" ruler according to standards internal to the realm of politics. Machiavelli generally used the term *virtù* to refer to a morally neutral set of bold and enterprising personal qualities that enable the ruler to adapt to unpredictable and mutable circumstances, a kind of virtuosity that allows the ruler to make the most out of available opportunities.[8] As J. G. A. Pocock explains, it was the *virtù* of princes that would enable them to manage (if not quite subdue) the "malignity" of *fortuna*.[9] Machiavelli's conception of *virtù* connoted flexibility, impetuousness, boldness, decisiveness, and other aggressive qualities necessary to deal with the seemingly random and violent vicissitudes of politics. In that respect, *virtù* was the mirror image of *fortuna*.

Even though Machiavelli's innovative and provocative use of the term *virtù* drew upon notions associated with the morally infused concept of *virtus* found in medieval and Renaissance advice-books for princes (of which *The Prince* is the best-known exemplar), his amoral conception of *virtù* repudiated the traditional understanding, shared by ancient and Christian writers alike, that ordinary moral norms should serve as regulatory ideals in politics.[10] Writers who contributed to the advice-books genre, which instructed princes on the importance of acquiring virtue to become more effective rulers, tended to draw an analytical distinction between the political virtues of rulers and the private virtues of subjects (or citizens), but Machiavelli described his notion of *virtù* without any positive reference to the Christian and ancient virtues that were still important to the humanist writers of such advice books for princes. He emphatically rejected the prevalent notion that princes who steadfastly dedicate themselves to upright lives of moral virtue would necessarily be more effective rulers as an unrealistic piece of utopian naiveté that conflicts with the harsh realities of experience. Concessions to necessity were common even in the traditions of Christian moral philosophy that Machiavelli subverted, but he transformed what was an exception to moral principles into the essential doctrine of politics.[11] Once expediency became the new rule, the moral virtues (for example, honesty, liberality, justice, clemency, piety) that humanist writers believed were indispensable to safe and effective governance became expendable if not downright dangerous constraints.[12]

Machiavelli's greatest influence on later theorists of executive power was based primarily upon his discussion of the unsettling contingency of politics and has had less to do with his amoral account of *virtù*. Most readers recoiled at Machiavelli's disturbing portrait of executive cruelty and immorality and decried his infamous counsel that "a ruler who wishes to maintain his power must be prepared to act immorally when this becomes necessary."[13] Such an image was anathema to those who were loath to empty politics of moral content. It was one thing to violate certain conventions of morality and justice when the welfare of the public was at stake, quite another to treat considerations of virtue in purely instrumental terms or to bracket them altogether. Machiavelli seemed to offer little more than a prudential regard for public opinion—and the not inconsequential fear of popular revolt—to restrain executive power.[14] Many doubted that an executive capable of unconscionable acts of cruelty and wickedness would actually promote the genuine welfare of the community. Machiavelli's suggestion that the preservation and expansion of a prince's own personal power, as opposed to loftier objectives like the promotion of the common good or the pursuit of national glory, constituted the very substance of politics repulsed those who believed that politics is a dignified and noble endeavor. However, many thinkers were more receptive to the proposition that the executive should be prepared to exceed and violate *legal* norms for the good of the community—if only in limited circumstances.

For many seventeenth-century English political thinkers, executive power would remain something of a constitutional anomaly, a necessary evil that defied the nature, limits, and functions of law.[15] Writers who viewed themselves as part of the same republican tradition as Machiavelli accepted many of his teachings on liberty and corruption in free states, but they never managed to reconcile his insights on executive power with the principles of constitutional government that they endorsed. The enormous and unchecked discretionary powers wielded by Machiavelli's prince were anathema to John Milton, Algernon Sidney, and others who railed against the royal prerogatives claimed by the Stuart kings. Moreover, the wanton (and largely self-serving) immorality of Machiavelli's prince offended the moral sensibilities of Puritans like Milton, who admired the austere and self-effacing virtues extolled by the ancients and exemplified by the early Christians. What Caroline Robbins has called the "republican insistence upon definition" in restrictions on government probably hampered the development of a full-fledged republican theory of executive power.[16] Suspicion of executive power ran so deep in republican waters that Sidney made no provision for an independent magistracy to administer and execute the law without the advice (in reality, supervision and oversight) of a council connected to the legislature. Republicans who did acknowledge the need for an executive restricted that officer to the seemingly narrow function of law enforcement: in Milton's words, "to keep the laws which the people have made."[17] With a few exceptions (discussed in chapter 2),

Whigs were generally just as hostile to executive power. In fact, they coalesced around their opposition to abuses of royal prerogatives during the Exclusion Crisis. They achieved their greatest triumph with the passage of the 1689 Bill of Rights, which carefully defined the limits of certain royal prerogatives and explicitly revoked many others. It codified the principle that the king was firmly under the law and rejected the idea that the executive could override or suspend the law without parliamentary approval.[18]

Their struggles against the constitutional abuses and excesses of the monarchy made English republicans unwilling to permit the executive, whether hereditary or elected, much latitude. They conceived of the executive as little more than a law enforcement agent subordinate to the popular assembly. Their belief in the sacredness of political foundations, which was inspired by Roman thought and example, predisposed them to suspect anything that operated outside the original frame of laws and institutions as a threat to the freedom that these sacred orders were supposed to preserve. When they did contemplate the use of extraordinary power, they looked to the Roman dictator as their model. Appointed by existing authorities on a strictly temporary basis to deal with a crisis that they had already declared to exist, the dictator was expected to wield his unlimited powers for the strictly conservative task of restoring the legal and constitutional status quo ante and to relinquish his post as soon as the crisis passed.[19] A reputation for superior public virtue made Romans more confident that a dictator like the celebrated Cincinnatus would use his extraordinary powers only for the sake of the public good.[20] But English republicans expressed wariness of executive power, no matter who wielded it. It was up to thinkers far less conservative than republicans in their outlook on law to incorporate Machiavelli's lessons on executive power into a viable theory of constitutional government suitable for the rapid and unpredictable pace of change in the modern world.

Thanks especially to the pioneering work of Pocock, it is widely understood that Machiavelli's insights into the particularity and contingency of secular political time, especially the notion of revolutionary foundings, had a profound influence on the political thought of English republicans concerned about the dangers of corruption to the stability and very survival of the commonwealth,[21] but scholars have not sufficiently appreciated the extent to which Machiavellian ideas shaped the understanding of early liberal political thinkers.[22] A Machiavellian sensitivity to political contingency pervades liberal political thought from John Locke to the Federalists—especially Alexander Hamilton, who was likely exposed to Machiavelli's works at an early age.[23] The worldview of liberals such as Locke, Hume, Blackstone, and James Madison generally disposed them to look for evidence of rational, harmonious, and law-like order and regularity in the natural and political worlds, but it did not prevent them from recognizing signs of irrationality, discord, and disorder, as Carl Schmitt alleged.[24] Their observations on the vicissitudes and fragility of politics indicate that liberal constitutionalists in this period were highly attuned to the problems of contingency. It would be mind-boggling if thinkers who personally witnessed or participated in the upheavals associated with the sanguinary religious conflicts, treacherous political intrigue, violent uprisings and insurrections, perilous struggles for independence, burgeoning industrialization, and accelerated urbanization of the seventeenth and eighteenth centuries did not confront the problem of contingency. Their overriding aim was to establish a political order that could "secure the Blessings of Liberty" in ordinary and extraordinary circumstances alike.

Unlike their republican counterparts, these liberals accepted the need for extraordinary executive action to deal with the unforeseeable contingencies of politics. In general, they were much more receptive to the positive contributions that a strong—though not unfettered—executive could make to a viable constitutional system. The importance they attached to contingent events distinguished their conceptions of political time from certain Enlightenment articulations of universal history, which tended to downplay the significance of particular events. To paraphrase Alexander Hamilton, they hoped that there could be a place in politics for sedate "reflection and choice," but they also feared that "accident and force" were inescapable.[25] In that respect, these liberals can be fairly described as post-Machiavellian.

There is perhaps no philosophical position more antithetical to post-Machiavellian notions of contingency than the Hegelian conceit that we have arrived at the end of history, an end-state in which contingent events amount to little more than momentary turbulence on the inexorable flight of Absolute Reason through history.[26] Disruptions in the stream of historical time were matters of grave concern even for those post-Machiavellian liberals with a progressive view of history, because these disruptions could pose serious setbacks to the advancement of freedom. Their conviction that such disruptions are an everpresent possibility that could derail the progress of liberty meant that extraordinary acts of intervention would always be necessary to set things right. Whenever it was impossible for the legislature to provide a quick or effective legal remedy in genuine cases of emergency, liberals were willing to allow the executive to act unilaterally even if that meant acting outside the law. In that respect, they shared Machiavelli's reluctance to restrict the means available to the executive, since, they believed, it is sometimes necessary to exceed the formal bounds of the law for the sake of higher interests. As Locke explained, prerogative is not intended to place the executive above the law but to ensure that the law does not undermine the welfare of the people when unexpected "Accidents and Necessities" arise.[27]

A significant—and perhaps surprising—difference between Machiavelli and the liberals who shared his views on the inescapability of contingency is that the liberals sometimes expressed *greater* confidence that a capable executive could actually deal effectively with sudden emergencies. Even though Machiavelli acknowledged that *fortuna* "lets us control roughly . . . half" of our actions, *The Prince* as a whole underscores the futility of even the most virtuosic action when confronted by the overwhelming force of haphazard and uncontrollable events.[28] As the fate of Machiavelli's "model" prince Cesare Borgia demonstrates, even the most cunning and enterprising executive is vulnerable to a sudden change of luck. Despite Machiavelli's lessons on the intractable contingency of politics, liberals seemed confident that the executive could "do something" to "tame" *fortuna*. Perhaps as a consequence, they were even more amenable to extralegal action than Machiavelli, who warned against the dangers of setting such precedents in his *Discourses*.

This willingness to entrust the executive with the discretion to act outside the law is surprising in light of liberal constitutionalism's origins as a revolt against the excesses and abuses of executive power. But it is important to bear in mind that they never revolted against executive power as such. They generally adopted an instrumental approach toward both legal rules and executive power that made it easier for them to contemplate and accept tradeoffs between the two when higher values were at stake. In fact, they never relied exclusively on the law to check the executive. Unlike many of those who revolted against royal prerogative in the seventeenth century, liberals from Locke onward generally eschewed legalistic restrictions that rely on overly determinate rules to circumscribe the proper limits of executive power, preferring a system of checks and balances that relies on the good political judgment of the people and their representatives. Compared to those who associated the law with divine will, superhuman reason, or ancient wisdom, even those liberals who subscribed to natural law doctrines took a much more positivistic view of human law that left them unsure of both the wisdom and justice of rigid adherence to established rules. This does not mean that any of them intended to place the executive "above the law," only that the kinds of legalistic restrictions favored by many republicans would make it impossible to establish a government that was strong and energetic enough to protect the public from foreign and domestic threats in cases of actual emergency.[29]

The problem was figuring out how to keep the executive in line during an emergency. One of the most significant differences between Machiavelli and the liberals who shared his understanding of contingency in politics was that the latter still retained more or less universal notions of justice and morality that served as regulatory ideals, if not absolute standards, in politics. Even though Machiavelli never explicitly denied the existence of natural law or any other eternal standard of morality, his assertion that politics is independent of conventional standards of morality was a proposition that liberals were not prepared to accept.

In ordinary circumstances, institutional arrangements and practices such as the separation of powers, judicial review, and periodic elections could be relied upon to prevent abuses of executive power. But in extraordinary circumstances, liberals found it necessary to look beyond such devices. The recognition that the regular operation of the laws and the system of checks and balances would likely be destabilized during an emergency led liberals from Locke to Hamilton to endorse the right of the people to overthrow an oppressive or tyrannical government. Not only would extraordinary occurrences overwhelm the capacity of legally and institutionally prescribed powers and procedures to handle invasions, insurrections, and other emergencies, but such events would also strain the ability of ordinary legal and institutional arrangements to check potential abuses of power by the executive. When that happened, it would be necessary to rely on extralegal and extra-institutional checks that would keep the executive from exploiting the situation for personal gain or political self-aggrandizement.

Republicanizing the Executive

The liberal constitutionalists whose ideas have had the greatest influence in shaping the American presidency—Locke, Hume, Blackstone, Hamilton, Madison, and Gouverneur Morris—were deeply concerned about the character of executives rather than just their technical abilities. They agreed with

Machiavelli's suggestion that a ruler "must be prepared to vary his conduct as the winds of fortune and changing circumstances constrain him," but they flatly rejected his idea that the executive should "be capable of entering upon the path of wrongdoing when this becomes necessary," where that meant committing cruel or immoral deeds that violate natural law or other fundamental norms.[30] It was one thing to accept a certain level of necessary illegality; it was an entirely different thing to tolerate any degree of calculated immorality. Believing that the regular legal and institutional checks on the executive would often prove inadequate in just those moments when the powers of the executive would be at their highest pitch, they looked to the personal qualities of the executive as a supplementary check against the abuses of power that extraordinary occasions seem to invite. Despite the trend toward a "scientific" approach to politics that aimed to devise institutional arrangements based on the universal patterns and regularities of human behavior, eighteenth-century accounts of political development were still dominated by humanist conceptions of politics as an elite affair shaped by the force of personality.

Due to the inability of strict formal rules and institutional arrangements to regulate extraordinary exercises of executive power, many writers who rejected the tyrannical tendencies of the Machiavellian prince raised the question of character as a serious constitutional concern. The virtue of the executive was a matter of extreme constitutional importance for Locke, Hume, Blackstone, and their followers in America. The responsibilities for dealing with the irregular and unpredictable occurrences of politics were such that ordinary legal and institutional checks on power could not be counted on to constrain an executive who was determined to expand his or her own power at the expense of the public and its freedoms. Since it was impracticable to do without executive power, it was impossible to dispense with virtue. Given the tremendous fear and uncertainty that people experience in times of emergency, the executive might even be able to usurp and abuse power with the approval of the public itself.[31] In such extraordinary circumstances, the character of a virtuous executive might provide the only constraint against excessive or abusive exercises of power.

Liberals have always claimed that virtues such as tolerance, open-mindedness, mutual respect, and respect for law among ordinary citizens are critical to the welfare and flourishing of a liberal society, but what has been generally overlooked is that they also believed that modern politics could not do without at least a modicum of virtue in its leaders—and, where the executive is concerned, a good deal more. Experience, knowledge, wisdom, and prudence were all considered desirable qualities in any public officer, but no more so than those qualities imbued with a distinctively moral meaning: honesty, moderation, frugality, patriotism, self-control, disinterestedness, justice, and humanity. In fact, moral qualities were often stressed at the expense of more obvious leadership qualities. Hume went so far as to claim that "the governing of Mankind well, requires a great deal of Virtue, Justice, and Humanity, but not a surprising Capacity." [32]

When liberals went on to specify the most important moral qualities that made up the "political virtues," they often singled out certain virtues closely associated with republican ideals. Even though these liberals were deeply skeptical about some of the basic assumptions and lessons of republicanism regarding institutional design, the meaning of the public good, and the role of the citizenry in a free state, they tended to invoke the republican virtues of patriotism, disinterestedness, and love of liberty in their discussions of executive character. [33]

What all of the these "political virtues" have in common is the expansion of one's temporal and spatial horizons, that is, the ability to look beyond the immediate gratification of selfish, parochial, or partisan appetites for the good of the community and the long-term preservation of freedom. As explained by Montesquieu, the touchstone on so many questions of free government for Americans of the Founding generation, republican virtue requires "a continuous preference of the public interest over one's own." [34] The *Encyclopédie* echoed the theme of sacrifice for the common good implicit in any specification of political virtue. [35] "Patriotism" was used most generally to refer to love of one's country, but it was also associated with an abiding commitment to the constitutional principles necessary for the preservation of the country's freedom, as against loyalty to the particular government in power. [36] A "patriot" was one who stood up for freedom against all forms of tyranny. "Disinterestedness," which was opposed to the pull of partial or parochial interests associated most directly with factions, referred to the ability to rise above considerations of private profit, sectarian attachment, or partisan advantage. [37] At a minimum, explained the libertarian Commonwealth writers John Trenchard and Thomas Gordon in their celebrated and widely cited essays in *Cato's Letters*, disinterestedness implies "that the turn of [a man's] mind is toward the publick, and that he has placed his own personal glory and pleasure in serving it." [38] "Love of liberty" described a habitual disposition to promote the long-term survival of public freedom when imperiled by rival considerations, such as security, wealth, or convenience. Love of liberty was not to be confused with a love of ease or contentment; in fact, it could be quite difficult and demanding. What made these virtues so desirable was also what made them so rare. As Montesquieu observed, "Political virtue is a renunciation of oneself, which is always a very painful thing."[39]

Like their republican counterparts, Locke, Hume, and Blackstone intuited that virtue was needed to prevent corruption. Corruption, as it was understood by James Harrington and others who took to heart Machiavelli's admonitions to nurture the virtue of citizens, referred to any practices that subverted the conditions for freedom in a republic. The understanding of corruption transmitted to Americans most directly through the writings of Opposition writers such Lord Bolingbroke, Jonathan Swift, and Trenchard and Gordon, who championed the cause of freedom against emerging concentrations of power in ministerial government and the commercial economy, was not limited to bribery and other obvious forms of malfeasance but included systems of patronage and influence that undermined the independence of officeholders and voters alike. The main object of fear in this case was not outright oppression by a dictatorial government but the insidious corrosion of the social, political, economic, and cultural preconditions of freedom. As Pocock explains, the term was "used to denote a disturbance of the balance of the constitution."[40] As opposed to bribery, corruption in this larger sense was far more dangerous, because it infected the very core of the political system, making it difficult, if not impossible, to extract once it took hold. The corrosive effects of corruption are put into motion whenever the people or their governors lose their virtue and begin to exhibit a disposition to place the narrower considerations of self, family, party, religion, or geographic section above the welfare of the nation as a whole.

Although the relationship between virtue and character is a complicated one that was never fully theorized or definitively spelled out, the general impression these writers convey is that virtues are constitutive elements of an individual's overall character. In a long line of thinking dating back to antiquity and confirmed by modern (eighteenth-century) psychology,[41] it was believed that an individual's character is reflected in that person's "enduring traits," which are themselves manifested in certain habitual patterns of behavior.[42] The ontological assumption that there is such a thing as character, which is stable, coherent, and consistent over time, was often accompanied by the equally problematic epistemic belief that it was possible to make dependable predictions about conduct in both private and public life. A "fit character," as the Federalists called it, was comprised of salutary moral virtues that were acquired and cultivated over an entire lifetime and revealed through habits and dispositions that were assumed to be relatively stable and durable over time. As is evident most clearly in the writings of the Federalists, a reputation for virtue was often regarded as reliable evidence of the real thing. They believed, perhaps naively, that a genuine reputation for virtue could be reliably distinguished from mere popularity, which could be the result of demagoguery or the kind of dissimulation described by Machiavelli.

These writers regarded all the virtues that comprise good character as interrelated and mutually reinforcing, but they placed special emphasis on the political virtues of patriotism, disinterestedness, and love of liberty when it came to the executive. Early liberals believed that such virtues were politically important because only an executive with a "fit character," one believed to be capable of looking beyond narrow and immediate interests and constitutionally incapable, so to speak, of deliberate trespasses against the public, could safely be trusted to exercise extralegal powers. The presence of virtue would thus compensate for the deficiencies of law in regulating executive power during an emergency. In a rambunctious political culture that abhorred and punished seditious speech because it undermined the authority—and hence the effectiveness—of government, it was imperative to select leaders who had well-established reputations for selfless public service if they were to be trusted with the dangerous discretionary powers that might be required in an emergency.[43]

In that respect, liberal justifications of virtue in the executive were directly opposed to Machiavelli's account of *virtù* in the prince. Whereas the *virtù* of the prince could be gauged by the extent to which it mirrored *fortuna* in adjusting to the fluctuations of politics, the virtue of the liberal executive could be measured by the extent to which it served as an anchor of stability in the midst of political flux, in much the same way that the rule of law is supposed to stabilize the political order in normal circumstances. The awareness that executive power is highly personalized and resistant to institutional formalization led them to the conclusion that the executive ought to be held to much higher standards of virtue, rather than the conclusion that more juridical constraints ought to be imposed, as might be expected from their espousal of the "new science of politics." Unlike Machiavelli, and contrary to the expectation that liberal writers would lower expectations for virtue, these liberals *raised* expectations for virtue where the executive power was involved.

Reserving Public Virtue for Elites

Liberal constitutionalism is credited by its proponents—and vilified by critics such as Schmitt—for introducing a form of politics that relies heavily on the impersonal institutional machinery of government to check and balance power. However, the difference between the liberal supporters of a strong executive and writers in other traditions does not lie in their use of countervailing institutions as means of checking and balancing power. Such devices had been recommended by thinkers as diverse as Polybius, Gasparo Contarini, Charles I, and James Harrington.[44] The exact nature of the checks and balances may have varied from one thinker to the next, but the idea of using opposing forces to counteract different political powers was one that modern liberals shared with ancient and medieval political thinkers. The main difference was that early liberals, and especially the Federalists, emphasized the role of virtue among the *governors* rather than among the *governed*.

Republican thinkers from Cicero to Milton were preoccupied with the mortal dangers of corruption in a republic that failed to maintain the virtue (along with the independence and equality) of its citizens.[45] Aristotle and others had even suggested that the acquisition of civic virtues was essential to the fulfillment of man's nature as a political being. Starting with the revival of classical ideals of citizenship in Renaissance political thought, the energies of republican thinkers in the modern era had been focused on the cultivation of the citizen "as a conscious and autonomous participant in an autonomous decision-taking political community," because it was believed that the fate of the republic ultimately depended on "a partnership in virtue among all citizens."[46] The notion of civic interdependence was central to republican political thought, which postulated that "one's virtue depended on cooperation with others and could be lost by others' failure to cooperate with one."[47] Since a virtuous citizenry was the *sine qua non* of personal and political liberty, republican writers focused on ways to nurture and preserve civic virtue in the entire citizenry. The virtue of rulers was a subsidiary concern, since active and vigilant citizens were expected to be capable of and responsible for guarding their independence and liberty against potential assaults by corrupt rulers. Indeed, most republican thinkers believed that the presence of virtue among citizens would ensure the presence of virtue among rulers. Republican writers prescribed institutional practices such as selection by lot and frequent rotation precisely to maintain that moral link between citizens and their rulers. The possibility that any citizen could become an officeholder and the requirement that officeholders relinquish their posts after brief tenures were supposed to make it less likely that rulers would develop interests or dispositions at odds with those of ordinary citizens. If the people lacked virtue, then so would their rulers.

A remarkable shift in thinking about the scope of republican virtue occurred in the writings of liberal constitutionalists. They became increasingly disillusioned with the civic ideals of republicanism, but they did not repudiate or revise traditional understandings of republican virtue itself. Instead, they modified their views about who could be realistically and reliably expected to possess those qualities. Where once the virtues of patriotism, disinterestedness, and love of liberty had been expected of all citizens in republicanism, liberals from Locke to the Federalists now moved toward an elitist conception of virtue that would be concentrated in government. They directed their search for republican virtue away from the citizenry as a whole and pointed it toward those who would occupy the highest political offices. The most forceful advocates of a strong executive in America preserved their commitment to virtue by reserving it mainly for the president. The Federalists continued to believe that the vigilance and virtue of citizens were indispensable to the long-term viability of the new republic, but the virtue of citizens was constitutionally peripheral to their interest in establishing virtue in government, especially in the presidency. In that respect, these were no longer civic virtues in the strictest sense. But these virtues were still undeniably republican inasmuch as they oriented individuals toward the pursuit of the public good even when that demanded the sacrifice of private interests.

There is perhaps no better indication of this change than the fact that nearly every appearance of the word *virtue* in the *Federalist* refers to the people's representatives rather than the people themselves. When it appears in *Federalist* 10, the essay that sounded the death knell of republicanism in America, it refers only to "our most considerate and virtuous citizens" and to "representatives whose enlightened views and virtuous sentiments render them superior to local prejudices and to schemes of injustice," not to ordinary citizens.[48] Indeed, one of the only instances in which the term *virtue* is used in connection with the people at large appears in *Federalist* 6, where Hamilton confessed that, contrary to revolutionary hopes, Americans "are yet remote from the happy empire of perfect wisdom and perfect virtue."[49] Federalists no longer perceived virtue in relational terms that stressed the mutual interdependence of virtue among the many but now began to regard virtue as a special quality possessed only by the few.

The transition from a civic to an elitist conception of republican virtue corresponds to a more basic transformation in liberal political thought that radically reversed the relationship between the public and the private. Distinctions between the public and the private realms stretch back as far as the ancient Greeks, but the relationship between them was considered complementary, not antagonistic or indifferent.[50] The private realm was subordinated to the public realm in Greek and later republican thought not to suppress or stifle the development of the former but to serve the latter. For instance, the habits and virtues formed in the private realm were thought to contribute indirectly to or make possible the vitality of the public realm. Even though a thinker like Aristotle could draw significant distinctions between the "good man," who possesses qualities that are esteemed in "man" as such, and the "good citizen," who embodies those qualities that are singularly well-suited for a particular regime type, the ancient ideal usually sought an alignment of the two figures.

Not only did liberalism reverse the ordering of these two realms by privileging the private over the public, it also drew such a sharp distinction between them that they began to appear separate and entirely unrelated. Some virtues—honesty, frugality, and industry, to name a few—were endorsed in both public and private life, but others would increasingly be relegated to separate spheres. When the public realm is no longer the privileged arena for the full realization of one's essential nature as a political being and political participation becomes optional, it is no longer necessary for all individuals to possess both sets of virtues. In some ways, this bifurcation demoted civic virtue from the privileged perch it occupied within republicanism, but in other ways it elevated the importance of republican virtue when it came to public officials. If liberals gravitated toward a republican conception of virtue when considering the qualities necessary in public officials, it was probably because those virtues are oriented toward the pursuit of relatively uncontroversial secular public goods that can garner widespread support in a pluralistic society.[51] As exemplified by the Clinton-Lewinsky affair and other sex scandals dating back to the Founding, the public-private distinction has also made it possible for liberals then and now to argue that personal deficiencies and vices that are confined to the private sphere have little bearing in politics.[52]

Liberalism's reappraisal of private life and its repudiation of politics as an ideal way of life for all citizens also means that there is potentially an unbridgeable moral gap between the people and their executive as far as public virtues are concerned. The irony is that the ideal modern executive may be just as morally unreachable as the ideal medieval king—if not more so. The medieval ruler was idealized as "the perfect impersonator of Christ on earth," but he was also supposed to serve as an.exemplar of virtue to his people.[53] Anointed to rule by the grace of God, the medieval king was expected to epitomize all the virtues so that his subjects would have a model to emulate. The ideal may have been unattainable (for both the king and his subjects), but it was promulgated to encourage the development of virtue in the people. The modern executive, in contrast, is supposed to possess republican virtues precisely so that liberal individuals can go about their own business as parents, business owners, wage earners, or churchgoers, who do not necessarily need to be paragons of strenuous public virtue. The public-spiritedness expected of executives was partly a response to the people's shortcoming in this respect, while also making it unnecessary for them to rectify those shortcomings.

The ability to take an enlarged perspective, the ability to look beyond the narrow and immediate interests of the self, has always been a hallmark of virtue in political thought. But this does not mean that such virtue required the abnegation or debasement of the self. The self-sacrifice required to live up to this notion of virtue—for example, in terms of one's pecuniary interests, familial obligations, or partisan attachments—was encouraged by the identification of the self with the public. Appeals to honor and fame made service to the public—the only place where these goods could be acquired—essential to their satisfaction. Virtue for the Founders was not a completely selfless matter, though. The "love of fame" exalted by Hamilton was a spur to patriotic public service and sacrifice for select Americans in the Revolutionary generation. The desire for the remembrance and veneration of posterity may have been grounded in concern for the self, but it provided an invaluable incentive to virtuous conduct in public life. The ability to discern and act in one's long-term, even posthumous, self-interest by pursuing the long-term interest of the public was a constitutive feature of a "fit character" as the Founders understood it.[54] Although proto-liberal thinkers like Hobbes had attempted to substitute the (self-)destructive impulses of social passions like glory and *amour-propre* with the supposedly innocuous calculations of rational self-interest,[55] most liberal thinkers, including Locke, Hume, and Adam Smith, regarded concern for one's reputation and the opinions of others as a legitimate source of moral motivation in public and private life.[56] Virtue for these liberals was a thoroughly social concept that required the recognition of others. Unlike Christian notions of virtue, whose authenticity diminished with public exposure, virtue in the Age of Reason did not exist unless it was visible to others.[57]

Despite the significance they attached to virtue in the executive, liberals at the time generally did very little to nurture that virtue. Many of them simply assumed that public virtue could thrive under the less-than-favorable conditions of modern life, which included the emergence of a centralized government that left less room for political action by ordinary citizens, new financial and commercial relations premised on the naked pursuit of self-interest, and the increasing privatization of religion and other practices that contributed to a withdrawal from public life. The hope was that individuals endowed with public-spirited virtue and patriotism would continue to sprout up and thrive in political soil that was no longer cultivated to grow virtuous citizens with the aid of traditional republican nutrients like civil religion, sumptuary laws, and civic education. That may go some way toward explaining why the linkage between republican virtue and executive power has received such little attention in scholarship on liberalism and the American Founding.

The Machinery of Government in Liberal Constitutionalism

Republican Revisionism

For the past several decades, scholarship on the intellectual foundations of early American political thought has been divided over the influence of classical republican ideas on members of the Founding generation. Disagreement has been particularly intense over the place of republican virtue in late eighteenth-century American political thought. One group of scholars contends that the adoption of the Constitution represented the repudiation of virtue in politics, while another argues that virtue endured as the organizing principle (if not the reality) of much American political thought into the Jefferson administration. However, both schools of thought think of political virtue as a treasured landmark that has disappeared from the political scene.

Perhaps the most important reason for this is that both camps tend to understand political virtue only as *civic* virtue.[58]

Republican revisionists such as Bernard Bailyn, Gordon Wood, J. G. A. Pocock, and Lance Banning have radically transformed the study of American political thought by drawing attention to its classical and civic humanist roots in Aristotle, Cicero, Plutarch, and Tacitus.[59] In particular, they have demonstrated the primacy of virtue in political discourse during this period. However, republican revisionists have had virtually nothing to say about the discourse on the virtue of representatives independent of civic virtue. Their primary focus has been on the reasons that a political discourse of virtue was discontinued rather than on the ways it might have been transformed in response to political experiences during and after the Revolution. As a result, many revisionists have been able to see virtue within the republican framework of citizenship or not at all. They have generally overlooked the critical shift in emphasis from the virtue of citizens to that of their representatives in the political writings of the Federalists. When they do acknowledge that the Founders expected virtue from their representatives, these scholars still locate that virtue within the context of civic virtue, as when Bailyn argues that the machinery of the Constitution "would depend in the end on the character of the people who managed it and who allowed themselves to be ruled by it."[60]

Another group of scholars denies that virtue would have much, if any, place at all in the new system of government, arguing that the Constitution "makes no provision for men of the founding kind."[61] This view is most commonly associated with scholars who lean toward Louis Hartz's liberal thesis. Scholars who insist on the liberal (specifically Lockean) character of the American Founding have sometimes been downright dismissive of virtue. Robert Dahl argues that the Madisonian system places its entire confidence in institutional checks and balances to the neglect of social or moral ones.[62] Paul Rahe suggests that the main expositors of the "new science of politics" in America "looked to constitutional machinery as a cure for all ills."[63] Samuel Beer flatly dismisses the notion that "superior virtue" was expected to play any role in the new government, contending that "the overwhelming attention [Madison] devoted to the structures and processes of representation, separation of powers, and federalism" proves how little the Virginian expected from the virtue of representatives and "how much he trusted to the institutions within which they operate."[64] John P. Diggins echoes the views of his republican revisionist adversaries when he concludes that "in the Constitutional era the proposition that the new Republic had to depend upon a virtuous citizenry was considered, debated, and ultimately rejected."[65]

However, the following chapters show that Locke, Hume, Blackstone, and those Federalists who most vigorously supported the institution of a strong national executive doubted that impersonal constitutional mechanisms would be sufficient to check political power. As discussed in chapters 5 and 6, waning confidence in the ability of ordinary citizens to exercise strenuous republican virtues gave way to a more elitist conception of virtue among leading nationalists by the time the Constitutional Convention met in 1787. Just as Locke, Hume, and Blackstone focused their discussions of character on the executive rather than the people, Federalists continued to talk about republican virtue but narrowed its scope.

The conventional view is that liberal constitutionalism relies on the impersonal "machinery of government" to ensure that the political system runs smoothly and safely. This pervasive mechanistic metaphor has often been interpreted to mean that more or less interchangeable individuals can be plugged into an automated system that steers their behavior in predictable directions. Judith Shklar, for one, has claimed that the framers "followed the wisdom of the modern age and planned a political system that did not require great statesman in order to succeed in its aims."[66] However, the Constitution was not designed to be "a machine that would go of itself."[67] Quite frequently, references to the complexity and enormousness of the constitutional machinery called attention to the importance of the main operator, who was usually designated as the executive. No matter how well-designed and well-oiled the machine, much would be left up to the discretion of the executive. Secretary of the Treasury Hamilton indicated just how incomplete and inert the machinery of government would be without the proper personnel to operate it when he explained that "there is no law providing for a thousandth part of the duties which each [executive] officer performs in the great political machine & which unless performed would arrest its motion."[68] And when it comes to the chief executive, who not only is responsible for the day-to-day routines of administration but also has to deal with unexpected occurrences, the personal qualities of the officer become even more vital.

Shklar and other scholars seem to miss the continuing need for personal discretion in liberal constitutionalism for two reasons. First, they misconstrue the nature of the aims pursued by the Framers of the Constitution. The most important aims—to take just those cited in the Preamble to the

Constitution—were articulated in terms of general principles rather than specific goals or precise formulas for action. Most of these aims are readily identifiable with fundamental commitments of liberalism like "Justice," "domestic Tranquillity," "common defence," and "the Blessings of Liberty," but others hearken back to the values of republicanism, as with "a more perfect Union" and "the general Welfare." The supporters of the Constitution were under no illusions that such general and abstract aims could be faithfully and successfully pursued without the requisite public virtues of patriotism and disinterestedness. James Madison, James Wilson, and other Federalists acknowledged that the machinery of government would become "an engine of tyranny" if "fit characters" could not be identified to operate it in a "responsible" manner. It was understood that the aims of the political system would not be realized unless politicians were animated by the proper motives and passions before they assumed office. They were unsure that improper motives and passions could be checked or redirected in a positive direction during those moments of crisis that tend to disrupt the delicate machinery of the constitutional system.

Second, in playing up the undeniable and enormous influence of the "new science of politics" in liberal constitutional thought, remarks like Shklar's end up downplaying the continuing hold of classical ideas in the post-Revolutionary American imagination.[69] Madison's research into the nature of ancient and modern confederations in preparation for the Constitutional Convention should be enough to disprove Shklar's claim that the Constitution "would all have to be their own invention."[70] In the decade leading up to the Constitution, ancient writers like Plutarch and Cicero were cited more often than the Whig martyr Algernon Sidney and quintessentially modern "scientific" writers such as Thomas Hobbes.[71] To be sure, frequency of citation in itself provides no evidence that references to these writers were anything more than ornamental. However, Plutarch's *Lives,* which extolled the virtues of great statesmen, exerted a powerful and palpable influence on American statesmen like Hamilton and Washington.[72] Plutarch's accounts of the lives of great Greek and Roman figures presented ancient paragons of virtue and models of statesmanship that continued to inform the values and shape the perceptions of Americans. Ancient depictions of virtuous statesmen were reproduced in modern portrayals of patriotic kingship by Opposition writers like Bolingbroke and Jonathan Swift.[73] The Roman hero Cato was a particularly popular figure in dramatic, literary, and political works and served as a model of republican virtue for many Americans, including Washington, who had Jóseph Addison's eponymous play performed regularly to inspire the soldiers under his command.[74]

Analytical and categorical distinctions between liberalism and republicanism, individual rights and public virtues, are useful in understanding the relationships and antagonisms between different ideas during the American Founding, but they sometimes obscure the extent to which eighteenth-century writers were able to combine ideas from varying traditions without any sense of contradiction.[75] Americans were able to absorb the lessons of both the ancients and the moderns without experiencing any cognitive dissonance over the tensions between their republican admiration for the heroic ethos of self-sacrifice and their liberal acceptance of an egoistic psychology grounded in self-interest. Federalists could simultaneously defend the new system of government as a *novus ordo seclorum* built on the progressive advances of the modern science of politics and continue to espouse values and principles gleaned from the writers of antiquity.

The expectation of virtue in the executive should not be seen as an outmoded relic of a bygone ideology but as a crucial complement to the institutional mechanisms associated with an ascendant liberal constitutionalism. The character of the executive could provide some warranty for liberty at exactly those moments when the rule of law seems to wane in strength. Belief in the stability of character made it possible for modern writers to assign it a constitutional role comparable to that of the rule of law: the constancy and fixity of moral character would promise a degree of stability and predictability in exceptional times comparable to what the rule of law provides in normal circumstances.

The Rule of Law and the Problem of Discretion

The rule of law has always been a central component in any theory of constitutionalism that aims to establish a limited government.[76] It is considered indispensable to the establishment of a stable and predictable order necessary for the preservation of freedom. As A. V. Dicey explained, this venerated ideal offers the best protection for individual freedom by requiring government to operate according to determinate rules applicable to all rather than extemporary decrees limited to specific individuals and groups.[77] The idea that government is subject to law actually draws upon two distinct but related senses of the rule of law, especially within liberal constitutionalism. On the one hand, the rule of law refers to the principle that citizens should be governed only according to general and prospective rules established by legitimate law-making authorities. On the other, it refers to the principle that government itself should operate only in accordance with prescribed rules. In other words, the rule of law implies that citizens are to be ruled *by* law while government is to rule *through* law. Adherence to both senses of the rule of law is considered essential to the preservation of liberty against the arbitrary "rule of men."

The historical and theoretical opposition of the rule of law to any form of rule based on arbitrary will is frequently translated into general hostility toward any form of discretionary action. Indeed, the rule of law occupies such an important position within modern constitutional theory and practice that it becomes difficult to conceive of legitimate exercises of constitutional powers outside of a juridically oriented framework that minimizes, if it does not deny, the role of discretionary action.[78] The rule of law is an appropriate and indispensable benchmark for the protection of individual rights—historically speaking, the *raison d'être* of the rule of law in liberal political thought—but it provides little guidance for the actual operation of government in moments of emergency. Unfortunately, this admirable emphasis on the centrality of the rule of law in liberal constitutionalism tends to obscure the fact that so much governmental activity—especially as it relates to the executive—is fundamentally irreducible to law. The tendency to view constitutional questions through such legalistic lenses means that political theorists who took an interest in constitutionalism prior to September 11 often devoted a good deal of attention to the rule of law but had little or nothing to say about executive power.[79] It was not unusual for scholars to describe the Constitution in extremely narrow legalistic terms that leave little room for discretionary action, long regarded as inimical to the rule of law.

The writings of early liberal constitutionalists suggest that many of the most crucial functions of government are not amenable to neat legal categories or precise juridical formulas. The rule of law rightly demands that government officials be subordinate to the law, but it cannot fully define all of their responsibilities in terms of the law. This is not simply because the rule of law is a logical "impossibility" or, like any other ideal, practically "unattainable."[80] Indeterminacy is also an inescapable feature of the law. Whether it takes the form of rules that prescribe specific outcomes in advance, standards that set rules of thumb to guide action, or principles that articulate ideals to strive for, law cannot avoid the ambiguity and uncertainty inherent in any use of language, general or otherwise.[81] And indeterminacy is even more difficult to avoid in a constitution. In fact, much of the indeterminacy resulting from the use of highly abstract and general provisions is deliberate. Because it is almost never as easy to amend a constitution as it is to alter or even repeal an ordinary law, it must be flexible enough to deal with myriad unforeseen and unforeseeable political problems, which makes some degree of vagueness a good thing. A complete and precise enumeration of all the things a government is expected to do not only is impossible but may also be undesirable. This is so for many of the same reasons that some liberals have opposed attempts to develop a comprehensive catalogue of individual rights: something important invariably gets left out, leaving the erroneous impression that it is not guaranteed at all or entitled to a much lower level of protection than what is actually enumerated. In ordinary circumstances, it would give government too much power; in exceptional circumstances, it might not give it enough.

Even though there are far greater dangers to liberty and the public good when powers are defined too broadly, liberal thinkers from Locke to Hamilton realized that liberty can also be endangered when powers are defined too narrowly because the government would have to resort to expressly prohibited powers in an emergency. One reason for this is that respect for constitutional limits tends to erode when the government is compelled to take actions in response to emergencies that clearly exceed those limits.[82] Clear rules may be essential in the area of criminal law and the protection of civil liberties and civil rights, but "such details, definitions, and rules, as appertain to the true character of a law" (which James Madison believed were "essential to the nature and character of law") were considered unsuitable in a constitution.[83] Constitutional indeterminacy was the price that the early liberals were willing to pay for constitutional viability.

Just as Machiavelli had provided a powerful justification for the necessity of extraordinary exercises of discretion in extreme circumstances, so too did he make a compelling case for the need to leave some constitutional matters up to the discretion of political actors. He drew an important distinction in his *Discourses on Livy* between the "orders" and the "modes" of a political system that found its way into liberal constitutional thought. "Orders" refer to the laws, procedures, and institutions formally established by the founders of a constitutional system. In the case of the U.S. Constitution, these would include the presidential veto power, the appointment power of the president, and the two-thirds requirement for treaty ratification specified in the U.S. Constitution. "Modes" refer to the constructive manner in which these formal orders are actually implemented. They correspond roughly to what Keith Whittington has described as constitutional "construction," as opposed to "interpretation."[84] This distinction recognizes that orders (like ordinary laws) are neither self-interpreting nor self-executing and that certain questions are deliberately—and necessarily—left unresolved by orders. As Harvey Mansfield and Nathan Tarcov explain, Machiavelli "stresses that political orders are not enough and do not last. Orders must be accompanied by 'modes' of political activity that give effect to the orders, interpret them, manipulate them."[85] For instance, presidents customarily reserve the veto only for constitutionally questionable legislation and enactments that seriously conflict with very important policy preferences, even though the Constitution places no explicit restrictions on the subjects in which the president can use it. Many common forms of presidential direct action (executive orders, presidential memoranda, national security directives, and presidential signing statements) are simply not spelled out in the Constitution at all but have become accepted modes of presidential politics.[86] It took an extensive debate in the First Congress to decide whether or not the president's shared appointment power implies an exclusive power of removal. Matters are even murkier in the realm of foreign affairs: executive agreements have become the preferred means of reaching agreements with foreign states even though the treaty provisions of the Constitution make no mention of this practice. Some of these practices, such as the use of presidential signing statements to thwart the will of Congress, may very well be unconstitutional, but the point is that the text of the Constitution lends itself to modes of action that may depend more on the person in office than on any established orders.

Innovative and creative uses of existing laws and institutional resources in ways unimagined and perhaps unintended by lawmakers are characteristic of the open-ended nature of modes. Despite their susceptibility to abuse, changes in the modes obviate the need for direct changes in the orders, thus preserving the appearance (if not the reality) of the continuity critical to the stability of every political system. Machiavelli's discussion of political modes and orders is particularly relevant to analyses of executive power because it highlights that many features of a constitutional system are worked out and institutionalized only in practice, which creates opportunities for exercises of power determined largely by informal and personal particularities and not formal and official criteria. Mansfield makes the provocative suggestion that "Machiavelli's constitution is composed of ordinary orders that permit, indeed encourage, extraordinary actions by an ambitious prince."[87] Those Americans who believed it was critical to the success of the new government that the highly respected and virtuous George Washington become the first president realized that, to a much greater degree than other constitutional institutions, the extent and scope of executive power is determined more by modes of conduct that vary with the personal qualities of the executive than by established orders designed for all cases.

In light of the fact that the full scope of executive power is determined by uncertain modes, it should be no surprise that executive power is so difficult to reconcile with the rule of law. Indeed, there is a two-fold tension between executive power and the rule of law. First, the inevitable indeterminacy of laws invites the very discretion that the rule of law is supposed to minimize if not eliminate. As scholars of the judiciary are aware, indeterminacy in the law makes legal interpretation a doubtful and contentious enterprise even if there are principles that can offer guidance in "hard cases."[88] Even if, as Locke always insisted, the right answer to difficult legal and political questions could be found by appealing to principles contained in natural law, the invocation of anything as vague and indefinite as natural law involves an exercise of constructive interpretation that necessarily lacks the formality of ordinary statutory interpretation.

Needless to say, the proper exercise of executive power is much more of an art than a science. Since the province of executive power is not defined by any particular subject matter, and in fact has the potential to range over the entire field of governmental responsibilities, it is difficult to imagine what it would mean to train individuals to become good executives in the way that individuals who acquire a certain level of legal expertise and internalize certain professional norms can be trained to become good judges. Thus, executive power conflicts with the rule of law in a second and more interesting sense to the extent that it is largely irreducible to general rules. Although it is possible to specify constitutionally the exact procedures a legislature must follow in enacting laws, it is exceedingly difficult to specify constitutionally the exact procedures an executive must follow in executing and administering laws without producing absurd or unjust results. The appropriate course of legislative action usually follows the same general pattern, but the appropriate course of executive action is frequently dictated by the particulars of concrete events that might never be repeated. Legislative action revolves around laws, but even outside the realm of foreign affairs, where the discretion of the executive is at its height, the executive is frequently pulled beyond the gravitational field of laws by the vortex of contingency. Post-Machiavellian theorists of executive power understood that the executive often has to deal with multifarious crises that exceed the competence of the law.

Not only must the executive act where the laws offer little or no guidance, but—more importantly—the executive must sometimes act directly contrary to the laws. Locke's conception of executive prerogative, which was the theoretical starting point for subsequent reflections on the emergency powers of the executive in early liberalism, is premised on the shortcomings and failures of ordinary legal norms. But the inapplicability of positive legal norms did not result in the abandonment of norms altogether. For Locke and his American adherents, natural law compensated for any inadequacies in positive law. For those liberals (like Hume) who raised questions about natural law, normative guidelines could be found in general principles like the ancient maxim *salus populi suprema lex est* ("the welfare of the people is the supreme law"). Because it is the duty of the executive to preserve the safety of the people, these writers admitted that the executive would sometimes have to exceed the law to fulfill this sacred duty.

As important as the rule of law was to early liberals, it must not be forgotten that they advocated rebellion and dissent in the name of fundamental principles that superseded established forms of law. It comes as no surprise that revolutionaries like Jefferson expressed such a view of the law: "Should we have ever gained our Revolution, if we had bound our hands by manacles of the law, not only in the beginning, but in any part of the revolutionary conflict? There are extreme cases where the laws become inadequate even to their own preservation, and where, the universal recourse is a dictator, or martial law." [89] The doctrine that the ends (often) justify the means was an essential part of early liberal thought, though it was qualified in ways that Machiavelli would have rejected. [90] Necessity provided a well-recognized exception to the inviolability of established rules. Post-Machiavellian thinkers rejected the legalistic maxim *fiat justitia ruat coelum* ("let justice be done though heaven may fall") as dangerously naive. As Hume explained, "By sacrificing the end to the means, [it] shews a preposterous idea of the subordination of duties." [91] Since early liberals understood that law and morality were analytically distinct (albeit related), violating the law was not quite as problematic for them as it was for republicans, who were much more likely to revere law as the foremost expression of the ethical values of the community. This is not to suggest that they permitted violations of the law in less than exceptional circumstances, only that their attitude toward the law could be better described as instrumental rather than reverential.

It is that distinction between law and morality that made the character of the executive a matter of vital constitutional significance. If the law could not always provide the proper moral guidance or serve as an effective check against abuses of power, it was imperative that the person who had to decide when it was necessary to exceed the law possess the right virtues. The expectation was that those virtues would harmonize with the spirit of the law without being in thrall to the letter of the law.

CHAPTER TWO

"Without the Prescription of the Law"

Virtue and Discretion in Locke's Theory of Prerogative

> This Power to act according to discretion, for the publick good, without
> the prescription of the Law, and sometimes even against it, is that which is
> called Prerogative.   JOHN LOCKE

The Rule of Law in Lockean Liberalism

The liberal conception of limited government is perhaps most closely associated with its commitment to the "rule of law." The rule of law is frequently (and rather indiscriminately) identified with the advancement of democracy, justice, and a host of other lofty ideals, but within liberalism it is
most closely associated with juridical guarantees of individual freedom
against public and private exercises of tyrannical power.[1] The *locus classicus*
of this ideal appears in Locke's *Two Treatises of Government*, where the freedom
enjoyed under the rule of law is contrasted with subjection to the arbitrary
rule of private will: *"freedom of men under government* is, to have a standing
rule to live by, common to every one of that society, and made by the legislative power erected in it; a liberty to follow my own will in all things, where
the rule prescribes not; and not to be subject to the inconstant, uncertain,
unknown, arbitrary will of another man" (Locke, *Two Treatises*, II, § 22).[2]
Lockean constitutionalism gives institutional expression to the rule of law
primarily through the codification of "settled and standing rules" designed to
circumscribe the discretion of public authorities.[3]

Despite Locke's insistence that the powers of government "ought to be exercised by *established and promulgated laws*" (II, § 137), he permitted the executive to exercise enormous discretionary powers in times of emergency. He endorsed an extralegal conception of prerogative that would allow the executive "to act according to discretion, for the publick good, *without the prescription of the Law, and sometimes even against it*" (II, § 160; italics added). This grant of power is so extraordinary that it seems to contradict Locke's understanding of the rule of law as an impersonal standard of legitimacy. The apparent theoretical inconsistency led Carl Schmitt to conclude that "the exception was something incommensurable to John Locke's doctrine of the constitutional state."[4] Even those who are more receptive to Lockean liberalism tend to regard prerogative as yet another example of his many theoretical inconsistencies.[5]

Locke's retention of prerogative is especially puzzling in light of the historical and political circumstances surrounding the composition of the *Two Treatises*. After all, he conspired with other radical Whigs to put an end to persistent abuses of royal prerogative.[6] The prorogation and dismissal of Parliament, the suspension and selective enforcement of laws, the granting of indulgences to nonconformists, and other policies carried out by the Stuart king Charles II reignited a blistering debate over the origins, scope, and purpose of royal prerogative that had blazed earlier in the century. Much of this debate was fueled by the posthumous publication of Sir Robert Filmer's absolutist defense of royal prerogative in his treatise *Patriarcha*. By locating the source of royal power in the absolute right of life and death that fathers enjoy over their children, Filmer's patriarchalist apology for the divine right of kings made monarchical power virtually independent of all institutional foundations and juridical checks.[7] Locke's argument for the rule of law is a direct repudiation of the Filmerian idea that political power rests on the personal attributes or identity of public officials: "For all the power the government has, being only for the good of society, as it ought not to be *arbitrary* and at pleasure, so it ought to be exercised by *established and promulgated laws*: that both the people may know their duty, and be safe and secure within the limits of the law, and the rulers too kept within their bounds, and not to be tempted, by the power they have in their hands, to imploy it to such purposes, and by such measures, and they would not have known, and own not willingly" (II, § 137).

Until recently, Locke scholars have had surprisingly little to say about this apparent anomaly. Although scholars of the American presidency have fixed upon Locke's discussion of prerogative as an important theoretical basis for some of the powers of the president, there has not been a serious effort to reconcile prerogative with the fundamental premises of Locke's theory of constitutional government.[8]

Lockean constitutionalism, like liberal constitutionalism more generally, is frequently construed in such impersonal and legalistic terms that it gets defined more by its formal rules than by its substantive principles. But a closer look at Locke's constitutional ideas suggests that Locke differed from later liberals in refusing to surrender politics to "a legalistic or jurisprudential paradigm of political philosophy."[9] Instead of viewing Locke's endorsement of prerogative as a contradiction of his basic constitutional ideals, it might be more accurate to view it as an expression of his pragmatism and flexibility concerning the best ways to realize and uphold fundamental liberal values. It is indisputable that formal rules play a major role in Lockean constitutionalism, but those rules themselves contain and are based on higher substantive principles that precede them. Understanding the centrality of substantive principles over formal rules in Locke's constitutionalism is essential to understanding why prerogative is not a deviation from his substantive aims but an alternate route to their fulfillment.[10]

In matters constitutional and moral, the ultimate source of substantive principles for Locke is natural law, which provides the supreme, incontrovertible, universal, and unexceptionable criteria of right in Locke's theory.[11] Locke explained that "the *first and fundamental natural Law,* which is to govern even the Legislative it self, is *the preservation of the Society,* and (as far as will consist with the publick good) of every person in it" (II, § 134). Collective self-preservation and the general welfare are superior even to individual self-preservation or the protection of individual rights, which are usually considered paramount in liberal doctrine.[12] Exercises of prerogative by the executive are constitutionally permissible as long as these activities do not conflict with the fundamental substantive principle of natural law: *salus populi suprema lex,* "the welfare of the people is the supreme law."[13]

The general principles contained in the laws of nature supply both the normative foundations of his jurisprudence and the justification for departures from the strict letter of the law. Given the ruling force of natural law, the temporary suspension or interruption of positive law is not dispositive proof of illegitimacy. Prerogative can be understood as an extralegal means of serving the ends of the constitution, which is not an end in itself but a means of serving the ends directed by natural law. Despite its extraordinary character, the proper employment of prerogative remains in strict compliance with the moral and legal order that matters most. In that respect, as Larry Arnhart observes, prerogative "is not a *substitute* for law" but "a *supplement* to law," where the relevant law is to be understood as natural law.[14]

But that prerogative is such an informal and highly personalized type of power made it necessary for Locke to resort to supplementary checks that were just as informal and personalized. Locke sensed that the external constraints that keep the executive and other public officials in check in normal circumstances might not be up to the task in unusual circumstances. The people's right to overthrow a tyrannical executive constituted the last line of defense against abuses of prerogative or any other powers, but the first line of defense would be the virtue of the executive. And just as natural law helps define the substantive ends of the community and the legitimate uses of government power, so, too, does it set the standards of virtue required in the executive. It is these standards of "Vertue," which "every-where correspond with the unchangeable Rule of Right and Wrong, which the Law of God hath established; there being nothing, that so directly, and visibly secures, and advances the general Good of Mankind in this World, as Obedience to the Laws, he has set them."[15]

The susceptibility of prerogative to abuse makes it imperative that government be filled with rational and virtuous individuals who recognize that their own happiness depends on their success in promoting the happiness of the community. These internal constraints turn out to be just as important in Locke's understanding and expectations of limited government as all those external mechanisms of control usually identified with liberal-constitutional government—the separation of powers, checks and balances, the rule of law. Locke's equivocal use of the term virtue does not alter the fact that it constitutes a safeguard against abuses of prerogative that is every bit as important—and informal—as the powers it is supposed to check.

Perhaps the most surprising—and unsettling—aspect of Locke's defense of prerogative has less to do with the nature and limits of positive law in dealing with the unexpected contingencies of life than with the determinants of power in cases of emergency. Not only does Locke's conception of prerogative permit the executive to circumvent the law in certain instances, but *the scope of this power itself depends on the character of the individual wielding it.* His rejection of Filmer's position on the personal foundations of political power notwithstanding, Locke's account of prerogative suggests that the full extent of prerogative depends on more than legal and institutional factors. It turns out that prerogative is a highly personalized form of power that depends on the personal qualities of the executive. The greater the virtue of the executive, the greater the latitude that executive ought to possess in exercising this discretionary power.

The Politics of Prerogative Prior to Locke

The deeply divisive and sometimes violent English struggle over royal prerogative—a well-documented history that helps explain the deep-seated suspicion of executive power among Americans in the eighteenth century— forms the backdrop for Locke's own reformulation of prerogative.

Royal prerogative referred to a wide array of royal powers and privileges that the monarch could exercise concerning the meeting of Parliament, the suspension of laws, the making of war, and the granting of monopolies, among the more controversial practices. The central questions in debates over prerogative concerned its relation to law. Was prerogative a part of the law or outside of it? Could it be defined by law? Was prerogative subordinate to law? Did it authorize the king to set aside or break the law? The answers to these theoretical legal questions had serious practical political implications for the rights, privileges, and property of the people, of the Parliament, and of the monarchy.

In medieval England, it was frequently argued that royal prerogative placed the king outside the law, but legal thinkers often claimed that this did not make prerogative unlimited inasmuch as its purpose was limited to promotion of the common good—a point similar to one that Locke would make.[16] The difficulties of reconciling prerogative with the law forced advocates into some bizarre legal contortions. Emblematic of the medieval penchant for arcane legal formulations was John of Salisbury's assertion in the twelfth century that the king's prerogative gave him absolute power insofar as he acted as "the minister of the public utility," but that the king was also absolutely limited by the law.[17] The theory that the king was absolute as long as he acted within certain legal boundaries defined by the rights of subjects predominated for several centuries but increasingly came under attack for leaving too much arbitrary discretion in the hands of the monarch.[18] In the fifteenth century, Sir John Fortescue reluctantly acknowledged the potential need for some kind of discretionary power in the king to deal with emergencies but considered such cases abnormal and not worth his sustained attention since he believed that "a perfect law always exists and can be found to define the rights and duties of all individuals and constitutional agencies in England."[19] The abundance of medieval legalisms was matched only by the dearth of effective constitutional sanctions to check abuses of prerogative. Even as late as the Tudor period, prerogative was curbed only by "a body of rules of statute and common law that provided a part of the legal framework within which a monarch was required to move."[20] However, the effectiveness of these legal rules rested more heavily on their hortatory force than on any real enforcement mechanisms.

The guiding principle of legal and political thought regarding royal prerogative during the Stuart era was the maxim that "the king's prerogative stretcheth not to the doing of any wrong,"[21] an idea that was affirmed even by the divine right absolutist King James I.[22] But this is not to say that prerogative was directly subject to law. Some powers were viewed as part of the monarch's "ordinary" prerogative, which fell within the purview of the common law, while other powers were seen as part of the monarch's "absolute" prerogative, which fell outside the common law.[23] In a series of landmark court cases, Sir Edward Coke and other jurists drew a distinction between the king's "ordinary" prerogative and his "absolute" prerogative to argue that the former was subject to judicial review, but the latter was not. James I infuriated parliamentarians when he asserted an exclusive right to judge the outcome of disputed elections as part of his prerogative, provoking even more resentment when he dismissed what he considered a truculent Parliament. These disputes, which squarely pitted royal prerogative against parliamentary privilege, hampered the king's ability to raise the funds he needed and to carry out his policies.

James' son and successor Charles I fared even worse. Like his father, he refused to relinquish any part of his prerogative, believing that it issued directly from God. When Charles imposed a ship money tax without parliamentary approval because the Crown's finances were in such terrible arrears, he failed to impress his critics with appeals to precedent and national emergency. The struggle over prerogative became one of the key issues that polarized the disputants when the Civil War finally erupted. Following the final defeat of his armies and a trial whose legitimacy he never acknowledged, Charles was executed on January 20, 1649, for treason and "other high crimes against the realm of England."

The failed republican experiment during the Interregnum made few lasting changes in prerogative. Almost immediately after the Restoration, Charles II used his prerogative to grant an indulgence to religious dissenters by suspending penal laws against those who refused to adhere to the modes of worship prescribed in the Conventicle Act and other parliamentary enactments. When Charles II invoked his prerogative to issue a Declaration of Indulgence in 1672 without parliamentary approval, many of the king's eventual opponents (including Anthony Ashley Cooper, better known as the First Earl of Shaftesbury and Locke's patron) interpreted this as part of a larger conspiracy to restore "popery" to England. These politicians were aghast at the religious, social, and constitutional implications. Identified with tyranny, foreign subjection, absolutism, and arbitrary government, popery was seen as a grave threat to the English form of government and English liberties. Much of the hostility to royal prerogative in this period arose out of an abhorrence of what Catholicism seemed to represent.[24]

The indulgence issue produced a peculiar political dilemma for Shaftesbury and his allies. Their support for toleration toward dissenters inclined them to approve the suspension of penalties against nonconformists who violated the Conventicle Act, but their opposition to arbitrary power disposed them to reject this (or any) exercise of royal prerogative. Some dissenters, who directly benefited from the indulgence, denied that "the king *had* the constitutional power to suspend the law through an act of his arbitrary will, even when the consequences of such an action carried obvious political benefits for themselves."[25] However, when Charles asked Shaftesbury for his opinion on the legality of the indulgence, Locke produced a draft for Shaftesbury that supported the king's power to suspend penalties against nonconformists because the benefits to the public secured by prerogative in this instance outweighed the dangers inherent in any augmentation of royal power.[26] Shaftesbury ended up supporting the continued existence of prerogative because it was the only way petitioners could have their grievances redressed when Parliament was not in session and because such discretionary power was more acceptable than the alternative: a legislature in permanent session.[27] Nevertheless, Shaftesbury regarded prerogative as only a temporary expedient and favored parliamentary action to give legal ratification to exercises of prerogative.

Some Whigs eventually resigned themselves to the usefulness of prerogative, but the prospect of a Catholic monarch was unpalatable to nearly all non-Catholics. Hysterical fears of a Catholic monarch who might restore the despotism of popery to England prompted Whigs to propose a bill of exclusion to prevent James from succeeding his brother. Charles refused to give his assent. Only six days after the election of 1681, he dissolved Parliament (the second Parliament in only three months) and resolved "never to call another."[28] At this point Shaftesbury's party—which included Locke—formulated plans for armed resistance against the king's subversion of constitutional government. As Richard Ashcraft pointed out, the avowed impetus for armed resistance "was the king's use of the prerogative to call and dissolve government in such a way as to defeat the purposes of representative government."[29] During this crisis, Locke and Shaftesbury suggested that the legitimacy of any particular exercise of prerogative depends on its conformity to higher substantive ends—an idea that would become a crucial part of Locke's argument in the *Second Treatise*.

The abortive Rye House Plot, which included plans for assassination and a general insurrection, was the first attempt at armed resistance. It was followed in 1685 by Monmouth's Rebellion, which also ended disastrously for the conspirators. James, now king, used his prerogative to issue a general pardon to the rebels and to grant indulgences to dissenters in the hopes of winning their support, which some gave, much to the chagrin of Locke and fellow radicals.[30] The dispute over prerogative was not resolved until after 1688, when James II "abdicated" and his successor William of Orange agreed in the following year to a bill of rights that narrowly circumscribed the royal prerogative.[31]

The Lockean Defense of Prerogative

It does seem puzzling, in light of this history and Locke's own involvement in radical Whig politics, that his *Second Treatise of Government*, a politically engaged text that gave theoretical expression to the objectives of many revolutionary Whigs, would incorporate the same power whose abuse provoked the radicals to take up arms against their king.[32] He did not merely allow prerogative as a necessary evil; he endorsed it as an indispensable—albeit potentially dangerous—tool of governance. For one thing, he permitted the executive to circumvent duly enacted laws. For another, he allowed the executive to dismiss the legislature, historically the most important and effective check on royal power. Moreover, his conception of prerogative was so highly personalized that it put him uncomfortably close to his chief antagonists, patriarchalists such as Filmer, who maintained that all power was personal.[33] It requires an expansion of just the sort of discretion that his doctrine of the rule of law is supposed to curtail. In many respects, prerogative seems to undercut the limited and impersonal government he set out to create, making it hard to avoid the impression that prerogative is a political and constitutional anomaly.

The Functions of Executive Power

It is impossible to understand the role of executive power, let alone prerogative, without getting a clear grasp of the purposes of constitutional government in Locke's political theory. According to Locke, individuals establish political society "for the mutual *Preservation* of their Lives, Liberties and Estates" (II, § 123). Even though individuals in the state of nature are entitled by the laws of nature to protect their rights to each of these goods, the uncertainty of those laws and the partiality of individuals lead to potentially violent disagreements that make those goods insecure. Government is instituted specifically to prevent and resolve these and other kinds of disputes through the codification and enforcement of clear and impartial laws. The rule of law thus becomes the *sine qua non* of legitimate government. In a system that establishes the rule of law, "all private judgment of every particular Member [is] excluded, [and] the Community comes to be Umpire, by settled standing Rules, indifferent, and the same to all Parties" (II, § 87).

The source of authority in such a government comes directly from the people themselves. In opposition to royalist claims about the divine right of kings or the patriarchal origins of political power, Locke argued that the authority of government is derived from the natural right of each individual to enforce the laws of nature, specifically the right to "do whatsoever he thinks fit for the preservation of himself and others within the permission of the *Law of Nature*" and "the *power to punish the Crimes* committed against that Law [the law of nature]" (II, § 128). These rights, or powers (Locke often used the terms interchangeably), are consistent with the fundamental duty and right to preserve individuals and mankind as a whole from the depredations of anyone who has "declared War against all mankind" by violating the laws of nature (II, § 11). Locke referred to the right to enforce the laws of nature against transgressors as the "Executive Power of the Law of Nature" (II, § 89).

One of the best guarantees of personal and collective security, Locke believed, is the functional separation of powers between the legislative, the federative, and the executive (which encompasses judicial functions). In spite of the functional differences between the executive, which enforces "the Municipal Laws of the Society *within* its self," and the federative, which manages "the *security and interest of the publick without*" (II, § 147), reasons of expediency and practicality make it necessary to combine these powers in one body.[34] Because they both draw upon "the force of the Society for their exercise," Locke argued that it would be "almost impracticable to place the Force of the Commonwealth in distinct, and not subordinate hands" (II, § 148). As a result of this combination of powers, the executive ends up representing the collective force of the commonwealth, both externally and internally. The historically contingent fact that these powers are often combined is not as consequential for Locke as the practical requirement that the government perform these functions with dispatch.

The apportionment of these powers between the legislative assembly and the executive magistracy is essential to his constitutional scheme, for without it "no Appeal lies open to any one" with grievances against the government (II, § 91). Locke's functional separation of powers also reflects the political wisdom that no one should be the judge of one's own case, which is bound to occur when power in concentrated in a single body. However, Locke deviated from his own principle in giving the executive some powers that directly affect the composition and the operation of the legislative power. Locke's executive has far more power to act independently of the legislature and sometimes even against its express enactments than one would expect in light of his claim that "the *first and fundamental positive Law* of all Commonwealths, *is the establishing of the Legislative* Power" (II, § 134, emphasis in original). After all, his basic assumption is that individuals establish government under the rule of law to escape those concentrations of power that render the state of nature so dangerous to liberty.

While the legislative assembly establishes the rules that will govern individuals in political society, just as the laws of nature direct them in the state of nature, the executive enforces civil laws, just as individuals punish violations of the natural law in the state of nature. As Jeremy Waldron argues, the primary responsibility of the legislature is not to substitute positive rules for the laws of nature but to make them "more determinate."[35] Despite the formal separation of powers, though, the executive is invested with the responsibility of convoking the legislative assembly (II, § 154) because there is more to be feared in the "Constant *frequent meetings of the Legislative,* and long Continuations of their Assemblies" (II, § 156), than in violating the separation of powers in this manner. Even though "the Original Constitution [might] require[ ]

their *assembling* and *acting* at certain intervals" (II, § 154), Locke thought that
it would be impossible "that the first Framers of the Government should, by
any foresight, be so much Masters of future Events, as to be able to prefix so
just periods of return and duration to the *Assemblies of the Legislative*" and
certainly not better "Masters of future Events" than the executive, "whose
business it was to watch over the publick good" (II, § 156). These remarks are
noteworthy for two reasons. One is that they reveal Locke to be much more
suspicious of legislative power than republican thinkers, who regarded legislative assemblies as bulwarks of liberty.[36] Another, more significant reason is
that they express Locke's anxieties about the unpredictability and unmanage-
ability of politics through "settled standing Rules" (II, § 87) alone.

Even more remarkable is the role assigned to the executive in effecting
electoral reform. In a passage reminiscent of Machiavelli's comments on the
need for periodic returns to first principles, Locke assigned the executive responsibility for eliminating rotten boroughs and reapportioning electoral districts to restore a fair and equal system of representation.[37] Like any exercise
of prerogative, this one is justified only insofar as it serves the legitimate
ends of the community:

> If therefore the Executive, who has the power of Convoking the Legislative,
> observing rather the true proportion, than fashion of *Representation*, regulates,
> not by old custom, but true reason, the *number of Members,* in all places, that
> have a right to be distinctly represented, which no part of the People however
> incorporated can pretend to, but in proportion to the assistance, which it af-
> fords to the publick, it cannot be judg'd, to have set up a new Legislative, but to
> have restored the old and true one, and to have rectified the disorders, which
> succession of time had insensibly, as well as inevitably introduced. (II, § 158)[38]

For the liberal Locke, "old custom" was largely irrelevant to determining the
propriety of a practice.[39] What matters here and in other contexts is conformity to a different standard of right. In a refrain that appears throughout the
Second Treatise, Locke proclaimed that "whatsoever cannot but be acknowledged to be of advantage to the Society, and People in general, upon just and
lasting measures, will always, when done, justifie it self" (II, § 158). Locke's
discussion of the relationship between the executive and the legislature in
these passages indicates that the executive has a special supervisory role over
the entire government to ensure that the aims of the constitution are being

served—at least where "private interests" impede legislatively enacted reform (II, § 157). This particular oversight function undoubtedly violates the separation of powers in giving the executive some say over representation in the legislature, but it satisfies Locke's demand for legitimacy because it promotes the original purposes of the constitution and serves the best interests of the community.

Contingency and Necessity

Locke's willingness to entrust such extraordinary responsibilities to the executive reflects his belief that the contingent nature of politics—and perhaps life more generally—leaves few other options. The executive's power to assemble and dismiss the legislative does not make the executive supreme, insisted Locke, but is only "a Fiduciary Trust, placed in him, for the safety of the People, in a Case where the uncertainty, and variableness of humane affairs could not bear a steady fixed rule" (II, § 156). The executive must be entrusted with such powers in order to deal effectively with the "Exigencies of the Commonwealth." Since settled institutional arrangements are not always adequate to this purpose, "the best remedy [that] could be found for this defect, was to trust this to the prudence of one, who was always to be present, and whose business it was to watch over the publick good" (II, § 156).

But Locke's views on contingency were not limited to the observation that gradual changes eventually make many long-established institutional routines and legal rules obsolete.[40] His views on contingency were much more radical than that. Not only is the world vulnerable to the slow processes of decay that time brings to all things, it is also exposed to sudden and unexpected changes that threaten to disrupt and destroy even recent innovations.[41] In what is perhaps the most melancholy passage in all of Locke's political writings, he laments the impermanence, insecurity, and utter fragility of a world that is never fully within human control or comprehension: "Things of this World are in so constant a Flux, that nothing remains long in the same State. Thus People, Riches, Trade, Power, change their Stations; flourishing mighty Cities come to ruine, and prove in time neglected desolate Corners, whilst other unfrequented places grow into populous Countries, fill'd with Wealth and Inhabitants" (II, § 157). The notion that even the best-laid designs are vulnerable to unpredictable disruptions might strike some readers as surprising for an otherwise optimistic rationalist work that constructs a system of politics out of the immutable laws of nature and the universal inclinations of mankind, for instance, sociality and understanding (II, § 77). But it would be even more surprising if Locke did not appreciate the vicissitudes of politics given what he had personally witnessed and experienced. This and other passages in the *Second Treatise of Government* echo a common motif in the literature that grew out of the extreme disturbances that rocked seventeenth-century England, including urban riots, terrorist plots, assassination attempts, and, of course, civil war.[42] Indeed, Locke's views on contingency betray a Machiavellian sensibility that was likely reinforced by his study of the Italian's political writings.[43] The parallels between Locke and Machiavelli are not all that unusual, since Locke confronted a problem, according to Pocock, that preoccupied Machiavelli too: "The continuation and stabilization of civic bodies in intimate tension with thought aimed at the understanding of rapid and unpredictable change."[44]

As early as his *Letter from a Person of Quality,* which he is believed to have coauthored with Shaftesbury, Locke came to terms with the idea that historical and political change is unavoidable and even salutary. In response to the argument of some clergymen that government must make no alterations in the structure of the church, since it has been ordained by God, Locke asked, "For what is the business of Parliaments but the alteration, either by adding, or taking away some part of the Government, either in Church or State? And every new Act of Parliament is an alteration; and what kind of Government in Church and State must that be, which I must swear upon no alteration of Time, emergencie of Affairs, nor variation of human Things, never to endeavor to alter?" Answering his own question, he stated that "such a Government should be given by God himself," but as the things and affairs of this world are transient, humans must adapt to change and be ready to make necessary alterations.[45]

This understanding of contingency goes a long way toward explaining Locke's views on the limitations of legislative or statutory action: "For since in some Governments the Law-making Power is not always in being, and is usually too numerous, and too slow, for the dispatch requisite to Execution: and because also it is impossible to foresee, and so by laws to provide for, all Accidents and Necessities, that may concern the publick; or to make such Laws, as will do no harm, if they are executed with an inflexible rigour, on all occasions, and upon all Persons, that may come in their way, therefore there is a latitude left to the Executive power, to do many things of choice, which the

Laws do not prescribe" (II, § 160). This passage is remarkable not just for its blunt pessimism about the inadequacies of legislative action but even more so for its evident aversion to uniformly rigorous execution of the law. Locke suggested that even where an applicable law exists, strict enforcement of that law might be harmful to a particular individual or even to the community as a whole. Unlike arguments from equity that counsel against the application of the law in the interest of justice toward a particular individual, Locke's argument advises against the application of the law in the interest of the community as a whole, regardless of what a particular individual deserves in a given case. Contrary to Harvey Mansfield's insistence that extraordinary violence is the consummate expression of executive power, Locke indicated that showing leniency "to mitigate the severity of the Law, and pardon some Offenders" (II, § 159) is just as important as vigor in the exercise of executive power.[46] Prerogative is a Janus-faced power that sometimes displays a merciful visage, at other times a cruel countenance. The executive decides which side to show based on a judgment of what is "for the good of the People, and not manifestly against it" (II, § 161).

Prerogative is no ordinary power of government. Indeed, it is literally defined by the concrete contingencies that call it forth. It is "a Power in the hands of the Prince to provide for the publick good, in such Cases, which depending upon unforeseen and uncertain Occurrences, certain and unalterable Laws could not safely direct" (II, § 158). Prerogative is justified by the fact that the extraordinary is an ordinary part of politics. As Larry Arnhart puts it, "Executive prerogative is a political response to that flux in the world that runs against the fixity of law."[47] Even though its aim is to rectify "the disorders, which succession of time had insensibly, as well as inevitably introduced" (II, § 158), prerogative itself cannot be ordered or controlled through ordinary means. It is not opposed to the established order, but it is not a regular part of that order, either.

In characterizing prerogative in such elastic terms, Locke's explanation calls to mind Machiavelli's dictum that the ends should never be subordinated to the means.[48] Contrary to conventional opinion about the supposedly legalistic character of liberal political thought, early liberals like Locke evinced a Machiavellian attitude toward the instrumental character of legal and institutional forms. For these two thinkers and later post-Machiavellian liberals, the contingencies of politics made it impractical and dangerous to codify rules of political action that would have to be violated in certain circumstances. Even though Locke relied on the rationality of natural law to help stabilize social and political relations, like Machiavelli he recognized the ineliminable human element that is simultaneously the cause of and the remedy for the inconstancy of politics. Like Machiavelli, Locke's views on the openness and incompleteness of political life give his thought what Peter Laslett has described as an "anti-synthetic quality" that makes it possible to see him as "Machiavelli's philosopher."[49] Neither the Florentine nor the Englishman accepted the idea that magistrates could serve themselves or the public well simply by memorizing and following a set of political rules.[50] Despite their differences on the scope and limits of executive power, both thinkers accepted the need for extraordinary exercises of discretionary power to deal with emergencies.[51]

Another indication of Locke's attitude toward contingency appears in the language of "necessity" that pervades his discussion of executive power.[52] This political idiom became pronounced during the Civil War, when the king's opponents invoked an array of ideas borrowed from the *raison d'état* tradition to justify rebellion.[53] Locke's political thought has much more in common with *raison d'état* thinkers on the Continent who stressed the need for constitutional flexibility to deal with the exigencies of politics than it does with English common law thinkers who insisted that customary constitutional forms were adequate. However, the flexibility of Lockean constitutionalism did not translate into the kind of moral flexibility that Machiavelli infamously advocated. Locke never accepted "the necessity for a *prince* to preserve himself as a head of state at all costs," because he did not believe that the interests of the prince and the state were inextricably united.[54] As we shall see, he suggested that it would be easy to distinguish between executives acting purely in their own self-interest from those acting in the best interests of the community. Consistent with the *raison d'état* tradition, though, Lockean constitutionalism does not constrain the executive from acting without legal precedent or the expectation of subsequent parliamentary approval. Locke's innovation was to reconcile the seemingly antithetical doctrines of necessity and constitutionalism by making the constitution subservient to the same master served by necessity: *salus populi*, as defined by the laws of nature.[55]

The Informality of Prerogative

In an important sense, the law defines the regular responsibilities of the executive. The main responsibility of the executive, after all, is to enforce the laws of the commonwealth. However, the executive's responsibilities are not limited to the law, because the world itself cannot be limited by the law. As a consequence, the executive must also act where the law is silent.[56] In contrast to the practice of Roman dictatorship, the executive, not the legislature, gets to decide whether there is a state of emergency and what to do about it. Locke explained that "*Prerogative* can be nothing, but the Peoples permitting their Rulers, to do several things of their own free choice, where the Law was silent, and sometimes too against the direct Letter of the Law, for the publick good; and their acquiescing in it when so done" (II, § 164). There are two types of legal silence relevant here. The first is the absence of a law regulating the particular case at hand. The second denotes the absence of formal guidelines regulating the use of prerogative. Unlike the ordinary powers of the executive, which are largely legal in focus and in operation, prerogative is an extralegal power in these respects.

Unlike theorists of royal prerogative who drew a distinction between legal, or ordinary, prerogative defined by the common law, and extralegal, or absolute, prerogative beyond the common law, Locke restricted his use of the term to extralegal exercises of power.[57] In fact, he redefined the term altogether by "wrenching it from the constellation of legal rights for which the king could demand respect and unquestionable obedience."[58] Not only does prerogative permit the executive to act in the absence of legislative authorization (that is, when the laws are silent), but, as already noted, *it even allows the executive to act contrary to the explicit commands of the law.*[59] Locke expressly defined prerogative as the interruption of civil laws: "This Power to act according to discretion, for the publick good, without the prescription of the Law, and sometimes even against it, *is that which is called Prerogative*" (II, § 160). In spite of his own admonition that the "*Legislative cannot transfer the Power of Making Laws* to any other hands" (II, § 141), Locke gave the executive indirect legislative powers to make exceptions to the duly enacted laws of the commonwealth when strict adherence to them would undermine the public good.

While it might be tempting to regard prerogative as an exception to, or even an aberration from, a model of government structured around determinate laws and formal institutions, the informality of prerogative is actually integral to Locke's model of government. Locke resisted the temptation to make a fetish of civil laws and cautioned against rigid adherence to artificial rules where it would damage the public good.[60] In his thinking, it is contrary to the public good to permit the laws to interfere with the very *raison d'être* of government. To him it made no sense to sacrifice the public good for the means that were designed to serve it. Whatever is for "the good of the Community"—whether it is a constitutional limitation of executive power or a well-meaning exercise of prerogative—"cannot be an *incroachment* upon any body" (II, § 163). Even though Locke never completely abandoned his commitment to consent as the ultimate terrestrial justification of authority, he declared that the people should acquiesce when it benefits the public good, as he believed they would.[61]

But in noting approvingly that "the People are very seldom, or never scrupulous, or nice in the point" (II, § 161), Locke seemed to promote, or at least to depend upon, the political apathy and indifference of the people to make prerogative possible.[62] He took it for granted that the people would simply know when their magistrates had gone too far, and he assumed that exercises of prerogative that "cannot but be acknowledged to be of advantage to the Society, and People in general, upon just and lasting measures, will always, when done, justifie itself" (II, § 158). Locke probably wanted to stress the informality of prerogative, but he ended up accentuating its undemocratic features, for unlike legislative enactments, exercises of prerogative are approved or disapproved by the people only after the fact and do not establish precedents that future executives can cite to justify their own actions. Moreover, he made no attempt to resolve the apparent inconsistency with his earlier prohibition against rule "by extemporary Dictates and undetermined Resolutions" (II, § 137). However, it is clear that the target of his attack is arbitrary rule, rather than discretionary action per se. The crucial difference is that arbitrary power conforms neither to determinate rules nor to the general ends of society, whereas discretionary power, however informal and indeterminate, can be instrumental to the preservation of the community.[63]

One of the key difficulties in appreciating the full implications of Locke's theory is that it is not entirely clear how far the emergency powers of the executive extend. Nor is it obvious which circumstances warrant an exercise of prerogative. The trouble is that Locke provided only one concrete example of an event that would call forth a justifiable exercise of prerogative. He gave the case of an accident, "wherein a strict and rigid observation of the Laws may do harm; (as not to pull down an innocent Man's House to stop the Fire, when the next to it is burning)" (II, § 159). Compounding the difficulty of interpreting this passage is the fact that Locke uses the example to justify the use of the pardon power to exonerate private individuals who breach the laws of the state to uphold the laws of nature rather than to illustrate how the executive might use prerogative powers to intervene in an emergency.

Despite the questions that Locke leaves unanswered in this particular example, the overall context of Locke's discussion indicates that the class of events that call for the use of prerogative is quite limited, if not quite well defined. However, it does appear that such events are distinguished from ordinary occurrences along two dimensions: time and severity. The event must happen quickly, coming as something of a surprise. And it must be an extreme event, one that exposes the community to an "eminent hazard" (II, § 156). The example of the burning house, along with the discussion that precedes it, strongly suggests that prerogative is restricted to sudden and life-threatening emergencies that exceed the competence of the law. Locke's references in this context to the "Fundamental Law of Nature and Government, *viz.* That as much as may be, *all* the Members of the Society are to be *preserved*" reinforces the impression that prerogative is summoned in matters of life and death (II, § 159). It is not just any unexpected event that justifies the use of prerogative, but only a "quick turn of affairs" where any delay in the meeting of the legislature "might endanger the publick" (II, § 156). In other words, prerogative is to be used only when time is of the essence and the events are of such an extraordinary nature that ordinary laws provide little to no effective guidance. In Locke's own words, prerogative is to be used when "unforeseen and uncertain Occurrences" make it impossible to follow "certain and unalterable Laws" without doing further harm to the public good (II, § 158).

Alternative Positions

Locke's incorporation of prerogative into his constitutional scheme of government was politically curious, to say the least. This personalized conception of political power surpasses anything contemplated or even tolerated by English republicans, whose quasi-democratic preferences inclined them to regard law—insofar as it constitutes the ultimate expression of public will—as the only appropriate source and benchmark of legitimate power. That Locke permitted prerogative to vary according to the personal characteristics of the executive distinguishes him from most of his contemporaries and actually places him closer to his political and ideological enemies, the royalists. Both the radicals of his own day and the parliamentarians of previous generations were more likely to favor legal or legislative alternatives to executive discretion in an emergency.

One of the most prominent critics of the royalist position on prerogative prior to the Civil War, James Whitlocke argued that even the king's absolute prerogative was defined by law. He asserted that "Our rule is in this plain commonwealth of ours, '*oportet neminem esse sapientorem legibus.*' [No one should be wiser than the laws.] If there be an inconvenience, it is fitter to have it removed by a lawful means, than by an unlawful." [64] In 1610 Thomas Hedley had maintained that the common law narrowly circumscribes the sphere of discretionary activity and always regulates it. Even those who did accept the necessity for prerogative generally preferred legislative action to executive discretion. On the whole, they denied that emergency discretionary powers were "legal." [65] By 1640, however, leaders in the Commons came to insist that the law defined the proper limits of prerogative and liberties alike, asserting that they "would accept only those prerogatives which were embedded in the law." [66] Parliamentarian Henry Parker proclaimed that "in times of national emergency, 'the supreame judicature,' as well in matters of State as matters of Law' must lie with the two Houses of Parliament as representatives of the ultimately sovereign people." [67] Locke, of course, would disclaim the idea that legal regularization of prerogative is possible.

The common law offered an alternative way to deal with unforeseeable emergencies. Sir Matthew Hale argued that the slow and impersonal accretion of customary law, which embodies both the reason and experience of an organic body, could handle the contingencies of politics better than abstract reasoning. This adaptive approach, he maintained, was better suited than individual reason to deal with "the Multitude of successive Exigencies and Emergencies, that in a long Tract of Time will offer themselves." [68] But Locke accepted only one half of the common law formula of adaptation and preservation where prerogative was involved. Each exercise of prerogative constitutes an attempt to adapt to particular exigencies, but no exercise of prerogative is to be preserved as a precedent or incorporated into the body of national law. Locke's refusal to grant exercises of prerogative any precedential value is of a piece with his skepticism toward the value of precedents embodied in the common law through long usage. His refusal also reflects his understanding that all political and legal acts involve particular exercises of personal judgment, both by legislators who enact statutes and by the executive who generally enforces (but sometimes finds it necessary to circumvent) them for the safety of the community. In either case, individual judgment is involved in a way that the common law tradition denies or conceals.

Locke's views on prerogative probably differ most markedly from those of his republican contemporaries. A brief comparison of Locke's theory with Algernon Sidney's *Discourses concerning Government* is instructive in clarifying just how unusual Locke's position was for someone of his political stripe. A comparison of these contemporaries, who were committed to many of the same political principles (rule of law, consent of the governed, equality, rational liberty, resistance against tyranny), highlights the stark differences between republican and liberal attitudes toward the law.[69] The legalistic inflexibility and rigor of Sidney's thought accentuates the greater flexibility and suppleness of Locke's constitutionalism and helps explain the disparities in their conceptions of executive power.

Like Locke, Sidney required virtue in rulers as a supplement to the protections of the rule of law, but his meritocratic conception of legitimate rule left little or no room for executive discretion. Sidney asserted that the magistrate "has no other power than what the law allows," for "we have no other notion of wrong, than that it is a breach of the law which determines what is right."[70] The executive, "under what name soever he was known . . . is circumscribed by such rules as he cannot safely transgress."[71] Furthermore, "The laws of every place show what the power of the respective magistrate is, and by declaring how much is allowed to him, declare what is denied."[72] Sidney explained that "if the safety of the people be the supreme law, and this safety extend to, and consist in the preservation of their liberties, goods, lands and lives, that law must necessarily be the root and beginning, as well as the end and limit of all magisterial power, and all laws must be subservient and subordinate to it."[73]

Lacking Locke's supreme confidence in the knowability of natural law or any other inexplicit standard of right, Sidney was unable to conceive of any viable limits on political power other than the public laws. To the extent that he discussed prerogative at all, he did so with so much skepticism—if not outright hostility—that it became unthinkable to incorporate it into any rational scheme of government. Sidney stated ironically that this power belongs "to him only, who is so adapted for the performance of his office" by divine grace.[74] The idea that anyone is actually endowed by God with such abilities is a proposition he emphatically denied on egalitarian, epistemological, and historical grounds throughout his *magnum opus*. As far as those individuals naturally, if not divinely, endowed with extraordinary abilities are concerned, Sidney clung to his conviction that no one is authorized to act contrary to the laws, which are sanctified as expressions of "that eternal principle of reason and truth, from whence the rule of justice which is sacred and pure ought to be deduced."[75]

For the republican Sidney, rule *by* law is the essential element of the rule of law. Thus, kings "have no power but what is given by the laws."[76] Similarly, John Milton insisted that "the Law was set above the Magistrate" in the beginnings of government because of "the danger and inconveniences of committing arbitrary power to any,"[77] while Neville stated that the jurisdiction of kings over their subjects does not extend beyond the laws, by which he meant those laws "made . . . in parliament and duly published."[78] Prerogative was antithetical to the republican notion that constitutional government was limited to government by strict rules. Because prerogative is, by its nature, an extralegal power, Sidney could not countenance its constitutionality. Sidney and Milton required *prior* consent (that is, "an explicit act of approbation") for any just exercise of political power since individual judgment was equated with mere will.[79] Sidney's belief that government under the law leaves little or no room for discretion to anyone explains his blithe indifference to the question of a single or plural executive.[80] Although he reluctantly granted the executive a power to pardon, it could be exercised only according to rules laid down by Parliament, which possesses the exclusive "power of altering, mitigating, explaining or correcting the laws of England."[81] In fact, the people ought to take precautions that the magistrate has no opportunity to subvert the constitution by loose interpretations of the laws, which should be "deaf, inexorable, [and] inflexible."[82]

Like most republicans, Sidney's distrust of the executive did not extend to Parliament, whose numerical size, he believed, made it less susceptible to corruption than a single individual or a small group.[83] Notwithstanding the enormous importance Sidney attached to the character of officeholders, he was unwilling to endow them with powers that had not been explicitly pre-approved by the people or that would contravene the laws of the commonwealth.

In case of emergency, Sidney did allow the temporary expedient of a dictator. Sidney followed Roman practice in reserving this extraordinary office to one who had "given great testimonies of his virtue" but deviated from the Romans in demanding tight legal constraints. His dictator would enjoy only those powers "limited in time, circumscribed by law, and kept perpetually under the supreme authority of the people."[84] Magisterial power "hath its exercises and extent proportionable to the command of those that institute it."[85] Without actually specifying the limits he had in mind, Sidney proclaimed that those nations which have "endeavoured to supply the defects, or restrain the vices of their supreme magistrates . . . have always flourished in virtue, power, glory, and happiness."[86] In effect, the kind of executive that republicans like Sidney preferred was one who has no independent will but simply carries out the will of the legislature.

Locke differed dramatically from the republicans not only because he considered prerogative indispensable—and not inimical—to the preservation of liberty but also because he accepted exercises of individual political judgment and discretion in a way that they fundamentally rejected. In some respects, Locke's theory of prerogative bears a closer resemblance to the arguments of royalists than to those of republicans, with whom he shared many more political and ideological aims. For instance, the royalist Thomas Fleming stated in Bates's Case:

> The absolute power of the King is not that which is converted or executed to private use, to the benefit of any particular person, but is only that which is applied to the general benefit of the people, and is *salus populi*; as the people is the body, and the king the head; and this power is guided by the rules, which direct only at the common law, and is most properly *Pollicy and Government*; and as the constitution of this body varieth with the time, so varieth this absolute law, *according to the wisdom of the king*, for the common good; and these being general rules and true as they are, all things done within these rules are lawful.[87]

As noted earlier, it was the royalists who emphasized the personalized nature of power. Royalist defenses of prerogative also invoked *salus populi* as often as they appealed to the king's emergency powers.[88] Although Locke never accepted the royalist argument that the king was absolute within his "realm" (those areas of government that made up the exclusive province of the king)—and would certainly have rejected the claims of parliamentary supremacy made by Henry Parker and others—his theory of executive power seems to argue for a conception of prerogative even more expansive in some ways than that of some royalists.

Extraconstitutional Criteria of Legality

The question, of course, is what can prevent the executive from abusing this extraordinary power in the middle of a crisis? John Dunn has argued that Locke intended the rules formally "specified in a set of written documents" to operate as checks. According to Dunn, who refers to English constitutional practices at the time to buttress his claims, prerogative is a "rule-bound" practice whose "legal authority is determined by the constitution."[89] It is, Dunn acknowledges, "totally unregulated" in "the mode of its exercise," but "the limits within which this exercise may take place" are definitely regulated by human law.[90]

Unfortunately, Dunn's interpretation is unconvincing. For one thing, historical practice cannot serve as a reliable guide to understanding Locke, not only because his avoidance of direct historical references makes it difficult to know his position on particular practices, but also because he rejected the idea that established practices have an automatic claim on our ideas.[91] Moreover, the textual references used in support of the contention that the *constitution* itself is supposed to delimit prerogative are oblique at best. For another thing, Locke explicitly and repeatedly states that prerogative entails action "without the prescription of the Law, and sometimes even against it" (II, § 160). And as the burning house example illustrates, the legitimate extralegal uses of prerogative even extend to the violation of specific laws that protect property rights when higher-ranking interests, such as the right to life, are at stake. Unable to muster a sturdy defense of his claim, Dunn himself ends up acknowledging that the "bland assumption that there must be a legal criterion is simply rejected by Locke."[92]

Notwithstanding his wholehearted support for the rule of law, Locke's account of prerogative exposes the limitations of human law. Not only is prerogative a response to the insufficiencies of man-made laws, it is also resistant to regulation by these laws. Even though it is possible to use the law to punish the executive for abuses of prerogative after the fact, the extraordinary circumstances in which it is used generally do not permit the law to operate with its usual effectiveness during an emergency. Moreover, Locke's discussion of prerogative makes it clear that adherence to positive laws is neither a primary nor a necessary criterion of legitimacy. In fact, Locke's own involvement in the Exclusion Crisis testifies to his view that legal and constitutional rules must yield to higher interests. That prerogative often operates outside the public law does not *ipso facto* make it an act of tyranny. A violation of positive law is a powerful *indication* that a king might be a tyrant, but it is not in and of itself *proof* of tyranny.

But this does not mean that prerogative is wholly unregulated. The absence of *legal* prohibitions on the executive does not mean that there is an absence of all *normative* prohibitions. Even when it becomes necessary to violate the legal restrictions imposed by the civil law or the constitution, it is never permissible to violate the moral restrictions imposed by the laws of nature. Adherence to the precepts of natural law is, in fact, an unconditional requirement of all action—public or private.

Locke consistently maintained a distinction between two systems of law, the human law and the natural law. While human laws are historically contingent, changing, fallible, and potentially breakable, the laws of nature are permanent, unvarying, inerrant, and inviolable.[93] Natural law provides the ultimate standard of legitimacy even after a full-fledged system of positive law has been established. Indeed, natural law forms the basis of human law. "Certainly," Locke commented in his *Essays on the Law of Nature,* "positive civil laws are not binding by their own nature or force or in any other way than in virtue of the law of nature."[94] The first commandment of natural law is the welfare of the people. "*Salus Populi Suprema Lex,* is certainly so just and fundamental a Rule, that he, who sincerely follows it, cannot dangerously err" (II, § 158).

This normative standard is built right into Locke's definition of prerogative. And in the final analysis, it is the only unassailable limitation on the exercise of prerogative. (Even the people's consent—or lack thereof—might be wrong.) When Locke stated that "Prerogative is nothing but the Power of doing publick good without a Rule" (II, § 166), he seemed to be referring to man-made rules, not the rules that natural law might prescribe. As Locke explained, "'tis fit that the Laws themselves should in some Cases give way to the Executive Power, or rather to this Fundamental Law of Nature and Government, *viz.* That as much as may be, *all* the Members of the Society are to be *preserved*" (II, § 159).

The non-institutionalized, informal nature of prerogative and the restraints on it give no reason to conclude, however, that Locke "*constitutionalizes* the necessity of tyranny."[95] Although there are serious epistemological—not to mention political—problems involved in correctly determining exactly what the laws of nature demand of either the people or their rulers in any given situation, the centrality of natural law in Locke's scheme belies Harvey

Mansfield's suggestion that prerogative is legally unrestricted. Mansfield simply does not take Locke's use of natural law seriously, so he misses its role as a normative constraint on prerogative. Instead of the unalterable and ultimate standard of normativity that it is for Locke, natural law becomes in Mansfield's interpretation a manipulable instrument of the self-interested and a pretext for self-righteous aggression. He alleges that Lockean freedom originates in the "doctrine that each man executes the law of nature for himself: although executing nature's law, one is set free by the necessity of doing so oneself. In short, Locke's idea of freedom seems to imply what we have called executive ambivalence. Weak insofar as it recognizes man's submission to the law of nature, it is strong insofar as the execution requires discretion and assertiveness."[96] Here Mansfield confuses the *de facto* discretion that is exercised in the state of nature with the *de jure* enforcement that ought to be practiced. As a result he asserts that "in executing the law of nature, men are merely following their own necessity."[97] But this is not what Locke claimed.

Locke frequently insisted (albeit unpersuasively) that God has provided individuals with a perfectly intelligible and accessible law to govern their actions and preserve peace (II, § 12). "The *State of Nature* has a Law of Nature to govern it, which obliges every one: And Reason, which is that Law, teaches all Mankind, who will but consult it, that being all equal and independent, no one ought to harm another in his Life, Health, Liberty, or Possessions" (II, § 6). The law of nature, "discernible by the light of reason," is the absolute, objective, and unavoidable measure of normativity. Without it, there is no such thing as morality at all, but Mansfield emphasizes its potential manipulation over its actual observance in the state of nature.[98] In order to give effect to this law, there has to be a perficient power to enforce it. The universality of executive power in the state of nature is a necessary consequence of the duty and correlative right of humans to preserve themselves and others: "And that all Men may be restrained from invading others Rights, and from doing hurt to one another, and the Law of Nature be observed, which willeth the Peace and *Preservation of all Mankind*, the *Execution* of the Law of Nature is in that State, put into every Mans hands, whereby every one has a right to punish the transgressors of that Law to such a Degree, as may hinder its Violation" (II, § 7).[99] It is precisely because different individuals have conflicting interpretations of the laws of nature that an impartial umpire in the form of a limited government is established to ensure that they are not manipulated by self-serving individuals.

Of course, the interpretive obstacles present in the state of nature do not disappear in political society. Determining exactly what natural law demands is a problematic task. Even though the meaning of civil laws is not always transparent, they are open to inspection in a way that the laws of nature are not. Notwithstanding his repeated assertions that natural law is "plain and intelligible to all rational creature" (II, § 124), Locke never provided a thorough specification of the substantive contents of the law of nature. Nor did he maintain a consistent position on its accessibility to the ordinary human intellect. He acknowledged the pervasive disagreement among even the concerned and the learned over its contents as well as the numerous epistemological problems associated with attempts to discover the law of nature.[100] However, as discussed below, his educational writings indicate that it is possible to overcome these difficulties with the proper training.

Even though the legislature is charged with enacting civil laws that conform to the natural law, situations will inevitably arise where the public welfare is better served and the natural law is more faithfully observed by *disregarding* the civil law. Locke believed that these two systems of law will often coincide, but when they do not, *the executive is expected to enforce the natural law instead of the civil law.* For instance, the executive ought to ignore or violate even a perfectly valid civil law protecting private property that would otherwise hinder the executive's ability to fulfill the more fundamental duty to preserve life, as in the example of burning house. Since there is no formal or institutional oversight of prerogative, it means that the executive is constrained by the very same law that he or she is charged with interpreting and enforcing.

The Personal Foundations of Executive Power

Prerogative is an utterly contingent power. It is contingent on the events that call it forth, contingent on the changing nature of those events, and contingent on the person who wields it. Thus, each use must be judged on a case-by-case basis. The specific actions carried out in the name of prerogative cannot be defined or prescribed in advance but depend on the actual circumstances confronting the community. For much the same reason that it is impossible to plan for or control sudden unexpected disturbances through ordinary law, it is impossible to specify in advance exactly what powers and actions might be necessary to handle those disturbances. In that respect, prerogative is beyond institutional formalization and is irreducible to law.

One of the most important factors to consider in determining whether such an exercise of prerogative should even be permitted is the personal character of the executive.

Locke's account of prerogative is suffused with references to the significance of personal character in determining the full extent of extralegal power. Due to the inherent and potentially lethal dangers of prerogative, the executive is given free rein to exercise this enormous discretionary power only where the people have confidence in the virtues of the executive. The full potential scope of prerogative does not belong to the executive office as a latent reservoir of power that the executive can freely access whenever the need arises. The ability to take full advantage of prerogative depends largely on the personal resources of the executive. Indeed, an executive who possesses the right personal qualities can expand the limited institutional resources contained in the office. And only those executives with the right personal qualities can be trusted to draw from this vast well of power without draining it all for themselves or poisoning the groundwater that nourishes the liberty of individuals in the process.

One of the things that might have made it difficult to recognize this feature of Locke's political thought is its resemblance to premodern traditions and ideas that liberalism is believed to have rejected. Locke's conception of prerogative is predicated on a critical distinction between the person and the office of the executive, much like the medieval doctrine of the "King's Two Bodies." As Ernst Kantorowicz explains, the (mainly English) medieval bifurcation of the monarch into the person of the king and the office of the Crown was based on a distinction between the "body natural" and the "body politic" of the king.[101] Unlike medieval theorists, however, Locke considered the person and the office clearly separable, despite their close links.[102]

There is an "intermingling of formal and personal political requirements" in Locke's theory of prerogative.[103] Both the person and the office determine the legitimacy of certain exercises of executive power. His agreement with the saying "the Reigns of good Princes have been always most dangerous to the Liberties of their People" demonstrates just how personalized and individualized his conception of prerogative is: "For when their Successors, managing the Government with different Thoughts, would draw the Actions of those good Rulers into Precedent, and make them the Standard of their *Prerogative*, as if what had been done only for the good of the People, was a right in them to do, for the harm of the People, if they so pleased; it has often occasioned

Contest, and sometimes publick Disorders, before the People could recover their original Right, and get that to be declared not to be *Prerogative,* which truly was never so" (II, § 166). The exercise of prerogative for the public good demands evidence of certain dispositions and characteristics that allow the executive to manage the affairs of government skillfully and in a manner consistent with its ends. Not surprisingly, familiar attributes of leadership, such as prudence and experience (being "acquainted with the state of public affairs"), are among the most important of these traits (II, § 156).[104] What Locke seems to have in mind is not just the technical ability to deal with emergencies but also the perspicacity to recognize that such a state exists in the first place. However, the greatest stress is placed on moral virtues. The presence of virtue provides some assurance that what prudence and ability initiate will be carried out in the best interests of the community as a whole and not simply for the benefit of the executive or one segment of that community.

For Locke, the personal moral qualities of the executive play a significant—even decisive—role in establishing the legitimacy of a particular exercise of prerogative. To a large degree, the moral qualities of the executive determine the functional status and reach of prerogative. The character of the executive provides a good indication that such powers would be exercised for legitimate ends, as specified by the laws of nature and the rightful aims of the constitution. Prerogative power is invested in the *person* as well as the *office*; it is not an inherent right that belongs to the office as such. Locke's contrast of the different styles of rule between a "good Prince, who is mindful of the trust put into his hands, and careful of the good of his People" and "a weak and ill Prince, who would claim that Power, which his Predecessors exercised without the direction of the Law, as a Prerogative belonging to him by Right of his Office" shined a spotlight on the way that differences in character produce differences in governance (II, § 164). Locke seemed to suggest that one was as incorruptible as the other was incorrigible. The "good Prince" exercises prerogative selflessly for the benefit of the community, whereas the "weak and ill Prince" exploits prerogative to increase his own power.

Locke went on to argue that differences in the moral qualities of executives would also lead to decisive differences in the amount of leeway the people give them to exercise such extraordinary discretion. In an unusually direct reference to English political history, Locke approvingly noted that "he, that will look into the *History of England,* will find, that Prerogative was always *largest* in the hands of our wisest and best Princes: because the People observing the whole tendency of their Actions to be the publick good, contested not what was done without Law to that end" (II, § 165). In other words, the "wisest and best Princes" enjoy the greatest latitude in the use of their powers by the people's permission. "The People . . . let them inlarge their *Prerogative* as they pleased, judging rightly, that they did nothing herein to the prejudice of their Laws, since they acted conformable to the Foundation and End of all Laws, the publick good" (II, § 165). Because of their unimpeachable moral character, these princes are more secure in the use of power than their vicious counterparts, who face the possibility of popular resistance and legal sanction (II, § 164).

And when it comes to the question of imposing legal constraints on those "God-like Princes" set apart by their "Wisdom and Goodness," Locke's response left little doubt that they were entitled to greater latitude than their morally deficient counterparts. He stated that it is "very possible, and reasonable, that the People should *not* go about to set any Bounds to the *Prerogative* of those Kings or Rulers, who themselves transgressed not the Bounds of the publick good" (II, § 166, emphasis added). One of the things this means is that no exercise of prerogative should set a precedent for future use by a different executive. Instead, each exercise of prerogative ought to start from scratch. There is no precedential value established for subsequent executives by previous exercises of prerogative, either to justify executive action, based on the example of those "God-like Princes [who] indeed had some Title to Arbitrary Power," or to constrain it. No extralegal exercise of executive power can be claimed "as a Prerogative belonging to [a prince] by Right of his Office, which he may exercise at his pleasure" (II, § 164), since that would be to define this extraordinary power without any reference to the purposes that justify—and limit—it.

The upshot of Locke's argument is that knowledge of an executive's character obviates the need to assess each and every single act of prerogative.[105] Confidence in the executive's character is a proxy indicator of the likely justifiability of a discretionary act. Since the power of prerogative accrues to the person, it is crucial that the supreme magistrate be a trustworthy person, or else the community will be deprived of the full potential use of this power.

Curbing the Executive

The main objective of the *Treatises* was to find some prophylactic device, institutional or otherwise, to prevent the outbreak of political violence. According to Locke, political society is set up specifically to settle disputes through impartial laws, yet prerogative threatens to bring back the uncertainties and dangers inherent in the state of nature. If prerogative is an extralegal power, *how* is it to be judged? In the absence of an impartial umpire between the people and their executive, *who* is to judge when prerogative is misused or abused? Locke's response is not very heartening: "I Answer: Between an Executive Power in being, with such a Prerogative, and a Legislative that depends upon his will for their convening, there can be no *Judge on Earth*: As there can be none, between the Legislative, and the People, should either the Executive, or the Legislative, when they have got the Power in their hands, design, or go about to enslave, or destroy them. The People have no other remedy in this, as in all other cases where they have no Judge on Earth, but to *appeal to Heaven*" (II, § 168). God remains the supreme judge and final arbiter of such disputes, but the people have a right to revolution if their trust is violated. The most viable check on the executive operates outside the structure of government and is predicated on a possible return to the state of nature. The dispute is taken to the tribunal of natural law, "a Law antecedent and paramount to all positive Laws of men" (II, § 168). However, that remedy is activated only when people are already placed in the state of nature, for resistance presupposes the dissolution of government. As a result, Locke provided for the preservation of life only by opening up the possibility of a lapse into the state of nature where life is vulnerable and enforcement of the laws of nature is precarious.

When the legislative or the executive branch contravenes the ends for which government was instituted, it puts itself into the state of nature—indeed, a state of war—vis-à-vis the people. Locke argued that anyone who makes a design on one's liberty (or property) can be supposed to have designs on one's life as well: "In all States and Conditions the true remedy of *Force* without Authority, is to oppose *Force* to it. The use of *force* without Authority, always puts him that uses it into a *state of War*, as the Aggressor, and renders him liable to be treated accordingly" (II, § 155). And since the legislature is the guardian of the people's freedom, an attack upon the legislative is tantamount to an attack upon the life, liberty, and estate of the people.

Upon the dissolution of government, the people resume the executive right and are authorized to defend themselves (II, § 212–19). As Locke famously argued, though, the fundamental law of nature to preserve mankind gives the people[106] an inalienable right to defend themselves with force.[107] As Grant

puts it, "The justification for a given power is also the justification for the limitations on that power. In other words, there is a duty to obey under certain
conditions for the same reason that there is a right to resist when the conditions are not met."[108] Furthermore, the "doctrine of trust" implies a right to
depose tyrants. Locke insisted that it is "those, whoever they be, who by force
break through, and by force justifie their violation of them [the Constitutions
and Laws of the Government], are truly and properly *Rebels*," and this includes members of government themselves (II, § 226). Properly speaking, it is
the mischievous executive who rebels, not the people.[109]

Richard Ashcraft offered the possibility that the legislature could remove
an executive for maladministration or usurpation of power, which would obviate an appeal to natural law. Based largely on Locke's remark that "when the
Legislative hath put the *Execution* of the Laws, they make, into other hands,
they have a power still to resume it out of those hands, when they find cause,
and to punish for any mall-administration against the Laws" (II, § 153), Ashcraft claimed that the legislature is equipped to deal with usurpation by the
executive. However, the passage that Ashcraft cites does not describe a typical instance of executive malpractice. How could it, in light of contemporary
events, such as repeated prorogations and dissolutions of Parliament? Ashcraft's view (and, in this particular passage, Locke's) presupposes a legislative
authority in existence, that is, one that has not been dismissed. But that was
not the situation Locke and the radicals faced in the 1680s, nor was it one that
Locke could or did count on. Ashcraft assumed that the original constitution
would provide regular meeting times for the legislative, but that is exactly
what Locke denied in his repeated profession of the inability to provide for or
foresee every contingency. He was very clear on this point: "For it not being
possible, that the first Framers of the Government should, by any foresight, be
so much Masters of future Events, as to be able to prefix so just periods of return and duration to the *Assemblies of the Legislative,* in all times to come, that
might exactly answer all the Exigencies of the Commonwealth; the best remedy could be found for this defect, was to trust this to the prudence of one,
who was always to be present, and whose business it was to watch over the
publick good" (II, § 156). When Locke did consider the possibility of legislative
oversight, he did so in tentative and conditional terms: "either the Original
Constitution requires their *assembling* and *acting* at certain intervals, and then
the Executive Power does nothing but Ministerially issue directions for their
Electing and Assembling, according to due Forms: Or else it is left to his Pru-

dence to call them by new Elections, when the Occasions or Exigencies of the publick require the amendment of old, or making of new Laws, or the redress or prevention of any inconveniences, that lie on, or threaten the People" (II, § 154). Locke even pointed out that, historically speaking, this matter was "not settled by the original Constitution" (II, § 156).

Ashcraft's contention is also belied by Locke's recurrent references to "the appeal to Heaven," a euphemism for violent resistance, which reveal Locke's convictions more clearly than a single tentative remark. Locke simply provided no internal mechanism to adjudicate constitutional disputes the way the judiciary in the United States is often expected to.[110] It is fair to say that Hume and the Federalists improved upon Locke's design of executive power by instituting what Madison called "auxiliary precautions." Locke simply underestimated the efficacy of possible institutional checks like impeachment.

None of this means that Locke was indifferent or hostile to legal or institutional checks. Far from it. But he seemed to understand that the circumstances in which such checks become necessary are probably not going to be conducive to their efficacy or their judicious exercise. Not surprisingly, the most effective check on potential abuses of this power—popular resistance— parallels prerogative in its contingency, its informality, and, above all, its extremity.[111] However, the costs and uncertainties associated with this ultimate check make it such a risky and irregular undertaking that many misuses of prerogative (or any other power) "will be *born by the People,* without mutiny or murmur" (II, § 225).

This may help explain why the same Locke who took up his pen to refute Filmer would look to the personal qualities of the executive to serve as an internal check. Virtue, as Locke conceived it, is the least disruptive check of all, because it operates so steadily and silently. Even though it was not an institutional or legal check, it could be expected to operate with even greater regularity and reliability—where it is present.

The Political Psychology of Virtue

Locke's explanation of the way that the threat of revolution checks abuses of power seems to contradict my claim that virtue was a necessary, let alone effective, check on the executive. After all, he relied on the crass inducements of self-interest, not the fine motivations of virtue, when he argued that "the properest way to prevent the evil, is to shew them [potential rebels] the danger and injustice of it, who are under the greatest temptation to run into it" (II, § 226). Here as elsewhere, Locke sought to link the self-interest of rulers with the interests of the community as a whole by appealing to their desire to avoid terrible punishment. In this respect, Locke appears to exemplify Stephen Holmes's claim that the "classical liberal theory of self-interest" is "a normative doctrine . . . not a descriptive one," whereby many liberals sought "to bridle [the] destructive and self-destructive passions" of individuals by harnessing their self-interest to discourage vicious or destructive conduct.[112] Holmes claims that this obviates the need for extraordinary moral qualities in leaders, as liberals have rejected the idea that kings possess any special virtues that distinguish them morally from ordinary individuals.[113]

But Locke's demystification of regal power does not mean that he rejected the idea of virtue itself, or, as Pocock suggests, that he exhibited "indifference to virtue."[114] In fact, virtue figures prominently in his discussions of politics. Even in those passages that focus on calculations of self-interest, Locke frequently attributed the goodness and badness of political conduct to underlying character traits, including "the Pride, Ambition, and Turbulency of private Men," "the Peoples Wantonness," "the Rulers Insolence" (II, § 230), the "prudence" of the executive (II, § 156), and the "Goodness and Vertue" of the first rulers (II, § 94). As Locke explained, the principle "That all Men by Nature are equal" does not extend to virtue, which "may give Men a just Precedency" (II, § 54). In fact, the very origins of government can be explained by the fact that "some one good and excellent Man, having got a Preheminency amongst the rest, had this Deference paid to his Goodness and Vertue, as to a kind of Natural Authority, that the chief Rule, with Arbitration of their differences, by a tacit Consent devolved into his hands, without any other caution, but the assurance they had of his Uprightness and Wisdom" (II, § 94). Of course, Locke went on to point out that the folly of trusting one person with all the powers of government is what led people to adopt constitutional safeguards, but he returned to virtue as a safeguard in his defense of prerogative.

In keeping with the egalitarian nature of his moral and psychological thought, Locke explained disparities in virtue among individuals as "the product of exercise" rather than the heritage of "natural endowments."[115] However, he occasionally acknowledged that nature itself may account for some of the differences in virtue among individuals. Locke observed that "nine parts of ten are what they are, good or evil, useful or not, by their education," but the rest are so "well framed by nature" in both "body and mind" that "the strength of their natural genius . . . carrie[s them] towards what is excellent."[116] But whatever the reason for these differences, Locke expected those entrusted with power to surpass other individuals in virtue.

Locke's analyses of political problems often included an assessment of character. On the brink of the Exclusion Crisis he wrote: "Since most of the wrong judgments that are given in the world are rather the faults of the will than the understanding, to have justice well administered care should be taken to choose rather upright than learned men."[117] These sentiments were echoed in the *Treatises,* where Locke placed more blame on the presence of a few bad individuals than on any incentive structures for disruptions to the peace and harmony of the state of nature. He likened these rotten apples to "Beasts of Prey, those dangerous and noxious Creatures" who "are not under the ties of the Common Law of Reason, [and] have no other Rule, but that of Force and Violence" (II, § 16). These epithets apply with special emphasis to those magistrates who expose the people "to the boundless will of Tyranny," and who are "justly to be esteemed the common Enemy and Pest of Mankind" (II, § 229, 230). The comparison to beasts and brutes suggests that the main defect of these malefactors lies in their inability to control their impulses and subordinate their passions to reason. Locke explicitly ascribed the causes of tyranny to defects in the character of rulers, whose "Commands and Actions" are directed to "the satisfaction of his own Ambition, Revenge, Covetousness, or any other irregular Passion" (II, § 199). Since moral reformation and rehabilitation are simply out of the question for "any savage ravenous Beast," Locke recommended swift extermination of those noisome pests who have "quitted Reason" (II, § 181, 172)!

The use of such vituperative rhetoric, unusual for Locke, underscores his conviction that personal character plays a critical role in politics. His tendency to assign praise and blame to the dispositions of individuals suggests that the explanation for particular actions depends as much, if not more, on the moral character of individuals as it does on the structure of external conditions. Perhaps the best evidence of this belief is his surprising claim that voluntary subjection to a ruler unchecked by any determinate limits is perfectly rational if that ruler possesses the attributes of goodness and wisdom. In the context of his discussion of prerogative, Locke asserted that where "a Rational Creature . . . finds a good and wise Ruler, he may not perhaps think it either necessary, or useful to set precise Bounds to his Power in all things." Indeed, "a good Prince, who is mindful of the trust put into his hands, and careful of the good of his People, cannot have too much *Prerogative,* that is, Power to do good" (II, § 164). Just as irredeemable vice disqualifies a ruler from the exercise of even ordinary powers, exemplary virtue justifies the use of even extraordinary powers.

Virtue for Locke resides in dispositions that manifest themselves in habits rather than in "essences" that might remain hidden from view. Proper habits are vital to the formation of good character by virtue of their ability to overcome bad predispositions and impart good ones.[118] In this respect, Locke's conception of virtue has certain affinities with Aristotle's. Both thinkers argued that virtues were developed through and exhibited in habitual practices, and both rejected the notion that virtue could be reduced to a set of moral rules or precepts. "The knowledge of *virtue,*" Locke explained in *Some Thoughts concerning Education,* is taught "more by practice than rules."[119] However, the aim of virtue differed significantly for these thinkers. Locke was interested in the virtues primarily because they tell us how to *act.* Aristotle was also interested in this question, but his primary interest in the virtues was because they told us how to *be.* As Alasdair MacIntyre explains, Aristotelian ethics focuses on the question: "what sort of person am I to become?"[120] Locke's promotion of the virtues did not have such lofty ontological aspirations. Nor did his conception of virtue correspond to a perfectionist ideal of human excellence.[121]

The practical nature of virtue is also connected with its usefulness to the community as a whole. According to Locke, God "joined *Virtue* and publick Happiness together; and made the Practice thereof, necessary to the preservation of Society."[122] Like Aristotle's conception of virtue, Locke's is also concerned with the social impact of personal habits and dispositions. For Locke, there is always a dimension of virtue that is other-directed. The personal qualities that Locke adumbrates in his discussions of executive power—"wisdom," "prudence," and especially "goodness"—justify the confidence of the people because these virtues orient the executive toward the public good. This understanding of virtue is detectable in the *Second Treatise,* but it is most evident in Locke's educational writings.

Locke's educational texts were written specifically to help "produce virtuous, useful, and able men" who would be ready to take up the "gentleman's calling" of service to the public.[123] However, these writings are crucial to our understanding of prerogative because they contain Locke's most detailed and comprehensive account of the kinds of virtues that would be necessary in an executive who might have to act outside the law in an emergency. Even though these writings focus on the qualities required in "gentlemen," they establish the minimum baseline for the virtues that any leader, including the executive, ought to possess if they are to look after the public good. The education of these future rulers of England is critical, argued Locke, because it is upon them that "the welfare and prosperity of the nation so much depends."[124]

Among the most striking things about Locke's educational writings is how much they reverberate with distinctively republican overtones. *Some Thoughts concerning Education* frequently laid stress on duty, public service, self-denial, and other ideals geared toward the benefit of the community over that of the individual. The tone is set immediately in Locke's dedication, which preached that it is "every man's indispensable duty to do all the service he can to his country."[125] The books and courses of study he advised for gentlemen reinforce the disposition to place the public good before private interest. In addition to the modern classics of natural law theory, Locke recommended the reading of the republican masterpiece Cicero's *Offices* to "be informed in the principles and precepts of virtue for the conduct of his life." And the study of law was advised, not to learn how to evade one's duties but to learn "wherein he may be serviceable to his country."[126] Even though Locke did not directly teach the public virtues of patriotism and disinterestedness, he—and his followers in America—expected them to emerge if the other moral virtues were present in sufficient strength.[127]

The virtues that were most important to Locke's political thought usually require the subordination of the selfish passions to the rule of reason. A proper education leads to the realization that "the great principle and foundation of all virtue and worth is placed in this, that a man is able to *deny himself* his own desires, cross his own inclinations, and purely follow what reason directs as best though the appetite lean the other way."[128] In fact, one of the reasons that the study of Latin is valuable is that it gives the student an opportunity to reflect on and absorb the wisdom of the Roman saying "*Dulces sunt fructus radix virtutis amara*": "Sweet are the fruits of virtue, but bitter its root."[129] But the way to virtue must first be paved by the right habits and dispositions: "Teach him to get a mastery over his own inclinations and *submit his appetite to reason*. This being obtained, and by constant practice settled into habit, the hardest part of the task is over."[130] Once acquired, virtue manifests itself negatively, in terms of what individuals *deny* themselves. Above all, individuals must be taught to deny their "love of *power* and dominion." Dominion "is the first origin of most vicious habits that are ordinary and natural" and must be eliminated, or else individuals will seek "nothing but to have their *wills*."[131]

Since the love of dominion is detrimental to everyone, it is politically imperative to make sure that it has been thoroughly suppressed: "He that has not a mastery over his inclinations, he that knows not how to *resist* the importunity of *present pleasure or pain* for the sake of what reason tells him is fit to be done, wants the true principle of virtue and industry and is in danger never to be good for anything."[132] In a political context, "the importunity of *present pleasure or pain*" manifests itself as that "Passion" which makes individuals go "too far" in pursuing their own interest and "too remiss, in other Mens" (II, § 125). The implication is that virtue in a political context consists in the pursuit of more long-term and broadly based interests. (This idea reappears in the writings of virtually all liberal proponents of prerogative up to and including Hamilton's discussion of the presidency.) Vice, in contrast, generally consists in the pursuit of short-range and narrowly construed interests that conflict with the happiness of the community.

Tyranny, the cardinal sin of politics, can be understood as the most extreme form of vice. In fact, Locke describes it as a political form of excessive individualism characterized by the ruler's use of power "for his own private separate Advantage."[133] Throughout the *Treatises* this lack of self-control is identified with a propensity to violence. In fact, anyone who makes an "unjust use of force" is considered to have "quit[ ] reason" and is no better than "any savage ravenous Beast" (II, § 181). The love of dominion causes enough problems in the state of nature, but its deleterious effects are compounded when joined with actual political power, hence the desire for revenge exhibited by many princes. The self-denial of shortsighted and impetuous appetites, such as the love of dominion, "the first origin of most vicious habits," is such an important part of Locke's moral and political system that he doubted that anyone incapable of self-denial could be capable of virtue at all.[134] He "who prefers the short pleasures of a vicious Life," that is, one which revolves around the gratification of immediate passions, is sadly impoverished and shortsighted.[135] As we shall see in chapter 6, most Federalists understood virtue and vice in precisely these terms, stressing the need for a chief executive with a demonstrated ability to look beyond the satisfaction of those narrow and immediate appetites and interests that generally conflict with the common good of society.

The idea that virtue entails a cognitive and dispositional reorientation of priorities away from the satisfaction of immediate appetites and interests toward the consideration of distant objects is itself not new, but Locke gave it a new psychological foundation. An important aspect of this orientation for Locke was proper training in the ability to discern the true light of reason, the law of nature. Once the proper habits began to take hold, individuals would be equipped to use reason to discover the moral precepts behind their habitual conduct. Without that "large, sound, round-about sense" that enables us to see beyond the narrow horizons of self-interest and partisanship, we are bound to be "short sighted."[136] In fact, "the true principle and measure of virtue" is knowledge of natural law, which promises rewards only in the afterlife.[137] The notorious difficulties associated with discerning the requirements of natural law can be mitigated, if not surmounted, by training the faculty of reason to examine problems with open-minded detachment, or "Indifferency."[138] The ability to do this comes about only as a result of extensive "industry and application" of the faculties "perfected by habits."[139] Effort and education are required to learn how to make "proper use of the faculties [one] is endowed with by nature" in order to discover the principles of natural law.[140]

Locke is famous for his view that the human mind is at first a "white paper," a literal *tabula rasa,* ready to be inscribed with experiential knowledge and open to modification like a palimpsest. Proper habituation and education account for the greatest part of the moral and intellectual differences among individuals, enabling them to rise above their animal instincts and base inclinations. In response to the question "Whether it be in a Man's power to change the pleasantness, that accompanies any sort of action?" Locke responded that "in many cases he can. Men may and should correct their palates, and give a relish to what either has, or they suppose has none."[141] In explaining that "Pains should be taken to rectify" the "wrong Notions" and "ill habits" that "Fashion and common Opinion have settled" and "education and custom" have instilled, Locke made an almost imperceptible shift from the individual to the collective interest. Education should aim at making these corrections because they are "necessary, or conducive to *our* Happiness."[142] It is the happiness of all, not the happiness of the individual per se, that drives this endeavor. Collective happiness depends on the promotion of virtuous conduct among individuals who have been tutored in the habits of self-discipline and trained in the proper use of reason to overcome their appetites and prejudices. For Locke, virtue is not an end in itself, but a means toward happiness: "I place *virtue* as the first and most necessary of those endowments that belong to a man or a gentleman, as absolutely requisite to make him valued and beloved by others, acceptable or tolerable to himself. Without that, I think, he will be happy neither in this nor the other world." [143] The explicit linkage of happiness and virtue has definite political implications for the kinds of qualities the people should look for in the executive. Not only is a virtuous executive expected to be more happy, but the executive's virtuous conduct contributes to the happiness—that is, to the safety and security—of the entire community.

The instrumentalism of Locke's account of virtue distinguishes it from certain classical accounts of virtue that justify it as an end in itself. Philosophers like Plato sometimes pointed to the personal and communal benefits of virtue, but these were mainly incidental to the primary interest of fostering moral persons as such, whereas Locke justified the virtues almost exclusively in terms of their contributions to the external manifestations of happiness in the individual and the community alike. This instrumentalism should come as no surprise given that Locke's ethics builds on his psychology. To the extent that the hedonic principles of Lockean psychology are oriented toward the attainment of extrinsic rewards and avoidance of punishments, external considerations have a prominence in Locke's theory of virtue that are downplayed by thinkers like Plato who are more interested in the intrinsic rewards of virtue. For Locke, external rewards and punishments are significant—and legitimate—motivational forces.

One of the most severe threats, or deterrents, that face the potentially rebellious executive is the loss of "Reverence, Respect, and *Superiority*" (II, § 235). In an unpublished fragment Locke made the striking claim that "the principal spring from which the actions of men take their rise, the rule they conduct them by, and the end to which they direct them, seems to be credit and reputation, and that which at any rate they avoid, is in the greatest part shame and disgrace." [144] Locke indicated that a king who provokes his subjects could be reduced to the level of an ordinary man, which itself constitutes serious, though not necessarily sufficient, punishment for his injustices. In "A Letter from a Person of Quality," Locke and Shaftesbury advised the king against overreaching his power, because this will lessen the esteem the people hold for him: "when it is considered that every deviation of the Crown towards Absolute power, lessens the King in the love, and affection of his People, makeing Him become less their Interest, A wise Prince will not think it a Service done Him. . . . [to] endeavor to give more power to the King, then [*sic*] the

Law and constitution of the Government had given."[145] The none-too-subtle message here, of course, is that a prince who loses the people's esteem is a weak prince, and a prince who lacks virtue is vulnerable to violent resistance. Locke warned, "In whatsoever he has *no Authority*, there he is no *King*, and may be *resisted*: For *wheresoever the Authority ceases, the King ceases too*, and becomes like other Men who have no Authority" (II, § 239).

Locke's educational and philosophical writings support the view that concern for one's reputation will lead one to consider praise and blame as significant rewards and punishments.[146] This idea, a clear antecedent to Hamilton's notion that "love of fame [is] the ruling passion of the noblest minds," indicates how crucial it is for an executive to value intangible and distant rewards, which always seem to be associated with the good of the public. Locke recommended a judicious use of esteem by educators to elicit virtuous conduct. His remark that a desire for esteem replaces the predilection for mastery is particularly instructive for political relations between the people and their magistrates. "*Esteem* and *disgrace* are, of all others, the most powerful incentives to the mind, when once it is brought to relish them."[147] Even as early as his "Letter from a Person of Quality," Locke had cautioned the king to moderate his ambitions for power, "when it is considered that every deviation of the Crown towards Absolute power, lessens the King in the love, and the affection of his People, makeing Him become less their Interest, A wise Prince will not think it a Service done Him" to have others "endeavor to give more power to the King."[148] This theme recurs in the writings of virtually all the liberal theorists of executive power and virtue.

However, this admonition is clearly in tension with the liberal individualist impulse to think and act independently. The executive's concern for reputation and the love of the people is not easy to square with Locke's general injunction in *Of the Conduct of the Understanding* and *An Essay concerning Human Understanding* to examine all opinions "indifferently." Although it is intended as an additional check on executive power, the problem with the kind of concern for reputation that Locke sought to instill is that it has the potential to undermine the independence expected of the executive. Another problem is that the people sometimes misconceive their own long-term interest and the common good. There is no guarantee that an executive who makes a difficult but ultimately beneficial political decision would receive the approval of the public. Locke never made it clear whether the prospect of punishment (for example, public disapproval or worse) or the habitual disposition to consider the long-term good would prevail if the executive were faced with such a difficult decision.

The Virtue of Auxiliary Precautions

It is noteworthy that the even the more familiar checks Locke devised to regulate political power were described in terms of virtue. In accordance with his hedonic understanding of the human mind, Locke sought to make virtuous behavior more rewarding and pleasurable and vicious behavior more costly and painful.[149] The political upshot of this doctrine is that the calculations of costs and benefits associated with certain political acts can be reconfigured in such a way that rulers feel compelled to pursue the common good and avoid whatever detracts from their happiness and well-being—even if they have not received a proper moral education. The assumption that individuals possess a modicum of instrumental rationality means that the administration of power does not have to depend entirely or exclusively on the preexisting virtue of magistrates, although the proper dispositions and habits make it much less likely that an executive would exploit an opportunity for self-aggrandizement at the expense of the public will, or even contemplate such a thing. The threat of revolution is crucial in modifying the dispositions of governors. It makes it more costly for governors to violate the trust of the people.[150] Still, Locke assumed that rulers would want the fame and honor that accrues to good leaders and avoid the dishonor and ignominy that follow bad ones. He hoped they would adopt a long-term perspective, one that is conducive to their own good and that coincides with the welfare of the people.[151]

Locke's equivocal use of virtue sometimes reduces it to a kind of instrumental rationality that predisposes the individual to respond properly to a given configuration of potential rewards and punishments. This is a far cry from classical theories that justify virtue as an end in itself. Locke's scheme amounts to a kind of psychological subterfuge whereby (it is hoped that) executives *will bind themselves* for their own good (for example, the avoidance of punishment or the preservation of a good reputation), which in turn benefits the people as a whole. Locke's admonitions to parents apply with equal validity to the community: "The restraints and punishments laid on children are all misapplied and lost as far as they do not prevail over their wills," that is, regulate actual conduct, which is the outward expression of the will.[152] The threat of punishment, the transfer of executive power back to the people upon the forfeiture of that right by an abusive executive magistrate, provides the ultimate security Locke seeks. After all, pain operates on the mind more profoundly than pleasure.[153] But these hedonic psychological mechanisms work in conjunction with virtue, even as they shape it. The great genius of Christianity, Locke opined, is that the "view of heaven and hell will cast a slight upon the short pleasures and pains of this state, and give attractions and encouragements to virtue, which reason and interest and the care of ourselves cannot but allow and prefer."[154] As he explained in the *Essay concerning Human Understanding*, "The motive to change, is always some *uneasiness*: nothing setting us upon the change of State, or upon any new Action, but some *uneasiness*. This is the great motive that works on the Mind to put it upon Action, which for shortness sake we will call *determining of the Will*."[155] Missing from this account of human motivation is any reference to an idea of the good that inspires individuals to follow a course of action for its own sake or for the achievement of an end that does not bring a near-term psychic or material reward. Nothing operates as powerfully on the mind as uneasiness, which is often precipitated by the desire to avoid some present or potential pain—in this case, removal from power and other punishment. As Locke asserted with regards to the legislative, "*This Doctrine* of a Power in the people of providing for their safety a-new by a new Legislative, when their Legislators have acted contrary to their trust, by invading their Property, is *the best fence against Rebellion*, and the probablest means to hinder it" (II, § 226).[156] This applies with equal force to the removal of the executive, which is the theme that concludes the *Treatises*. The hope is that the self-regulation of executive power forestalls the need for resistance against the executive.

Locke's treatment of moral relations demonstrates the need to attach rewards and punishments to the observation or violation of the law:

> For since it would be utterly in vain, to suppose a Rule set to the free Actions of Man, without annexing to it some Enforcement of Good and Evil, to determine his Will, we must, where-ever we suppose a Law, suppose also some Reward or Punishment annexed to that Law. It would be in vain for one intelligent Being, to set a Rule to the Actions of another, if he had it not in his Power, to reward the compliance with, and punish deviation from his Rule, by some Good and Evil, that is not the natural product and consequence of the Action it self. For that being a natural Convenience, or Inconvenience, would operate

of it self without a Law. This, if I mistake not, is the true nature of all *Law*, properly so called.[157]

When the logic of this argument is extended to politics, it is clear that only the people are fit to judge whether an executive has abrogated the people's trust. The rational executive is expected to adhere to self-restrictions that will be advantageous to both the people and the executive. However, as Locke himself indicated, defects in rationality are characteristic of tyrants. If it is true that some individuals are simply deficient in rationality, it is not at all clear that the threat of punishment would be effective without the habitual disposition toward virtuous conduct that Locke endorsed.

Locke's redefinition of virtue as a kind of hedonic rationality raises some important questions. Is this really virtue at all? Does mere abstention from self-interested, appetitive behavior qualify as virtue? Is virtue nothing more than dutiful obedience to the dictates of reason? Locke was equivocal in his answers. He seemed to distinguish among three categories of executives on the basis of their relative virtue: (1) those "God-like princes" who fully embody virtue; (2) those ordinary executives who are simply rational enough to figure out that their own self-interest coincides with that of the polity and act accordingly; and (3) those degenerates who pursue their self-interest at the expense of the public. The first class enjoys the widest latitude in the exercise of prerogative; the rest are to be kept on a short leash. In the latter case, though, the community is deprived of a valuable resource insofar as the ordinary executive lacks the leeway to act freely in usual circumstances. This explains why Locke's educational project is so intimately connected to his political project, for without the right rulers, a political society cannot be assured of the most extensive happiness. Although everyone is not equally qualified to judge what the law of nature requires in a particular situation, Locke implied that character is transparent enough for anyone to judge accurately. The hope—and that is all it is—is that character is a reliable enough proxy indicator of the propriety of political actions to preclude disputes over the meaning or applicability or natural law.

But another problem remains. Locke appeared to offer two not entirely consistent arguments why virtue is strongly correlated with conformity to natural law, and each of them is open to different objections. The first argument, that a virtuous person is one who has been habituated to act in a manner consistent with the demands of natural law, minimizes the role of reason that is so important to Lockean liberalism. The second argument, that a virtuous person is one trained in the proper application of reason, is open to the objections noted above and presupposes a kind of individual voluntarism that is not entirely consistent with the role of habituation. The first notion makes virtue a product of unconscious and impassive habituation, whereas the second identifies it with deliberate and rational calculation. In fairness to Locke, the relationship between these concepts is much more complex than the schematic summary presented here suggests, but it is undeniable that Locke failed to connect these disparate strands of his thought. Ultimately, Locke seemed to suggest, neither proper habituation nor ratiocination alone is sufficient to generate virtue. Both are necessary. Presumably, the virtuous executive will possess the right combination of both qualities.

Conclusion

I have attempted to demonstrate in this chapter that most of the ostensible contradictions and inconsistencies in Locke's theory of prerogative are only apparent, not real. But if contradictions and inconsistencies remain, the fault may not lie with Locke. If it is difficult to square his theory of prerogative with his constitutional ideals, that may have more to do with the complexity and irrationality of the world than any shortcomings or oversights on his part. Prerogative is an imperfect solution for an imperfect world. However, it is important not to dismiss it out of hand as a feeble or craven concession to danger without bearing in mind that its ultimate purpose is to promote the welfare of the community, including the liberties of its members.

Lockean constitutionalism can perhaps best be understood as an attempt to respond to the necessities and exigencies of political life that the strictest legal formalism cannot accommodate. Constitutional forms alone are only indicative of, but never definitive of, legitimate political action for Locke. His discussion of prerogative reminds us that the administration of government depends on the judgments and character of particular individuals because the rule of law is neither impersonal nor self-executing.

It is also important to keep in mind that prerogative is not supposed to be used to undermine the law even when it contradicts the law. But the law that is most relevant for Lockean constitutionalism is contained in the substantive principles of natural law, not the formal rules of human law. To the extent that the laws of nature establish the ultimate measure of the rule of law, it avoids that "political vacuum" in which other modern theories of the rule of law get lost, according to Judith Shklar. In Locke's political universe, the higher purposes of law are never subordinated to formal rules or juridical formulas.[158] It is a constitutional vision in which legal rules serve ends higher than themselves.[159] Locke taught the American Founders that it was possible to pursue legitimate ends through unauthorized means without making a sacrifice of morality on the altar of necessity as long as the governor presiding over the delicate process was virtuous. "God-like Princes" are in short supply, but the shortage is not really felt until a crisis or an emergency arises that demands extraordinary and sometimes extralegal action. In such a situation, however, it is just as dangerous to trust an executive of questionable character as it to question a trustworthy executive because the result is the same: it becomes more difficult to take necessary action for the welfare of the community.

However, it was Hume who demonstrated empirically what Locke had postulated in theory, namely that superior virtue in an executive was possible. Even more so than Locke, Hume showed that the preservation of a free and regular government depends almost as much on the character of the executive as it does on the checks contained in the constitution.

CHAPTER THREE

"All Was Confusion and Disorder"

Regularity and Character in Hume's Political Thought

> No government, at that time, appeared in the world, nor is perhaps to be
> found in the records of any history, which subsisted without the mixture of
> some arbitrary authority, committed to some magistrate; and it might
> reasonably, beforehand, appear doubtful, whether human society could
> ever reach that state of perfection, as to support itself with no other
> controul than the general and rigid maxims of law and equity.
>
> DAVID HUME

Hume's Political Skepticism

There is general agreement among scholars that the guiding principle of
David Hume's political philosophy is the proposition that "politics may be
reduced to a science." Hume's claim that the scientific study of politics would
make it possible to deduce "consequences almost as general and certain . . .
as any which the mathematical sciences afford us" meant that "stability" in
"human affairs" would not have to depend on "the casual humours and characters of particular men."[1] The understanding that "politics admit of general
truths" that can be expressed in terms of universal axioms and scientific principles opened up the exciting possibility of discovering permanent solutions
to the perennial problems of politics.[2] The same kinds of methods that Newton had used in physics could be applied in politics with remarkable practical
results.[3] According to the standard interpretation of Hume's claim, the "experimental" study of politics leads to the discovery that the maintenance of
public virtue and liberty depend on nothing more than "well-conceived and
well constructed political machinery."[4] Hume's observation that "laws and
forms of government" have "a uniform influence upon society" suggested that
it would be possible to achieve enduring stability, regularity, and predictability

in government once the personal idiosyncrasies of particular individuals were rendered moot by the proper arrangement of public institutions.[5]

The notion that institutional design ultimately matters more than personal character in politics is not only thought to be Hume's most significant achievement as a liberal political philosopher, it is also considered his single greatest contribution to the political thought of the American Founding.[6] Ever since Douglass Adair demonstrated the influence of Hume's ideas on James Madison's famous solution to the problem of factions in *Federalist* 10, scholars have traced the source of many important political ideas and arguments during the American Founding back to Hume.[7] As much of this scholarship has shown, American readers took great interest in Hume's new science of politics because it promised to substitute the uncertain irregularities associated with premodern forms of personal rule with the predictable regularities that accompany impersonal institutional mechanisms.[8] American receptiveness to Hume's mechanistic solutions seemed only to increase as their disillusionment with republicanism increased following the start of the American Revolution.

Much of Hume's work was explicitly opposed to the classical ideas revived by modern republicans in their moralistic critiques of modern commercial society. His unromantic understanding of the passions that explain human motivation directly contradicted the rosy assumptions and unrealistic expectations of republican writers. Where republicans generally looked to the virtue of the people to prevent corruption and safeguard liberty, Hume looked to institutional arrangements based on a more realistic appraisal of human nature as the most reliable and durable safeguards of liberty.[9] Unlike the scientific approaches of James Harrington and Montesquieu, who had also relied on devices such as institutional balances and the separation of powers to protect liberty from the predations of tyrants, Hume's science of politics seemed to obviate the need for republican virtue or any selfless qualities whatsoever. It is for such reasons that Hume's political writings are regarded as a vindication of the values correlated with an emerging liberal order largely indifferent to considerations of character in politics.

However, Hume's confidence in the "science of politics" was tempered by a healthy dose of skepticism that filters through his philosophy.[10] Even though he believed that the new science of politics was a vast improvement over previous approaches in politics—including those associated with classical and modern republicanism—Hume remained deeply skeptical about the ability of his own or any other theoretical framework to provide definitive answers to the unexpected questions that are bound to arise in politics. As a historically minded empiricist who disdained all forms of dogmatism, he recognized that abstract theory must yield to concrete facts. His search for general patterns did not blind him to the presence of exceptions in morals or in politics.[11] He did not pluck the universal principles of politics from the airy perches of theoretical abstraction. Instead he laid the foundations of his science of politics in the solid ground of historical detail and empirical particularity.[12] Any attempt to erect a constitutional edifice that was stable and uniform would have to contend with the shifting and uneven terrain of the political world. Like Machiavelli and Locke before him, Hume faced up to the fact that contingencies constantly disrupt even the most rational and carefully formulated plans. There are "some critical Times" when so much is out of human control because "Fortune does, at least, one Half of the Business."[13]

There is no doubt that Hume's explanations of political behavior emphasized "the primacy of political institutions," but this does not mean that he downplayed or ignored the role of cultural, historical, and personal factors that operate alongside or even against prevailing institutional arrangements.[14] And even though he always stressed the decisive role of impersonal trends and structural processes in charting the course of historical development, he often noted how specific accidents and individual personalities end up steering this development in unusual and unexpected directions. Such contingencies are simply irreducible to social scientific principles or universal maxims. Whenever the facts failed to support one of his generalizations, Hume was quick to qualify his claims, which is why his historical writings so often appear "untidy."[15] Nearly the entire corpus of his political and historical writings demonstrates the limitations of a science of politics capable of overcoming or controlling the vicissitudes of politics.

It is in connection with these observations on contingency that Hume addressed the topic of executive power. At the time that Hume wrote his six-volume *History of England* and his *Essays,* the two works that represent the culmination of his political philosophy, prerogative was no longer the focal point of political and constitutional controversy in England. The major dispute now centered on the patronage powers of the first prime minister, Sir Robert Walpole. Supporters of Walpole defended his efforts to "influence" the Commons through the use of place bills as essential to the effectiveness of government, whereas critics led by Viscount Bolingbroke decried Walpole's uses of patronage as unconstitutional measures that undermined liberty by destroying the independence of Parliament.[16] Even though Hume was deeply engaged in these debates, he did not avoid the larger topics involving the nature and responsibilities of executive power.[17] Far from being "silent on the subject" and therefore of little guidance to constitutional debates in America, Hume's scattered references to the executive reveal that its powers, especially in emergencies, are shaped by the unavoidable irregularities and uncertainties of politics.[18]

Though he never theorized executive power or emergency action with the same care as Locke before him or Hamilton after him, Hume's historical studies provided strong empirical support for the idea that fixed laws and institutions often fall short in handling emergencies without the discretionary intervention of the executive. There would always be room for personal factors in politics because institutions only condition—never determine— the scope of political action. Notwithstanding his disdain for utopian idealizations of human nature and for unrealistic republican expectations of virtue in ordinary citizens, Hume's attentiveness to deviations from general principles of politics and psychology indicated that the virtuous executive was nonetheless a definite—albeit exceptional—possibility. Hume offered copious empirical demonstrations of what he himself was reluctant to admit in theory: the preservation of liberty would still depend to some degree on the character of statesmen.

Hume's *Essays* and his monumental *History of England* show that the contingent element of individual personality is often decisive in determining the course of political history. Even though his philosophical principles recommended a historiographical methodology that would have focused on the impersonal forces of historical change, J. G. A. Pocock points out that Hume "adopted from the outset—and surely not unthinkingly—the convention of writing history by reigns," with the result that his *History of England* became "a narrative of human deeds."[19] These texts, which were even more popular in eighteenth-century America than his philosophical treatises, illustrate that the character of the chief executive (for example, any of the English monarchs, Oliver Cromwell as the Protector of the Commonwealth, or Robert Walpole) has been a crucial determinant of historical progress and constitutional development.[20] This is precisely the feature of Hume's writings that infuriated the egalitarian Jefferson, but was so instructive to creators of the presidency such as Madison and Hamilton.[21] It is significant that his historical account of each English monarch concludes with an extensive discussion of the character traits that contributed to the monarch's success or failure and, concomitantly, to the nation's political happiness or misery. According to Hume, history shows that personality is often converted into policy—albeit under historical conditions that constrain the effects of personality.[22]

One of the lessons Hume drew from his study of history is that good character strengthens government because virtuous rulers tend to enjoy more latitude than vicious ones. This is an aspect of Hume's writings that has been overlooked even by scholars who have taken note of his political concern for the character of ordinary citizens and subjects, but it is consistent with the empirico-historical orientation of Hume's writings.[23] Perhaps the most compelling evidence that Hume's historical writings aimed to teach the political importance of virtue appears in a philosophical essay on the study of history in which he remarked that "the historians have been, almost without exception, the true friends of virtue." Clearly expressing his preference for "that experience which is acquired by history" over the speculations of abstract philosophy, Hume explained that history affirms the reality of virtue, whereas philosophy sometimes "go[es] so far as to deny the reality of all moral distinctions."[24]

Hume's remarks on the irregularity of government under feudalism nicely encapsulate his views on the connection between personality and politics, which this chapter will explore:

> If a prince, much dreaded and revered like Henry [II], obtained but the appearance of general consent to an ordinance, which was equitable and just, it became immediately an established law, and all his subjects acquiesced in it. If the prince was hated or despised; if the nobles, who supported him, had small influence; if the humours of the times disposed the people to question the justice of his ordinance; the fullest and most authentic assembly had no authority. Thus all was confusion and disorder; no regular idea of a constitution; force and violence decided every thing.[25]

Though a great deal had changed since Henry's time to make the regularity of government less dependent on the tempers and humors of its chief executives, character would continue to exert a powerful influence on the shape of government and help guide the course of constitutional development. As

Hume noted in a discussion of royal prerogative, "All human institutions, and none more than government, are in continual fluctuation."[26] For that reason, it is highly improbable that we will ever see the permanent elimination of prerogative.

The Uncertain Science of Politics

Since Hume never systematically laid out a theory of constitutionalism in any single work or even provided definitions of such key concepts as "constitution," "prerogative," or "liberty," it is necessary to reconstruct his views on constitutionalism from his analyses of particular political situations and historical events in the *Essays* and *The History of England*. The particularism and contextualism of Hume's empirico-historical approach eschews the kind of rationalistic, a priori, deductive approach typical of many natural law thinkers during the Enlightenment. Hume explained that "use and practice" are the true rules of government because "Reason is so uncertain a guide that it will always be exposed to doubt and controversy."[27] If Hume devoted an inordinate amount of attention to monarchs as opposed to other kinds of executives, it was because his method focuses on empirically verifiable material gleaned from history rather than suppositious abstractions or "counter-factual conditionals" such as the "state of nature."[28] Nevertheless, Hume insisted on the possibility of deriving some uniform and universal principles of politics that apply generally across cultures and over time. His political and constitutional ideas are of a piece with his philosophical ideas. They seek to provide an account of the general principles that structure and delimit particular, observable variations.[29] In a remark that Hamilton would echo in the opening of the *Federalist*, Hume explained that the first step in the social sciences is "to distinguish exactly what is owing to *chance*, and what proceeds from *causes*," for to "say, that any event is derived from chance, cuts short all farther enquiry concerning it."[30]

Following his own advice that "no criticism can be instructive, which descends not to particulars, and is not full of examples and illustrations," Hume provided a detailed elucidation (and popularization) of his philosophical and political ideas in his *History of England*.[31] As he saw it, the primary use of history "is only to discover the constant and universal principles of human nature."[32] Whatever occurs on a sufficiently large scale is susceptible of scientific inquiry and allows for the discovery of general rules and principles.[33] Even though "human society is in perpetual flux," it is possible to discern patterns in this turbulence.[34] It is from the contingent details of accidental events, "by following the experimental method, and deducing general maxims from a comparison of particular instances," that Hume was able to develop a general theory of politics and history at all.[35] It is easy to get lost in the thicket of historical details of *The History of England* and lose sight of the general principles that course through the entire environment, but it is in history that the possibilities—as well as the limitations—of political science become evident.[36] That is why no account of Hume's political philosophy is complete without an examination of both his political essays and his historical analyses.

Delving beneath the surface of events is crucial because, "of all sciences there is none, where first appearances are more deceitful than in politics."[37] Nowhere is the deceptiveness of politics more evident than in Hume's own essay, "That Politics May Be Reduced to a Science," a polemical as well as a philosophical work that exemplifies the very same maxim it explicates. The ostensible subject of the essay concerns the question whether the goodness or badness of government depends more on its "form" or on "the character and conduct of the governors."[38] Hume seems to side with those who place the emphasis on forms, but it becomes clear that things are not so simple.

The essay begins with the sorrowful observation that some believe "human affairs admit of no greater stability, than what they receive from the casual humours and characters of particular men," but it concludes with an unrepentant endorsement of the very form of government that seems most highly dependent on the "humours and character of particular men."[39] His opening remarks lead one to expect that Hume would champion republican forms of government because they make it "the interest, even of bad men, to act for the public good," but instead he went on to advocate a monarchical form of government. As it turns out, that republican governments are so dependent on institutional forms makes them extremely susceptible to "disorder" and injustice "where either skill or honesty has been wanting in their original frame and institution."[40] When all things are considered, Hume concluded that hereditary monarchy suffers from the fewest inherent inconveniences and ought, for that reason, to be retained over its republican rivals! The "experimental method of reasoning" in politics proves that the form of government *most dependent* on personal "administration," whether by the king himself or by his prime minister, is actually the best instituted.

This curious conclusion leads one to suspect that there is more at stake in this essay than merely a comparison of the relative advantages and disadvantages of republican and monarchical forms of government. As James Conniff explains in his analysis of "That Politics May Be Reduced to a Science," Hume's aim is to demonstrate that "abstract reasoning in politics" is absurd.[41] Hume's ostensibly "scientific" essay satirizes the scientific pretensions of republican writers like Harrington by demonstrating that their theoretical generalizations simply fail to withstand empirical scrutiny.[42] But Hume's point was not simply to rail against the absurdities of other thinkers; it was to reveal the limitations of any science in politics. The point comes out more explicitly in a different essay, where Hume averred that any attempt "to make a full comparison" of political systems "would, in all probability, be refuted by further experience, and be rejected by posterity."[43] The history of philosophy demonstrates that theoretical claims that "have prevailed during one age" are always being "exploded" by scientific revolutions that occur in a later age.[44]

"That Politics May Be Reduced to a Science" also derides those who eulogize the perfections of the British Constitution yet blame Robert Walpole's vicious character for all the problems in government. If Walpole's administration is either as wicked as his detractors allege or as wise as his supporters claim, then "the constitution must be faulty in its original principles," because it never would have permitted such a man to govern for so long.[45] Though Hume's own position is somewhat equivocal in "That Politics May Be Reduced to a Science," his character sketch of Walpole, which originally appeared as a footnote to that essay, leaves no doubt that the prime minister's personal virtues and vices *did* matter: "During his time trade has flourished, liberty declined, and learning gone to ruin."[46] A constitution can mitigate the effects of character, but it can not—and should not—entirely eliminate the effects of character.

One of the things Hume demonstrated was that the inescapable contingencies, uncertainties, and complexities of politics are simply not amenable to the kind of scientific approach that would permit confident predictions or facile manipulation. Some republican writers were foolish enough to think they could "foretel the situation of public affairs a few years hence," but Hume believed that "no prudent man, however sure of his principles, dares prophesy concerning any event, or foretel the remote consequences of things."[47] If

Hume had a model of science in politics, it was not to be found in the experimental technical manipulations of Francis Bacon's New Organon but in the rich cultural details of Montesquieu's comparative history, which permits generalizations while avoiding predictions. The Scottish philosopher never exhibited as much confidence in the "science of politics" as did subsequent political writers who employed the phrase. For instance, Jean-Louis de Lolme, a Swiss admirer of the British Constitution who was frequently cited during the ratification debates on questions concerning executive power, adhered to the more optimistic view that "the science of politics, considered as an *exact science,*—that is to say, as a science capable of actual demonstration,—is infinitely deeper than the reader suspects."[48] As chapters 5 and 6 show, even many of those Federalists who applied this new science in creating the Constitution actually displayed Humean skepticism toward their own activity.

To understand Hume's own position, it is necessary to realize that he had an ulterior political motive in dressing up an argument in favor of hereditary monarchy in scientific clothing. Hume's ostensibly scientific and philosophical (that is, "detached") essay is an act of political intervention. His statement of ideals is not to be taken seriously as a realistic political prescription, but only as a standard by which to judge existing institutions.[49] Even though "it must be advantageous to know what is most perfect in the kind [of government], that we may be able to bring any real constitution or form of government as near it as possible," it is only so that it may be done "by such gentle alterations and innovations as may not give too great disturbance to society."[50] As several scholars have shown,[51] Hume sought to inject a dose of "moderation" into contemporary political debates over the nature of the British Constitution, which were all too often "interested" (in the sense of "partisan") and violent.[52]

As a skeptic and as a conservative, Hume favored established forms of government that had been tried and tested over long periods of time to those experimental innovations, which often create tumults. Thus, he concluded his plea for moderation with a suggestion that the "best civil constitution" (that is, the British Constitution) should not be altered: "I would only persuade men not to contend, as if they were fighting *pro aris & focis,* and change a good constitution into a bad one, by the violence of their factions."[53] As Hume saw it, the least institutionally formal government is more suitable for Britain than one with the most "particular checks and controuls."[54] Such a government enjoys so many advantages that the alternatives simply pale in comparison.

Because the constitutional monarchy of Britain is no longer inimical to liberty, as it was during much of the seventeenth century, when absolutist doctrines of royal power were at their height, the argument in favor of republicanism is moot. Since the Glorious Revolution, "public liberty, with internal peace, has flourished almost without interruption." In addition, "So long and so glorious a period no nation almost can boast of: Nor is there another instance in the whole history of mankind, that so many millions of people have, during such a space of time, been held together, in a manner so free, so rational, and so suitable to the dignity of human nature."[55] The British constitution had achieved a state of ordered liberty that Hume was loath to jeopardize.

In his "Idea of a Perfect Commonwealth," Hume admitted that there are several "inconveniences" associated with a limited monarchy. One of these is that "the king's personal character must still have great influence on the government."[56] But that is a problem endemic to all governments with a single executive, not just monarchies. For that reason, Hume's ideal executive would consist of a plural council.[57] However, such an innovation would require so many alterations in the rest of the constitution that it would be better to keep the established form of government. The conservatism expressed in this and other political statements is given philosophical support in *A Treatise of Human Nature*, where Hume wrote: "No maxim is more conformable, both to prudence and morals, than to submit quietly to the government, which we find establish'd in the country where we happen to live, without enquiring too curiously into its origins and first establishment."[58]

Why is the science of politics—or philosophy, for that matter—so invaluable to Hume? Why go through all the arduous rhetorical contortions only to "prove" that political science suffers from inherent and unavoidable limits? Part of the answer lies in the fact that philosophy is a form of political practice for Hume. Philosophy depends on a disposition Hume sought to extend into and promote in politics: moderation. "Philosophy," in contrast to the superstitions of the ignorant multitudes, "can present us only with mild and moderate sentiments."[59] Moderation is of inestimable importance in politics as in philosophy because, for all its advantages, philosophy is still an uncertain, and therefore fallible, practice. Therefore, the philosophical outlook recommends skepticism: "A true sceptic will be diffident of his philosophical doubts, as well as of his philosophical conviction; and will never refuse any innocent satisfaction, which offers itself, upon account of either of them."[60] Hume recommended diffidence in politics because zeal leads to a dangerous belief in one's own infallibility. According to Hume's logic, the error committed by most zealots and partisans in politics is that they fail to appreciate the delicacy and fragility of political innovations, which are not only untested but also lack firm public support. That is a deadly combination that makes inventions in politics prone to premature obsolescence. Whereas Locke remained skeptical about the ability of any formal institutions to meet all the exigencies of government, Hume was especially suspicious about the ability of institutional innovations to live up to early expectations. That diffidence in institutional devices translated into support for the discretionary powers of the executive for both Locke and Hume. During the struggle over constitutional ratification, Humean skepticism manifested itself in the writings of all those Federalists who insisted that "perfection" could not be expected of a constitution designed by imperfect humans. Although the framers and supporters of the Constitution could not have accepted Hume's defense of monarchy as the most durable form of government, they could and did accept his argument that executive power could be made compatible with liberty and free government.

Constitutional Regularity and the Rule of Law

As noted earlier, the rule of law is such an important facet of modern constitutionalism that it often becomes the prism through which the entire system is viewed. But the tendency to define constitutionalism exclusively in terms of juridical limits on government induces a kind of analytical myopia that leads many observers to overlook (or simply to dismiss as illegitimate) many of the informal or implicit powers contained in constitutions. This tendency is evident even in some scholarship on Hume, even though he rejected this one-sided perception of constitutionalism.[61] His political writings show that grants of power and limitations on its exercise form a complex constitutional chiaroscuro. In Hume's view, a constitution is necessarily composed of negative, power-denying elements and positive, power-granting elements. These elements correspond to the key constituents of Hume's constitutional theory: liberty and authority. These, he believed, are interdependent features of nearly every political system: "In all governments, there is a perpetual intestine struggle, open or secret, between AUTHORITY and LIBERTY; and neither of them can absolutely prevail in the contest. . . . liberty is the perfection of civil society; but still authority must be acknowledged essential to its very existence."[62]

Even though he rejected the doctrine of natural rights championed by Locke and other liberals, he still esteemed liberty as a universal value whose "progress and security, can scarce be too fondly cherished by every one who is a lover of human kind."[63] Liberty is essential to the happiness of society not only because the love of liberty is rooted in human nature but also because it is so closely associated with human progress.[64] This view of liberty as a universal and progressive value set Hume apart from republicans who prized liberty as the historic birthright of particular peoples, such as Romans, Venetians, or Englishmen.

But as Hume never tired of pointing out, the precondition of liberty is order, which itself requires strong political authority.[65] It is for that reason that the preservation of liberty ultimately depends on "obedience" to political authority. Indeed, "society could not subsist otherwise."[66] He reminded those zealots for liberty that the maxims of the Tories are essential to the "very existence" of the Whigs and their doctrines.[67] However, this does not mean that authority should ever "become quite entire and uncontroulable," because that would destroy the very liberty that authority is established to serve.[68]

Although liberty does not quite qualify as the *summum bonum* for Hume, principally because he recognizes that there is a plurality of inestimable goods and values in a society, each of which contributes uniquely to human happiness, disorder easily qualifies as the *summum malum*. Like liberal theorists before and after him, Hume believed that liberty could not exist without law, which establishes and preserves order in society and politics. In the absence of well-executed and judiciously administered laws, there can be only license and the disorder that it brings. Although he devoted more attention to the positive, power-granting side of constitutionalism than other liberal theorists, it is important to stress that this difference was only a matter of degree, not of kind. If Hume tended to focus more intently on the positive, power-granting side of constitutionalism, it was because he was convinced that liberty could not even exist in the absence of adequate authority. The proper balance between the two is critical if a system of government is to achieve regularity, the *sine qua non* of constitutionalism for Hume. Regularity provides a useful measure in gauging both the stability of authority and the vigor of liberty in a political system.

Regularity refers to the stability, reliability, and predictability that adherence to established laws, precedents, customs, and institutions brings to government. Regularity is a matter of degree—in government as in nature. The more closely government operates according to normal routines, the greater its regularity. Law is the chief instrument for the achievement of regularity.[69] Hume stated plainly that "we must govern ourselves by rules, which are more general in their application, and more free from doubt and uncertainty" than subjective determinations of "fitness or suitableness."[70] The durability and resilience of the law are its main virtues, as "it is not preserved with the same difficulty, with which it is produced; but when it has once taken root, is a hardy plant, which will scarcely ever perish through the ill culture of men, or the rigour of the seasons."[71] The systematic and comprehensive application of the rule of law, "the salutary yoke of law and justice," is undoubtedly the ideal condition because it offers the proper balance of order and liberty.[72] Hume accepted the truism, "which we readily admit as undisputed and universal, that a power, however great, when granted by law to an eminent magistrate, is not so dangerous to liberty, as an authority, however inconsiderable, which he acquires from violence and usurpation. For, besides that the law always limits every power which it bestows, the very receiving it as a concession establishes the authority whence it is derived, and preserves the harmony of the constitution."[73] Every grant of power through the law is simultaneously a limitation of that power inasmuch as the law defines both the purpose and the range of any power.

Regularity is thus closely related to the rule of law, but it is more comprehensive than its juridically oriented relative.[74] It encompasses the legal and structural arrangements that have come to be institutionalized in the rule of law and the separation of powers as well as the social and political practices that have developed into national customs and manners. The juridical rules contained in political documents such as the Magna Carta, the Petition of Right of 1628, and the Bill of Rights of 1689 are simply not enough to explain the regularity of the British Constitution. Customary practices, internalized norms, and national manners also play a significant role in maintaining the balance between liberty and authority. In Machiavellian terms, a constitution consists of both orders and modes. As noted in chapter 1, the orders, which consist of formally established laws and institutions, are animated by customary modes of political action. Hume saw both the orders and the modes of the constitution developing in an uneven and contingent manner. Because the orders, or institutions, of a constitution are not self-activating or self-interpreting, they ultimately depend on the intervention and interpretation of political actors. The policies and practices of these actors—themselves conditioned by these institutions—are capable of setting important precedents that breathe life into an otherwise inert constitution. Hume, like Machiavelli, reminded readers that government is administered by individuals who energize and vivify lifeless institutions. Would government in the reign of Henry II have been so regular were it not for the reverence the people paid to the king?[75] And would the system of patronage have even taken hold were it not for the political skill and cunning of Walpole?

Hume generally expressed a strong preference for a constitution that specified the powers of government according to strictly defined orders over one that left the powers of government up to open-ended modes, but he conceded that this was an unrealizable ideal. The full realization of the rule of law entails the elimination of discretionary powers, but perfection in the law (or anything else for that matter) is simply impossible.[76] Hume noted that "even the general laws of the universe, though planned by infinite wisdom, cannot exclude all evil or inconvenience in every particular operation."[77] Since irregularity is one of the more regular features of human affairs, it should come as little surprise that "that imperfect and irregular manner which attends all human institutions" is so prevalent in government.[78]

Because it would be impossible to eliminate all discretion in the administration and enforcement of law, it would be necessary to seek an additional source of regularity outside the law. That could be found in the character of public officials. Hume suggested that the character of magistrates often determines whether or not the laws actually achieve the regularity they were designed to produce. Thus, it is critical that those individuals charged with the administration and execution of laws exhibit a commitment to the spirit and reason of the laws. Even when he recommended the rule of law over more personal forms of rule, Hume was careful not to overstate the superiority of the former over the latter: "All general laws are attended with inconveniences, when applied to particular cases; and it requires great penetration and experience, both to perceive that these inconveniences are fewer than what result from full discretionary powers in every magistrate; and also to discern what general laws are, upon the whole, attended with fewest inconveniences."[79] Here Hume juxtaposed general laws to an undesirable extreme that had few serious spokespersons in England at the time he was writing: *full* discretionary power of the kind only found in arbitrary governments.[80] It may be true that "Monarchy, when absolute, contains even something repugnant to law," but that was not a plausible threat in Great Britain.[81] Besides, noted Hume, monarchy is an even more predictable form of government than a republic, which is why Cromwell was eventually offered the crown: the people at least know what to expect from a king, whereas "every undeterminate power, such as that of a protector, must be arbitrary."[82] In Hume's account monarchy was more trustworthy than a protectorate because the former had settled into certain routines conducive to the certainty and predictability associated with the rule of law.

Hume's historical investigations led him to the conclusion that the executive is generally the single most important determinant of regularity in any form of government with a single executive. However much the particulars of executive power vary according to historical circumstance, the need for an executive authority with some degree of discretionary power remained a constant in Hume's theory of constitutionalism. The problem with the discretionary powers of the executive, however, is that they are necessarily irregular, or at least less regular, than more rule-bound, more highly institutionalized forms of power because so much depends on the personal character of the executive.

Personal Administration and Political Psychology

One of the things that makes Hume's political thought so difficult to summarize is that his empirical and historical analyses tend to undercut the feasibility of his stated political and constitutional ideals. This is particularly true of his reflections on the relationship between institutional forms of government and the actual administration of government by individual statesmen. Even though he flatly rejected Alexander Pope's famous dictum about the irrelevance of political forms of government, Hume recognized that the actual realities of politics provide some support for the notion that "Whate'er is best administer'd is best."[83]

Much of Hume's reputation as an institutionalist committed to eliminating the influence of personal factors in politics rests on the arguments presented in his "Idea of a Perfect Commonwealth," the essay "that most stimulated James Madison's thoughts on factions."[84] As the title suggests, the essay investigates "the most perfect of all" forms of government in order "to bring any real constitution or form of government as near it as possible." [85] In a perfect commonwealth, the balance and regularity of government would be independent of "the abilities and behaviour of the sovereign; which are variable and uncertain circumstances." [86] But as Hume was accustomed to pointing out, perfection is not to be found in politics (or anything else, for that matter). The imperfections of the real world make it an inhospitable place for the fanciful models concocted by speculative philosophers from Plato to Sir Thomas More. Far from recommending the form of government that he himself devised, Hume ended up recommending the form of government already in place. At the very outset of the essay he advised against any rush to abandon the prevailing system of government, no matter how flawed, because it always "has an infinite advantage" over untried experiments "by that very circumstance of its being established." [87] By the end, he strongly discouraged the adoption of any system that was too intricately designed, because "rust may grow to the springs of the most accurate political machine, and disorder its motions." [88] Such is the nature of the world itself, which "probably is not immortal." [89] As we will see in chapter 5, similar arguments were made by Americans who came to realize that the republican experiment in government following the Revolution was simply unworkable without the discretionary executive powers they had eliminated under the Articles of Confederation.

One of the chief considerations in deciding on the best form of government is the regularity it manages to produce. Arrangements that minimize if not eliminate the unsteady and uncertain effects of character are preferable to those that leave too much up to "the casual humours and characters of particular men." [90] However, Hume's pessimistic assessment of the actual prospects for perfection in politics led him to the somber but unavoidable conclusion that regularity in government would always depend to some degree on the vagaries of personal character. Even in his own scheme for reforming the British Constitution, Hume was forced to admit that "the king's personal character must still have great influence on the government." [91] The belief that a constitution can operate justly or effectively without people of good character turns out to be just as erroneous as the assumption that a durable constitution can be based on the expected virtue of politicians alone. [92] To Hume, institutional and legal arrangements that aimed to turn government into an automated machine were silly.

But even when Hume restricted his analysis to the plane of theory, he could not bring himself to endorse all measures aimed at liberating government from the effects of personal character. The system of rotation was one that republican philosophers had always recommended as a chief means of preserving equality and preventing corruption in office. But the very first objection that Hume raised in his critique of James Harrington's republican utopia, *The Commonwealth of Oceana*, was its reliance on a system of rotation. The problem is that rotation is based on a notion of equality that denies any meaningful distinctions among officeholders. In a remark that Federalists would echo in defending the president's unlimited re-eligibility for office, Hume explained that "rotation is inconvenient, by throwing men, of whatever abilities, by intervals, out of public employments."[93]

There may have been another consideration in Hume's mind when he repudiated rotation. In a number of his other writings, Hume stressed the importance of personal allegiance to both the legitimacy and the strength of government. By automatically turning individuals out of office so regularly, rotation tends to attenuate the people's attachment to their rulers. In other words, by making government less personal, rotation renders republics less stable. One of the greatest advantages of monarchical over republican forms of government is that allegiance in the former is more personal—and therefore more durable—than it is in the latter.

Hume's defense of limited monarchy over republican alternatives drew upon psychological insights that looked beyond standard political arguments about strength, unity, and stability. Limited monarchy was more realistic because it was more compatible with human nature. In fact, there are powerful epistemological-psychological reasons in favor of hereditary monarchy. Among other things, it is the "most easily comprehended" and conforms to the "natural prepossessions" of the people.[94]

Hume's most spirited defense of monarchical government appeared not in his political or historical writings but in his philosophical tome, *A Treatise of Human Nature*. He suggested that this form of government is more "natural," psychologically speaking, than the alternatives. Even though he had in mind a hereditary monarch, many of Hume's remarks on the psychological advantages of monarchy apply with equal force to any single and relatively permanent executive because the same kinds of cognitive and affective mechanisms are at work in both cases. The mind is "more apt to over-look in any subject, what is trivial, than what appears of considerable moment," just as we are more inclined to think immediately of Jupiter when looking upon one of its many satellites than we are to remember any of its moons when observing the great planet. Because "the fancy passes with more facility from the less to the greater," it is no surprise that the idea "of the subject carries our view to the prince."[95] There are powerful psychological forces that explain the identification of the people with a single executive but militate against a corresponding identification in the other direction.

What seems to be at stake politically in these psychological processes is respect for governors. The implication of Hume's argument in *A Treatise of Human Nature* is that it is much more difficult to establish and maintain respect for a mere servant of the people who is periodically returned to their ranks than for an individual who enjoys an aura of superiority by dint of his or her distance from the people. In other words, the egalitarian presuppositions of republicanism seem to undermine its durability since it is so difficult to elicit loyalty from people who regard their governors as no different from themselves. Hume stated that esteem seems to diminish in direct proportion to the similarity between subjects and their rulers. "Nothing has a greater tendency to give us an esteem for any person, than his power and riches," which naturally excite our sympathy.[96] All kinds of greatness elicit this cognitive-emotional response, since "the fancy passes with more facility from the less to the greater, than from the greater to the less."[97] "Heights" and "elevation" also have a considerable influence on the imagination. "Any great elevation of place communicates a kind of pride or sublimity of imagination, and gives a fancy'd superiority over those that lie below." Just as we associate heaven with elevation, "Kings and princes are suppos'd to be plac'd at the top of human affairs."[98]

With such powerful psychological predispositions drawing continued attention to objects of grandeur, it is only natural that Hume's own theory of constitutional development should revolve around the central role of the chief executive. Although Locke was also concerned with the availability of "God-like princes" who could be trusted to wield extraordinary powers, he was less interested than Hume in providing formal, institutional supports for esteem, which he believed had to be personally earned. With the possible exception of Hamilton, Hume's American followers would have flatly rejected the idea that a monarchy was the best way to elicit and maintain loyalty to government, but they would come to accept his claim that republicanism is self-defeating insofar as it undermines respect for and allegiance to public officials. Although there were obvious class implications in Hume's psychological account of esteem for governors, his analysis pointed mainly to the need for an executive of superior virtues to maintain the authority of government.

Character and the Possibility of Virtue

Hume is well known for his thoroughly modern repudiation of republican moralism. Instead of seeking a general moral reformation along the lines of Harrington or Bolingbroke, scholars have argued, Hume sought to link the existing passions and self-interest of rulers with a concern for the public good as the best way to regulate against potential abuses of power.[99] He was emphatic that the prospects of changing human nature are exceedingly slim. Just as "'twou'd be in vain, either for moralists or politicians, to tamper with us, or attempt to change the usual course of our actions, with a view to public interest," attempts to transform the characters of politicians would be equally quixotic. In the absence of rulers stimulated by "virtuous motives," he suggested, "All they [or we] can pretend to, is, to give a new direction to those natural passions."[100] And as "Nothing is more certain, than that men are, in a great measure, govern'd by interest," partial to "their nearest friends and acquaintances" and short-sighted even as regards their own long-term interests, it is necessary to reconfigure those interests for the sake of the common good.[101] The solution Hume offered for this dilemma is the one that James Madison ultimately endorsed in the *Federalist*:

> as 'tis impossible to change or correct any thing material in our nature, the utmost we can do is to change our circumstances and situation, and to render the observance of the laws of justice our nearest interest, and their violation our most remote. But this being impracticable with respect to all mankind, *it can only take place with respect to a few, whom we thus immediately interest in the execution of justice. There are the persons, whom we call civil magistrates, kings and their ministers, our governors and rulers, who being indifferent persons to the greatest part of the state, have no interest, or but a remote one, in any act of injustice*; and being satisfied with their present condition, and with their part in society, have an immediate interest in every execution of justice, which is so necessary to the upholding of society. . . . They cannot change their natures. All they can do is to change their situation, and render the observance of justice the immediate interest of some particular persons, and its violations their more remote.[102]

Hamilton's account of the long-term, or enlarged, perspective that presidents ought to take presupposes the sharp distinction Hume drew between the interested many and the "indifferent" [disinterested] few. The critical challenge for Hume and his American followers on this issue was to make sure that the few who were capable of justice were kept that way. As discussed in chapter 6, the framers followed Hume's advice and sought to connect "the interest of the man . . . with the constitutional rights of the place."

As daunting a task as it is, the duty of free governments is to make "it the interest, even of bad men, to act for the public good."[103] As discussed above, institutions play a key, but not exclusive, role in ensuring that individuals pursue the public good. Laws are necessary "because, if men had been endow'd with such a strong regard for public good, they wou'd never have restrain'd themselves by these rules."[104] Hume was clear that his solution is a political expedient and not an attempt at moral reformation, for "those, whom we chuse for rulers, do not immediately become of a superior nature to the rest of mankind, upon account of their superior power and authority. What we expect from them depends not on a change of their nature but of their situation, when they acquire a more immediate interest in the preservation of order and the execution of justice."[105] What is a remote interest among the mass of humankind becomes the immediate interest and province of a small—or even singular—minority. Because we tend to "yield to the sollicitations of our passions, which always plead in favour of whatever is near and contiguous," it is imperative to bring the public interest as close as possible to rulers.[106]

It is important to keep in mind that Hume wrote these words in the hopes of influencing contemporary politics in Britain. Since he was dealing with a hereditary monarchy, there was nothing he could realistically say to change the identity of the monarch. Thus, it made sense for him to concentrate on institutional and other impersonal variables that could contribute to regularity in government. It is likely that, had he been dealing with an elective monarchy, he would have been more explicit about the desirability of finding virtuous candidates for the office in the first place. Nevertheless, he did provide some indications of the kinds of qualities that would be necessary in an elected executive in his short essay on Robert Walpole.

Walpole was a flawed man, but his intellectual mediocrity did not trouble Hume as much as his moral shortcomings, which manifested themselves in just those qualities that should distinguish public officials from ordinary, self-interested, and often narrow-minded citizens. The very same virtues that might have made Walpole a good friend made him a bad public servant. For one thing, the generosity of his private character manifested itself in nepotistic policies pernicious to the public. For another, his concern for the welfare of his contemporaries was disadvantageous "for posterity."[107] Walpole's solicitude for the immediate welfare of those around him was opposed to the long-range interests of the nation as a whole—the proper object and aim of any good executive. In terms of Hume's general moral philosophy, it was clear that Walpole possessed many of the qualities that Hume claimed were most "intitled to the general good-will and approbation of mankind" but lacked that essential ingredient of "public spirit" that "proceeds from a tender sympathy with others, and a generous concern for our kind and our species."[108] Though legal and institutional constraints could mitigate some of the worst tendencies of Walpole's flawed character, Hume offered no hint that such constraints could transform him into a virtuous man.

Notwithstanding the promises made by his "science of politics," there is no indication that Hume expected legal and institutional arrangements to eliminate virtue as a check on political power. Hume's antipathy toward republican writers and their preoccupation with morals and manners did not make him indifferent to the personal character of princes. Contrary to Forbes's contention that a civilized monarchy for Hume is one in which "the personality of the ruler hardly matters," a more careful reading of Hume's works suggests that a civilized monarchy rendered personality *less* important, not *un*important.[109] The very survival of the constitution would no longer hang so precariously on the personal characteristics of a king as it did during the constitutional struggles of the seventeenth century, but the regularity of government would always depend to some extent on the personal qualities of the chief executive, whether that was the king or a minister. As Garry Wills observes, "For Hume, who saw the force of personal attachment in the whole range of political ties, it was hard to distinguish government (always to be supported) from governors (who are opposable)."[110]

To the extent that personality still matters in politics, personal character and virtue would continue to be crucial considerations in preventing tyranny and preserving liberty. Hume denied that the spartan virtues demanded by republicanism were either feasible or desirable ideals for the vast generality of humankind, but he admitted that some individuals are capable of achieving those qualities and that it is proper to esteem them. Thus, it would be wrong to say that "Hume has virtually no affinities with the Machiavellian moralists and corruption mongers of his age."[111] He developed a postrepublican conception of virtue that would appeal to leading nationalists in America, who were becoming increasingly disenchanted with the prospects of republicanism during the 1780s. Hume's insistence on the importance of the personal qualities of a ruler, especially in times of national crisis, called into question some of the most cherished convictions of republicans, who considered *national* character decisive in determining the outcome of war, for instance. Hume's position on leadership was an oblique critique of the republican stance on civic virtue. Successive reigns in the fourteenth century "are a proof, how little reason kingdoms have to value themselves on their victories, or be humbled by their defeats; which in reality ought to be ascribed chiefly to the good or bad conduct of their rulers, and are of little moment towards determining national characters and manners."[112] Politics for Hume was clearly driven from the top down, but this did not spell the end or insignificance of virtue, only shift the focus when it came to those qualities treasured by republicans.

Hume's remarks on the possibility of publicly oriented virtue localized in the few or even the one would have a great impact on Federalist conceptions of the presidency. His moral philosophy reoriented the focus of political ethics away from its traditional emphasis on mutually shared civic virtue understood as an indispensable prerequisite of freedom toward an emphasis on the universal principles of human nature. In a typically modern move that suggests the extent to which moral philosophy had abandoned the central concerns of classical republicanism, Hume shifted attention to man "as he really is" away from man "as he ought to be," which had been defined in markedly political and teleological terms since Aristotle.[113] The best that can be hoped for, Hume observed, is "to give a new direction to those natural passions, and teach us that we can better satisfy our appetites in an oblique and artificial manner, than by their headlong and impetuous motion."[114] Hume shared Machiavelli's vision of developing a science of human nature, but he was unwilling to state categorically that the patriotism and disinterestedness valued by republicans was unachievable. Even if it was unrealistic to expect it from the multitudes, Hume recognized that it was attainable by a few.

Hume's theory of human psychology revolves around the interplay of the passions. The most important distinction for political purposes is that "betwixt a calm and a weak passion; betwixt a violent and a strong one."[115] Hume's preference for "the prevalence of the calm passions above the violent" is directly related to the desideratum of moderation in politics noted above.[116] While a violent passion threatens political stability, a calm passion tends to support it because it "takes a comprehensive and distant view of its object."[117] One of the most powerful determinants of the violence of a passion is the proximity in time and space of the object of a passion to the individual. Propinquity has a tendency not only to excite the passions but also to divert an individual's attention from important long-term interests. According to Hume, the multitudes are preoccupied with "their present and immediate interest" and "prefer any trivial advantage, that is present, to the maintenance of order in society, which so much depends on the observance of justice."[118] More often than not, these sentiments undercut civic virtue, though custom and convention can overcome or redirect the natural impulse of the passions up to a point.[119] Republican virtue is at odds with the basic foundations of human psychology insofar as it requires the extension and expansion of one's temporal and spatial horizons beyond the present, narrow concerns of the self.

The political implications of this psychology are clear: it is hopeless to expect the majority of individuals to exhibit the publicly oriented virtues prized by republicans. Civic virtue entails the ability and the inclination to surmount the low and narrow impulses of self-interest, which constitute the starting point of modern psychology. In effect, Hume had demonstrated that republican virtue is incompatible with the general cognitive orientation toward spatially narrow and temporally immediate concerns, as indicated by the powerful effects of "partiality" and "selfishness."[120]

Even though there are universal features of human nature that oppose the development of an orientation toward either long-term or general interests that extend beyond the self, Hume insisted that there was plenty of room for individual variation within the framework of the passions. The Hobbesian notion of a humankind so benighted that nothing short of external restraints could bridle its destructive urges was anathema to Hume. The Scottish philosopher believed that these external restraints might not always be necessary to promote pro-social behavior, provided that other motivations were in place. There were some "virtuous motives" that had a more powerful influence in directing the conduct of some individuals over others. In terms reminiscent of Lockean psychology, he stated that "nothing can be more real, or concern us more, than our own sentiments of pleasure and uneasiness; and if these be favourable to virtue, and unfavourable to vice, no more can be requisite to the regulation of our conduct and behaviour."[121] One of the things that gives us pleasure, noted Hume, is a favorable opinion of one's character. A well-deserved reputation for virtue provides one of the most enduring sources of pleasure, and almost nothing contributes to such a reputation as much as public acknowledgment and appreciation for service to the public.[122]

Although Hume did not explicitly draw out the implications of this insight for the possibility of virtuous statesmen in the *Treatise,* his historical surveys provide ample documentation that monarchs disposed to virtue have always looked after the public interest. For instance, he showered warm praise on Alfred the Great, who "seems indeed to be the model of that perfect character, which, under the denomination of a sage or wise man, philosophers have been fond of delineating, rather as a fiction of their imagination, than in hopes of ever seeing it really existing."[123] As "unusual" as such individuals have been, their virtuous conduct testifies to the possibility of virtue. Far from ignoring the role of virtue in politics, Hume's "attempt to introduce the experimental method of reasoning into moral subjects"—the subtitle of his *Treatise*—called for closer scrutiny of the dispositions and motives of rulers. As already noted, Hume concluded his account of the life and reign of each monarch with a review of their public and private virtues and vices. He frequently attributed the successes and failures of their reigns to their personal qualities, which were no less important than general historical and constitutional developments in maintaining the proper balance between liberty and authority.

Hume explained that character is crucial in politics—as in moral evaluations—because it provides the only justification for the assignment of praise or blame.[124] The reason for this is that actions reflect the underlying character of an actor, which Hume believed to be relatively inflexible, constant, and predictable. [125] "If any *action* be either virtuous or vicious, 'tis only as a sign of some quality or character. It must depend upon durable principles of the mind, which extend over the whole conduct, and enter into the personal character."[126] Some characters are less firm and inflexible than others, and all characters are subject to change, but, Hume argued, character is still a reliable predictor of behavior. Repeated actions eventually habituate us to act in certain ways even when the passion that may have initially inclined us to behave in a particular way is no longer present.[127]

The upshot of Hume's theory about the fixity of character is that certain individuals are constitutionally incapable of wickedness. They are predisposed to behave in certain ways, and there is little (but by no means nothing) that can be done to change their orientations. But how, it might be asked, is it possible to reconcile this observation with Hume's discussion of the relation between opinion and virtuous conduct? If character is truly fixed, then what sort of effect could public opinion be expected to have on the behavior that flows from character?

Hume's account of character seems to suggest that individuals of poor character are indifferent to the opinions of their fellows, whereas individuals of good character are good precisely because they care about their reputations. The latter desire the pleasure that comes from public esteem more than the pleasure that comes from satisfying their hunger for power or wealth. Outside the context of character, it is neither sensible nor possible to ascribe either merit or demerit to those actions, which "are by their very nature temporary and perishing; and where they proceed not from some cause in the characters and disposition of the person, who perform'd them, they infix not themselves upon him, and can neither redound to his honour, if good, nor infamy, if evil."[128] The relative consistency of actions flows from an individual's character, which is the only thing that makes genuine responsibility for actions possible. Hume insisted that "we are never to consider any single action in our enquiries concerning the origin of morals; but only the quality or character from which the action proceeded."[129] Hume observed that "men are less blam'd for such evil actions, as they perform hastily and unpremeditately, than for such as proceed from thought and deliberation. For what reason? but because a hasty temper, tho' a constant cause in the mind, operates only by intervals, and infects not the whole character."[130] Although Hume had stressed the influence of external factors in his more political writings, the most important factor in determining behavior seems to be personal character. Quite often, a person's character consists of enduring motives that are resistant to the influences of material rewards and punishments that diehard utilitarians like Bentham sought to manipulate. As a result, it is necessary to consider personal qualities as well as institutional arrangements in determining the trustworthiness of officeholders.

The Character of Kings and Statesmen

Throughout his historical surveys, Hume suggested that the best monarchs—those who made the most lasting positive contributions to the nation's economic, cultural, and political development—were those who consistently exhibited those virtues that contributed to the long-term collective welfare of the community, as opposed to those who were overly emotional, erratic, or parochial in their outlooks.[131] Contrary to Machiavelli's advice that the prince ought to be impetuous and flexible, Hume advocated moderation and constancy.[132] Hence, it was imperative that a ruler possess a calm and rational mastery over his or her passions.[133] These predispose the magistrate to focus on "distant pursuits" and long-term collective objects, rather than the satisfaction of immediate private interests.[134] In fact, Hume often extolled many of those virtues exalted by republican whenever he observed them.

Perhaps the reason that Hume's endorsement of these republican-sounding dispositions has gone unnoticed is that he did not condemn individuals for exhibiting their "natural" tendencies toward selfishness, as republican writers frequently did. As Annette Baier explains, "there is a realism constraint built into his theory, which amounts to the requirement that vice be the exception, virtue the rule."[135] The difference between Hume and republican thinkers was that he opposed those rigorous standards of virtue that set people up for failure. Where republicans consistently defined the virtues up, Hume usually defined them down. As a result, Hume's catalogue of virtues was much more inclusive and, on the whole, less political than the list of virtues acclaimed by republicans. But this did not stop Hume from castigating individuals who were self-serving or egotistical and lauding individuals who were altruistic or public-spirited.

Hume sounded much like his intellectual and political enemy Bolingbroke when he wrote, "The Idea I form of a political Whig, is that of a Man of Sense and Moderation, a Lover of Laws and Liberty, whose chief Regard to particular Princes and Families, is founded on a Regard to the publick Good," a predisposition all the more important in rulers.[136] Like Bolingbroke, Hume criticized the English minister Robert Walpole for his nepotistic policies, which showed a marked disregard for the public good.[137] A public official who lacks republican virtue may be just like everyone else, and may even be a good person in other respects, but makes for a bad statesman. That is to say, Hume applied a double standard to public officers. He did not necessarily expect them to possess any special talents or technical expertise, but he did expect them to exhibit superior moral virtues. Hume opined that "the governing of Mankind well, requires a great deal of Virtue, Justice, and Humanity, but not a surprising Capacity."[138] Virtue for Hume is not so much an end in itself as a means toward happiness, or a "tendency to the good of mankind."[139] Although

Hume applied the label "virtue" rather promiscuously to moral and nonmoral qualities, to mental and physical qualities, what all these virtues have in common is that they may be useful or agreeable (or both) to others. Like everything else, Hume judged virtues by their consequences. Indeed, nonmoral leadership qualities are valued mainly for their contribution to more directly moral qualities. "Knowledge in the arts of government naturally begets mildness and moderation, by instructing men in the advantages of humane maxims above rigour and severity, which drive subjects into rebellion."[140]

As Hume demonstrated throughout his historical surveys, a lot is at stake in the character of an executive. One reason character is important is that a king should always provide a moral example to his people.[141] The observance of the laws by a monarch will inspire similar obedience by subjects otherwise disinclined to obey.[142] More important, the personal character of an executive often determines the extent of his or her authority. Elizabeth is the most prominent but certainly not the only example of this phenomenon. Throughout his detailed account of the queen's reign, Hume made it clear that her political longevity and success were attributable to her reputation for superior personal qualities, which included political savvy as well as moral rectitude. The virtue of Henry V buttressed his questionable title to the throne and earned him the universal assent of his people: "Virtue now seemed to have an open career, in which it might exert itself: The exhortations, as well as example, of the prince gave it encouragement: All men were unanimous in their attachment to Henry; and the defects of his title were forgotten, amidst the personal regard, which was universally paid to him."[143] Because "this prince possessed many eminent virtues," Parliament submitted to many of his requests for "extraordinary supplies" and even acquiesced in his violations of the law. It tolerated his invocation of the right of levying purveyances, which "had been expressly guarded against by the Great Charter itself."[144]

Hume devoted attention to the opposite phenomenon, as well. The historian lamented that "by the example of Charles II. and the cavaliers, licentiousness and debauchery became prevalent in the nation."[145] The nation suffered a precipitous decline in moral standards because the king himself was a lecherous hedonist, though Hume admitted that this moral decline was a predictable reaction to the severe austerity of life under a commonwealth of pretended Puritan "saints." As sympathetic as Hume was to the Stuart monarch, he noted that Charles' personal failings had a pernicious moral influence, and he agreed that "his character, though not altogether destitute of virtue, was in the main dangerous to his people."[146] The upshot was that the public's aversion to his character exacerbated its disaffection with his policies. He endured chronic civil unrest and assassination attempts because his defective character never gave opponents any excuse to think twice about getting rid of him.

Hume cited many other examples that showed that an executive with bad character becomes an embattled, hence a weak, executive. For instance, he attributed the deposition of Edward II in 1326 to the weakness of his character and his personal incapacity to govern, not to any infractions he had committed.[147] Hume also indicated that moral turpitude has often delegitimized even a rightful ruler. King John's murder of his nephew almost completely undermined his authority: "All men were struck with horror at this inhuman deed; and from that moment the king, detested by his subjects, retained a very precarious authority over both the people and the barons in his dominions."[148] This is an egregious case, but Hume repeatedly showed how personal failings have contributed to political failure even when there was no controversy over a rightful claim to power. Henry III was a failure because his soft temperament made him unfit to exercise regal authority. This monarch lacked the toughness, activity, and vigor necessary to carry out his policies. His irresolute manner, complaisance, and passivity exacerbated the "inconveniences" that were already plaguing government in those times.[149] Henry III "had not prudence to chuse right measures, [and] he wanted even that constancy, which sometimes gives weight to wrong ones."[150] Had Henry been a stronger, more determined leader who exhibited less "variableness" in his conduct, the twenty-four barons selected by the "mad parliament" would never have usurped power and disrupted the balance of the constitution.[151]

In contrast to his hapless father Henry III, and despite his many faults, Edward I "possessed industry, penetration, courage, vigilance, and enterprize," which enabled him to restore "authority to the government" and plant the seeds of a viable legal system. The "correction, extension, amendment, and establishment of the laws, which Edward maintained in great vigour, and left much improved to posterity . . . gained to Edward the appellation of the English Justinian." His resolute character helped the principles of law take root in ground that had been morally barren.[152]

Significantly, the fixity of character, especially resolution in a magistrate, are important for the same reason as the rule of law. Without the predictability and certainty that they provide, political life would be thrown into confusion. Although Hume did not draw out the full implications of this similarity, it should be noted that the predictability and certainty provided by a stable and constant character are beneficial only if that character is virtuous, just as the predictability and certainty of the rule of law are only as salutary as the substantive content of the laws themselves. Just as uniform adherence to the formalities of law tends to reinforce respect for the law by giving people confidence that particular laws are not being applied against them in a discriminatory fashion, the fixity of character enhances respect for statesmen by assuring people that their rulers are impartial, or disinterested.[153] Hume more or less took it for granted that character and the rule of law would contribute to the stability and order he valued so highly only when their substance was as good as their form.

Character as a Check

Much like Locke, Hume was dubious about excessively legalistic checks, which tend to impose overly rigid standards of propriety that hamper the executive's ability to deal effectively with critical situations. Only a consistent pattern of pernicious behavior signifying a defective character—not a single, aberrational instance of indiscretion—justifies the incrimination of a political leader. If "nothing can oppose or retard the impulse of passion, but a contrary impulse," the only way to prevent abuses of discretionary powers is to make sure that public officials possess the appropriate mix of passions.[154] Although improvements in the regularity of government minimize dependence on the character of politicians, the passions have such a powerful influence that a politician with the inclination and the opportunity could wreak unspeakable havoc.

While the proper institutional arrangements and constitutional checks are capable of reorienting these passions toward the public good to some extent, Hume never argued that they made character considerations in politics obsolete. As Hume noted in his *Treatise,* "'tis not contrary to reason to prefer the destruction of the whole world to the scratching of my finger."[155] History is fraught with instances of massively destructive behavior, which Hume attributed to the defective characters of political figures ranging from the inept John I to the nefarious Richard III, from the fanatical Oliver Cromwell to the bigoted and imprudent James II. As happens all too often, individuals "often act knowingly against their interest: For which reason the view of the greatest possible good does not always influence them."[156] Each of these historical figures lacked virtue to the extent that they failed to be useful and agreeable to themselves *and to others,* the essential criteria of virtue. Without the ability or willingness to consider the welfare of others, one of the most important checks on power is missing.

One of the most significant personal checks on public officials is their own self-perception, which is based partly on the opinion of others. One's self-perception is very closely connected to one's reputation within the larger community. "When a man is prepossessed with a high notion of his rank and character in the creation, he will naturally endeavor to act up to it, and will scorn to do a base or vicious action, which might sink him below that figure which he makes in his own imagination."[157] The bases of reputation vary according to social and political standing. A hereditary monarch will naturally have a different self-perception than an urban merchant or even a country gentleman. Like the rest of Hume's moral system, this sentiment is highly interpersonal. In fact, Hume's account of sympathy shows the complex and mutually reinforcing interactions between self-esteem and the esteem of others. "Men always consider the sentiments of others in their judgments of themselves."[158]

The "love of fame" and the love of others are also dramatic spurs to virtuous conduct: "There are few persons, that are satisy'd with their own character, or genius, or fortune, who are not desirous of shewing themselves to the world, and of acquiring the love and approbation of mankind."[159] Alexander Hamilton's comment that the "love of fame" is "the ruling passion of the noblest minds" is very similar to—if not actually derived from—Hume's discussion of this sentiment in *An Enquiry Concerning the Principles of Morals,* where Hume contended that "a desire of fame . . . seems inseparable from virtue, genius, capacity, and a generous or noble disposition."[160] It is easy to see why Hamilton would find Hume's discussion so appealing and relevant to the creation of the presidency when one considers its role in promoting virtue. As Hume explained, "This constant habit of surveying ourselves, as it were, in reflection, keeps alive all the sentiments of right and wrong, and begets, in noble natures, a certain reverence for themselves as well as others, which is the surest guardian of every virtue."[161] This aspect of Humean moral psychology anticipated the main features of Adam Smith's more familiar notion of the "impartial spectator."[162] For both philosophers, the process at work involves continual adjustment between one's own perceptions of moral conduct and the (often idealized) opinions of observers. It is through this process,

Hume suggested, that individuals bring their conduct in line with the moral expectations attached to their particular situation or station in life. In the case of an executive, this entails living up to standards of behavior that apply with special force to one in that position of authority. Ideally, executives would try to live up to those moral expectations even if, like Henry V, they had failed to exhibit the relevant moral dispositions in the past.

Hume observed the paradox contained in the maxim that *"every man must be supposed a knave*: Though at the same time, it appears somewhat strange, that a maxim should be true in *politics,* which is false in *fact*."[163] The adage is true only because the social nature of politics tends to insulate individuals from the shame they would otherwise experience when pursuing the same illicit activities individually. There tends to be a diffusion of responsibility in political aggregations that removes, or at least reduces, the moral constraints that ordinarily check individual behavior. Because of the pernicious dynamics of group psychology, it is necessary to develop a form of government in which responsibility is readily identifiable and blame easily assignable. (This analysis of pernicious group behavior and individual responsibility was later picked up by Madison and other delegates to the Constitutional Convention who condemned the behavior of legislative assemblies and recommended a single executive as a safer alternative to a plural executive.)

Hume went even farther, noting that the official authority of the executive must be unambiguous, or else the impact of virtue will be negligible: "Though *affection* to wisdom and virtue in a *sovereign* extends very far, and has great influence; yet he must *antecedently* be supposed invested with a public character, otherwise the public esteem will serve him in no stead, nor will his virtue have any influence beyond a narrow sphere."[164] A clear investment of authority is a precondition not only for the full exercise of talents but for the public accountability of leaders as well. When power is contested, responsibility is destroyed. In one version of the "Idea of a Perfect Commonwealth," Hume stated that "a wise politician is the most beneficial character in nature, if accompanied with authority; and the most innocent, and not altogether useless, even if deprived of it."[165] As important as the wisdom and virtue of magistrates are to consolidating and defining the extent of executive power, not surprisingly, these are of negligible influence without an "antecedent" investment of authority.[166] In light of the kinds of executive powers this liberal theorist advocated, it should come as no surprise that maintaining the authority of the executive was a primary concern for Hume.

Prerogative in Historical Context

Hume's views concerning the relationship between authority and liberty and between regularity and prerogative are complex. As noted above, Hume believed that there was an antagonistic relationship between liberty and authority, but he also believed that ample authority was a precondition of liberty, especially as it developed in England.[167] He approved of the constitutional changes that had taken place since the great seventeenth-century struggles over prerogative and parliamentary privileges, but he did not regard prerogative with the same abhorrence his contemporaries exhibited. He thought many of the constitutional changes concerning prerogative were salutary—especially those that protected the rights of citizens from arbitrary practices—but he defined the class of dangerous prerogatives rather narrowly. Contrary to Locke's more general usage, Hume used the term to refer to specific royal privileges disputed during the seventeenth century and limited the dangerous ones to: "the dispensing power, the power of imprisonment, of exacting loans and benevolences, of pressing and quartering soldiers, of altering the customs, or erecting monopolies." Exercises of prerogative that touch upon these areas are not *ipso facto* antithetical to free government, but they are suspect because they affect the rights of subjects. Perhaps even more important, these prerogatives are objectionable because they involve what are now regarded as legislative powers. They are not discretionary powers so much as powers to rule by fiat. Even though Hume approved the elimination of powers that directly touch the most cherished rights of citizens, he was less enthusiastic about efforts to curb the general discretionary powers of the executive since they are *not necessarily* inimical to liberty or to the principles of free government.

According to Hume, the constitutional propriety of any given practice depends on a variety of particular circumstances—social, cultural, political, and historical. In contrast to Locke, who abstractly defined prerogative in terms of substantive ends defined by natural law, Hume offered a relativized account of prerogative defined in terms of customary constitutional practices. He judged prerogative mainly according to standards internal to the constitution broadly understood, not the external standards of a narrowly defined morality. One of Hume's political purposes in writing *The History of England* was to debunk the popular Whig myth that the people enjoyed their liberties uninterrupted and unmolested under the ancient constitution until the Stuarts overreached the proper limits of royal prerogative and encroached on the privileges of Parliament.[168] He argued that popular rights and privileges were virtually nonexistent under the feudal system, when the administration of justice was so irregular and undependable that nearly all the inhabitants of England had to seek protection from "some particular nobleman . . . whom they were obliged to consider as their sovereign, more than the king himself, or even the legislature," which itself bore only a slight resemblance to the revered institution of Whig lore.[169] "The pretended liberty of the times," wrote Hume, "was only an incapacity of submitting to government."[170] The "rude" state of society in earlier periods of English history justified the more expansive notion of prerogative that prevailed at the time. Insofar as exercises of prerogative power depend on the will of the monarch, they can be regarded as irregular, or less regular than government according to well-established legal rules, but Hume denied that exercises of prerogative are necessarily or altogether irregular. In fact, instances of prerogative were more or less regular according to historical precedent, accepted practice, and the character of the monarch.[171]

In politics as in morality, context makes all the difference in determining what kinds of rules should be in place and whether they should be followed. In Hume's opinion, the institutionalization of the rule of law is an undoubted improvement upon those forms of government that depend more heavily on human judgment and royal discretion. The Magna Carta, "a kind of epoch in the constitution," was a monumental step along the path to the full realization of "a new species of government, and introduced some order and justice into the administration."[172] However, Hume did not object to the use of prerogative in eighteenth-century England because it offended his principles but because it was no longer necessary. This explains the neutral tone in which Hume described exercises of prerogative in circumstances very different from the ones that obtained in his time. The simplicity of the ancient governments created a greater need for wide-ranging discretionary powers.[173] There was little alternative to the "sole discretion" that monarchs possessed during times of emergency in those periods when "the imperfect and unformed laws left, in every thing, a latitude of interpretation; and when the ends, pursued by the monarch, were, in general, agreeable to his subjects, little scruple or jealousy was entertained with regard to the regularity of the means."[174]

The frequency of legally binding proclamations issued in former periods is explained by "the extreme imperfection of the ancient laws, and the sudden exigencies, which often occurred in such turbulent governments, [and] obliged the prince to exert frequently the latent powers of his prerogative."[175] Not only did subjects implicitly validate exercises of discretion, but wide discretion was also a political necessity when government was still irregular.[176] The question, of course, is whether discretion would ever be appropriate in a more regular government.

Regularity and Discretion

The principle of regularity literally seemed to rule out the kind of discretionary action associated with executive prerogative. Hume's political conservatism made him more receptive to the claims of authority, but he was still too much the liberal to accept a form of power that threatened the claims of liberty. Sounding much like the Whigs he often needled with his historical corrections to their constitutional myths, Hume advised that "an eternal jealousy must be preserved against the sovereign, and no discretionary powers must ever be entrusted to him, by which the property or personal liberty of any subject can be affected."[177]

Even though Hume was adamantly opposed to legal grants of wide discretionary power of the sort that royalists had defended during the reign of the Stuarts, he seemed to be open to the possibility that occasional exercises of extralegal prerogative might be necessary and appropriate in certain circumstances. He never systematically investigated or theorized the problem of emergencies, but his writings are full of brief but telling references to exceptional circumstances that justify limited departures from established rules of law. These admissions are often made with evident reluctance, but that does not diminish their significance, especially when one considers the role of regularity in his constitutional theory. In one of his more explicit remarks on contingency in politics, Hume seemed to set the bar for exceptions from the law extremely high. "Nothing less than the most extreme necessity," he asserted, "can justify individuals in a breach of promise, or an invasion of the properties of others." But in the sentence immediately preceding this one, Hume seemed to allow for somewhat greater flexibility. He observed that "all politicians will allow, and most philosophers, that reasons of state may, in particular emergencies, dispense with the rules of justice, and invalidate any treaty or alliance, where the strict observance of it would be prejudicial, in a considerable degree, to either of the contracting parties."[178]

It would be tempting to conclude that the main difference between the two cases is that one pertains to domestic affairs, where the rules are usually clear and well established, while the other pertains to foreign affairs, where the rules are more ambiguous and less entrenched—where they exist at all. But Hume does not make much of this difference, here or elsewhere. The real distinction seems to lie in the positions of the individuals who would have to decide between whether to follow the rules or to disobey them in particular circumstances.

The threshold for ordinary citizens is always much higher than it is for public officials. As carefully qualified as Hume's articulation of the reason of state doctrine is, the exception he allowed for individuals is so narrowly circumscribed that it precludes nearly all exercises of individual judgment contrary to rules. Only an "extreme necessity," such as a direct threat to self-preservation for the individual or the community, absolves the ordinary individual from following the rules of justice.[179] However, Hume believed that occasions giving rise to such threats would be extremely rare in a well-regulated society.[180] Moreover, giving individuals any more leeway than this would make regularity virtually impossible. The general social costs of allowing individuals to decide for themselves on an *ad hoc* basis when a particular breach of the rules might actually do more good than bad almost always outweigh any potential benefits to themselves or others directly involved.

But that is not the case for public officials. There are acknowledged costs to the rule of law in allowing them to make the same kinds of decisions, but the costs are more likely to be outweighed by the potential benefits to society as a whole. The kinds of emergencies that public officials are forced to deal with affect not just their own personal welfare; they impinge on the welfare of the entire society. As a result, catastrophic consequences for the entire society might follow if a public official had to show the same scrupulous regard for rule-following that is expected of ordinary citizens. That is the reason that it had always appeared so "doubtful, whether human society could ever reach the state of perfection, as to support itself with no other controul than the general and rigid maxims of law and equity."[181] A departure from settled laws and routines by anyone is going to have some impact on regularity, but it seems that the overall negative effect is expected to be more limited when the decision is restricted to public officials.

Hume's discussion of the rules of justice clarifies his position on the purpose of rules more generally. The same principle that justifies the rules of justice in the first place—"the convenience and necessities of mankind"—also explains the reason for its violation: "The safety of the people is the supreme law: All other particular laws are subordinate to it, and dependent on it: And if, in the *common* course of things, they may be followed and regarded; it is only because the public safety and interest *commonly* demand so equal and impartial an administration."[182] As far as ordinary individuals are concerned, the overall scheme of justice should be observed because "the advantage of society results only from the observance of the general rule."[183] General rules are made for the generality of mankind. Exceptions are allowed only to the exceptional.

Hume employed a more expansive notion of necessity when dealing with the discretionary powers of public officials. In a discussion of the "latent powers, which might be exerted on any emergence," the historian made the unequivocal remark that "in every government, *necessity, when real, supersedes all laws, and levels all limitations.*"[184] Hume's occasional references to "reasons of state" suggest that serious threats to the public good that fall short of life-threatening emergencies might justify the violation of legal and institutional rules. Even the use of arbitrary power did not automatically invalidate extralegal action in cases of necessity: "I reckon not among the violations of the Great Charter, some arbitrary exertions of prerogative, to which Henry's [Henry III] necessities pushed him, and which, without producing any discontent, were uniformly continued by all his successors, till the last century."[185] The restraint of law must yield to the pressures of necessity identified by the king in the interests of the public. Thus Hume acquitted Charles I of many accusations against him, including violating the Petition of Right, because it was justified by "the necessity of his situation."[186]

Discretionary powers are justified not only by indeterminate reasons of state, but also by specific customs and conventions supported by public opinion. Much to the chagrin of his Whiggish contemporaries, Hume demonstrated that many of the worst offenses committed by the Stuarts were actually well-established conventions practiced as recently as in the reign of the beloved Queen Elizabeth. Although her policies did not go unchallenged, Elizabeth's exercises of royal prerogative never generated the kind of opposition that her Stuart successors faced. "Even though monopolies and exclusive companies," the banes of early seventeenth-century Parliamentarians, "had already reached an enormous height, and were every day encreasing, to the destruction of all liberty," members of Parliament were not even allowed to contest these policies without fears of serious reprisal by the queen. In addition to exacting forced loans from the populace, demanding benevolences, and imposing a brand of ship money, Elizabeth peremptorily denied Peter Wentworth's insinuations that Parliament enjoyed any special privileges or exemptions against the Crown. She asserted that Parliaments were summoned only to expedite policies formulated by the queen and her ministers.[187] Parliament would wage war against Charles I for much less than this, yet Elizabeth encountered relatively little opposition, aside from a handful of persistent Puritans. The legal grounds for Elizabeth's conduct were just as weak as they were for Charles I, but her reputation for virtue made the very same conduct more acceptable to the people. As Hume explained, "Elizabeth continued to be the most popular sovereign that ever swayed the scepter of England; because the maxims of her reign were conformable to the principles of the times, and to the opinion, generally entertained with regard to the constitution."[188]

Hume's account of the "transactions" between Elizabeth and her Parliaments illustrates the importance of context in determining the constitutionality of a particular exercise of power. Constitutionality is simply not equivalent to legality, no matter how important legality is to either constitutionality or regularity. Elizabeth's nearly unquestioned assertions of arbitrary power confirm Hume's proposition that certain exercises of arbitrary power are consistent with prevailing constitutional practices and doctrines, if not with the demands of legal exactitude.[189] Hume never said that Elizabeth's actions were inconsistent with the constitutional principles of her day, only that she "exercised the royal authority in a manner so contrary to all the ideas, which we *at present* entertain of a *legal* constitution."[190] It is a modern—though not exclusively liberal—prejudice to deny the status of constitutionality to anything that does not conform to the strictures of law. Hume certainly preferred the more regular "legal constitution" that obtained in his time, but he acknowledged the validity of other kinds of constitutions. When there is an "extreme imperfection" in the laws, as was the case during the feudal period in England, "sudden exigencies" may compel the prince to resort to extralegal measures.[191] It all depends on context. As a result, a disruption in the steady and progressive development of regularity in government that Hume recounted in so much detail might justify the use of discretionary powers that were thought to be a thing of the past.

The legal and political structures in place are not the only things that shape the context in which prerogative occurs. The state of learning, the progress of the arts, the standing of religion, and the condition of the economy are all important determinants. The decisions made about these and other matters will have a definite impact on the regularity of government. Making greater resources available to the executive is one way to bypass the need for discretionary executive violence. Charles II should not be condemned for some of his arbitrary policies since "it may be doubted, whether the low state of the public revenue in this period, and of the military power, did not still render some discretionary authority in the crown necessary to the support of government."[192] Hume insisted that people are faced with the unavoidable choice of either vesting discretionary, and necessarily arbitrary, power in their monarch, or establishing a large revenue and military to support the prince: "And it seems a necessary, though perhaps melancholy truth, that, in every government, the magistrate must either possess a large revenue and a military force, or enjoy some discretionary powers, in order to execute the laws, and support his own authority."[193] The implication seems to be that the legislature has an interest in maintaining the strength of the executive because an executive that feels more secure is more likely to be a friend of liberty.

In general, though, it is the responsibility of the legislature to check the ambitions of the executive and prevent encroachments on the liberty of the people. The legislature abdicates that responsibility when it gives legal warrant to otherwise extralegal activities. Hume would sometimes go out of his way to criticize legislatures for their incompetence and excesses in pursuing liberty, but he never missed an opportunity to chastise them for their failures in curbing the excesses of executive authority. He castigated the Tudor Parliaments for passing a law that "gave to the king's proclamations the same force as to a statute enacted by parliament; and to render the matter worse, if possible, they framed this law, as if it were only declaratory, and were intended to explain the natural extent of royal authority."[194] Combined with the dispensing power of the crown, this proclamation power gave the crown "full legislative authority," reduced Parliament to a mere source of revenue, and enthroned the will of the monarch as the only rule for the nation.[195] It should come as no surprise, Hume opined, that the monarch should ignore the liberties of the people when "the parliament itself, in enacting laws, was entirely negligent of it."[196]

Hume's scornful critique of this "servile and prostitute parliament" fore-shadowed contemporary quarrels about the normalization of emergency powers.[197] His principal objection was not that the parliament's obsequious act of political self-abasement basically rendered it useless to the cause of liberty but that the legal recognition of the monarch's superior ability to deal with "sudden emergencies" was effectively a means of "having tyranny converted into law."[198] Hume acknowledged the need for executive discretion in times of emergency, but insisted on the importance of maintaining the distinction between regular and irregular, legal and extralegal. As he explained, "there was a difference between a power, which was exercised on a particular emergence, and which must be justified by the present expedience or necessity; and an authority conferred by a positive statute, which could no longer admit of controul or limitation."[199] Once an extraordinary act of discretion is given the cover of law, there is little to prevent it from becoming an ordinary part of government. And once that occurs, it becomes more difficult to raise consequential constitutional objections due to the habits of obedience that get formed.[200] It is worth bearing in mind that for Hume the key criterion of constitutionality is established practice: "In the particular exertions of power, the question ought never to be forgotten, *What is best?* But in the general distribution of power among the several members of a constitution, there can seldom be admitted any other question, than *What is established?*"[201] There is nothing in Hume's theory that precludes the possibility of change, but his analysis suggests that it is probably best to eliminate the need for change in the first place.[202]

The ultimate check against abuses of extralegal power may be just as irregular as extralegal power itself. Unlike conceptions of constitutionalism that define the extent and legitimacy of political power according to formal criteria stipulated in written instruments, Hume's conception gives pride of place to the informal normativity of public opinion.[203] The "easiness with which the many are governed by the few" is explained by the fact that, "as FORCE is always on the side of the governed, the governors have nothing to support them but opinion. *It is therefore, on opinion only that government is founded.*"[204]

As suggested above, public opinion also determines the extent and legitimacy of discretionary powers insofar as officials with reputations for virtue enjoy more leeway in discharging their duties. It took only a few decades to undo centuries of accepted constitutional practice in the seventeenth century once the Puritans, common law jurists, and others succeeded in convincing the people (through the force of arms as much as arguments) that they possessed certain privileges—all of which Hume insisted were recent fabrications. For Hume, rules are not the only sources of political legitimacy. As Richard Flathman notes, indeterminate criteria of legitimacy (like public opinion) are not meaningless criteria in either an epistemological or a political sense.[205] In the end, one of Hume's most important contributions to constitutionalism may consist in his demonstration that the ultimate foundations of prerogative and other forms of political power rest on the shifting ground of public opinion. In that fact lies both the greatest hope and the greatest despair concerning the prospects of liberty.

Conclusion

By now a pattern has begun to emerge. It is clear the earliest varieties of liberalism were amenable to discretionary power. The first liberals were preoccupied with the uncertainties and contingencies of politics, and they recognized the limitations and inconveniences associated with formal procedures and institutional structures of government. Locke's political theory is closely identified with the rule of law, and Hume's is associated with the machinery of government, but both thinkers demonstrated the need to depart from these ordinary forms in extraordinary circumstances. Contrary to conventional opinion, these philosophers also sought to supplement the formal checks on power with those character requirements that would render the potentially extralegal discretionary powers of the executive safe(r).

Perhaps the most important lesson Hume taught his American readers was not that the proper arrangement of political institutions or the right ordering of social practices could solve all political problems but that perfection could not be expected from any human invention.[206] Constitution-makers had to learn that institutional machinery could never entirely replace the role of individual character in determining the safety or quality of government. It would sometimes be necessary to fall back on human intervention in the form of executive discretion, especially when emergencies arise. For Hume, constancy of character could provide a degree of regularity in government comparable to that afforded by more formal and impersonal institutions. He had demonstrated that there are exceptional individuals who possess the public virtues required to maintain a regular administration even in highly irregular times, but he never explained how such individuals could be located in the first place. That was the challenge that Hume's American followers would have to meet.

CHAPTER FOUR

"The King Can Do No Wrong"

Blackstone on the Executive in Law

> The mass of men will be apt to grow insolent and refractory, if taught to
> consider their prince as a man of no greater perfection than themselves.
>
> WILLIAM BLACKSTONE

The Constitutional Primacy of the King

Popular assemblies have been celebrated as bastions of freedom against the
encroachments of monarchs and ministers in a variety of political traditions that predate the rise of parliamentary government. Throughout the seventeenth century, Anglophone political thinkers typically looked to legislative
assemblies as the guardians of liberty and sought to enhance their constitutional powers vis-à-vis the executive. Even those early eighteenth-century Opposition thinkers who bewailed the state of corruption in Parliament tended
to place the blame on the pernicious influence of royal ministers and sought
greater independence for Parliament. By the end of the eighteenth century,
the doctrine of parliamentary supremacy had become an "irresistible" staple
of English constitutional thought.[1] Perhaps no other work contributed as significantly to the ascendancy of this doctrine in the second half of the eighteenth century as William Blackstone's *Commentaries on the Laws of England*.

Based on a series of lectures he gave as the first chair established for the
study of English law, Blackstone set out to educate those gentlemen in Parliament whom he considered "the guardians of the English constitution" about
the meaning, structure, and value of the common law (I, 9).[2] His monumental

study of the English system of government and law found an eager audience in colonial and revolutionary America, where readers were already receptive to the Lockean proposition that "the principal aim of society is to protect individuals in the enjoyment of those absolute rights, which were vested in them by the immutable laws of nature" (I, 120). As Blackstone repeated throughout his multi-volume work, the chief instrument of that hallowed responsibility was a mixed system of government weighted heavily toward the legislature, or the King-in-Parliament, to use his preferred term.[3] With good reason, Blackstone has been considered a preeminent eighteenth-century expositor of "Old-Whig" values and an important contributor to the development of both a rights-based Anglo-American liberalism[4] and a legislative-centered constitutionalism, both of which emerged as responses to the dangers of executive power.[5]

However, for all the attention that Blackstone's putative Whiggism has received, scholars have taken relatively little notice of his surprisingly expansive notions of executive power in general and royal prerogative in particular.[6] This neglect is especially surprising considering his enormous contributions to American notions of executive power.[7] After Montesquieu, he was the author cited most frequently at the Constitutional Convention and throughout the ratification debates, and his influence, as measured by frequency of citations, surpassed that of all other writers in the period after the adoption of the Constitution.[8] This influence was not limited to discussions of property rights, criminal procedure, and the law of nations but extended to the topic of executive power, especially in Alexander Hamilton's writings.

What is so remarkable about this influence is that Blackstone's theory of executive power was modeled on seventeenth-century notions of royal prerogative that had been repudiated in Whig doctrine and abolished in practice. Far from minimizing the role and powers of the executive, as most Whigs had done, Blackstone made executive power the centerpiece of the constitution and favored an extension of executive powers beyond anything contemplated by other common law writers. To describe the powers of the king, Blackstone used the notion of "royal prerogative" in two different senses, both of which stretched the current meaning of the constitution. Not only did he borrow explicitly from Locke's *Second Treatise* to develop an extralegal conception of prerogative for use in emergencies, he also identified and endorsed specific legal powers available during normal times that were derived from outdated constitutional practices and doctrines. In the first volume of his *Commentaries,*

Blackstone stated that English liberties are well protected because the king's prerogatives are bound by law, but he proceeded almost immediately to describe a set of powers that were either no longer authorized by law or had not been exercised in decades. Moreover, he ignored the existence of cabinet government and other developments in eighteenth-century British politics, which was increasingly centered on ministerial government. The irony is that the great expositor of the common law was even less willing to reduce the powers of the executive to legal rules than Locke and Hume, neither of whom was very favorably disposed to common law approaches to constitutional problems.

Some contemporaries disapprovingly noted Blackstone's outmoded views on executive power, but he supported so many doctrines favored by liberal reformers that they could safely ignore what they found objectionable. For instance, the oft-quoted Opposition writer James Burgh had criticized Blackstone for his undemocratic receptiveness to prerogative in one passage but cited him approvingly in the rest of his *Political Disquisitions*.[9] Twentieth-century critics also noted the anachronistic qualities of Blackstone's account of royal power. For instance, Harold Laski noted that "the powers of the king are described in terms more suitable to the iron despotism of William the Norman than to the backstairs corruption of George III," without offering a satisfactory explanation for Blackstone's anachronistic description of executive powers.[10] A large part of the explanation for this may lie in the easy assumption that Blackstone's support for the doctrine of parliamentary supremacy somehow entailed a repudiation or diminution of executive power. In fact, close examination of Blackstone's considered views on the legislature reveals a skepticism that occasionally descends into outright contempt. A few Anti-Federalists noted Blackstone's royalist propensities, but to no avail. His reputation as a defender of liberty and proponent of natural rights was too well established in America after the Revolution to cast any serious doubt on his commitments to all the right principles.[11]

As scholars have noted, Blackstone was a liberal in the classical sense, but a conservative in his politics. Nowhere is this conservatism more evident than in his constitutional apologetics. He was an unstinting defender of the prevailing system of English law, especially those "fundamental maxims and rules of the law" that "are now fraught with the accumulated wisdom of the ages" (IV, 435).[12] Insofar as the existing system of English law exhibited "the perfection of reason" (I, 70), anything that introduced permanent or significant change would have detracted from the harmony and order of this system. In a complaint that James Madison would repeat in his analysis of the vices of the American system under the Articles of Confederation, Blackstone denounced what he considered to be the excesses and ineptitude of legislative intermeddling, as evidenced by the profusion of irrational laws passed since the Glorious Revolution. Although Blackstone admitted the need for reforms in the criminal law, he lamented the fact that Parliament had taken "too little care and attention in framing and passing new ones" (IV, 4). Since the law's "symmetry has been destroyed, it's [sic] proportions distorted, and it's majestic simplicity exchanged for specious embellishments and fantastic novelties" (I, 10), he advised legislative restraint and "quiescence" to prevent further tampering with the "perfection" and beauty" of the legal structure.[13] Those legal reforms that Blackstone did favor did not entail any significant structural changes in the constitutional system.

This conservatism towards the law helps explain why Blackstone often preferred extralegal executive action that made no lasting institutional changes to legislative action that instituted permanent changes in the legal structure. He was worried more by the prospect of an overbearing legislature than by the discretionary intervention of a powerful executive.[14] Echoing Locke's account of the unavoidable turbulence of politics, Blackstone acknowledged that all states are subject to "numberless unforeseen events" (IV, 2) that demand immediate attention. No matter how rational the constitutional order, it would still require a "vigorous" and "independent" executive, capable both of stemming the tide of ill-advised change initiated by an overactive, incompetent Parliament and of making the periodic adjustments necessary to keep the machinery of government in working order. He suggested that the proper use of prerogative powers would preclude the need for noisome legislative intrusions into the "old Gothic castle" of the common law (III, 268). Where Locke had emphasized the practical limitations of legislative action in dealing with domestic emergencies, Blackstone stressed the inherent incompetence of the legislature.

Blackstone not only stressed the role of the executive as a check on an overactive legislature, but he also conceived of the executive as the fulcrum of the constitutional balance. The political primacy and supervisory role of the executive in Blackstone's theory of constitutional order reflect his aversion toward large-scale legal and political reformism.[15] His image of the constitution as a "machine" whose "energy" is supplied by the executive indicates the centrality of the executive in maintaining the constitutional order. A single, unified executive possesses the requisite "energy," "dispatch," and "vigour" to carry out the necessary tasks of government. Echoing Hume's discussion of the psychological advantages of a single executive, Blackstone added that "an elective monarchy seems to be the most obvious, and the best suited of any to the rational principles of government, and the freedom of human nature" (I, 185). As the title of the concluding essay of the *Commentaries* indicates, Blackstone acknowledged that the laws of England have been subject to "Progress, and Gradual Improvements," but he pointed out that many of them had been initiated by monarchs.[16] Even though discretionary exercises of prerogative constitute implicit acknowledgments of the imperfections of the prevailing legal and political system, Blackstone considered them less disruptive to the overall harmony and balance of the English system than the sweeping changes favored by reformers like Jeremy Bentham.[17]

Blackstone's justification of such extraordinary executive powers is in some ways even more remarkable than the scope of the powers themselves. Perhaps no phrase recurs more often throughout all four volumes of the *Commentaries* than the hoary maxim "the king can do no wrong." According to Blackstone, the idea "that the king can do no wrong, is a necessary and fundamental principle of the English constitution" (III, 254). The purpose of the doctrine after the Glorious Revolution was to maintain stability in government by immunizing the monarch as a person from punishment for the misdeeds of the Crown as an institution. Instead, ministers were liable to impeachment and subsequent punishment for wrongdoing.[18] This particular usage was an integral part of Blackstone's account, but he invoked this doctrine over and over again in a manner suggesting he meant something more than sovereign immunity from the law.

This maxim was closely connected to Blackstone's conception of "royal dignity." Although he referred to the notion of executive character in more formal terms than either Locke or Hume, the legal scholar's account of royal dignity suggests that he also worried about the ability of the executive to carry out certain duties without the extra public support that good character tends to generate. Blackstone used the concept of royal dignity and relied on the legal fiction that the king can do no wrong to justify his claim that the king possesses a superior character and ought to be regarded as such. His remark that "the law deems so highly of his [the king's] wisdom and virtue, as not even to presume it possible for him to do any thing inconsistent with his station and dignity" (IV, 33) was more than a straightforward explication of the existing constitutional doctrine. It was a description of the qualities the executive must (be believed to) possess in order to operate the machinery of government smoothly and without interference from "idle enquiries" into his character. Blackstone seemed to fear that the king would not enjoy the latitude necessary to exercise his ordinary powers under law—let alone the extraordinary powers of prerogative—without the supposition that the king's character makes him incapable of violating the public good. Though he rarely used the rhetoric of virtue, Blackstone did help establish a link between (general belief in) superior personal qualities and extraordinary powers that was even more explicit than anything found in either Locke or Hume.

Blackstone's Constitutional Apologetics

In considering Blackstone's conception of executive power, it is important to keep in mind his admonition that "without contemplating the whole fabric [of the law] together, it is impossible to form any clear idea of the meaning and connection of those disjointed parts, which still form a considerable branch of the modern law" (III, 196). An appreciation of the importance he assigns the executive requires an understanding of his general views on the constitution, which he also referred to as the "English system." This system forms an organic whole enlivened by the animating principle of liberty under law. Consistent with the Enlightenment impulse to understand the world in terms of rational principles and systematic categories of thought, he set out to demonstrate that England enjoyed a genuine *system* of law, not merely a confused conglomeration of conflicting customs, preposterous practices, and obsolete statutes.[19] At the rhetorical level, at least, there is probably no better example of that "deistic view of the world" that Carl Schmitt identified with the rationalism of eighteenth-century liberal thought.[20] But as discussed below, the maddeningly inconsistent Blackstone tended to confine his optimistic rationalism to his pious panegyrics to the English system.[21]

If there is a precedent for Constitution worship in the United States, it is Blackstone's unrivalled idolatry of the British constitution. In dealing with the constitution, description was often equivalent to prescription. Blackstone usually took as his ideal what he set out to describe and justify, conflating "is" and "ought" without hesitation or regret. Like Hume, Blackstone was skeptical of rationalistic appeals in politics—in spite of his own gestures toward a rationalistic worldview. He distrusted abstractions that had not been confirmed by experience and history, so he eschewed attempts at reform based on rationalistic abstractions and untried theories.[22] This is one reason that critics have accused him of being so "conservative and complacent" regarding the question of reform. His former student Jeremy Bentham reviled the teacher as a "tranquil copyist and indiscriminate panegyrist" who exhibited a pathological "hydrophobia of innovation."[23] There is a kernel of truth in this criticism. After all, Blackstone adamantly maintained that any detectable constitutional defects are attributable only to the "curious refinements of modern art . . . or the rage of unskilful improvements in later ages." The presumption was that existing institutions, which have been tested and sanctified by time, deserve veneration.[24] Thus, it was necessary for gentlemen in Parliament to adopt a historical appreciation of the law, lest they persist in introducing reforms inconsistent with the prevailing system and principles of the law.

Blackstone exalted the English constitution because he believed it embodied "that spirit of equal liberty which is the singular felicity of Englishmen" (III, 423). The separation of powers was an essential part of the constitution, but the main reason it was conducive to liberty was its mixed nature.[25] As a mixed form of government, it manifested "the three grand requisites . . . of wisdom, of goodness, and of power" characteristic of "the three regular forms of government": democracy, aristocracy, and monarchy (I, 48, 49). These forms are represented by the Commons, the Lords, and the king, respectively. Together they constitute the King-in-Parliament. But because "this aggregate body" is composed of three distinct branches, Blackstone argued, "there can no inconvenience be attempted by either of the three branches, but will be withstood by one of the other two; each branch being armed with a negative power, sufficient to repel any innovation which it shall think inexpedient or dangerous" (I, 51). What is noteworthy about Blackstone's account is not just his articulation of the way checks and balances operate but also his suggestion that the king has a share (albeit a negative one) in the legislative powers. Even though the royal veto power had not been used in decades, Blackstone wrote as if the king were still an active participant in the legislative process.

The current state of the legislature was the major source of Blackstone's discontent. In a letter he wrote to one Mr. Richmond in 1745, Blackstone opined that knowledge of history deepened the study of law, for without it, one's "learning will be both confused & superficial." But history was also important to Blackstone for reasons other than intellectual refinement: It is in the recesses of the past that one discovers the perfection of the law and the constitution.[26] Blackstone's "science of the law" was premised on "the primitivistic conviction that the original form of the legal system had been one of pure and rational simplicity."[27] He used a vivid architectural metaphor to express his wonderment at the harmony and balance that had typified the law before so many unnecessary and irrational embellishments were superadded to the splendid structure. His words are worth quoting at length:

> I have sometimes thought that ye Common Law, as it stood in Littleton's Days, resembled a regular Edifice: where ye Apartments were properly disposed, leading one into another without Confusion; where every part was subservient to ye whole, all uniting in one beautiful Symmetry: & every Room had its distinct Office allotted to it. But as it is now, swoln, shrunk, curtailed, enlarged, altered & mangled by various & contradictory Statutes &c; it resembles ye same Edifice, with many of its useful Parts pulled down, with preposterous Additions in other Places, of different Materials & coarse Workmanship: according to ye Whim, or Prejudice, or private Convenience of ye Builders. By wch means the Communication of ye Parts is destroyed, & their Harmony quite annihilated; & now it remains a huge, irregular Pile, with many noble Apartments, tho' awkwardly put together, & some of them of no visible Use at present. But if one desires to know why they were built, to what End or Use, how they communicated with ye rest, & ye like; he must necessarily carry in his Head ye Model of ye old House, wch will be ye only Clew to guide him thro' this new Labyrinth.[28]

What began as a tribute to the common law quickly turned into a bitter indictment of legislative activity. Blackstone specifically mentioned "various & contradictory Statutes" as causes for the decline of the law, while other causes merited nothing more than a perfunctory "&c." His nostalgic encomium to a past before the law had been deformed by the interference of legislators who do not fully understand or appreciate the delicate structure of the constitution calls into question the advisability of much legislative reform. The law used to be a rational and orderly—hence more intelligible—whole before statutory interference deranged its elegant and simple foundations.

In the *Commentaries,* he was somewhat more forgiving of those "superfluities" and "little contrarieties, which the practice of many centuries will necessarily create in any system," but he still blamed legislators for the "mischiefs that have arisen to the public from inconsiderate alterations in our laws" (I, 30, 10). Blackstone objected to statutory interference on aesthetic as well as intellectual grounds. The simplicity that made the ancient laws so beautiful had been replaced by an unsightly complexity that conformed to no apparent design. He attributed these changes to individuals acting on private motives— "Whim, or Prejudice"—as legislators are wont to do. But besides recommending training in the law to overcome the "confusion introduced by ill-judging and unlearned legislators" (I, 10), Blackstone never expressed any interest in addressing the underlying moral defects of legislators. Where legislators were concerned, he sought intellectual rather than moral reformation. Like Locke and Hume, he focused on the overall personal qualities of the executive instead.

Blackstone was a notoriously inconsistent thinker, but, in fairness to him, he was dealing with material that was impossibly inconsistent. In direct contradiction to his remarks in the letter to Richmond and to similar statements in the *Commentaries,* Blackstone claimed at one point that the complexity of the legal system was precisely what made it a paragon of free civilization. Ever the apologist, he asserted in the third volume that the "multiplicity of the English laws . . . is essential to a free people" (III, 327). The complexity and intricacy of the law are constitutive of English liberty and indicative of England's cultivation, in contrast to the simplicity of the laws in uncultivated nations, which know nothing of freedom (III, 326–27). He explained away instances of "contradiction or uncertainty" in the English system as something that "must be imputed to the defects of human laws in general, and are not owing to any particular ill construction of the English system" (III, 328).

In spite of this and other glaring contradictions, one element of his account remained fairly consistent throughout: the blame he cast on the legislature for defects in the English system. He was particularly aggrieved by the incompetence of ordinary members of parliament. His refusal to include the king in his indictment comes as no surprise, considering his conviction that belief in the legal maxim that the king can do no wrong is a precondition of constitutional legitimacy. Although Blackstone was considerably more circumspect about criticizing Parliament in the *Commentaries,* he did occasionally disclose sentiments similar to those evident in the letter cited above. Even when he tried to mute his criticisms, he ended up chastising legislators for their tampering and blaming "the sentiments or caprice of successive legislatures," among other things, for "the uncertainty of legal proceedings" (III, 325). He warned that the gentlemen who "represent . . . their country in parliament" should be very cautious in introducing constitutional or legal "innovations" (I, 9) in the future. After all, it was their fault that the law's "symmetry has been destroyed, it's proportions distorted, and it's majestic simplicity exchanged for specious embellishments and fantastic novelties" (I, 10).[29] The thrust of Blackstone's argument was to discourage structural reform and innovation, as "the mischiefs that have arisen to the public from inconsiderate alterations in our laws, are too obvious to be called in question" (I, 10). Instead, lawmakers should strive to preserve the status quo: "They are the guardians of the English constitution; the makers, repealers, and interpreters of the English laws; delegated to watch, to check, and to avert every dangerous innovation, to propose, to adopt, and to cherish any solid and well-weighed improvement; bound by every tie of nature, of honour, and of religion, to transmit that constitution and those laws to their posterity, amended if possible, at least without any derogation" (I, 9). Even when he acknowledged the positive role of legislators as guardians of English liberty, he emphasized that their most important function was to preserve the existing order and harmony of the English system with minimal modifications.

As Blackstone understood the English system, constitutional changes enacted by the legislature are fraught with risk. Because so many features of English law "have their root in the frame of our constitution," they "therefore can never be cured, without hazarding every thing that is dear to us" (III, 267). Accordingly, Blackstone preferred executive intervention to "the difficulty of new-modelling any branch of our statute laws" (III, 267). Although he acknowledged without any obvious hint of disapproval that judges often remedy defects in the law in order to maintain "the coherence and uniformity of our legal constitution" (III, 271), he insisted that it is the executive as custodian of the constitution who makes the periodic repairs that keep the constitutional machinery in good working order. Prerogative is integral to this scheme of constitutional government: "The enormous weight of prerogative (if left to itself, as in arbitrary government it is) spreads havoc and destruction among all the inferior movements: but, when balanced and bridled (as with us) by it's [sic] proper counterpoise, timely and judiciously applied, it's operations are then equable and regular, *it invigorates the whole machine, and enables every part to answer the end of it's construction*" (I, 233, emphasis added). Prerogative is indispensable because it enables the executive to preserve the integrity of the existing constitutional order through periodic adjustments that obviate the need for the more dramatic and permanent changes that legislative action brings in its wake. To put it in Machiavellian terms, Blackstone believed that unobtrusive changes in constitutional modes are almost always preferable to more obvious and disruptive changes in constitutional orders. Neither Locke nor Hume envisioned the broad range of executive functions that Blackstone endorsed so enthusiastically in preserving the existing constitutional orders.

Blackstone was an apologist with an agenda. Instead of merely outlining the main features of the constitution, he supplied his own justifications and rationales for those aspects that he found agreeable. Moreover, he sometimes justified powers that had not been exercised in a long time or did not even formally exist anymore. Nowhere is this more evident than in his treatment of executive power. He defended and extended the powers of the crown by invoking both outdated political arguments and the latest idioms of modern science. His position on executive power cannot be fully understood without comprehending the mechanistic Newtonian underpinnings of his constitutional theory.

The Political Newtonianism of Blackstone's Legal Science

One of Blackstone's chief strategies in validating the unmatched beauty and order of the common law was to demonstrate that its study could be developed into a systematic science.[30] It is for that reason that the rhetoric of Blackstone's *Commentaries* is suffused with scientific metaphors and technical imagery. As Dicey explained, Blackstone "lived at a time when the learned world was still a reality, when there was an established standard of style and when men of letters could address themselves, even when writing on such a subject as law, neither to experts, nor to practitioners, nor to that unsatisfactory class now known as general readers."[31] A common idiom of learned discourse, Newtonian science constituted one of the branches of knowledge familiar to eighteenth-century gentlemen.[32] Blackstone not only shared many of its central assumptions, but he also borrowed freely from its vocabulary, as evidenced by his recurrent references to "the laws of motion, of gravitation, of optics, or mechanics" and related concepts (I, 38).[33]

Blackstone analogized the law-making power of the government to the law-making power of God, who "impressed certain principles upon that matter [the universe]," much as "when a workman forms a clock, or other piece of mechanism, he establishes at his own pleasure certain arbitrary laws for it's [*sic*] direction" (I, 38).[34] Blackstone had a penchant for mixing metaphors and sometimes employed conflicting images, but when it came to executive power, they all conveyed a consistent message about its constitutional primacy. The effect of these metaphors is characteristic of all ideological expositions: to naturalize what is contingent and conventional. Contrary to Carl Schmitt's claim that mechanistic imagery in eighteenth-century jurisprudence signified an attempt to eliminate the need for personal decisions by the executive by turning government into a "machine [that] now runs by itself," Blackstone's Newtonian rhetoric always pointed to the centrality of executive power in the constitutional balance and the everpresent possibility of extralegal action.[35] This was a point well understood by Americans like James Wilson, who noted in his *Lectures on Law* that Blackstone's executive is not "set in regular motion by the laws" but "is the first mover, who regulates the whole government."[36]

Blackstone was not a proponent of the strict theory of the separation of powers, but he did subscribe to a theory of checks and balances.[37] It is his formulation of the latter that best illustrates his views on the constitutional role of the executive. Although he discussed the impeachment of ministers as an essential check on abuses of executive power, Blackstone spent much more time justifying and elaborating on the executive's powers over the legislature. He advocated the king's power to prorogue or dissolve Parliament as a safeguard against a "perpetual" legislature, a fear also shared by Locke but rarely voiced by republican writers. A perpetual legislature "would be extremely dangerous, if at any time it should attempt to encroach upon the executive power" (I, 180). Even though England was a mixed monarchy, Blackstone was more troubled by the possibility of legislative tyranny than executive tyranny, as evidenced by his critical references to the Long Parliament (I, 150). According to his formulation of checks and balances, the executive's power was analogous to the gravitational force of the sun, which keeps the political planets in their proper orbits and prevents them from spinning out of control. This heliocentric conception of executive power illustrates not only its centrality but also the idea that it is the vital, activating principle of the system as a whole. This was particularly true in foreign affairs: "In the king therefore, as in a center, all the rays of his people are united, and form by that union a consistency, splendor, and power, that make him feared and respected by foreign potentates; who would scruple to enter into any engagements, that must afterwards be revised and ratified by a popular assembly" (I, 245).[38]

Blackstone did not limit his rhetorical comparisons to interplanetary metaphors. Varieties of the orbital metaphor are evident throughout the *Commentaries*, but it is the mechanical imagery of balances, equipoise, and springs that is most revealing of the jurist's idea of executive power. His preference for mixed government is revealed in his assertion that "it is highly necessary for preserving the ballance of the constitution, that the executive power should be a branch, though not the whole, of the legislature" (I, 149). The legislative power of the king is limited to "the power of *rejecting*, rather than *resolving*," for "the crown has not any power of *doing* wrong, but merely of *preventing* wrong from being done." In this instance, Blackstone did minimize the functions of the monarch—but only for the moment. He continued: "Herein indeed consists the true excellence of the English government, that all the parts of it form a mutual check upon each other" (I, 150, emphasis in original). They do this by "mutually keep[ing] each other from exceeding their proper limits; while the whole is prevented from separation, and artificially connected together by the mixed nature of the crown, which is a part of the legislative, and the sole executive magistrate. *Like three distinct powers in mechanics, they jointly impel the machine of government in a direction different from what either, acting by themselves, would have done; but at the same time in a direction partaking of each, and formed out of all; a direction which constitutes the true line of the liberty and happiness of the community*" (I, 151, emphasis added). In Blackstone's presentation, the Crown serves as the centripetal, gravitational force in the constitutional system that limits the centrifugal tendencies of the legislature and oversees that system, just as the "supreme being . . . superintends . . . every action in human life" (IV, 43).

The checking power of the executive, made necessary by the propensity of the legislature to disrupt the harmony of the system, was not an automatic process. It required constant and active supervision by the executive. Blackstone typified a particular strand of political Newtonianism described by Richard Striner thus: "Newtonian imagery was used not only by people who were susceptible to visions of an automatic social balance but also by those for whom the cosmic metaphors underscored suspicions that society's machinery could not be made automatic and that the best results of political or constitutional engineering would still require steady vigilance and even modification by watchful citizens and statesmen."[39]

Blackstone used a variety of other metaphors to establish the constitutional primacy of the executive. In his discussion of the king "as the fountain of justice and general conservator of the peace," he noted that the king "is not the spring, but the reservoir; from whence right and equity are conducted, by a thousand chanels, to every individual" (I, 257).[40] This metaphor reappeared in the third volume: "The course of justice flowing in large streams from the king, as the fountain, to his superior courts of record; and being then subdivided into smaller channels, till the whole and every part of the kingdom were plentifully watered and refreshed" (III, 30–31). In this vision of society, justice does not emerge from the spontaneous interactions of diverse individuals but emanates from a single royal center "to every part of the nation by distinct, yet communicating, ducts and chanels" (IV, 404).[41]

The political primacy of the executive is evident in Blackstone's discussion of the pardon power as well. He wrote: "In monarchies the king acts in a superior sphere; and, *though he regulates the whole government as the first mover,* yet he does not appear in any of the disagreeable or invidious parts of it" (IV, 390–91, emphasis added).[42] The king's primacy in government is evident not only in his vast powers but also in the fact that prosecutions for criminal offences are carried out in his name "as the person injured in the eye of the law" (I, 259). The king is never absent from the courts of justice; indeed, "the legal *ubiquity* of the king" is an essential presupposition of judicial proceedings (I, 260; emphasis in original). In the courts, the king "is there represented by his judges, whose power is only an emanation of the royal prerogative" (III, 24). Members of Parliament may *represent* the nation, but "the king, in whom centers the majesty of the whole community," (IV, 2) embodies it.

Spheres of Sovereignty

Blackstone's theory of government is more than just another theory of mixed monarchy; it is a theory of mixed sovereignty. This would suggest that sovereignty is dispersed or shared among several different parts of government, but Blackstone's usage is more complicated and confusing than this.[43] He applied the term *sovereign* both to the legislature as a whole (King-in-Parliament) and to the king alone. On the one hand, he asseverated that "legislature [*sic*] . . . is the greatest act of superiority that can be exercised by one being over another. Wherefore it is requisite to the very essence of a law, that it be made by the supreme power. Sovereignty and legislature are indeed convertible terms" (I, 46). On the other hand, he repeatedly called the king "sovereign" even when acting in a purely executive capacity without the participation of the legislature.

This discrepancy may be explained by the fact that sovereignty for Blackstone is not limited to the supreme lawmaking power but applies to different spheres of governmental action. Within its proper sphere, each of these powers is absolute. Neither the legislature nor the executive is answerable to any external authority for what it does within its own exclusive sphere. However, that sovereignty within the legislature is shared by the king, the Commons, and the Lords means that each of these constituent parts is subject to an internal set of institutional checks and balances that prevents any one of them from acting without the cooperation of the rest. But because executive power belongs to the king alone, there is no corresponding set of internal institutional checks and balances. "In the exertion therefore of those prerogatives, which the law has given him, the king is irresistible and absolute, according to the forms of the constitution" (I, 244).

Even Blackstone's arguments in favor of parliamentary supremacy provided indirect support for the idea of royal supremacy. If judicial review was objectionable because it implied judicial supremacy over the legislature (I, 91), then what does it mean to have an executive whose actions cannot be checked by the legislature? If the requirement of royal consent to legislative action is one of the things that contributes to "the true excellence of the English government" (I, 150), then what does it mean when the executive can act without the consent of the legislature? To the extent that Blackstone's understanding of supremacy rules out the kinds of checks that apply to the other parts of government, his theory of sovereignty seems to bear a closer resemblance to medieval conceptions than to the Whig doctrine that gained ascendancy after the Glorious Revolution.[44] The jurisdiction of the king was limited, but within his proper sphere of action, the king was practically absolute because there were no effective sanctions that could be enforced against him.

The Political Perfection of the King

Neither recent practice nor contemporary doctrine entirely justified Blackstone's account of executive power. In fact, his argument was a throwback to the debates of the previous century. He employed quasi-Filmerian arguments to justify the powers and status of the king. In doing so, he resorted to a variety of legal fictions that becloud his commitment to English liberty and constitutional balance. On the one hand, he seemed firmly committed to the principles of the Glorious Revolution, but on the other hand he seemed displeased that the prerogative powers of the crown had been severely curtailed. Somewhat less explicitly than Hume, the jurist suggested that the powers decried by most Whigs were actually essential to the liberty they potentially threatened. Indeed, Blackstone's aim was to show that executive power is a protector, if not a precondition, of liberty.

In order to justify his extravagant claims regarding the king's responsibilities within the English system, Blackstone had to convince his readers that the king was a "superior being" who could be trusted not to abuse his station. Before he could do that, he had to demonstrate and defend the singular character of the king.

One of Blackstone's main arguments in support of a single executive rested on the pragmatic point that it would be more efficient to leave the execution and administration of the laws to a single person. "Were it placed in many hands," the jurist explained, "it would be subject to many wills: many wills, if disunited and drawing different ways, create weakness in a government: and to unite those several wills, and reduce them to one, is a work of more time and delay than the exigencies of state will afford" (I, 242–43). According to Blackstone, one of the happy facts of the British Constitution is that "with us the executive power of the laws is lodged in a single person, [so] they have all the advantages of strength and dispatch, that are to be found in the most absolute monarchy" (I, 50).

But Blackstone's case for the single executive also rested on the claim that placing executive power in a single pair of hands would be safer. Contrary to the old republican commonplace that every concentration of any power constitutes a menace to freedom, Blackstone argued that the English king posed little threat to liberty precisely because he was a single executive. The legal fiction that "the king can do no wrong" was an integral part of this claim. To admit that someone can do wrong is to open up the possibility that they can be punished. But Blackstone could never allow the king as sovereign to be subject to punishment, since, following a Hobbesian line of reasoning, the idea of punishment presupposes a superior authority. For Blackstone, the king was that superior authority. Far from being a source of danger, the superiority of the king provided a source of security because an executive who already enjoys special privileges and exclusive prerogatives has absolutely no reason to encroach on the liberties and rights of subjects. It is simply inconceivable that someone who already has everything could desire more. Although he lacked the theoretical sophistication or intellectual rigor of Hobbes, Blackstone took an important, albeit unacknowledged, lesson from *Leviathan*: concentrated power is much safer than dispersed power. If the critics of "possessive individualism" are right in suggesting that competitive acquisitiveness is the distinguishing characteristic of the liberal individual, it appears that, for Blackstone at least, the desire for power ceases when the competition over power comes to an end.[45]

Even though Blackstone never fully explained why executive power was so conducive to liberty in England, this claim was elaborated by the Genevan political writer Jean-Louis de Lolme, who borrowed extensively (though not always explicitly) from Blackstone in his own comprehensive account of the English Constitution. Blackstone is cited by name only four times in *The Constitution of England*, which first appeared in 1784, but his influence can be detected in the formulation of de Lolme's own theory of constitutionalism and even in his use of the machine metaphor to describe the role of executive power in England.[46] De Lolme's views are relevant to this discussion not only because he was widely cited on questions pertaining to executive power during the American debates on constitutional ratification but also because his discussions of executive power accentuate the distinctive features of Blackstone's theory.[47]

According to de Lolme, the unity of the executive contributes to liberty in two ways. First, giving all executive power to "one great, very great man in the state" prevents the ruinous rivalry that results in republics where each citizen is presumed to be equal to and no better than any other.[48] Second, and more important, a single executive is a "responsible" executive. Not only is it easier to "confine" executive power when it is unified, it is also less necessary to do so. There is no need in England for the king to be repressive since there is no danger that this hereditary monarch will lose his power.

But this is where the agreement between Blackstone and his Swiss admirer ends. As important as the institution of executive power was to de Lolme's explanation of English liberty, he was no great supporter of executive power per se. The secret of English liberty was that executive power was so easy to restrain because it was unified. Its unity, according to de Lolme, made it easier for individuals to unite in their opposition to a common enemy.[49] Blackstone recognized the right of revolution, but, ironically, he refused to acknowledge any direct check against the person of the king that fell short of this extraordinary recourse to force.

Although de Lolme was skeptical about "the natural weakness of power which is not founded on virtue," he did believe, *pace* Blackstone, that the favorable "opinion and reverence of the people" was crucial to the stability of executive power, which is itself a prerequisite of general political and constitutional stability. [50] But unlike his English counterpart, de Lolme did not attempt to justify the powers of the king in terms of any special attributes, personal or otherwise. He was too firmly committed to a scientific and institutional approach to politics to rely on the actual or ascribed personal qualities of rulers as reliable checks on power. Because of his pessimistic view of a uniform human nature, de Lolme denied that any public officials were different from ordinary individuals in their abilities to look beyond short-term interests—perhaps the main criterion of executive virtue for other liberal writers. Contrary to popular opinion, "The truth is, that ministers, in all countries, never think but of providing for present, immediate contingencies."[51] Unlike the English-speaking liberals who wrote on executive power, de Lolme found it difficult to discuss virtue outside the context of civic republicanism, which he criticized for being unscientific in its assumptions about human nature.[52] Whereas the Genevan refused to accept the possibility that noninstitutional factors could reliably make power safer, these liberals and their American readers looked directly to the (actual or imputed) personal qualities of rulers to render executive power safe.

Royal Dignity

Since Blackstone's purpose in writing the *Commentaries* was to expound the English constitution, not to write an original treatise on politics, one would expect him to focus on constitutional essentials rather than interject his own political views. That makes it all the more remarkable that Blackstone spent so much time justifying the mysterious maxim that "the king can do no wrong." The amount of attention he devoted to this legal fiction was out of all proportion to its actual legal significance in the English system, suggesting that his references to this numinous maxim conveyed his own ideas about the political value of respect for the executive.

Blackstone's primary legal objective in discussing the maxim that the king can do no wrong was to provide an explanation for the sovereign immunity that the person of the monarch enjoyed. That the king is considered sovereign within the sphere of executive power means that "no jurisdiction upon earth has power to try him in a criminal way; much less condemn him to punishment" (I, 235). Blackstone explained that the "law feels itself incapable of furnishing any adequate remedy" against "all oppressions, which may happen to spring from any branch of the sovereign power" (I, 237) because the power to punish the sovereign would make the agent of punishment itself the sovereign (I, 235).

None of this means that anything and everything done by the executive is constitutionally permissible. For to deny the possibility of constitutional wrongs is to deny the existence of constitutional rights. The idea that anything goes as far as the executive is concerned would subvert the very idea of constitutional government and vitiate the very purposes for which limited government was instituted in the first place. Besides, there is a law of nature, which "is binding . . . at all times," in all places, and without exception, that serves as the ultimate standard of right and wrong (I, 41). For that reason, any unconstitutional acts committed by the executive are attributed to "the advice of evil counselors, and the assistance of wicked ministers," who "may be examined and punished . . . by means of indictments, and parliamentary impeachments" (I, 237). Parliament enjoys the privilege "of enquiring into, impeaching, and punishing the conduct (not indeed of the king, which would destroy his constitutional independence; but, which is more beneficial to the public) of his evil and pernicious counsellors" (I, 151). Blackstone justified this extraordinary displacement of responsibility on the grounds that the king is incapable "even of *thinking* wrong," let alone doing wrong, without the sinister machinations of vicious advisers (I, 239).

Blackstone's account of the legal fiction that "the king can do no wrong" also served a critical political function in his theory of executive power. The discussion gave him the opportunity to explain why it was essential for the people to believe that their chief executive was endowed with such extraordinary qualities. If the people doubt the personal superiority of the king, they will be apt to distrust and even deny his use of certain powers, especially where the legality of his actions is in doubt. Demonstrating that an exercise of "supreme power" is formally justified under law is simply not enough to

guarantee popular acceptance, because the people are always going to distrust power that is susceptible to abuse. Blackstone explained that "such distrust would render the exercise of that power precarious and impracticable.
For, wherever the law expresses it's [sic] distrust of abuse of power, it always
vests a superior coercive authority in some other hand to correct it; the very
notion of which destroys the idea of sovereignty" (I, 237). Since Blackstone did
not consider the possibility of *popular* sovereignty as a way out of this constitutional conundrum, he was forced to look beyond the formalities of law to
provide against the subversion of the constitution by the executive.[53] The right
personal qualities would not only inhibit abuses of power, they would also
reinforce the people's trust in their king. Hence, the law ascribes to the king
"absolute *perfection*" (I, 238, emphasis in original). Since there is "in him is no
folly or weakness," the king is incapable of doing wrong in his public capacity
(I, 239).

The desideratum of trust in the executive made it critical to maintain the
king in his "royal dignity" (I, 234). As Blackstone claimed in a different context, "The most stable foundation of legal and rational government is a due
subordination of rank, and a gradual scale of authority" (IV, 104). The concept
of "royal dignity" was explicitly described as an attribute of royal prerogative
that distinguished the king from his subjects and from other members of government. One of the three divisions of prerogative along with authority and
income, royal dignity referred to that preeminence attributed to the "king's
royal *character*" which was "necessary, to secure reverence to his person"
(I, 233, emphasis in original). Royal dignity reinforced the belief that the king
is a being with "a great and transcendent nature" superior to his subjects in
both authority and character, a belief requisite to the "business of government" (I, 234). A king who is believed to possesses "certain qualities, as inherent in his royal capacity, distinct from and superior to those of any other individual in the nation," is one that enjoys the full benefit of the doubt in carrying
out his constitutional responsibilities (I, 234). In fact, Blackstone defined prerogative in terms of privilege and preeminence associated with royal dignity:
"By the word prerogative we usually understand that special pre-eminence,
which the king hath, over and above all other persons, and out of the ordinary
course of the common law, in right of his regal dignity. It signifies, in it's [sic]
etymology, (from *prae* and *rogo*) something that is required or demanded before, or in preference to, all others. And hence it follows, that it must be in it's

nature singular and eccentrical; that it can only be applied to those rights and capacities which the king enjoys alone, in contradistinction to all others, and not to those which he enjoys in common with any of his subjects." (I, 232).

The reason that the king's judgments are (or ought to be) unimpeachable is that he is entrusted with the constitutional responsibility of making what are often unilateral decisions about what is in the public or national interest. The king's judgment on these matters should not be subject to debate. Debate is essential to the legislative function, but it is an impediment to the function of the executive, which requires secrecy and dispatch. Excessive deliberation *within* the executive branch is bad enough, Blackstone believed, but excessive deliberation *concerning* the executive branch is even worse. It tends to diminish the "superior . . . dignity" of the executive, who is "the first person in the nation" and "is said to be *caput, principium, et finis*" (beginning, foundation, and end; I, 146, 149). Blackstone sought support for this idea within the English system, but it seems to apply in other political systems as well: "distinction of rank is necessary in every well-governed state," because "such a spirit, when nationally diffused, gives life and vigour to the community" (I, 153). As Blackstone explained later in his *Commentaries*: "The law will not cast an imputation on that magistrate whom it entrusts with the executive power, as if he was capable of intentionally disregarding his trust: but attributes to mere imposition (to which the most perfect of sublunary beings must still continue liable) those little inadvertencies, which, if charged on the will of the prince, might lessen him in the eyes of his subjects" (I, 239).

Blackstone continued his defense of royal dignity by explicitly linking personal attributes (or ascriptions, in this case) to the performance of executive functions. He unreservedly approved the fact that "the law deems so highly of his wisdom and virtue, as not even to presume it possible for him to do any thing inconsistent with his station and dignity; and therefore has made no provision to remedy such a grievance" (IV, 33). But since the law is a necessary but not a sufficient condition of effective government, Blackstone turned to the personal qualities of the executive to enhance its vigor: "The law therefore ascribes to the king, in his high political character, not only large powers and emoluments which form his prerogative and revenue, but *likewise certain attributes of a great and transcendent nature; by which the people are led to consider him in the light of a superior being, and to pay him that awful respect, which may enable him with greater ease to carry on the business of government*" (I, 234, emphasis added). Where Locke and other Whigs generally sought to demystify political power by locating its source in the consent of the people, Blackstone revived archaic royalist rhetoric that related the king to God in His splendor and perfection.[54] Maintaining an aura of executive infallibility and preserving the mystique of royal power insulate the king from challenges to his authority from the people. Despite his acknowledgment that "a philosophical mind" remains skeptical about the mystery of majesty, he insisted that "the mass of mankind will be apt to grow insolent and refractory, if taught to consider their prince as a man of no greater perfection than themselves" (I, 234).[55]

In general, Blackstone's strategy was to emphasize the special singularity and "personal perfection" (I, 239) of the king before he proceeded to specify and expand upon the powers that constitute royal prerogative.[56] From the beginning Blackstone made it clear that prerogatives of all kinds belong to the person of the king as "parts of the royal character" and not simply as parts of his formal legal authority (I, 232). But all aspects of the king's prerogative (dignity, authority, and revenue) are equally necessary "to maintain the executive power in due independence and vigour" (I, 233), because "the king is always busied for the public good" (I, 240) and should not be bothered with petty distractions like prolonged lawsuits.[57] (Perhaps President Clinton could have benefited from Blackstone's services.) It is "in his capacity of supreme governor, and *pater-familias* of the kingdom," that the king possesses the exclusive right to punish public nuisances, for instance (III, 220). Blackstone spent a lot of time specifying and defending the various sources of royal revenue, including some bizarre ones like "royal fish," because they were vital to maintain the independence of the executive in order to avoid the recurrence of seventeenth-century conflicts (I, 271–326).

The highly personalized nature of this power is also evident in the fact that subjects owe their allegiance to the person of the king rather than to an abstraction called the "state." "Allegiance is the tie, or *ligamen*, which binds the subject to the king, in return for that protection which the king affords the subject" (I, 354, emphasis in original).[58] The "care and protection of the community" are committed to the executive, and in return, the king receives the "duty and allegiance of every individual" (I, 183). Even the king's "general superintendence of all charities" is explained by the fact he is regarded as the "*parens patriae*" (III, 427).

This personalized conception of executive power creates certain advantages for both the executive and the community. Insofar as the king is regarded as a "superior being," he is less likely to arouse the kind of suspicion or resistance that can hamper the fulfillment of his responsibilities. A king who is above reproach is thus more likely to be a strong and effective executive. And inasmuch as the king feels personally tied to his subjects, he is less likely to violate the trust reposed in him. Blackstone's remarks on executive ministers reinforce the idea that the public good is connected to the personal status of the king. Because of their privileged position as the king's most trusted advisors, the members of the privy council served at the king's pleasure and took an oath that required them "to advise for the king's honour and good of the public" (I, 223). Ministers serve at his pleasure, that is, they are removable at will, because the executive must constantly evince the dispatch, energy, uniformity of will, and singularity of purpose that are trademarks of executive power.

Notwithstanding these extraordinary claims, Blackstone was no reactionary. Even though the law itself provides no direct formal penalties against a tyrannical king, Blackstone adopted the Lockean position that "the prudence of the times must provide new remedies upon new emergencies" and endorsed the right of revolution (I, 238). In those extreme cases where "unconstitutional oppressions, even of the sovereign power, advance with gigantic strides and threaten desolation to a state," it becomes necessary to look beyond the constitution for a solution. The Glorious Revolution is a case in point. Even though prevailing "political maxims" provided no relief and even prohibited resistance against the king, the Convention Parliament hit upon a solution that established a precedent for future use. Their declaration that James II had abdicated the throne allowed England to rid itself of the king without altering the fundamental laws (I, 238). But this is to be understood as an extralegal remedy for an extralegal malady. Short of such extreme cases where the fundamentals of the constitution are being subverted, it is imperative to accept that the king can do no wrong if the system is to run smoothly and effectively.

Executive Powers and the Law
The Power of Interpretation

Blackstone's account of executive power begins early in the first volume of the *Commentaries* and continues intermittently throughout all four volumes. Blackstone's starting point is the plain-sounding and predictable declaration that "the principal duty of the king is, to govern his people according to law" (I, 226), but his definition of the law and his understanding of executive power only complicate the issue. What is odd is that he cited the medieval jurists Henry of Bracton and Sir John Fortescue as legal authorities to support his uncontroversial claim that the king is to govern "according to law" and supplied very little commentary of his own to explain how the law guides or regulates executive action. In fact, he breezed through the chapter on the king's duties in four brief and perfunctory pages, which consist mostly of quotations taken from the medieval thinkers and from the king's coronation oath. In contrast, the very next chapter on the king's prerogative takes up forty pages of extensive commentary.[59]

Blackstone's chapter on royal prerogative ranges over a variety of privileges, powers, and immunities belonging to the king in foreign affairs, domestic policy, criminal proceedings, and ecclesiastical matters, where the king is "considered by the laws of England as the head and supreme governor of the national church" (I, 269). The list of these specific legal prerogatives includes the right to send ambassadors (I, 249); "the sole prerogative of making war and peace" (I, 249); the ability to grant "letters of marque and reprisal" (I, 250); the "prerogative of granting safe-conducts" (I, 251); the power to regulate the arms trade (I, 255); the power to veto legislation (I, 253); the exclusive "right of erecting courts of judicature" (I, 257); the power to issue proclamations in executing the laws (I, 261); "the regulation of weights and measures" (I, 264); the power to pardon offenders (I, 259); and the authority to convene, regulate, and dissolve "all ecclesiastical synods or convocations" (I, 269). According to Blackstone, each of these prerogatives is grounded in established law, but their exercise is determined not by law but by the sole judgment and discretion of the king. Even though the commentator claims at an earlier point in his text that the king's prerogative is limited "by bounds so certain and notorious, that it is impossible he should exceed them without the consent of the people," the discussion that follows in his chapter on royal prerogative indicates that the king is absolute within those bounds (I, 137). In fact, the theme of discretion recurs throughout this chapter and pervades his references to executive power.

Blackstone's conception of law helps explain the discretionary nature of executive power. Based on his definition of law as a command directed by "the supreme power in a state" (I, 44), the English executive is beyond the coercive reach of the law. According to Blackstone, the king *is* the supreme power in his capacity as executive, and he even shares a portion of supreme power in his legislative role. To allow another branch of government to review the acts of the executive would undermine the independence of the king and subvert the foundations of the English constitution. By (Blackstone's) definition, even the most basic functions of executive power require exercises of independent judgment, as in the decision whether or not to apply a particular law at all. The reason for this is that the meaning of the law is much more complicated than his positivistic definition would suggest.

The enforcement of the laws created by Parliament—and with the king's consent—is the main responsibility of the executive. However, the execution of the laws is far from automatic. The king has enormous room for discretion even in the most basic exercise of his most regular function because there is always ample room for interpretation of legal rules and judgments about the particulars of a concrete situation. Blackstone explained that "the manner, time, and circumstances of putting those laws in execution must frequently be left to the discretion of the executive magistrate. And therefore his constitutions or edicts, concerning these points, which we call proclamations, are binding upon the subjects, where they do not either contradict the old laws, or tend to establish new ones; but only enforce the execution of such laws as are already in being, in such manner as the king shall judge necessary" (I, 261). Blackstone recommended that the king follow the intent of the legislature to guide him in his interpretations of the law, but even this advice loosened the restraints of the law. To pursue legislative intent would potentially lead away from the literal letter of the law toward the substantive principles underlying the law.[60]

Like proponents of "equity" before him, Blackstone believed that it would sometimes be necessary to follow the "spirit" of the law over the letter of the law in construing the meaning of statutes. Whenever the two conflict, the "reason and spirit" of the law ought to prevail over the letter of the law: "From this method of interpreting laws, by the reason of them, arises what we call *equity*; which is thus defined by Grotius, 'the correction of that, wherein the law (by reason of its universality) is deficient.' For since in laws all cases cannot be foreseen or expressed, it is necessary, that when the general decrees of the law come to be applied to particular cases, there should be somewhere a power vested of excepting those circumstances, which (had they been foreseen) the legislator himself would have excepted" (I, 61, emphasis in original). The substantive considerations that were to guide the king in the use of his enforcement powers were not limited to principles of equity and justice, but included, above all, mercy: "This is indeed one of the great advantages of monarchy in general, above any other form of government; that there is a magistrate, who has it in his power to extend mercy, wherever he thinks it is deserved: holding a court of equity in his own breast, to soften the rigour of the general law, in such criminal cases as merit an exemption from punishment" (IV, 390).

But in defending the pardon power of the king, Blackstone was compelled to acknowledge that the legal system was imperfect—otherwise the power to pardon lawbreakers would be superfluous or worse (IV, 390). In any other thinker this would be unremarkable, but in Blackstone's case that admission only reinforced the primacy of the executive. This mark of imperfection provided further evidence that the king "regulates the whole government as the first mover" (IV, 391). In fact, the king's possession of a power that confirms the imperfection of the constitution enhanced his own position within the defective structure: "To him therefore the people look up as the fountain of nothing but bounty and grace; and these repeated acts of goodness, coming immediately from his own hand, endear the sovereign to his subjects, and contribute more than any thing to root in their hearts that filial affection, and personal loyalty, which are the sure establishment of a prince" (IV, 391).

Blackstone's willingness to contemplate departures from the strict letter of the law aligns him with the liberals discussed so far against those republicans like Algernon Sidney who believed that "the force and essence of all laws would be subverted, if under colour of mitigating and interpreting, the power of altering were allow'd to kings."[61] Nearly every republican thinker insisted on the strictest execution of the laws as the only way to preserve their integrity, whereas liberal writers from Locke to the Federalists recognized that it was occasionally necessary to mitigate the severity of the law in the greater interests of justice, humanity, or right. That required a degree of confidence in the discretion of executive power that republicans could not muster.

The Extralegal Character of Prerogative

Despite his initial claim that the executive is restrained "from acting either beyond or in contradiction to the laws," the general thrust of Blackstone's account leads to the conclusion that the prerogative powers of the Crown extend beyond those specific powers delimited by the constitution (I, 137). There are definite and sometimes detailed limits on the specific, enumerated powers of the king, but they apply only "in the *ordinary* course of law" (I, 243, emphasis in original). Just as he made an exception for "those *extraordinary* recourses to first principles, which are necessary when the contracts of society are in danger of dissolution, and the law proves too weak a defence against the violence of fraud or oppression" (I, 243), he allowed exceptions for extraordinary exercises of power by the executive in cases of emergency. What is noteworthy about this remark is that Blackstone deployed a radical Whig justification for revolution in his defense of prerogative. When the danger of degeneration into a state of nature—or, worse yet, a state of war—becomes evident, the powers of the executive cannot be limited by law, just as the right of the people to resist cannot be denied, even if it cannot be explicitly acknowledged in the law (I, 139; cf. I, 157). Indeed, the king even has the ability to grant exemptions from the law in times of war because he is "supposed the best judge of such emergencies" as threaten the peace of the nation (I, 252).

Despite his remark at the very beginning of his chapter on prerogative that explicit limitations on the king's prerogative constitute "one of the principal bulwarks of civil liberty" (I, 230), Blackstone ended up developing an explicitly Lockean defense of those prerogative powers that were not expressly provided for in the constitution. His chapter on the king's prerogative moves swiftly from the ways that the law constrains specific royal powers to the ways that prerogative introduces certain exceptions to the law (I, 231–33).

Blackstone blamed "over-zealous republicans" for spreading the erroneous and deleterious belief that executive violations of the law are never justifiable. They tend to forget "how impossible it is, in any practical system of laws, to point out beforehand those eccentrical remedies, which the sudden emergence of national distress may dictate, and which that alone can justify" (I, 244). Blackstone acknowledged the dangers in permitting the king to exercise powers that exceed the law, but he argued that republicans go "over to the other extreme" when they urge resistance against each and every deviation from a "general and positive" rule of law as if it forebodes the death of liberty (I, 244). In the end, Blackstone urged deference to the king in his handling of emergencies because "society cannot be maintained, and of course can exert no protection, without obedience to some sovereign power" (I, 244).

Whereas "over-zealous republicans" have worried that extralegal action would alter and even subvert the constitution, Blackstone endorsed prerogative because he believed that it was more likely than the alternatives to leave the existing constitutional structure intact. His reasoning against the introduction of innovations in the spiritual courts generally applies to his views on the law as whole: "Should an alteration be attempted, great confusion would probably arise, in overturning long established forms, and new-modelling a course of proceedings that has now prevailed for seven centuries" (III, 99). In good conservative fashion, Blackstone argued that it is more prudent to stick with proven institutions than to experiment with untested innovations introduced by the legislature. There was always the risk that legislative action would only exacerbate the problem of uncertainty in an emergency: "How impossible it is to foresee, and provide against, *all* the consequences of innovations" (II, 338–39, emphasis in original)! Prerogative offers an expeditious way to address political "inconveniences" without necessarily introducing permanent or irrevocable structural changes. Legal innovation and structural reform undermine the certainty that defines the freedom of the English (III, 327; II, 80), whereas executive tinkering with the machinery of government leaves its fundamental structure essentially unchanged.[62] And when legislative involvement is necessary, it is the king who has the power to convene the nobility "in cases of emergency" (I, 221).

On occasion, Blackstone also raised questions about the sanctity of legal checks on the king's power. He concluded his main discussion of royal prerogative by pointing out that "most of the laws for ascertaining, limiting, and restraining this prerogative have been made within the compass of little more than a century past," as if to suggest that these limitations are less hallowed for being more recent (I, 322–23). In the very next paragraph he mentioned that the king still possessed certain privileges established "by long usage" that maintain his "constitutional independence" (I, 323). Because the common law mentality privileges what has existed "from time immemorial," the antiquity of a practice was a weightier consideration in Blackstone's mind than its recency. But because these changes in prerogative, however salutary, hardly extend to the "time whereof the memory of man runneth not to the contrary" (I, 460–61), the implication was that the recently imposed limitations on prerogative do not merit the same kind of veneration that ancient practices do.

Liberty and Prerogative

Blackstone's struggle to formulate a legal and constitutional defense of executive powers compatible with the liberty of subjects provides an important lesson on the persistent difficulty of reconciling the inherent tension between prerogative and popular privileges. Laying the groundwork for the more elaborate argument that Hamilton would build in *The Federalist,* he tried to resolve this dilemma by arguing that liberty depends on the force of executive power. Adverting that "monarchical government is allowed to be the fittest of any for this purpose," that is, protecting "the weakness of individuals by the united strength of the community" (I, 254), he suggested that its enormous powers can also be deployed to preserve and protect individual liberty and not just to undermine and harass it, as republicans and many Whigs maintained. By assigning the king a task historically performed by Parliament, Blackstone suggested that liberty depends first and foremost on stability and the powers required to maintain it. It also reflects the fundamental liberal agreement with the Hobbesian sentiment that "any government is better than none at all" (I, 123).

There is no reason to doubt the sincerity of Blackstone's commitment to liberty. He wholeheartedly felt that "the law is always ready to catch at any thing in favour of liberty" (II, 94). Its relation to other constitutional and political values is a different matter altogether, though.[63] Blackstone denied that the historical opposition between prerogative powers and civil liberties is irrepressible or inexorable. In fact, he considered democracy a far greater threat to liberty than monarchy and explicitly contrasted the rule of law with the "wild and capricious" tendencies of the "multitude" (III, 379). He acknowledged that prerogative had been "strained to a very tyrannical and oppressive height" in certain reigns (IV, 424), but he treated such instances as constitutional aberrations. He seemed to go out of his way to point out the advantages of prerogative even when he was justifying the tight restrictions that had been placed on it: "And however *convenient* these [prerogatives] may appear at first, (as doubtless all arbitrary powers, well executed, are the most *convenient*) yet let it be again remembered, that delays, and little inconveniences in the forms of justice, are the price that all free nations must pay for their liberty in more substantial matters; that these inroads upon this sacred bulwark of the nation are fundamentally opposite to the spirit of our constitution" (IV, 344, emphasis in original).

Even though Blackstone acknowledged the tension between royal power and liberty, he tended to minimize the opposition between the two. Whenever he mentioned the explicit limits on executive power, he did so in the most perfunctory way. For instance, he noted casually and without commentary that a statute passed in the reign of William and Mary made clear the "pretended power of suspending, or dispensing with laws, or the execution of laws, by regal authority without consent of parliament, is illegal" (I, 138).[64] In those instances where Blackstone did not discuss the executive's ability to exceed the law, the often plain and incontrovertible language of these statutory restrictions left him little room to do much more than to restate the current law in detached and straightforward terms.

But even where Blackstone explicitly endorsed recent restrictions on royal prerogative, he raised the possibility that the executive might be justified in exceeding these restrictions under the right conditions. His ostensibly reassuring remark that royal prerogative was limited "by bounds so certain and notorious, that it is impossible he should exceed them without the consent of the people" (I, 137) suggests that violations of explicit legal limits on executive power may be acceptable as long as they receive public support. The notion of consent used here is reminiscent of Locke's claim that the people's acquiescence in certain discretionary acts is tantamount to consent. This notion of consent entails *post hoc* acceptance rather than prior or interim authorization of extralegal executive acts.

Considering that some Englishmen resented the restrictions imposed on royal power since the Bill of Rights of 1689, Blackstone often made it a point to demonstrate that the king's powers were still quite ample. There was no reason to fear that the king had been rendered impotent by these recent changes, Blackstone reassured his readers: "The instruments of power are not perhaps so open and avowed as they formerly were, and therefore are the less liable to jealous and invidious reflections, but they are not the weaker upon that account" (I, 324). But in Blackstone's view, not all of these changes were necessarily for the better. Not only had the new regime "given rise to such a multitude of new officers," which Blackstone found regrettable because it expanded the already pervasive presence of the government, but it also led to the establishment of a "disciplined army" (I, 324, 325), the bane of Whigs and republicans alike. A standing army of this type, "at the absolute disposal of the crown . . . is more than equivalent to a thousand little troublesome prerogatives" (I, 325). It was not prerogative power as such that disturbed Blackstone but its multiplication and dispersal among individuals who could not inspire the same degree of confidence or command the same degree of respect as a king who by definition could do no wrong.

Like Hume, Blackstone recognized that there was a tradeoff between discretionary prerogatives and the erection of new and entrenched institutions with vested interests in their own survival and extension. The creation of new offices was particularly insidious because it had "extended the influence of government to every corner of the nation" on a more or less permanent and general basis (I, 324).[65] The discretionary powers that Blackstone preferred operated on a more temporary basis, and only in particular circumstances. Here Blackstone's solicitude for English liberties explains his position on prerogative. The bureaucratic apparatuses that replaced some of the king's prerogatives as foundations of royal power made it more difficult to identify or ensure responsibility, which is essential to safe government. It now became necessary to "guard against corrupt and servile influence from those who are intrusted with it's [the crown's] authority." But as he was wont to do, Blackstone vacillated on (or simply tried to rationalize) the advantages of "any transactions in the last century. Much is indeed given up; but much is also acquired" (I, 325–26).

Conclusion

Blackstone's neglect of recent developments such as the introduction of cabinet government and the Court/Country debate of the early eighteenth century makes some sense in light of his insistence on the continuity of the English system. The emergence of cabinet government marked a radical change in the constitution whose full effects were only beginning to be understood when Blackstone was writing. But more was involved in his studious avoidance of this phenomenon than the analytical myopia that close proximity to events sometimes induces. Cabinet government was antithetical to many of the principles elucidated by the commentator. Eventually it would reduce the British monarch to a mere figurehead. Even the royal power to appoint the prime minister was fast becoming obsolete, as the electoral system and other changes, many of which Blackstone could not have foreseen and might not have endorsed, reduced the role of the monarch in British politics.[66]

Unlike the king, these ministers and politicians most definitely could do wrong—and suffer the consequences for it. Ministerial government was simply incapable of generating the same degree of respect people naturally exhibit toward kings. In theory, the "dignity" that surrounded the king insulated him from criticism in a manner that allowed him to carry out his duties unencumbered by the imperatives of ordinary politics. That "dignity" was not transferable to the king's ministers or other officials, whose persons were not sacred and whose acts were subject to scrutiny in a way the king's was not—

and should not be. The latitude that the king enjoyed in discharging his duties was one of its most attractive and important features to Blackstone, and the vicious partisan attacks on Sir Robert Walpole must have convinced him that ministerial government was inherently less stable and harmonious than truly royal government, regardless of its own peculiar problems.[67]

Even though Blackstone did not deal directly with the question of executive virtue, he addressed the dangers associated with a lack of reverence and awe for the executive in a forceful and forthright manner. Since it was impossible in a hereditary monarchy to find an individual virtuous enough to command the universal respect and reverence of the people, Blackstone sought the next best thing. He sought to buttress the monarch's claims to authority by enhancing the majesty of the crown. The importance of maintaining the illusion that the king is a special person is reflected in Blackstone's spirited defense of the "outward pomp and decorations of majesty" (I, 234). The ideological scaffolding he built around the office of the king was a safeguard against potential flaws in the underlying structure of the monarch's character.

Supporters of a strong national executive in the United States could never get away with advocating monarchy—as Hamilton found out after his widely reported encomium on the English constitution at the Constitutional Convention—but they did promote measures that would solidify the dignity of the executive.[68] John Adams's reasoning did not differ substantially from Blackstone's when he proposed that the president be addressed by a lustrous and honorific title.[69] Unless the executive enjoys some freedom from that constant scrutiny and distrust characteristic of republican thought, the executive will be incapable of exercising those awesome powers that are ultimately essential to the preservation of the very same liberty they place in danger.

Blackstone is worth reconsidering today because his formulation of the proper role of executive power in the constitutional order helps explain the conservative preference for expansive executive powers. These powers allow the executive to make necessary constitutional, legal, or political adjustments in a piecemeal fashion and obviate the need for more extensive, permanent, and democratic legislative reform. In a sense, Blackstone's conception of constitutionalism anticipated Hamilton's expansive theory of constitutionalism, according to which government inherently possesses certain broad if implied powers that obviate the need for constitutional amendment. It is easy to see why this conception of the executive's role would appeal to some American founders—and frighten others. According to Blackstone's formulation, executive power provided the constitutional flexibility that could make a system of government stable and durable, which would contribute to the rule of law. According to critics like Jefferson, though, it is that very same flexibility that detracts from the principles of constitutionalism and the rule of law. At stake in the debate over the proper role of the executive in the constitution is the question about the nature of the rule of law, an important question that the *Commentaries* never fully answered.

CHAPTER FIVE

"It Squints towards Monarchy"

Constitutional Flexibility and the Powers of the President

> Among other deformities, [the Constitution] has an awful squinting; it
> squints towards monarchy. . . . It is on a supposition that [y]our American
> Governors shall be honest, that all the good qualities of this Government
> are founded. . . . Shew me that age and country where the rights and
> liberties of the people were placed on the sole chance of their rulers being
> good men, without a consequent loss of liberty? . . . Away with your
> President, we shall have a King.
>
> PATRICK HENRY, THE VIRGINIA CONVENTION, JUNE 5, 1788

Centralized Government and the Need
for a Strong Executive

Americans at the time of the Founding were taught to be deeply suspicious
of executive power. Their knowledge of England's violent constitutional
struggle over royal prerogative in the seventeenth century, their acquaintance
with Commonwealth condemnations of the corruption wrought by ministerial influence, their intimate familiarity with Whig political thought, and
their own colonial experiences under royal governors who exercised "exorbi-
tant powers" that sometimes exceeded those of the king in England all alerted
them to the dangers that executive power posed to liberty.[1] After Thomas
Paine's explosive pamphlet *Common Sense* burst on the scene, the struggle for
Independence was just as much a revolt against the very idea of monarchical
power as it was against the oppressive policies of an unrepresentative and
unresponsive Parliament. The repudiation of monarchical forms was so thor-
oughgoing that the immediate reaction was to make the executive subordinate to the legislature in the states and to do away with it almost entirely at
the national level. The newly independent states adopted republican constitutions that either stripped their governors of virtually all of those powers

enjoyed by their colonial predecessors or established councils of state or a plural executive that rendered the executive weak and dependent.[2] Because the Continental Congress was the only national political institution under the Articles of Confederation, the responsibility for carrying executive functions fell to ad hoc congressional committees.

The stench of monarchy still lingered in the nostrils of individuals who had just carried out a revolution against the outrages of executive power when they began to sense that a strong executive might be necessary to ward off the even more pungent odor of chaos. It was fast becoming obvious: without a strong centralized national government, the fledgling republic could neither enforce its own laws nor protect itself from foreign attack. The single-chamber Congress was simply not up to the task of regulating commerce among the states, adjudicating conflicts between states, collecting revenue, conducting foreign policy, and maintaining national security under the current distribution of powers. To make matters worse, the thirteen states formed thirteen sovereign entities with separate militaries, separate currencies, separate land claims, and separate foreign policies that often brought them into conflict with one another. The rivalries among the states and the weaknesses of the national government led to fears that the states might disband and form alliances with foreign powers. To establish a strong central government capable of dealing decisively and effectively with these and other problems would require a powerful and energetic executive of the kind that the Articles of Confederation and the first state constitutions had soundly rejected.

This reconsideration of executive power coincided with a reappraisal of republicanism itself. Developments at the state and national levels raised serious doubts about the people's capacity for responsible and virtuous self-government. The appalling spectacle of legislatures in Rhode Island and other states rushing to pass ill-considered and unjust laws that violated property rights; the shameful display of cities like New York and Philadelphia erecting discriminatory commercial rates that exploited the dependence of neighboring states like New Jersey; the nauseating sight of national politicians pandering to the worst instincts of their constituents; the shocking scene of rioting mobs descending on the capital in Philadelphia to intimidate feckless legislators; the frightening prospect of war between the states; the terrifying news of Shays' Rebellion; and the prospect of lawless violence erupting in other states convinced many Americans that republican virtue as they knew it had expired.

There was a growing consensus among concerned nationalists that the majority of people and their representatives lacked the virtues necessary for self-government. At the start of the Revolution, Alexander Hamilton could confidently proclaim that "it is the unalienable birthright of every Englishman . . . to participate in framing the laws which are to bind him," but after less than a decade he and others began to assert that the people themselves were now the problem.[3] The decentralized system of authority established by the Articles of Confederation led to a diffusion of responsibility that fostered the growth of sectionalism and factionalism among the people and the representatives who yielded to their whims. "There are certain conjunctures," explained Hamilton, "when it may be necessary and proper to disregard the opinions which the majority of the people have formed."[4] Madison, Hamilton, and Washington now began to believe that the republican virtues that had inspired and animated the Revolution belonged only to a select few and that the current system of politics placed too many obstacles in the path of enlightened and effective statesmanship. Madison, in particular, found the system of rotation prescribed under the Articles of Confederation galling, because it forced out men of virtue and ability—such as himself—only to replace them with shameless demagogues and unqualified yahoos. Any effort at reform would have to find a way to attract and retain "fit characters" if the government was to be trusted with new and enlarged powers.

The subject of presidential character became a major source of controversy during the constitutional ratification debates that took place in the state conventions. Although there was probably more confusion than consensus on key questions concerning executive power throughout much of the Constitutional Convention in Philadelphia,[5] and although many Framers changed their minds on key issues along the way,[6] there was no doubt that the office which finally emerged would be powerful and "energetic." When the delegates completed their work in September 1787, Anti-Federalists, critics who opposed the ratification of the Constitution on a variety of grounds, accused them of betraying both the spirit of the Revolution and the principles of republicanism. Not only had the framers brazenly exceeded their limited mandate to propose revisions to the Articles of Confederation, but, Anti-Federalists charged, they had also dared to devise a government with ill-defined and unchecked powers that would endanger the very freedoms for which the Revolution had been fought. The specific powers granted to each of the three branches of the proposed government provoked a fierce outcry, but the vague and uncertain grants of power to the executive were just as troubling.

Even though the new executive was given the innocuous title of "president," the same designation used to refer to the relatively weak presiding officer of Congress under the Articles of Confederation, critics immediately recognized that the powers of this new office were unlike any seen before in the states or in Congress.[7] The creation of a single executive with largely undefined powers was a remarkable accomplishment in a society "culturally programmed to be ever on guard against the dangers of unlimited prerogative,"[8] but many Federalists, who believed that ratification of the Constitution was essential to the preservation of the Union, feared that the gains of the Revolution would be squandered and the United States would succumb to anarchy or internecine strife among the states without the energy and stability that only an "energetic" executive could provide.[9] As a result, many of them hinted at the notion that the president's powers to deal with domestic emergencies would be irreducible to law. It would have been exceedingly imprudent for any Federalist to admit outright that the president would possess extralegal powers, so direct and explicit references to Lockean prerogative were rare. However, the theory of constitutionalism they laid out left little doubt that the exercise of such extraordinary powers would sometimes be necessary to secure the legitimate ends of government.[10]

Although the Federalists went to great lengths to reassure Americans that the juridical rules and institutional mechanisms set up by the framers would provide adequate checks on presidential power, many of them also suggested that the powers of the president would be partially determined and controlled by the personal qualities of the chief executive. Like the liberal writers who preceded and influenced them, many Federalists doubted that all the necessary powers of government could be fully spelled out in advance or that institutional arrangements and legal rules would prove sufficient to check abuses and misuses of power in times of emergency. They sought to reconcile the tensions between the normative imperatives imposed by the rule of law and the objective demands for energetic and potentially extralegal action through the medium of virtue. Ideally, the president would embody those republican virtues that would enable and even compel him or her to place the general interests of the nation before the interests of self, party, or locality.[11] The patriotic statesmanship expected of the president was diametrically opposed to the demagoguery and crass partisanship rampant in the states and increasingly common in Congress.

The role that the Federalists assigned to virtue as a check against abuses of power indicates their views on the limitations of law and highlights one of their fundamental differences with the Anti-Federalists. The dispute between Federalists and Anti-Federalists over the presidency was ultimately a dispute over the extent to which executive power could be defined and circumscribed by legal rules. For most Anti-Federalists, who endlessly recited republican pieties about the sanctity of law, the legitimacy of any political power ultimately depended on its legality. Law enjoyed a privileged place in the political thought of the Anti-Federalists because strict adherence to the law was believed to be indispensable to the preservation of liberty. Their insistence on the need for greater specificity and determinacy in the Constitution became a mantra.[12] Because they conceived of a constitution principally as a legal document that carefully spells out the precise terms and conditions according to which political power is to be held and exercised, they tended to perceive discretionary power and other deviations from specific rules of law as fateful steps on the road to tyranny.

Federalists also demanded adherence to the law, especially in their insistence that states uphold rules protecting property rights, enforce private contracts, and abide by congressional enactments, but they differed from their opponents in rejecting law as an appropriate model of constitutionalism. In contrast to the dogmatic legalism of many Anti-Federalists, Federalists tended to exhibit a more pragmatic attitude toward constitutional questions.[13] Many of them had come to the conclusion that a constitution must allow for much greater flexibility than the law usually affords. Not all of their ideas on constitutionalism were fully worked out when the ratification process got under way, but the idea that "the construction of a constitution necessarily differs from that of law" was written into the "Draft Sketch of Constitution" that was used by the Constitutional Convention's Committee of Detail. That document advised that the constitution should contain "essential principles only; lest the operations of government should be clogged by rendering those provisions permanent and unalterable, which ought to be accommodated to times and events."[14] Nowhere was this advice followed more closely than in Article II on the presidency.

For Federalists, the indeterminacy of presidential power was not a sign of failure or a nefarious scheme to rob the people of their liberties but a necessary means of fulfilling the purposes of the Constitution. Underlying this conception of constitutionalism was the understanding that the contingencies of politics would often exceed the capacities of the law. It is impossible to appreciate their expectations of the presidency without understanding their views on the nature of constitutionalism. Before turning directly to debates over the scope of executive power, we must first consider arguments about the nature of constitutionalism.

Skepticism and the Limits of Political Science

The opening paragraph of the *Federalist* has often been interpreted as an expression of the confident rationalism and optimistic ideals of the Enlightenment, which held out the possibility that humans could order their lives through the proper application of reason. Hamilton remarked that the fate of mankind itself was implicated in America's answer to "the important question, whether societies of men are really capable or not of establishing good government from reflection and choice, or whether they are forever destined to depend for their political constitutions on accident and force."[15] Although Hamilton had hoped that history would vindicate "reflection and choice," he was acutely aware that "accident and force" would nonetheless continue to play a decisive role in human affairs. Hamilton's tumultuous personal history, which led him on an improbable journey from the West Indies, where he experienced the loss of both parents at an early age, to New York, where he was swept into revolutionary activity, probably predisposed him to the view that "changes in the human condition are uncertain and frequent," but he was certainly not alone among the Founders in doubting that institutions built on "reflection and choice" could ever entirely manage or eliminate the vicissitudes of "accident and force."[16] This view of contingency is reflected in the instructions that the Continental Congress gave to Washington at the start of the American Revolution: "Whereas all particulars cannot be foreseen, nor positive instructions for such emergencies so before hand given but that many things must be left to your prudent and discreet management, as occurrences may arise upon the place, or from time to time fall out, you are therefore upon all such accidents or any occasions that may happen, to use your best circumspection."[17] For a generation that had just experienced the violent vagaries and startling uncertainties of war, it was naive to think that any institutional arrangement could ever bring the world fully under control. This mindset goes a long way toward explaining why their conception of constitutionalism would permit so much discretionary power to the executive.

Even though the primary aim of the Federalists was to convince apprehensive Americans that the institutional machinery established by the proposed Constitution would meet the competing demands of liberty and security, the skepticism they exhibited in their own handiwork is nothing short of astounding. It is difficult to imagine another propaganda effort as forthright as this one was in acknowledging the limitations and imperfections of the system they were recommending. The unbounded optimism that Benjamin Franklin expressed on the final day of the Convention (Farrand II, 648) was shared by a number of Federalists, but it was by no means representative of the sentiments of the younger generation of statesmen who were much less confident than one would expect from men engaged in so novel and daring an enterprise. Indeed, the younger members of the founding generation were far less optimistic about the current enterprise than their elders were in forming the state constitutions following the break with England.[18] The enthusiasm of men like Madison and Hamilton for the Enlightenment project of rationalizing politics was dampened by cool reflections on the inherent limitations of and external impediments to an undertaking as bold as the construction of a regime founded on "the plainest paths of reason and conviction," which Hamilton distinguished from "too great abstraction and refinement" (XII, 134). If a sense of foreboding and trepidation characterized the mood of these individuals, it had as much to do with intellectual reasons as it did with a political awareness that the rough road to ratification would be strewn with obstacles.

Like the notions of executive power already examined, the ones articulated by the Federalists were premised on a belief that the unpredictability and contingency of events tend to disrupt even the best-laid plans, necessitating continuous exercises of individual discretion to set things right when institutions fail. This belief was axiomatic of skepticism in much eighteenth-century political philosophy. As Isaac Kramnick demonstrates, the character of political leaders is an overriding concern for political skeptics, who generally "envision[ ] government as primarily an act of management and administration" and renounce "abstract *a priori* blueprint[s]" for politics.[19] The rationalism of the American Founders was abated by a political and philosophical skepticism that has received relatively little attention in the scholarly literature on the American Founding.[20] Eighteenth-century skepticism (which should not be confused with the cynicism and pessimism characteristic of much Anti-Federalist thought) was a positive and constructive philosophical position that aimed to discover the limits of human reason and knowledge in order to establish what could be known—and accomplished—with certainty. It was opposed to speculative philosophical claims that abstract reason alone was sufficient to evaluate, formulate, and direct political practice. Many of the Founders eschewed the perfectionism and rationalism that bewitched eighteenth-century liberals like Bentham and Kant, who, for all their obvious differences, are perhaps the best representatives of that rationalistic impulse in politics that strives to eliminate, abridge, or displace contingency.[21] Skeptics like Madison expressed serious doubts about what rational designs could accomplish without developing the anti-rationalist propensities of conservative critics like Edmund Burke, who subordinated reason to the rule of prejudice.[22] This attitude is closely related to their conception of executive power. It is that part of government whose functions cannot be easily embodied in, reduced to, or derived from formulaic rules.

Many of the younger members of the Founding generation were skeptical about the ability of abstract reason to serve as a guide and a corrective to existing practices, even as they exalted reason above revelation, custom, and habit as the ultimate standard of right. It is important to remember that skepticism in politics developed right alongside the political rationalism that is so often regarded as emblematic of Enlightenment political philosophy. Quite often these attitudes appeared simultaneously in the writings of the same author. The Framers exemplified both attitudes in their application of abstract principles to a constitutional design that recognized and respected the inherent limits of rational planning and left ample room for the exercise of practical judgment based on the accretion of experience in particular circumstances. They disavowed the rationalist conceit that it was possible and desirable to anticipate and solve every problem as quixotic and dangerous. They deferred certain problems for the future and resolved to do only what was necessary to ensure that the ability to respond to unforeseeable problems in the future would not be hampered by anything done in the present. They left future generations the tools they would need to fix unforeseen problems, not a finished product that would solve all of their problems.

The most common manifestation of this outlook appears in the recurrent claim that "a faultless plan was not to be expected" (XXXVII, 242). In Federalist literature, the assertion that "pursuit of a perfect plan" is a "chimerical" and unattainable ideal in human institutions (LXXXV, 484) was perhaps matched in its frequency only by the dire warnings that disastrous consequences would follow rejection of the Constitution. There is little exaggeration in Hamilton's claim that the Anti-Federalists were making entirely unreasonable—and unrealizable—demands for perfection in the Constitution before they would consider it suitable for adoption. Future Supreme Court Justice James Iredell, whose "Marcus" essays rank second only to the *Federalist* in expounding the scope of executive power, showed little patience for concerns that certain powers would be subject to abuse, "since all power may be abused where fallible beings are to execute it." After all, he observed, "none but the Supreme Being himself is altogether perfect," which leaves only two alternatives: "either to have no government at all, or to form the best system we can, making allowance for human imperfection."[23] The Federalists' acknowledgment of the inherent limits of human reason gave them a better appreciation of what reason can and cannot accomplish in politics than the Anti-Federalists' dogmatic insistence on specificity would ever permit. Hamilton's confession that he "never expect[ed] to see a perfect work from imperfect man" (LXXXV, 484) was not an indictment of human frailties but an expression of a widely held and philosophically grounded position among Federalists that was used to justify flexibility and discretion in government.

It was Madison who developed the most sophisticated analysis of the various obstacles—affective, cognitive, linguistic, and epistemological—that ordinarily bedevil attempts to devise political institutions according to the dictates of reason and the lessons of history. He expounded the causes of obscurity in politics in *Federalist* 37, which begins the second half of the *Federalist* and initiates the explication of the powers and structure of the Constitution. The influence of Locke and Hume is apparent throughout the essay, by far the most philosophical in the entire series. That Madison introduced the part of the *Federalist* intended to offer clarification of the specific features of the Constitution with a discussion of the inevitable obscurity and difficulty "experienced in the formation of a proper plan," as the heading of *Federalist* 37 suggests, provides important clues into the nature and proper interpretation of the Constitution—at least as he understood it. Furthermore, that Madison—hardly an enthusiastic supporter of energetic government and outsized executive power—developed a sustained defense of energy in government in this essay also indicates the close connection between skepticism and the importance of executive power in "the very definition of good government" (XXXVII, 243).

Madison offered an explanation for the imperfections, and especially the obscurity, of the Constitution before actually explicating its specific provisions as if it were also necessary to justify any imperfections contained in the discussion. He attributed most of this unfortunate but unavoidable obscurity directly to the "imperfection of the human faculties." This imperfection is an insuperable and ubiquitous obstacle to the rational practice and science of politics. Given the imposing problems involved in even the ordinary task of framing "all new laws," it is not surprising that "the science of government" has been unable to resolve more fundamental problems in politics.

The shortcomings of political science are particularly acute when it comes to definitions of basic concepts, a major point of contention between the Federalists and the Anti-Federalists, for whom precision was an indispensable prerequisite of the rule of law and constitutionalism. Many delegates at the Convention had already begun to sense both the political and the intellectual difficulties involved in providing precise definitions. According to his Convention notes, Madison expressed both "a strong bias in favor of an enumeration and definition of . . . powers" and strong "doubts concerning its practicability" (Farrand I, 53). He later admitted that political science has "yet been unable to discriminate and define, with sufficient certainty, its three great provinces—the legislative, executive, and judiciary" (XXXVII, 244). Montesquieu notwithstanding, Madison found it nearly impossible to draw clear distinctions among the three powers, which "consist in many instances of mere shades of difference,"[24] and he doubted that a strict separation of powers could ever "in practice be duly maintained" (XLVIII, 308). Even though Hamilton acknowledged that the "science of politics . . . has received great improvement," he expressed his skepticism in the received wisdom of Montesquieu by noting that "there is no absolute rule on the subject" of confederacies (IX, 119, 121). James Iredell argued that "it is impracticable to define everything" in explaining why certain powers were not specified with the precision demanded by critics like George Mason.[25] James Wilson justified the discretionary powers contained in the Constitution on the grounds that "it is only in mathematical science that a line can be described with mathematical precision."[26] According to this line of reasoning, rules are inadequate because neat demarcations and fine distinctions—though possible in theory—are impossible to maintain in practice. Constitutional politics involves a constant process of adjustment and renegotiation in response to new and unforeseen situations.

Madison and the other Federalists repudiated the deductive and rationalistic model of politics associated with reformers like Bentham in favor of a more pragmatic approach based on the "experimental method of reasoning" associated with the Humean "science of politics." Nothing illustrates their approach better than their attitude toward law. In rather dismissive fashion, Hamilton stated that "the idea of governing at all times by the simple force of law (which we have been told is the only admissible principle of republican government) has no place but in the reveries of those political doctors whose sagacity disdains the admonitions of experimental instruction" (XXVIII, 204). Federalists like Hamilton were well aware that no collection of predetermined political formulas exists to guide them or future generations of statesmen. Instead, they would have to beat a path through the uncertain terrain of politics using a trial-and-error process. Madison was just now beginning to articulate the intellectual principles underlying the work of a constitutional convention that followed no preconceived plan, though many such plans were offered—and rejected—as impracticable. That is the decisive difference between the two models of political science represented by Anti-Federalists and Federalists: one puts a premium on certainty and rationality, while the other emphasizes practicality and feasibility. Where one seeks to settle matters in advance, the other recognizes the impossibility of doing so without impairing the government's ability to meet all exigencies. As Iredell explained in reference to the indeterminacy of the "necessary and proper" clause, "It was not possible for the Convention, nor is it for any body, to foresee and provide for all contingent cases that may arise."[27]

Madison felt that the plan ultimately adopted by the Convention was far from perfect and contained serious defects, but by the end of the summer he had come to appreciate that it was a more workable plan than anything he or the other delegates had contemplated individually before their collective deliberations began in May. Although the Convention had "been forced into some deviations from that artificial structure and regular symmetry which an abstract view of the subject might lead an ingenious theorist to bestow on a Constitution planned in his closet or in his imagination" (XXXVII, 246), the end result was on the whole practicable. The theoretical precision and rational order he had hoped to impart to the Constitution gave way to more practical necessities, including the conflicting imperatives to devise a system that would be acceptable to the people but adequate to the exigencies of government. This resulted in a document that was far vaguer than anything

Madison had expected. That ambiguity turned out to be both instrumental and potentially hazardous to popular acceptance of the Constitution. As far as the Federalists were concerned, ambiguity was a small price to pay to overcome the defects of the system in place.

Ambiguity and Undefined Powers

The most serious objections to the Constitution raised by Anti-Federalists—and even some supporters—concerned its potential threats to civil liberties. Critics pointed to the absence of a bill of rights, the perilous blending and confusion of powers within the national government, dangerous concentrations of power within each branch, and the erosion of state sovereignty as obvious threats to liberty, but there were many opponents who charged that "the ambiguity of the whole, is its greatest fault."[28] Anti-Federalists considered the detailed specification of constitutional powers absolutely essential to the rule of law and the preservation of liberty. They believed the indeterminacy of the Constitution was a repudiation of America's great contribution to constitutionalism: the written form. William Grayson spoke for many at the Virginia Convention when he remarked "that he did not believe there existed a social compact upon the face of the earth, so vague, so indefinite, as the one now on the table."[29] The "want of precision in defining the limits of the several departments," including the "complication of powers and prerogatives they have heaped on their Senate[,] President and Vice President," was taken as a sure sign that the framers had dishonorable intentions concerning the people's liberties.[30] The Anti-Federalist historian Mercy Otis Warren warned that "the undefined meaning of some parts, and the ambiguities of expression in others" would inevitably "terminate in the most *uncontrouled despotism.*"[31]

Complaints that the Constitution was "incomprehensible and indefinite" often focused on the presidency.[32] Luther Martin fulminated that the "*great and undefined powers*" of the government would pave the way for the "*introduction of monarchy.*"[33] The Anti-Federalist "Cato" alluded to the seemingly irreconcilable tension between presidential power and the rule of law in explaining that the "vague and inexplicit" language of Article II undermines the central values of constitutionalism: "Certainty in political compacts which Mr. Coke *calls the mother and nurse of repose and quietness,* the want of which induced men to engage in political society, has ever been held by a wise and free people as essential to their security; as on the one hand it fixes barriers which the ambitious and tyrannically disposed magistrate dare not overleap, and on the other, becomes a wall of safety to the community." [34]

Although there were as many differences among Anti-Federalists as there were between them and the Federalists, there was almost unanimous agreement among Anti-Federalists that the ambiguity of the Constitution was an intolerable defect. As noted earlier, they generally believed that it was both possible and highly desirable to frame strict and exact laws that would restrain "designing tyrants." [35] They were constitutional literalists who insisted on "strict adherence to original terms." [36] To the extent they tolerated indeterminacy in instruments of government such as the Articles of Confederation, they did so only because specific powers were reserved to competing systems of government, where discretionary powers were susceptible to more direct oversight by officials close to the people or by the people themselves. [37] To allow so much ambiguity and indeterminacy seemed to defeat the very purpose of a written constitution, which they naturally assumed was to define carefully the functions and extent of legitimate powers in order to prevent the kinds of fractious political disputes that characterized seventeenth-century constitutional struggles over the limits of royal prerogative and the proper balance of power between the Crown and Parliament. The history of Great Britain was sometimes cited to demonstrate the intrinsic dangers of leaving powers and rights open to interpretation, rather than defining them explicitly and very specifically. [38]

Madison squarely faced the task of justifying the "want of precision" in *Federalist* 37, which performed two crucial services: intellectually, it explained why some degree of obscurity is inevitable in politics; politically, it preempted criticisms of the *Federalist* papers themselves. (It is also of special relevance to any discussion of executive power because it is one of only two papers in which Madison used the term *energy*.) In anticipation of potential objections to subsequent essays in the *Federalist,* he stressed that the "unavoidable inaccuracy" of political discourse originates in three sources: "indistinctness of the object, imperfection of the organ of conception, [and] inadequateness of the vehicle of ideas." These limitations are so formidable that the meaning of "the Almighty himself . . . is rendered dim and doubtful by the cloudy medium through which it is communicated" (XXXVII, 245). Madison's strategy here was to shift debate away from the motives of participants, which were both diverse and inscrutable, toward the faculties of participants, which were common and observable to all, even if "the most acute and metaphysical philosophers" have yet to distinguish and define these faculties "with satisfactory precision." Everyone is subject to the same limitations of reason and language, so it is unrealistic, Madison implied, to expect a degree of precision and certainty from the Federalists that the Anti-Federalists themselves could never hope to achieve. As a result of the "imperfections of the human faculties" and the limitations of language, it is incumbent upon us to moderate "still further our expectations and hopes from the efforts of human sagacity" when it comes "to the institutions of man, in which the obscurity arises as well from the object itself as from the organ by which it is contemplated" (XXXVII, 244). Madison's explanation constitutes an admission of guilt to the charge that the Constitution is ambiguous, but it does adduce extenuating circumstances to show "that a faultless plan was not to be expected" (XXXVII, 242).

Madison's analysis may have successfully explained why definitions of human institutions are unavoidably indeterminate, but it utterly failed to explain why no definition of executive power was even proffered, either at the Constitutional Convention or in the ratification debates.[39] Furthermore, it seems somehow incomplete. A brilliant first attempt at political epistemology, it never provided final answers to the questions it raised. Madison's diagnosis of obscurity in politics did not take into account reciprocal interactions among the three sources of obscurity. He never developed a theory that might have explained the complex and mutually constitutive relationship between objects and words. Madison never developed the point that certain objects are constituted in and through language, that they have no independent existence outside the realm of human thought. His persistent (and persistently ignored) exhortation to define executive power was put to fellow delegates in a manner suggesting that the Convention had to *discover* rather than define or revise the meaning of executive power. However, there was no reason to think—then or now—that any of the "three great provinces" of government were pre-given or pre-discursive objects with fixed and objective meanings. Executive power was a conceptual coin that circulated with such celerity and ease that its users were apt to forget it had been minted only recently and could be re-minted for the new political market. It never occurred to Madison or to anyone else to utilize the same method of redefinition that he had employed with such great success in re-describing representative democracy as a republican form of government. Instead, it was left to participants in the ratification debates, including Madison himself, to offer definitions and explanations that frequently relied on and revised ideas found in Locke, Hume, Blackstone, and other familiar sources.

Although the delegates to the Constitutional Convention neglected to define executive power, Madison's remarks on the problem of indeterminacy in the law offer a potential solution to the problem of indeterminacy concerning executive power. A law that is ambiguous at the moment of its formulation can be clarified and corrected in its application: "All new laws, though penned with the greatest technical skill and passed on the fullest and most mature deliberation, are considered as more or less obscure and equivocal, until their meaning be liquidated and ascertained by a series of particular discussions and adjudications" (XXXVII, 245). The "complexity and novelty" of the Constitution render the task of liquidating and ascertaining its meaning even more cumbersome but no less imperative than it is where an ordinary law is concerned.[40] The Constitution may be guilty of ambiguity, but it is not incorrigible.

No one appreciated and exploited this opportunity as much as Hamilton, who did as much in his capacity as Secretary of the Treasury to settle and define the extent of executive power as any president would. In Machiavellian terms, the Framers left it to "modes" of political behavior to establish and extend the meaning of certain constitutional "orders." Certain aspects of the Constitution would ultimately be determined by actual practice rather than theory, which could offer guidelines but could not be expected to direct constitutional action. According to Madison, the Constitution's failure to specify the meaning of key concepts was not a fatal flaw in its design. It was up to statesmen to fill the lacunae of the Constitution even as they operated under its auspices. Others pushed this point even further by stressing the essential differences between an ordinary law and a constitution, which, as Edmund Randolph came to argue during the ratification debates, embraces a wider array of objects and "is to have a more liberal construction."[41] Madison concurred, arguing that the clauses regarding the presidency in particular claim "the indulgence of a fair and liberal interpretation" because of the "peculiar difficulty" in precisely defining the powers of the executive. There was nothing sinister involved in the ambiguity regarding the presidency since "precision was not so easily obtained."[42] Although this was far from Madison's ideal, it would have to suffice, since the alternative—a second constitutional convention to revise and refine the proposed system—would be politically unacceptable and even more theoretically disordered. Further tampering with the plan at this point would only create additional confusion and disrupt whatever

rational organization the Constitution exhibited. In light of the strong probability that George Washington would be the first president, this manner of
settling the extent of executive power did not seem so bad to Madison. The
expectation that the virtuous general would establish modes of executive
power compatible with republicanism made it much easier for Madison to
accept such indeterminacy.

The Defects of Legislatures

The Federalist conception of executive power, like Blackstone's, might be
best understood in contradistinction to their reflections on the legislature.
The growing disaffection and disillusionment of many Americans with their
popular assemblies at both the state and the national levels after the Revolution help account for the increasing willingness of influential leaders to reconsider the propriety and necessity of a single executive in a republic. As a result
of what Wood has called "the perversion of republicanism," Americans began
to lose confidence in legislative government.[43] State legislatures were especially prone to partiality and the perturbations of base passions, while partisan divisions and administrative incompetence prevented the Continental
Congress from accomplishing the most basic tasks.[44] Once the urgencies of
the war subsided, the inherent defects of popular assemblies became obvious
to leaders like Washington, Hamilton, and Madison. In addition to the necessity for internal institutional reforms (such as bicameralism), their analyses of
the country's plight suggested the need for an independent single executive
who could both check the malignant impulses of legislatures and compensate
for their inherent limitations. At the Constitutional Convention, the dangers
of legislative tyranny became an explicit justification for making the powers
of the executive "formidable" (Farrand II, 301).

For nationalists like Hamilton and Madison, recent experience confirmed
Hume's diagnosis of group dynamics: whenever individuals act together in
large numbers, the violent passions tend to overwhelm the voice of reason and
the better inclinations of the calm passions. Nationalists began to understand
that the problem was not necessarily the amount of power that any individual
or entity possessed but the institutional setting in which that power was to be
exercised. They stood the old argument, that power was necessarily safer
when it was widely diffused, on its head. The very size of legislatures, once
regarded as a major source of security, was now considered to be part of the

problem. As Madison observed in his "Vices of the Political System," the restraint of character "is diminished in proportion to the number which is to share the praise or blame." [45] In the *Federalist* he explained that "the more numerous any assembly may be, of whatever characters composed, the greater is known to be the ascendancy of passion over reason" (LVIII, 351). Not only did many individual representatives fail to live up to republican ideals, but their private passions were compounded by "the love of power or the desire of pre-eminence and dominion" that "operate upon the collective bodies of society" (VI, 104). Hamilton echoed Hume in contrasting the "angry and malignant passions" (I, 88) and the preoccupation with personal interest prevalent in popular assemblies with the reason and "calmer" passions possessed by "fit characters" acting alone. "Are not popular assemblies frequently subject to the impulses of rage, resentment, jealousy, avarice, and of other irregular and violent propensities?" he wrote (VI, 106).[46] In short, precisely because they were numerous, legislatures were actuated by the "common impulses of passion, or of interest," which Madison famously identified as the primary sources of factions in *Federalist* 10. Echoing Hume's analysis of group dynamics, the Virginian explained that the propensity of "numerous bodies" to be "actuated more or less by passion" disqualified them from possessing the pardon power.[47]

Madison argued that party spirit, one of the more politically pernicious passions, was not a natural human inclination but a phenomenon peculiar to groups. At the moment, "the public good [was being] disregarded in the conflicts of rival parties" (X, 123). Legislators placed the partial interests of party above the general good of the public, state assemblies pursued parochial interests over the national interest, and everywhere laws were passed that violated basic principles of justice. Madison was the most outspoken critic of the partiality and injustice of state legislative enactments (he was loath to dignify them as "laws") that promoted the interests of one segment of the community at the expense of another. He upbraided the state legislatures for the "multiplicity," "mutability," and "injustice" of their enactments, exemplified by the issuance of paper money, the "occlusion of Courts," and various debtor relief laws that harmed creditors. The "luxuriancy of legislation" alone was a matter of grave concern, but the injustice of the laws "brings more into question the fundamental principle of republican Government, that the majority who rule in such Governments, are the safest Guardians both of public Good and of private rights." Because "ambition" and "personal interest" have proven to be more "prevalent" motives than devotion to the public good, Madison concluded that the selfish passions predominate over reason in a popular assembly.[48] The problem was worse in the states, but Congress itself was divided by sectional differences and rancor over issues like navigation of the Mississippi and fishing rights for the New England states. Hamilton deprecated the ability and integrity of the legislature "on account of the natural propensity of such bodies to party divisions," which gives good "reason to fear that the pestilential breath of faction may poison the fountains of justice" (LXXXI, 452).[49]

Sectional and factional divisions within Congress were partly responsible for its inability to achieve important national objectives relating to treaties, commerce, and requisitions, but critics like Washington and Hamilton determined that a popular assembly was by nature fundamentally ill-suited to handle administrative and executive tasks. Congress was responsible for carrying out both legislative and executive functions at the national level, and its performance in both areas was poor. The working consensus that characterized the First Congress began to erode only a few years into the war and disappeared entirely by the end, so that little of national significance was accomplished after the conclusion of the war.[50] The situation was so desperate in 1781 that Richard Henry Lee proposed vesting Washington with dictatorial powers to coerce the states into meeting their obligations to the general government.[51] Experiments with executive committees directly accountable to Congress were unsuccessful because they lacked the independence and powers to carry out their functions efficiently and responsibly. Neither these committees nor Congress as a whole possessed the energy and dispatch required to perform those functions that demanded decisiveness and expediency. The inability of the national government to deal with several minor uprisings and outbreaks of violence in the states demonstrated the shortcomings of congressional dominance, but Shays' Rebellion exposed the desperate urgency for a remedy. Because Congress simply lacked the wherewithal to respond to this crisis or any other in a regular or efficacious manner, it had to call upon Washington once more to quell the uprising in western Massachusetts. That incident convinced many citizens that decisive action was imperative. In fact, most state legislatures voted to send delegates to Philadelphia while the crisis in Western Massachusetts was still in progress.[52]

Injustices in the states and factionalism at the national level convinced Madison that there was as much to be feared from legislative tyranny as there was from executive, for the "legislative department is everywhere extending the sphere of its activity and drawing all power into its impetuous vortex." Consequently, "it is against the enterprising ambition of this department that the people ought to indulge all their jealousy and exhaust all their precautions" (XLVIII, 309, 310). It may be true that "the latent causes of faction are thus sown in the nature of man" (X, 124), but factions and other evils cannot thrive without the proper institutional nourishment and political cultivation. Madison's analysis showed that the institutional design and dynamics of popular assemblies were responsible for the dissipation of republican virtue. But the implications of this insight were not completely discouraging, and it would not be right to conclude that critics of the legislatures abandoned their belief in virtue. It was not certain that any institutional design could generate virtue where it did not already exist, but the right institutional design could create a hospitable environment for virtue to flourish and thrive. The Federalists argued that virtue did have a place in modern politics, but they located it in the unlikeliest of places. It was no longer the legislature, the traditional bastion of liberty, that would be a home to virtue but the single executive, ostensibly the least republican institution of all.

More important, an independent executive with sufficient powers might be able to solve the immediate political problem posed by passionate legislators. Because legislatures "will constantly seek to aggrandize & perpetuate themselves," Gouverneur Morris argued that the executive could serve as an indispensable check. "It is necessary then that the Executive Magistrate should be the guardian of the people, even of the lower classes, agst. Legislative tyranny" (Farrand II, 52). Madison defended the proposed powers of the president as necessary *protections* against the "powerful tendency in the Legislature to absorb all power into its vortex" (Farrand II, 74). Before they could convince skeptics of the possibility of virtue in a single executive, though, its defenders had to prove that a single executive would supply the energy that the national government sorely lacked and that a single executive was actually safer than the institutional alternatives.

The Responsibility and Energy of the Single Executive

In spite of the deep-seated suspicion and animosity directed against the single executive, which was closely associated with monarchy, it was almost universally acknowledged to possess distinct advantages over alternative arrangements like the plural executive and competing branches like the legislature. Chief among these was the ability to act with sufficient energy.[53] The ability to summon the force of the entire community in maintaining internal and external security against domestic and foreign threats became the quintessential characteristic of energy in the executive. In fact, energy became so closely associated with executive power that it became identified with other qualities frequently mentioned in connection with executive power: secrecy, dispatch, decisiveness, vigor, and action. Not surprisingly, these qualities were contrasted—sometimes negatively—with the supposed hallmarks of legislative power: publicity, lethargy, indecision, moderation, and deliberation. Among those who believed a stronger centralized government was necessary to meet the challenges that faced the country, energy in the national government would be impossible without the energy that only a single and independent executive could supply. As Blackstone had argued, energy ought to pervade the entire government, and it was the executive that would invigorate it.

Most of the delegates to the Constitutional Convention were committed nationalists already convinced of the need for an energetic government. In his Circular to the States, Washington stated that the "distresses and disappointments" of recent years were attributable to "a want of energy, in the Continental Government."[54] By the second day of debate in the Convention, Randolph had already insisted on "the absolute necessity of a more energetic government" (Farrand I, 24). Even before turning to the presidency, Hamilton identified good government with the dominant characteristic of executive power, thereby creating an inseparable link between good government as a whole and one of its constituent parts.[55] Wilson expressed the prevailing view that "good laws are of no effect without a good Executive" (Farrand II, 538). In the very first installment of the *Federalist* Hamilton noted that free and effective government was impossible without two crucial ingredients: vigilance among the people and "vigor" in the government. As Blackstone had intimated, energy, or "vigor of government," is "essential to the security of liberty" (I, 89). Indeed, the notion that a strong government is essential to the preservation and promotion of liberty was the hallmark of Hamilton's statist political thought and practice.[56] "Experience," he explained, had taught the public "that greater energy of government is essential to the welfare and prosperity of the community" (XXVI, 197).

Of course, this was a remarkable transformation in American notions of executive power, which only a decade before was a constitutional anathema.

Now, Americans could mention liberty and energy in the same sentence without a sense of contradiction. Washington expressed his satisfaction that the delegates had formed a "government, where due energy will not be incompatible with the unalienable rights of freemen."[57] Even more impressive, Americans could mention liberty and monarchy in the same breath. Wilson commented that "by adopting this system, the vigor and decision of a wide-spreading monarchy may be joined to the freedom and beneficence of a contracted republic."[58] This was a far cry from the avowed principles of the Revolution, when Thomas Paine vehemently denied that "the *strength of government, and the happiness of the governed*" depend in any way on "the monarchical part of the constitution."[59]

Hamilton explicitly linked the overall quality of government with the strength of executive power in his discussion of the presidency: "Energy in the executive is a leading character in the definition of good government. It is essential to the protection of the community against foreign attacks; it is not less essential to the steady administration of the laws; to the protection of property against those irregular and high-handed combinations which sometimes interrupt the ordinary course of justice; to the security of liberty against the enterprises and assaults of ambition, of faction, and of anarchy" (LXX, 402).[60] Although he never specified how energetic government actually protects the community from the "assaults of ambition and faction," Hamilton's remark implied that Madison's solution to the problem of factions articulated in *Federalist* 10 essay was not the final word on the matter. Hamilton's apparent meaning is that a vigorous execution of the laws entails the equal and impartial application of general laws against any and all parties. This interpretation is supported by one of Hamilton's most important statements on the relation between good government and energy: "A feeble executive implies a feeble execution of the government. A feeble execution is but another phrase for a bad execution; and a government ill executed, whatever it may be in theory, must be, in practice, a bad government" (LXX, 402). In response to those who argued that a plural executive was more consistent with republican principles, Hamilton asserted that such an arrangement was likely to produce disastrous dissensions that "might impede or frustrate the most important measures of the government in the most critical emergencies of the state" (LXX, 404). Since the maximization of energy required the monarchical form, or the single executive, proponents of a strong government had to prove the counterintuitive proposition that a single executive could—and would—be a responsible executive.

Federalists worked hard to convince doubtful Americans that the presidency would be energetic enough to meet all the exigencies of government but safe enough to be entrusted with so many discretionary powers. They pointed to periodic elections, the impeachment process, and senatorial approval of treaties and nominations as reliable institutional checks on the president, but they offered definitions of limited government that often omitted any reference to the executive, confirming Anti-Federalists' worst fears about the potentially despotic nature of presidential power. Hamilton's definition of "a limited Constitution" was restricted to "one which contains certain specified exceptions to the legislative authority," making no mention whatsoever of the presidency (LXXVIII, 438). Similarly, reassurances that the *"ne plus ultra* of the powers of Congress, and of the judiciary of the United States, is expressly fixed" left one wondering why similar precautions were not taken to "fix" the powers of the presidency.[61] When it came to Federalist definitions of constitutionalism, their silence on executive power was deafening.

Defining Executive Power?

The Founders generally found it much easier to describe what executive power is not than to explain what it is. Those who drafted the state constitutions were certain of only one thing when it came to executive power: they did not want to entrust their executive officers with the full array of royal prerogatives found in the British Constitution. Jefferson's "Draught of a Fundamental Constitution for the Commonwealth of Virginia" was typical in denying the state governor "those powers exercised under our former government by the crown as of its prerogative." To render the office as safe as possible, the governor would possess "those powers only, which are necessary to execute the laws (and administer the government) and which are not in their nature either legislative or judiciary."[62] Many writers in the period between the Revolution and the Constitutional Convention described executive power in minimalist terms that reduced it to a subordinate agent of the legislature with no independent will of its own, which is exactly what most state constitutions did. With the possible exceptions of New York and Massachusetts, the powers of the governors were so weak and limited that the state constitutions provided little guidance on what an energetic executive might actually look like.[63]

One of the things that makes it so difficult to determine exactly how any group of Founders understood executive power in this period is that their discussions were often vague and unspecific. There were strong connotations—strength, vigor, force, energy, decision, and dispatch, to name a few—but few denotations. Sometimes, executive power referred to anything that was left over after the powers of the legislature and the judiciary had been specified. De Lolme's recent text on the English constitution reminded—and warned—readers that in most forms of government, "the executive power in the state is supposed to possess, originally and by itself, all manner of lawful authority: every one of its exertions is deemed to be legal: and they do not cease to be so, till they are stopped by some express and positive regulation. . . . The authority of the government, in short, is supposed to be unlimited so far as there are no visible boundaries set up against it; within which boundaries lies whatever degree of liberty the subject may possess."[64] Americans were used to the idea that the only way to make executive power conformable to liberty was to place explicit limits on it. Furthermore, its association with monarchy made it appear even more extravagant and arbitrary, hence antithetical to law. Although a handful of Anti-Federalists actually favored augmenting the powers of the national executive to form a check on the "aristocratic" tendencies of the Senate, which they believed was the real threat to freedom, most of them rehearsed the same objections to the self-aggrandizing tendencies of executive power that were voiced in 1776. It continued to arouse suspicion long after George III had been vanquished, but successful experiments in the states helped somewhat to dissociate executive power from monarchical models. In fact, the office of governor of New York proved so effective as a check against the excesses of legislatures common in other states that it became a leading model for reformers determined to eradicate the doctrine and practice of legislative supremacy.[65]

Entering the Convention, leading nationalists were unsure if the national executive ought to be limited to the administration and enforcement of laws or given additional functions. Shortly before the Convention, Madison confided to Washington, "I have scarcely ventured, as yet, to form my own opinion either of the manner in which [a national executive] ought to be constituted, or the authorities with which it ought to be cloathed."[66] At the Convention Madison repeatedly entreated fellow delegates to explain what they meant by executive power, but since his requests were ignored, it is difficult to extract many useful insights from the records of the Convention.[67] (The lack of a precise definition never seemed to bother Hamilton, who had confidently asserted as early as 1780 that "undefined powers are discretionary powers, limited only by the object for which they were given.")[68] Like the ratification debates that followed, discussions of executive power at the Convention were generally so vague that one wonders if anyone really had any idea what the term meant.[69]

Opponents of a strong executive had some definite ideas, but their conception of executive power would have reduced the presidency to "nothing more than an institution for carrying the will of the Legislature into effect" (Farrand I, 65). This suggestion was soundly rejected because it would have undermined the independence of the executive and rendered the separation of powers nugatory. However, proponents of a strong executive did not provide a clear alternative. Early in the Philadelphia Convention, Madison and Wilson sponsored an amendment to the Virginia Plan that did not define executive power but instead assigned the executive "such powers, not legislative or judiciary in their nature, as may from time to time be delegated by the national legislature" (Farrand I, 63). Wilson, one of the most outspoken proponents of a strong executive, opined that the "only powers he conceived strictly Executive were those of executing the laws, and appointing officers" (Farrand I, 66). But by the end of the Convention he was pushing for a notion of executive power far more expansive than this. What had changed over the course of the Convention was the delegates' understanding of the role of the executive in the new government as well as the relation between the people and the national government. After it had been decided, gradually and often grudgingly, that many of the new and improved powers of the national government would operate directly on individuals without the cooperation (or interference) of the states, the notion that the states were the exclusive centers of sovereignty began to fade. Once the Federalists adopted the view that sovereignty was located in the people, not the states, it became easier to conceptualize the proper role of executive power in the constitutional system.

The initial confusion over the nature of the executive was largely a result of the Framers' uncertainty over the proper location of sovereignty. Beginning with Jean Bodin and leading through Thomas Hobbes to (moments in) William Blackstone, sovereignty was identified so closely with the supremacy of legislative authority that it became difficult to reconcile the idea of indivisible sovereignty with the emergent doctrine of the separation of powers. The confusions in Blackstone's account of the British Constitution stem in large part from an analytical inability to disentangle the idea of sovereignty from the powers of the legislature. Wilson's powerful endorsement of the idea of popular sovereignty as the basis of national government was not an idea that came naturally to men used to thinking in terms of state sovereignty or even of legislative sovereignty, but as the summer progressed Wilson articulated this idea with increasing clarity and conviction as more and more delegates came around to his way of thinking. The idea that all political institutions, state and national, ultimately derived their authority from the sovereign will of the people was uncongenial to those who favored a pivotal role for the states in any new system of government. But once the Framers began to see the issue of sovereignty in these terms—if somewhat indistinctly and relatively late in the Convention—it became somewhat easier to resolve the theoretical dilemmas surrounding questions of executive power. If the executive branch ultimately derives its authority from the people by way of the Constitution, then it becomes easier to reconcile the idea of a vigorous executive with the principles of republican government. That is why the mode of presidential election (described in the next chapter) was such a decisive step toward the notion of popular sovereignty and away from the idea that the legislature was the sole repository of sovereignty or the exclusive representative of the people (much less the states). If the people were the ultimate fount of sovereignty, then any and all powers exercised by the different branches of government sprang from this same—hopefully unadulterated—source.

The halting steps taken by the Framers did not lead inevitably to an expanded notion of executive power, though. Even after many of them had begun to envision a new system of government firmly grounded in the principle of popular sovereignty, they still had to address the proper relation of the executive to that wellspring and to the other branches and levels of government. But each time they returned to the executive, they failed to resolve the fundamental question concerning the nature or essence of executive power, even if they had less difficulty determining the specific powers that the president would have once a clearer image of the Constitution began to emerge. The only thing they could agree upon was the uncontroversial, though not necessarily unproblematic, idea that the executive should be given powers to carry into effect the national laws. As participants on both sides of the ratification debates would later suggest, execution is not as simple or straightforward a matter as some delegates seemed to think, but there is no indication that anyone was especially troubled by possible complications. For attempts to conceptualize executive power, it is necessary to turn to the ratification campaign, where commentators could consider the nature of executive power in light of the specific powers of the presidency and the general framework of government established by the Constitution. Indeed, it is impossible to get a firm grasp on the Federalists' conception of executive power without understanding their conception of the purposes of the Constitution as a whole.

Where Madison provided the epistemological justification for constitutional ambiguity, Hamilton provided the practical justification. Never one to be deterred by epistemological or constitutional obstacles, Hamilton did not let the Constitution's reticence on any point silence him. Besides, circumstances did not afford him that luxury. On the one hand, he had to placate fears that the president possessed too many dangerous powers; on the other hand, he wanted to leave enough room for a generous interpretation of executive power.[70] The strategy he pursued was to make executive power seem as innocuous as possible even as he laid the groundwork for its expansion beyond anything explicitly authorized in the Constitution. *Federalist 75*, which deals with the treaty power, is a case in point. In that essay, he surmised that "the execution of the laws and the employment of the common strength, either for this purpose or for the common defense, seem to comprise all the functions of the executive magistrate" (LXXV, 425). The phrasing suggests that executive power is restricted to a limited set of responsibilities, but it leaves open the possibility that there may be other functions not readily apparent either to Hamilton himself or to those "writers on the subject of government" who would include the treaty power as one of these functions. A few years later, Hamilton forthrightly admitted "that there is and necessarily must be a great number of undefined particulars incident to the general duty of every officer, for the requiring of which no special warrant is to be found in any law," but at the moment he was less interested in the "endless variety of things unexpressed" than he was in explicating the larger purposes of executive power.[71]

Throughout his writings and statements on constitutional government, Hamilton maintained that a constitution was both empowered and limited by its purposes. His view of constitutionalism was that the functions, though not necessarily the powers, of the state were limited. As early as 1780, he had begun to formulate a theory of implied or inherent powers that would have allowed Congress to deal with exigent circumstances even when it lacked an express grant of formal powers. Anticipating the argument he would develop later in the decade, Hamilton argued that "undefined powers are discretionary powers limited only by the object for which they were given."[72] At the Convention he admonished fellow delegates against defining powers too carefully because "something will always be wanting" (Farrand I, 298). Although Madison and Hamilton both argued that a viable constitution must be adequate to its exigencies, Hamilton stressed the relation between means and ends as the crucial determinant of constitutionality. Even though a written constitution ought to provide adequate means to achieve the ends for which it is created, Hamilton believed that there would be cases where the achievement of those ends would require the development of new and unspecified means—as long as they "are not precluded by restrictions & exceptions specified in the constitution; or not immoral, or not contrary to the essential ends of political society."[73] As Hamilton had been arguing since the early days of the Revolution, certain ends are simply too important to sacrifice to a rigid legalism that would uphold the letter of the law but violate its spirit.[74]

Constitutional Means and Ends

The key to the Federalists' theory of executive power is the idea that a constitution is a purposive and flexible instrument of government. It is impossible to appreciate the role that Federalists envisioned for the president without grasping their view of the constitution as both a means and an end. As an instrument, the constitution is a means to higher ends, which are themselves partly defined in and by that very same instrument. Its ends are identified with "the general welfare," "the public good," "the commonweal," or "the national interest." These are all notoriously nebulous notions, but they underscore the idea that government exists for general rather than particular interests. The preamble to the Constitution articulates these ends in general terms, while the Articles that follow indicate the structure, functions, and powers of government in more specific terms. The means or instruments of government are subordinate to and dependent on higher ends outlined in the Constitution, which itself is a means to higher ends defined by the laws of nature, the principles of justice, or other notions of higher law.[75] But to say that the Constitution is a means is not meant to suggest that it is *merely* a means, as Mansfield suggests in contrasting Lockean constitutionalism to Federalist constitutionalism.[76] The Constitution is both a means and an end, depending on the object in question. It is a means with respect to liberty, but an end—albeit a proximate one—with respect to ordinary law. And it is worth keeping in mind that Article II, Section 1 of the Constitution requires the president to take an oath to "preserve, protect and defend the Constitution of the United States."

Madison accepted a version of the doctrine of means and ends as an axiomatic rule of construction, which stipulates that "where the several parts cannot be made to coincide, the less important should give way to the more important part; the means should be sacrificed to the end, rather than the end to the means" (XL, 260–61).[77] The argument concerning the relation between means and ends was used to defend both the selection of means specified in the Constitution and the transcendence of those very same means in cases of necessity. Sometimes they simply argued that the means established by the Constitution were justified by widely accepted ends, but at other times they suggested that these ends might justify the use of other means, means *not* authorized by the Constitution. The ability of Federalists to glide easily from one use of this axiom to the other allowed them to downplay the extralegal implications of this constitutional doctrine.

Federalists tended to regard governmental forms pragmatically, in terms of the ends they served, and not simply as ends in their own right. This is not to say that Federalists were unprincipled consequentialists ready to sacrifice the Constitution for any and all ends that a president or Congress could conjure. Their conception of the proper relation between means and ends was premised on an implicit distinction between derivative and subordinate principles, like the separation of powers or the rule of law, on the one hand, and what Sheldon Wolin has called "metaprinciples, superior to other principles," on the other.[78] The participants in the struggle over ratification followed the tradition of other liberal writers in defining constitutional government in terms of its ultimate purposes, which were nearly always defined by Anglophone writers as the preservation and extension of liberty, whether defined historically by immemorial custom or derived rationally from the laws of nature. Federalists and Anti-Federalists alike agreed that government was established to promote liberty, foreign and domestic peace, economic prosperity, and other lofty ideals, but they disagreed vehemently on the proper means of securing these vital ends. The crucial difference between them concerned the proper relation between lower-order means and proximate ends.

Unlike most Anti-Federalists, who continued to view constitutionalism through the prism of sacrosanct and inviolable law, most Federalists rejected juridical models of constitutionalism because they entail a degree of rigidity that threatens to undermine the long-term viability of constitutional government. The legalistic tendencies of the Anti-Federalists are most evident in their demands that both the ends and the means of the Constitution should be defined precisely and that the powers of the national government should not extend an inch beyond those specified expressly in the Constitution. Many of them insisted dogmatically on constitutional rigor because they considered alternative options to be far more dangerous to liberty than any inconveniences arising from strict adherence to legal forms.[79] In many respects, they were forerunners of the strict constructionist doctrines that Jefferson would oppose to the loose constructionism advocated by Hamilton. Even though Madison would later join Jefferson in contesting the elastic constitutionalism championed by Hamilton, he contributed to the development of those very same doctrines during his partnership with Hamilton in 1787 and 1788.[80]

As a result of their analysis of the relation between means and ends, the Federalists were compelled to reconsider the primacy of those neat juridical categories and precise legal demarcations that were always the ideal if not quite the actual practice of traditional conceptions of constitutionalism. The dispute revolved around the basic question whether the means specified in the Constitution were the only ones appropriate for government to use in pursuit of designated ends. As usual, Hamilton made the most forceful case for the idea that government could go beyond the express powers specified in the Constitution. Since "future necessities admit not of calculation or limitation" (XXX, 214), government should be "free from every other control but a regard to the public good and to the sense of the people" (XXXI, 218). Hamilton was not alone in emphasizing the instrumental character of those institutional forms codified in the Constitution. The future apostle of strict constructionism Madison himself asserted confidently that "no axiom is more clearly established in law, or in reason, than that wherever the end is required, the means are authorized; wherever a general power to do a thing is given, every particular power necessary for doing it is included" (XLIV, 290). Government, he stated, should be "commensurate to the exigencies of the Union" (XLIV, 292). Other Federalists concurred with Madison's assessment, but Hamilton differed from all of them in defining government according to its typical modes rather than its established forms. He seemed to value forms only insofar as they helped secure worthy ends and contributed to modes of governance that call to mind all the watchwords of Hamilton's political vocabulary: efficiency, vigor, dispatch, responsibility, firmness, and energy.

Executive power was always implicit in discussions of the higher ends of government, especially discussions of self-preservation. Madison echoed Locke's argument that institutional and legal forms must yield to substantive considerations in his references to "the great principle of self-preservation" and natural law, "which declares that the safety and happiness of society are the objects at which all political institutions aim and to which all such institutions must be sacrificed" (XLIII, 285). Madison acknowledged that "a power to advance the public happiness involves a discretion which may be misapplied and abused" (XLI, 266), but that discretion could not be eliminated without eliminating the means of happiness. He invoked the principle of self-preservation to justify the Constitutional Convention's superseding of the Articles of Confederation, but the principle is of such fundamental and foundational importance to government that it trumps legal and even constitutional considerations that conflict with its imperatives. "It is vain," according to Madison, "to oppose constitutional barriers to the impulse of self-preservation," since limitations on a government's ability to defend society only invite "usurpations of power, every precedent of which is a germ of unnecessary and multiplied repetitions" (XLI, 267). He flatly denied "that the solid happiness of the people is to be sacrificed to the views of political institutions" (XLV, 293). And because Madison often discussed self-preservation in connection with government's responsibility to secure internal and external security, the potential for presidential exercises of extralegal powers was always implicit in his analysis. Madison articulated his notion of constitutional flexibility in *Federalist* 44, which justifies the "necessary and proper" clause as an indispensable adjunct to Congressional power, but what he said there applies with equal—if not greater—force and propriety to the presidency. "No axiom is more clearly established in law, or in reason, than that . . . wherever a general power to do a thing is given, every particular power necessary for doing it is included" (XLIV, 290). It is the executive whose powers are expressed in such general terms that "in every new application of a general power, the *particular powers,* which are the means of attaining the *object* of the general power, must always necessarily vary with that object" (XLIV, 289).

Hamilton's resolute defense of "that fundamental maxim of good sense and sound policy, which dictates that every POWER ought to be proportioned to its OBJECT" (XXX, 214), is a familiar leitmotif of his constitutional theory, but it is striking how central these ideas were to Madison's arguments as well. Madison sounded like his coauthor when he noted that "tyranny has perhaps oftener grown out of the assumptions of power called for, on pressing exigencies, by a defective constitution, than out of the full exercise of the largest constitutional authorities" (XX, 171). Since emergencies will inevitably arise, it was thought best to vest the government, particularly the executive, with the powers required to deal with such contingencies, because tyranny was more likely to result from a "feeble" government than a strong and energetic one. Hamilton maintained that the powers of the proposed government were adequate to any contingency, obviating the need for extraordinary, or extra-constitutional, exercises of power in cases of emergency. But he did so only at the expense of considerable ambiguity and indeterminacy in his description of "executive power." This did not go unnoticed by Anti-Federalists. William Symmes argued that the constitutional requirement that the president take care that the laws be faithfully executed was not a restriction but an *extension* of power. The president could ignore the specific instructions of the legislature in construing and executing laws by pointing to this vague requirement. This single clause could potentially render him "to all intents & purposes absolute." [81]

Emergencies and the Exigencies of Government

The specter of Shays' Rebellion haunted the proceedings of the Constitutional Convention. Unless the new government was empowered to exorcise such demons, the Framers feared, the republic would be doomed. The fear that similar uprisings might materialize in other parts of the country prompted Edmund Randolph, the chief sponsor of the Virginia Plan, to warn of a potential "American downfal [sic]" if the delegates failed to act (Farrand I, 18). John Dickinson's "Plan of Government" made specific reference to "Emergencies of Invasion or Insurrection" in its proposal for a tripartite executive. [82] In an uncharacteristically anxious letter written to Thomas Jefferson at the start of the Convention, George Washington declared, "That something is necessary, none will deny; for the situation of the general government, if it can be called a government, is shaken to its foundation, and liable to be overturned by every blast. In a word, it is at an end; and, unless a remedy is soon applied, anarchy and confusion will inevitably ensue" (Farrand III, 31). Jefferson considered the Framers' reaction to domestic disturbances out of all proportion to the actual size and nature of the threat, but it was hard to deny that something was deeply wrong. [83] All of the delegates did not agree on the appropriate remedy, but they did agree that the nation was afflicted with a potentially life-threatening malady. Though a few left in protest and some refused to sign the Constitution, there was no question that the proposed government would be more "energetic" than the one it was meant to replace.

Unfortunately, none of the Federalists ever developed a full-fledged systematic theory of emergency. However, they said enough about insurrections, uprisings, popular tumults, financial crises, and invasions to allow fair inferences about the role of the executive in dealing with unforeseen and extraordinary events. In contrast to Machiavelli's account of contingency near the beginning his *Discourses on Livy*, Federalists generally conceived of emergencies as more or less isolated disturbances that interrupt the normal flow of politics, not as part of a cyclical or degenerative process of decay.[84] As a result, the task of the president would differ in significant ways from that of the prince. Both had to minimize the threats to the immediate and long-term welfare of the republic. However, because Machiavelli considered some (though not all) disturbances as symptomatic manifestations of an inexorable historical process of decline and eventual regeneration, the primary responsibility of his prince was to return a corrupted state back to first principles. The Federalists tended to view politics in episodic rather than cyclical terms. A process of irreversible decline was not out of the question for Americans, but domestic disturbances, especially in the form of popular uprisings and insurrections, were not necessarily portents of inevitable and irreversible deterioration. Consequently, the president's task would be to prevent domestic unrest from igniting a more general conflagration that would engulf the entire republic in a blaze of destruction. Some disturbances might be just minor outbursts, and it was the president's duty to extinguish these flareups in a manner that would prevent their spread or reoccurrence.

Contrary to Machiavelli and some of his interpreters, particularly Harvey Mansfield, this task requires a judicious mix of lenience and severity, of mild forbearance and forceful intensity. The Framers objected to a uniform policy of strictness because it could exacerbate a situation that requires careful consideration of all pertinent facts in the circumstances at hand as well as the long-term consequences of different courses of action. But either approach might force the president to go beyond the institutional confines of the Constitution. Mansfield's incantation that the Constitution "constitutionalizes necessity" simply fails to consider the way that institutional resources and the law can serve either to obstruct or to facilitate the president's task. He correctly recognizes that executive power highlights the "dispute between law and prerogative," but he falls into the common trap of reducing the constitution to law, when in fact, for both Locke and the Federalists, it was much, much more than that.[85] The Federalists made a decisive break with the legal-

istic constitutionalism of the past in establishing a flexible model of constitutionalism that treats law as a privileged but not exclusive modality of governance. The thrust of Hamilton's entire argument concerning executive power
and emergencies was that extra*legal* exercises of power were not necessarily
extra-*constitutional*, though (as we will see) he did raise the possibility that
even unconstitutional acts might be dictated by necessity.

The Federalists never claimed that a constitution could prevent emergencies, but they did contend that the proposed Constitution was adequate to any
exigency. In their view, a proper understanding of the purposes and nature of
a constitution would make it possible to deal with unforeseen emergencies
without undermining popular confidence in the Constitution. Unless the
powers of government are great enough to meet any challenge, argued Hamilton, necessity will dictate the violation of laws, which are hopelessly inadequate in dealing with those emergencies that "will sometimes exist in all societies" (XXVIII, 204). That, as much as anything else, explains why Article
II never specifies the meaning or accessories of executive power and contains
no explicit restrictions on executive power as such. As a general rule, Hamilton considered it unwise to impose restrictions that would hamper government's ability to respond to emergencies. For instance, despite his vigorous
"disapprobation" of poll taxes, Hamilton was unwilling to rule them out entirely: "There are certain emergencies of nations in which expedients that in
the ordinary state of things ought to be forborne become essential to the public weal. And the government, from the possibility of such emergencies, ought
ever to have the option of making use of them" (XXXVI, 240). The rule of
constitutional construction laid out here was based on the broad principle
that government retains all powers not expressly forbidden, rather than the
more stringent doctrine associated with Wilson that government possesses
only specifically enumerated powers: "Wise politicians will be cautious about
fettering the government with restrictions that cannot be observed, because
they know that every breach of the fundamental laws, though dictated by
necessity, impairs the sacred reverence which ought to be maintained in the
breast of rulers towards the constitution of a country, and forms a precedent
for other breaches where the same plea of necessity does not exist at all, or is
less urgent and palpable" (XXV, 196). Unless he was prepared to call into question his own wisdom and that of fellow delegates, the implication is that the
Constitution contains no absolute restrictions that would fetter the government's ability to deal with emergencies. The implication is that it would never

be necessary to violate the Constitution (though inferior laws are different matters altogether).

The question of course still remains where the authority to deal with necessity is located. Nearly every reference in the Constitution to potential domestic disturbances, as "in Cases of Rebellion or Invasion" appears in Article I, but the indeterminacy of the language makes it unclear, for instance, whether or not Congress has exclusive authority to suspend the writ of habeas corpus—an indeterminacy that Abraham Lincoln fully exploited during the Civil War. Hamilton's own preferences rested with the executive, but he was certainly not alone in suggesting that the primary responsibility for handling domestic crises rested with the president. For instance, Edmund Pendleton considered the presidency "admirably contrived to prevent Popular Tumults."[86] This is of course because "the President is to have the command" of the militia, hence is best equipped to employ force.[87]

The correspondence between an energetic executive and good government was so strong, intimated Hamilton in *Federalist* 23, that the executive's powers cannot properly be limited without threatening the very preservation of the union: "These powers ought to exist without limitation, *because it is impossible to foresee or to define the extent and variety of national exigencies, and the correspondent extent and variety of the means which may be necessary to satisfy them*" (XXIII, 184, emphasis in original). The argument "that there can be no limitation of that authority which is to provide for the defense and protection of the community" is made well in advance of the discussion on the executive, yet there is no doubt that this argument entails an expansion of executive powers. Hamilton's language here is equivocal enough to create some uncertainty as to whether it is the president or Congress that "will best understand the extent and urgency of the dangers that threaten" the public safety, but later essays in the *Federalist* leave little doubt that the president is in the best position to compass the general good. Not only is the chief executive expected to have the expertise necessary to ascertain the "national interest," but the office is also constituted in such a manner that the executive's interests will coincide with the preservation of the whole (XXIII, 186), unlike the more provincial perspectives of legislators who represent narrower constituencies.

Supporters of a strong presidency were preoccupied with the problem of emergencies. Iredell noted that "one of the great advantages attending a single Executive power is, the degree of secrecy and dispatch with which, on critical occasions, such a power can act."[88] The possibility—indeed the probability—

of emergencies was cited to justify both the specific and general powers of the president. Using all the familiar themes of executive power, Wilson contrasted the torpidity of the legislature with the dispatch of the president as his chief qualification for dealing with emergencies: "In planning, forming and arranging laws, deliberation is always becoming, and always useful. But in the active scenes of government, there are emergencies, in which the man, as, in other cases, the woman, who deliberates is lost. . . . How much time will be consumed! and when it is consumed, how little business will be done! When the time is elapsed; when the business is finished; when the state is in distress, perhaps on the verge of destruction; on whom shall we fix the blame? Whom shall we select as the object of punishment?"[89] At the Virginia Convention, future chief justice John Marshall strongly suggested that, of necessity, the president possesses plenary powers equivalent to those of a dictator in times of "danger."[90] A grant of general powers is necessary and unavoidable because even in England, "it is easier to enumerate the exceptions to [the king's] prerogative, than to mention all the cases to which it extends."[91]

The notion that emergencies fall within the special province of executive power was widely shared even by prominent opponents of a strong executive. As far as the records of the Philadelphia Convention show, George Mason never challenged the propriety of having the executive handle cases of emergency, but his belief in the corruptive nature of unchecked power and the incurable corruptibility of human nature led him to conclude that only a plural executive could suppress an insurrection with impartiality (Farrand I, 113). Anti-Federalists recognized that one of the president's functions would be to deal with emergencies and unforeseen events, but they saw this as an invitation to tyranny. Recalling the practice of Roman dictatorship, Patrick Henry argued that it would be more prudent to give the president necessary powers when the occasion for their exercise arises rather than to vest the president with discretionary powers subject to abuse in ordinary circumstances. Like most Anti-Federalists, he flatly rejected the notion that any president could ever be trusted with indefinite or extraordinary powers on the grounds that it was contrary to reason, experience, and human nature to expect an individual conferred with such great powers *not* to abuse them.[92]

There was little question among participants in the ratification process that the powers of the president would extend to unforeseen emergencies in large part because the executive represents the collective force of the community.[93] Some suggested that the energy, secrecy, and dispatch of the executive would uniquely enable it to handle "cases of emergency" as in the British government, but without "its defects."[94] William Grayson admitted that the president is "fettered in some parts, and as unlimited in others as a Roman Dictator."[95] Many Federalists sensed that the force necessary to enforce the laws potentially exceeds the law. The danger is always that the force upon which the law depends might supplant it, but Madison and others maintained that "public force must be used, when resistance to the law require[s] it, otherwise the society itself must be destroyed."[96]

Presidential Powers and Emergencies

The ability to deal with emergencies—whether by express grants of constitutional authority, delegations of power by Congress, or claims of inherent if unspecified executive power—was always an important consideration for proponents of a strong presidency. Even explicit grants of specific powers were frequently justified as emergency powers. The pardon power is a case in point. For instance, an anonymous pamphleteer in Virginia argued that the pardon power should be placed "in no other hands" than the chief executive "so long as laws can not provide for every case that may happen."[97] A "single man of prudence and good sense is better fitted" to exercise this power responsibly "than any numerous body whatever" because the "reflection that the fate of a fellow-creature depended on his *sole fiat* would naturally inspire scrupulousness and caution." "An Impartial Citizen" defended the pardon power on the grounds that "human sagacity cannot devise any law, but what, in its operations, may in some instances bear hard. It is impossible by any general law, to prevent punishments from being in some unforeseen cases, inadequate to offences."[98]

Contrary to Machiavelli's advice on the need for extraordinary punishments, Hamilton suggested that "the benign prerogative of pardoning" contributed to the maintenance of justice and respect for law, which would otherwise "wear a countenance too sanguinary and cruel" (LXXIV, 422). Hamilton rejected the idea that severity was always (or even usually) appropriate in those critical circumstances that seem to call for extraordinary displays of force and severity. Considerations of time were just as important to Hamilton as they were for Machiavelli in this context, but Hamilton came to the very opposite conclusion regarding the relative merits of leniency and severity: "the principal argument for reposing the power of pardoning in this case in the Chief Magistrate is this: in seasons of insurrection or rebellion, there are often critical moments when a well-timed offer of pardon to the insurgents or rebels may restore the tranquillity of the commonwealth; and which, if suffered to pass unimproved, it may never be possible afterwards to recall" (LXXIV, 423). The urgency of the situation is such that the "loss of a week, a day, an hour, may sometimes be fatal" (LXXIV, 423). This is exactly the same argument used in the Federal Convention. Other ordinary powers were also pressed into the service of the president's campaign against emergencies. Hamilton defended the president's power to make recess appointments as a useful expedient when "it might be necessary for the public service to fill [an office] without delay" (LXVII, 391). The power to convene Congress was also defended as a necessary measure to be exercised "on extraordinary occasions," as in cases of foreign attack or rebellion (LXIX, 397).

As already noted, there are aspects of Federalist constitutional thought that are inconsistent with the idea that constitutional government means a government of limited powers. Once again, it is Hamilton who exemplified this strain of Federalist thought. His narrow definition of a "limited Constitution" as "one which contains certain specified exceptions to the legislative authority" (LXXVIII, 438) directly contradicted the party line formulated by James Wilson that the proposed Constitution contained only enumerated powers. His exclusion of executive power from this formulation was no oversight. To carve out exceptions to executive power—as he understood it—would be contrary to both the ultimate ends of government and the essence of executive power. The executive is the part of government responsible for responding to emergencies, which recognize no limits or exceptions. Hamilton did not allow for the outright violation of express constitutional strictures, but he did permit a kind of flexibility inconsistent with perhaps the primary objective of a written constitution: to establish definite procedures and fixed rules for the activities of government. Wrote Hamilton: "Constitutions of civil government are not to be framed upon a calculation of existing exigencies, but upon a combination of these with the probable exigencies of ages, according to the natural and tried course of human affairs. Nothing, therefore, can be more fallacious than to infer the extent of any power proper to be lodged in the national government from an estimate of its immediate necessities. There ought to be a CAPACITY to provide for future contingencies as they may happen; and as these are illimitable in their nature, so it is impossible safely to limit that capacity" (XXXIV, 227). If a written constitution serves any purpose at all, it is to establish regularity in modes of governmental action and impose a modicum of order on the flux of politics, but the upshot of Hamilton's argument was that agents of government could exceed the strict bounds of their authority when dictated by necessity. The lesson of history, he claimed, is "that no precise bounds could be set to the national exigencies; that a power equal to every possible contingency must exist somewhere in the government" (XXVI, 198).

Roger Sherman addressed the topic of emergency powers in similar terms. He warned against placing too many restrictions on the power of government and even argued against a bill of rights because these limitations would not only hamper the government's ability to deal with unexpected contingencies but would also undermine the liberties of the people in the long run! In language reminiscent of Locke's discussion of prerogative, Sherman made the general point that "it is possible that in the infinite variety of events, it might become improper strictly to adhere to any one provision that has ever been proposed to be stipulated." [99] In discussing the constitutional role of the president, Iredell cautioned against placing too many limits on government power: "When a power is acknowledged to be necessary, it is a very dangerous thing to prescribe limits to it; for men must have a greater confidence in their own wisdom than I think any men are entitled to, who imagine they can form such exact ideas of all possible contingencies as to be sure that the restriction they propose will not do more harm than good." [100]

The debate in the Constitutional Convention on the presidential oath of office indicates that both the supporters and the opponents of a strong executive recognized the discretionary character of even ordinary exercises of executive power. The former favored language that would validate exercises of discretionary judgment, while the latter strived for wording that would constrain it as much as possible. The Hamilton Plan enjoined the president to swear to execute the *office* "to the utmost of his Judgment & power" (Farrand III, 624). This version of the oath would not only have made the president's personal judgment the standard of propriety, it also would have made the office rather than the Constitution the primary concern of the president. As an alternative, Mason and Madison proposed an oath requiring the president to swear that that he "will to the best of my judgment and power preserve protect and defend the Constitution of the U.S." (Farrand II, 427). The Committee of Style adopted this version in its draft of the Constitution, but the Convention ultimately substituted the subjective standard of "judgment" for the more observable standard of "abilities" (Farrand II, 621). Unfortunately, the records for the debate that day (September 15)—which lasted until 6:00, unusually late for the Convention—are extremely sketchy and offer few clues about the specific arguments that carried the day in favor of the change.

Given the enormous discretion that the president would have in carrying out both routine responsibilities and extraordinary tasks, it was well understood that the personal qualities of the president would be extremely important. But it was not simply a question of "specialized know-how," technical expertise, or long experience—as critical as these were to the administration of government.[101] It was also a question of moral character. The responsibilities of the president were so great, and the powers so ill-defined, that it became imperative to find the right person for the office. That is why virtue was so pivotal to this scheme of constitutional government. Virtue was supposed to help the executive resist temptations to exceed constitutional limits for the wrong reasons and encourage the use of power for the right ones. But the question is why the Framers or Federalists believed that any person could be trusted not to abuse such enormous powers. The answer lies in the notable qualities of George Washington.

Republicanism and Personal Government

George Washington stands as the towering figure in the debate over the role that virtue was expected to play in the formation of the young republic. The universal expectation that he would serve as the first president probably did more to allay fears about the powers of the presidency than all the speeches, pamphlets, and declarations of the Federalists put together.

An avid reader of Plutarch who scrupulously modeled his personal life and political conduct after the "great men" of antiquity, Washington himself came to epitomize the qualities of disinterestedness, patriotism, and probity he had emulated. He set a consistent example of virtue that not only vindicated republican aspirations and hopes but also justified the extraordinary powers vested in the executive. Iredell asked how anyone could possibly object to the potential influence of Virginia in the new government "on account of the high character of General Washington, confessedly the greatest man of the present age, and perhaps equal to any that has existed in any period of time."[102] The common conviction that the presidency and, more importantly, the Constitution would fail without him indicated not only the political fragility of the

Constitution but the inegalitarian implications of virtue as well. In a letter dated October 30, 1787, Gouverneur Morris implicitly acknowledged the unrepublican nature of the presidency when he told Washington that "your great and decided Superiority leads Men willingly to put you in a Place which will not add to your personal Dignity, nor raise you higher than you already stand: but they would not willingly put any other Person in the same Situation because they feel the Elevation of others as operating (by Comparison) the Degradation of themselves."[103] Morris's remark suggested just how dependent upon the force of individual personality and character the Constitution would be. It is simply not the case that the office of the presidency automatically confers its holder with authority and legitimacy, for the officeholder can actually enhance the legitimacy and authority of the office—or, perhaps fatally, diminish them. The weakened position of the presidency after Watergate validates Morris's idea that the dignity of the office would depend in some measure on the dignity of its occupant.

Morris's letter to Washington is important because it articulates clearly and explicitly a common Federalist attitude that there are inherent limits to the official, formal, and institutional sources of authority. Morris, Hamilton, and Iredell, among others, accepted the Lockean insight that personal character constitutes a basis of authority and power nearly as significant as those impersonal institutional sources contained in the Constitution or the laws. In this letter Morris explained why it was constitutionally imperative, and not simply politically expedient, that Washington assume the office of the presidency. In his closing paragraph, Morris combined the Blackstonean metaphor of constitutional machinery and the Humean psychology of custom and habit in a sexist plea to convince Washington of the thoroughly personalized nature of new governments:

> I will add my Conviction that of all Men you are best fitted to fill that Office. Your cool steady Temper is *indispensably necessary* [emphasis in original] to give a firm and manly Tone to the new Government. To constitute a well poised political Machine is the Task of no common Workman; but to set it in Motion requires still greater Qualities. When once a-going, it will proceed a long Time from the original Impulse. Time gives to primary Institutions the mighty Power of Habit, and Custom, the Law both of Wise Men and Fools, serves as the great Commentator of human Establishments, and like other Commentators as frequently obscures as it explains the Text. *No Constitution is the same*

on Paper and in Life. The Exercise of Authority depends on personal Character; [emphasis added] and the Whip and Reins by which an able Charioteer governs unruly Steeds will only hurl the unskillful Presumer with more speedy & head-long Violence to the Earth. The Horses once trained may be managed by a Woman or a Child; not so when they first feel the Bit.[104]

Morris repudiated the reasoning that motivated the Athenian lawgiver Solon, who had entered into voluntary exile after drafting the laws for Athens, and instead adopted the Machiavellian position that certain situations call for specific types of leaders because laws and institutions are not self-executing. As explained in chapter 1, it is the "modes" established by certain actors that animate the otherwise impersonal and inert "orders" of a constitution. The machinery of government would stall unless Washington gave it its first "impulse," because only he possessed the requisite skills and talents necessary to execute this crucial task.[105] While some hoped Washington would legitimize and augment the powers of the presidency, others appealed to him to set an example of modesty. The Marquis de Lafayette beseeched Washington to accept the office since "You only Can Settle that Political Machine" and mitigate "the Great Powers and Possible Continuance of the President."[106] If it is true that the Federalists "were mainly interested in the machinery of government," it was because a proper understanding of the mechanics of government was necessary to figure out who would make the best operator.[107]

Not everyone was placated by the prospect of Washington's presidency. Since many features of the presidency were designed or justified with Washington in mind, even many supporters of the Constitution worried that an office designed for virtuous individuals could do great harm if it fell into the wrong hands. Jefferson objected to "the perpetual re-eligibility of the same president, [which defect] will probably not be cured during the life of General Washington. [H]is merit has blinded our countrymen to the dangers of making so important an officer re-eligible."[108] He expressed disappointment that the re-eligibility of the president "has scarcely excited an objection in America." That Washington would undoubtedly become the first president posed certain dangers to the long-term stability and health of the nation, for "our jealousy is only put to sleep by the unlimited confidence we all repose in the person to whom we all look as our President. [A]fter him inferior characters may perhaps succeed, and awaken us to the danger which his merit has led us into."[109]

Fears that the presidency could become a lifetime or even a hereditary office were not necessarily based on paranoid speculation. The belief that Washington's virtues and abilities might be hereditary led Americans like Anthony Wayne to declare a "wish [that] he had a *son*."[110] Washington's character was such that it caused people to see hereditary government in a positive light and even, more alarmingly, to question the necessity of certain limits on executive power. Pierce Butler's remarks concerning the likelihood of a Washington presidency exemplify the ambivalence felt by many: "His Powers are full great, and greater than I was disposed to make them. Nor, Entre Nous, do I believe they would have been so great had not many of the members cast their eyes towards General Washington as President; and shaped their Ideas of the Powers to be given to a President, by their opinions of his Virtue. So that the Man, who by his Patriotism and Virtue, Contributed largely to the Emancipation of his Country, may be the Innocent means of its being, when He is lay'd low, oppress'd" (Farrand III, 302). As discussed in the next chapter, this and other acknowledgments that virtue plays a role in determining the scope of presidential power signified a major shift toward an elitist conception of representation anathema to egalitarian republicans.

Hamilton confirmed the idea that the full form of the system had not yet been determined when he noted "'tis time only that can mature and perfect so compound a system, can liquidate the meaning of all the parts, and can adjust them to each other in a harmonious and consistent WHOLE" (LXXXII, 458). In doing so he also repudiated the notion that government could ever be completely impersonal. His frequent use of the term *administration* reflected his conviction that the stability and legitimacy of political institutions depend on the character of those who fill its offices, not just their structural integrity. Administration, he explained, "in its most usual and perhaps in its most precise signification . . . is limited to executive details" (LXXII, 412), but, as we have seen, the meaning of "executive details" is neither simple nor straightforward. Administration for Hamilton signified much more than the mere implementation of the will of the legislature or some impersonal, bureaucratic ideal.[111] It denoted a form of rule that was highly personal. The choice of Washington to lead the new government would be critical to its success because a "good administration will conciliate the confidence and affection of the people and perhaps enable the government to acquire more consistency than the proposed constitution seems to promise for so great a country."[112] What is so interesting about this remark, contained in a note Hamilton wrote to himself and never published, is its combination of skepticism about the design of the Constitution and optimism that a good administration could compensate for its inherent defects and limits. Even though he considered Alexander Pope's famous couplet an overstatement of the ability of good administration to overcome the imperfections of a government, Hamilton nevertheless agreed that it contained some wisdom. He reminded his readers of the obvious but significant fact that republics are "administered by *men* as well as" monarchies (VI, 106). The people's "confidence in and obedience to a government will commonly be proportioned to the goodness or badness of its administration" (XXVII, 201).

The Pacificus-Helvidius Debate

Federalists like Hamilton, Madison, and Morris thought it was more prudent to create a flexible but limited constitution capable of meeting any crisis rather than fashion a legalistic constitution whose powers were narrowly defined and completely enumerated. Even Madison, who would later become a leading strict constructionist, opposed juridical limits on certain governmental functions during the ratification struggle. In *Federalist* 41 he observed: "It is in vain to oppose constitutional barriers to the impulse of self-preservation." In the very next sentence he took a position on this subject that would sharply divide Hamilton and Jefferson, who represented the different paths a Lockean approach to constitutionalism might take: "It is worse than in vain; because it plants in the Constitution itself necessary usurpations of power, every precedent of which is a germ of unnecessary and multiplied repetitions" (XLI, 267). All three men agreed with Locke's notion that the executive must sometimes exceed the law for the good of the community, but they disagreed over the constitutional implications of this idea.[113] Locke, who justified his political ideals in terms of natural law, formulated his ideas on the subject before written constitutions became commonplace, but the Americans took the idea of a written constitution for granted, so they had to decide exactly how much specificity would be appropriate when it comes to executive power. Their differences on this matter came to a head in 1793.

In that year, the American government had to decide whether to honor its treaty with Revolutionary War ally France and battle the British once again or to maintain neutrality and let the newly minted republic spread the values of the French Revolution on its own in the face of fierce European resistance.

This diplomatic crisis gave the Founders a practical opportunity to resolve some questions about the meaning of executive power the text of the Constitution failed to answer. With Hamilton's strong advice and encouragement, Washington issued a Proclamation of Neutrality designed to appease England and keep the fledgling republic out of war, but this act infuriated the Francophile Jefferson and his new protégé Madison. The controversy produced one of the most interesting and important debates on the nature of presidential power in the entire history of American political thought. The immediate issue in the pamphlet war that raged between the erstwhile colleagues was whether the president had the authority to issue the Proclamation, which arguably contravened a treaty with France, but the dispute had much broader implications for the nature and scope of executive power and the proper construction of the Constitution.

Writing under the pseudonym "Pacificus," Hamilton began the first essay by asserting the president's exclusive responsibilities in foreign relations, including the construction of treaties, but quickly launched into a dissertation upon the proper constitutional interpretation of executive powers more generally. He affirmed the president's power to interpret treaties as a corollary of his general power to interpret all laws he is charged with enforcing: "The President is the constitutional EXECUTOR of the laws. . . . He who is to execute the laws must first judge for himself of their meaning."[114] He contended that the president's power to issue the proclamation derives from a general grant of executive power and argued forcefully that the vesting clause of Article II gives the president vast powers incident to "the execution of all laws, the laws of Nations as well as the Municipal law, which recognises and adopts those laws."[115]·

Although the first essay in the "Pacificus" series makes it clear that the president possesses the full panoply of executive powers not shared concurrently with the legislature (for instance, the appointment power, the war powers, and the treaty power), it is still not entirely clear what specific powers that includes. Hamilton never offered a full specification of executive powers in law. Neither he nor anyone else could, according to him, because "the detail would be endless." This was a position he held consistently throughout his political life. In response to an earlier query by William Heth, Hamilton explained "that there is and necessarily must be a great number of undefined particulars incident to the general duty of every officer, for the requiring of which no special warrant is to be found in any law." If no "law could ever define the details of the duty of a Secretary of the Treasury," what hope is there that such a thing would be possible for the president? In no nation in the world does the law provide "for a thousandth part of the duties which each officer performs in the great political machine & which unless performed would arrest its motions."[116] Not only is express legal specification impossible, it is undesirable too. Formal rules and regulations, Hamilton insisted, are more likely to be hindrances than aids in dealing with unexpected occurrences. The discretionary nature of executive power allows for the possibility of a manual override where the machinery of government would otherwise stall or malfunction. To impose strict and insuperable legal restrictions on the executive would be to saddle that officer with the very same defects executive power is supposed to bypass.

Now that Hamilton was involved in an actual dispute with serious constitutional implications for the shape of executive power, he took the opportunity to advance even more forcefully and explicitly the theory of constitutionalism he and Madison both endorsed in the *Federalist*. Hamilton's key point was that enumerated powers did not exhaust the powers of government, at least not where the executive was concerned:

> It would not consist with the rules of sound construction to consider this enumeration of particular authorities as derogating from the more comprehensive grant contained in the general clause, further than as it may be coupled with express restrictions or qualifications; as in regard to the cooperation of the Senate in the appointment of Officers and the making of treaties; which are qualifica[tions] of the general executive powers of appointing officers and making treaties: Because the difficulty of a complete and perfect specification of all the cases of Executive authority would naturally dictate the use of general terms—and would render it improbable that a specification of certain particulars was designed as a substitute for those terms when antecedently used.[117]

Enumeration, Hamilton explained, serves as both a specification of and a restriction on powers. The general terms of the first clause in Article II are not merely prefatory or introductory; they make a general grant of power that belongs exclusively to the president.

Hamilton went on to explain that certain rules of interpretation are implied by the very structure and language of Article II. In contrast to the general grant of executive power, which must be construed generously, exceptions to the president's powers must be interpreted as narrowly as possible.

The enumeration ought rather therefore to be considered as intended by way of greater caution, to specify and regulate the principal articles *implied in the definition of Executive Power*; leaving the rest to flow from the general grant of that power, interpreted in conformity to other parts [of] the constitution and to the principles of free government. (Emphasis added)

The general doctrine then of our constitution is, that the EXECUTIVE POWER of the Nation is vested in the President; subject only to the *exceptions* and *qu[a]lifications* which are expressed in the instrument.[118]

Hamilton's "Pacificus" essays explicated much of what he was forced to leave implicit because of sensitive political considerations during the ratification struggle. The inability (or perhaps reluctance) of Founders like Hamilton to define executive power or specify its functions reflected the elusive and ineffable qualities of executive power as much as any deficiencies in the language or human faculties.

Madison challenged Hamilton's interpretation of presidential powers in a series of essays written under the pseudonym "Helvidius." He castigated the author of the "Pacificus" papers for advancing principles "which strike at the vitals of [the] constitution."[119] Although both men were guilty of demagoguery, Madison's impugned Hamilton's motives, accusing him of betraying the principles of republican government.[120] The Virginian quoted at length from *Federalist* 75 to expose Hamilton's alleged inconsistency, but the passage actually vindicates Hamilton's view that executive power cannot be reduced to precise rules. It must have pleased Madison immensely to be able to throw the following words back in Hamilton's face, but a careful reading of the excerpt shows that Hamilton never actually denied the president anything he was now affirming: "The essence of the legislative authority, is to enact laws; or, in other words, to prescribe rules for the regulation of the society. While the execution of the laws and the employment of the common strength, either for this purpose [making treaties] or for the common defence, seem to comprise *all* the functions of the *executive magistrate*" (emphasis in original).[121] Hamilton defined the very *essence* of legislative authority with total confidence and without qualification but ventured only a tentative statement of the functions of the executive. The typically bold and assertive Hamilton carefully proposed that "the execution of the laws and the employment of the common strength" only "*seem* to comprise all the functions of the executive magistrate," leaving open the possibility that there might be other functions.[122] And his reference to "the employment of the common strength" opened up vast possibilities that were explored in essays that did not deal explicitly with executive power but implied its use (most notably *Federalist* 23). The real inconsistency, if there was one, in Hamilton's writings was only in the confident certainty with which he now explained executive power.

In fact, it was Madison who retreated from his earlier position that practice would have to settle the meaning and scope of uncertain powers. He now reduced the executive to the function of executing laws and denied that executive powers were even involved where no laws were concerned. "The natural province of the executive magistrate is to execute laws, as that of the legislature is to make laws. All his acts therefore, properly executive, must presuppose the existence of the laws to be executed."[123] The boldness with which Madison expressed himself here was missing during the Constitutional Convention, where Madison futilely asked for clarification of executive power. Moreover, this remark conflicts with his stated position in the Convention that this would render the executive a subservient branch of government.

An additional indication of Madison's dramatic departure from earlier positions was his new hostility toward the use of certain modern writers, particularly Locke and Montesquieu. In contrast to his extensive reliance on ancient and modern authorities on government during the ratification struggle, Madison now summarily dismissed the use of political thinkers "not only because our own reason and our own constitution are the best guides; but because a just analysis and discrimination of the powers of government, according to their executive, legislative and judiciary qualities are not to be expected in the works of the most received jurists, who wrote before a critical attention was paid to those objects, and with their eyes too much on monarchical governments, where all powers are confounded in the sovereignty of the prince."[124] Madison now renounced liberal luminaries like Locke and Montesquieu on the grounds that they were "evidently warped by a regard to the particular government of England, to which one of them owed allegiance; and the other professed an admiration bordering on idolatry."[125] This is the same "celebrated Montesquieu" that Madison invoked more than once to buttress his claims about the attainability of an extended republic in the *Federalist*. Moreover, his insistence that all executive acts "must presuppose the existence of the laws to be executed" is diametrically opposed to his assertion in the *Federalist* that "it is in vain to oppose constitutional barriers to the impulse of self-preservation" (XLI).[126] Madison also denied that the Constitution permits the "intermixture and consolidation of different powers" in spite of his famous argument—ostensibly borrowed from Montesquieu—that the separation of powers only prohibits a single branch of government from possessing "the *whole* power of another department" where it already possesses the whole power of its department (XLVII, 304, emphasis in original).[127] Indeed, the entire thrust of Madison's argument in the "Helvidius" essays rests on premises that he had denied in his previous writings. His attempt to dissociate American constitutionalism from Locke and Montesquieu was a disingenuous—and unpersuasive—partisan ploy to discredit a political opponent who remained steadfastly committed to ideas the two had articulated during the ratification struggle.

In a strange way, Hamilton's nemesis Jefferson actually vindicated those ideas as president. Like Hamilton, Jefferson rejected the legalistic mindset so often associated with liberal constitutionalism and endorsed the Lockean proposition that "self-preservation is paramount to all law." "Should we have ever gained our Revolution," Jefferson asked, "if we had bound our hands by manacles of the law, not only in the beginning, but in any part of the revolutionary conflict? There are extreme cases where the laws become inadequate even to their own preservation, and where, the universal resource is a dictator, or martial law."[128] Jefferson recognized the paradox of law: it is an instrument for collective preservation that can undermine or impede the quest for preservation. In a famous letter to John B. Colvin, Jefferson emphasized that extralegal, and even illegal, actions by the executive are sometimes required to serve the purpose of the law.[129] Jefferson also indicated in the same letter that much less than dire necessity or self-preservation justifies expeditious extralegal executive action. Explaining his own thinking leading up to the Louisiana Purchase, Jefferson wrote that if the "Executive of the Union" had the opportunity to purchase "the Floridas for a reasonable sum" but knew that protracted congressional deliberations might nix the deal, the executive ought to act despite the prohibition of the law. "Ought the Executive, in that case, and with that foreknowledge, to have secured the good of his country, and to have trusted to their justice for the transgression of the law? I think he ought, and that the act would have been approved." The executive is justified in violating the law to enhance the long-term safety and security of the country even when it is not immediately threatened or at risk. All the examples cited by Jefferson "constituted a law of necessity and self-preservation, and rendered the *salus populi* supreme over the written law."[130] Ever the man of contradictions, the strict constructionist approved of violations of the law when required and justified by extra-constitutional considerations.

Even though both Hamilton's and Jefferson's positions were firmly rooted in Lockean soil, the Virginian never tried to justify extralegal executive actions in terms of a "general grant" of executive power or other questionable constitutional constructions.[131] Unlike Hamilton, he did not think a written constitution should permit anything beyond the four corners of the text. That is to say, he rejected the Federalists' flexible theory of constitutionalism, but he shared their conception of executive power—at least where extraordinary circumstances were concerned. As demonstrated in his "Opinion on the Constitutionality of a National Bank," Jefferson vehemently rejected attempts to stretch the meaning of the Constitution beyond the powers specifically enumerated in the text as undemocratic usurpations of authority.[132] Instead of distorting the meaning of the Constitution to justify necessary exercises of presidential prerogative, Jefferson preferred to have executives violate the law outright and let the public judge the propriety of their acts: "It is incumbent on those only who accept of great charges, to risk themselves on great occasions, when the safety of the nation, or some of its very high interests are at stake. An officer is bound to obey orders; yet he would be a bad one who should do it in cases for which they were not intended, and which involved the most important consequences." Jefferson further explained that "the good officer is bound to draw it at his own peril, and throw himself on the justice of his country and the rectitude of his motives."[133] If, as Locke suggested, the executive's actions and motives were good, then the public would approve. And, just as important for Jefferson, the integrity of the Constitution would be preserved.

The problem with Jefferson's conception of executive power, though, is that it turns the executive into a lawbreaker. In effect, Jefferson required presidents to throw themselves on the mercy of the court of public opinion. They would have to seek an indemnity, or "retroactive ratification," from the legislature for their admitted lawbreaking.[134] Even though actual "necessity" was supposed to be sufficient justification for what Jefferson regarded as unconstitutional exercises of power, his recommended policy left no doubt that the president had violated the law. Under Hamilton's more expansive reading of the Constitution, a president acting with the best intentions for the sake of the nation could always find justification for his actions in the Constitution itself.

There would be no need to resort to first principles or other political abstractions, since the Constitution was designed to meet any situation. Jefferson decried this approach because it vitiated the purpose of a constitution as he understood it. Both approaches have their merits, but each one comes with a distinct set of costs. Hamilton's insulates the president from accusations of criminality, but it turns virtue into the primary, if not the only, check on executive power. Jefferson's protects the integrity of the Constitution, but it renders it ineffective in dealing with the exigencies of politics. Moreover, it makes the character of the president even *more* important inasmuch as a president who lacks virtue will find it exceedingly difficult to convince the public—as Jefferson said he must—that his "motives" were pure. That is the implication, if not the stated purpose, of Jefferson's claim that the public would "judge the rectitude of his motives" rather than the merit of his policies. The Virginian acknowledged the critical importance of virtue in the entire executive branch, but he never explained if this was enough to overcome the accusations of criminality that his approach to prerogative invited.[135]

Conclusion

Hamilton is reported as having prophesied that the day will most assuredly come "when every vital interest of the state will be merged in the all-absorbing question of *who shall be the next* PRESIDENT?" (Farrand III, 410). Legal, political, constitutional, bureaucratic, and technological changes in government have minimized that dependence on the single individual dreaded by the Anti-Federalists, but the history of the presidency in the modern era has largely confirmed Hamilton's prediction. The system the Founders developed has adapted in ways they could not have foreseen, and some of its most indeterminate features have been "liquidated and ascertained" with varying degrees of permanence by custom (executive agreements, for instance), statute (the War Powers Act), adjudication (*Ex parte Milligan* and *In re Neagle*), amendment (Amendment XXV), and economic crisis (the Great Depression). Many others are still open to bitter contestation. The system was of course designed to minimize the inconveniences and uncertainties that result from unsettled and irregular practices, but a certain degree of flexibility at crucial moments was the price the framers and supporters of the Constitution were willing to pay to ensure the continuance and growth of the nation. Contrary to its critics, liberalism is not irrepressibly hostile to the uncertainties of politics. The first liberal Constitution designed to govern an entire nation is a testament to the complexity and ambivalence of early liberal political thought. It never finally resolved tensions between competing interests like the rule of law and executive power, liberty and energy, precisely because it recognized that they could not be resolved once and for all without serious harm to one or the other. As the next chapter shows, the best that American thinkers could hope for was that virtuous individuals would mitigate these problems to a tolerable degree.

CHAPTER SIX

A "Patriotic and Dignifying President"

Republican Virtue and the Presidency

> *Our President must be matured by the experience of years,* and being born among us, his character at thirty-five must be fully understood. Wisdom, virtue, and active qualities of mind and body can alone make him the first servant of a free and enlightened people.　　　TENCH COXE

The Crisis of Republicanism and the Redemption of Virtue

The conventional wisdom among eighteenth-century political writers was that the fate of free government ultimately depends on the public virtue of ordinary citizens. For Americans steeped in the writings of Aristotle, Plutarch, Cicero, Machiavelli, Harrington, Milton, and Sidney, virtue denoted a willingness to place the public good above private interest.[1] During the early stages of the American Revolution, supporters of independence frequently expressed their hopes that the noble struggle for liberty would inspire the people to exert themselves and make personal sacrifices for the good of their country. Men like John Adams invoked a highly demanding ideal of republican citizenship that required the subordination of private interests to the public good when they worried that liberty could not be preserved without "a possitive Passion for the public good . . . established in the Minds of the People."[2] Self-styled patriots believed that America could avoid the corruption and tyranny that had corroded liberty in Europe if it relied on the public virtue of dedicated citizens.[3] But the actual conduct of most citizens failed to live up to this high-minded republican ideal, leading some to suspect that Americans were no more virtuous than their decadent and licentious European counterparts.[4] Within a few years, James Madison and others were coming to the conclusion that the popular "rage for paper money," the "injustice" of the laws, and shameless profiteering at the public's expense signaled a "crisis" in republicanism.[5] The representatives of the people turned out to be no better. According to Madison, the propensity to place "personal interest" before the "public good" called "into question the fundamental principles of republican Government."[6]

It would have been easy to abandon all hope for virtue in a modern commercial society that condoned the self-interested and avaricious passions unleashed by the rise of capitalism, but national leaders like Madison, Hamilton, and Gouverneur Morris refused to accept the idea that each and every individual without distinction was motivated solely by narrow self-interest. But instead of revising their understanding of public virtue or replacing it with qualities more consistent with a self-interested, profit-driven mercantile society, they reconsidered their ideas about who could be expected to possess public virtue. Rather than look for such virtue in the citizenry as a whole, as republicans recommended, they restricted their search to those few who would occupy the highest offices of government. What had been a matter of general civic concern was now an elite affair to be centered on the presidency. As Gordon Wood has shown, many leaders "continued to hold out the possibility of virtuous politics," even though "only a few were liberally educated and cosmopolitan enough to have the breadth of perspective to comprehend all the different interests of society."[7]

The rhetoric of public virtue pervaded discussions of the presidency during debates over ratification of the Constitution. Hamilton, Morris, and other Federalists sought to placate the fears of a public that had been taught to be deeply suspicious of executive power not only by highlighting the legal and institutional checks on the office but also by stressing the likelihood that the president would be motivated by the public spirit that the people themselves lacked.[8] In contrast to the destructive passions of "mankind in general," Hamilton and like-minded Federalists indicated, "there may be in every government a few choice spirits, who may act from more worthy motives."[9] While some Founders still emphasized and worked to cultivate the civic virtue of ordinary citizens through the spread of public education, the establishment of a national university, and other schemes for the improvement of the people, the most outspoken champions of a strong national executive expected the presidency to be the primary repository of those republican virtues that they believed could no longer be realistically expected from ordinary citizens.[10]

Since executive power is so highly personalized and resistant to institutional formalization, it became critical to ensure that the person entrusted with this power would possess virtues conducive to responsible behavior, such that the new government would be energetic yet limited. Such virtues would be especially important in extraordinary circumstances, when the regular institutional checks and balances that normally constrain executive conduct might not work with their normal effectiveness—if at all. The virtue of the president would not replace institutional constraints, but it would make it unnecessary to resort to them in times of crisis, when maximum flexibility is required. And in ordinary circumstances, the expected virtue of the president would contribute to the smooth operation of the machinery of government. In the New York Ratifying Convention, Hamilton proclaimed that the proposed system was rendered "as perfect as human forms can be," in large part because the Constitution "connected the virtue of your rulers with their interest."[11] Virtue was both the first and last line of defense against the abuse of power: a representative who embodied republican virtue would not have to be checked in the first place, and only the virtue of such a representative would prevent him or her from abusing power when the normal operation of institutional checks and balances is disrupted.

A modicum of virtue was expected in all three branches of government, but the presidency was expected to be the "summit of republican renown."[12] Not only were the virtues of the president expected to exceed those of other national officeholders, they were also expected to be thoroughly republican in character. Most Federalists supposed that the president would embody "those principles of wisdom and virtue which form the pillars of republican government."[13] It was thus not so much the "popular" foundation of executive power in the United States that was supposed to make the presidency republican as its continued linkage to a quintessentially republican conception of virtue.[14] The argument put forth by Federalists was that the president would and should embody the republican virtues of patriotism, disinterestedness, and love of liberty, not to mention the related moral qualities of probity, honesty, and integrity that ought to be expected of any officeholder.

Contrary to the prevailing scholarly view that the institutional machinery of liberal constitutionalism in America was specifically designed to obviate the need for virtue in government, this chapter demonstrates that many Federalists expected this machinery to supplement, not supplant, virtue in the presidency. That is, the system would work best when it reinforced the republican virtues the president already possessed. The expectation was that institutional checks and balances would strengthen existing virtues, not make them unnecessary or generate them where they did not already exist. As discussed in chapter 5, many Federalists contended that there were definite limits to the capacity of institutional arrangements to control or redirect the dangerous passions. As confident as they were in the ability of the "new science of politics" to guide them in constructing a constitutional system that could safely channel the self-interests and base passions of officeholders toward the public good, the Founders attempted to build the requirement of virtue into the very structure of the liberal constitutional order they were establishing. In other words, the Constitution did not merely establish a minimum threshold of virtue or erect institutions that would merely elicit behavior that just appeared to be virtuous. Rather, the system was also designed to attract virtuous individuals and help keep them that way. A republican ideal of virtue was built into the structure of the Constitution as a standard according to which presidents could be judged.[15] It was unthinkable to place "so important a trust" (LXVIII, 393) as the presidency in an individual who did not exemplify the republican virtues of patriotism, disinterestedness, and love of liberty. But where such virtues were lacking, Federalists insisted that the Constitution's checks and balances would minimize the damage an ambitious or avaricious president could do by channeling their passions and interests in the right direction.

By relocating republican virtue to the presidency, Federalists reaffirmed its indispensability in free government but denied the idea that the existence of such virtue was necessarily dependent on or derived from the citizenry as a whole. In doing so, they severed the traditional link between republicanism and civic virtue. When Federalists like Madison did acknowledge the virtue of ordinary citizens, it was done not to imply that they could be trusted with political authority themselves but merely to affirm that there was still sufficient virtue to ensure the possibility of the right individuals for public office. Instead of an explicit denial of the Anti-Federalist charge that the supporters of the Constitution "expect nothing but the most exalted integrity and sublime virtue" as security against the abuse of power by representatives, Madison turned the table on his opponents by insinuating that they lacked his supreme republican confidence in the ability of the people "to select men of virtue and wisdom." But in offering his reassurance that "there [would] be sufficient virtue and intelligence in the community" to make a wise decision, Madison and other Federalists who made this point ended up acknowledging the gulf that the Constitution would open up between the people and their representatives.[16]

In fact, it was the Federalists—often noted for their quintessentially modern and "realistic" articulation of the role of selfish interests and ordinary passions in politics—who preserved a hospitable place for virtue in the office of the presidency. The great irony of American political thought in the Founding is that the supposed modernists were the ones who insisted that virtue was both desirable and possible in the highest levels of government, whereas the presumptive heirs of the republican legacy, the Anti-Federalists, generally had such a pessimistic conception of human nature that they denied the possibility of virtue where political power was concerned. A thorough examination of the ratification debates demonstrate that it was not the Federalists but rather their self-proclaimed republican antagonists who rejected virtue and promoted exclusively juridico-institutional solutions to the problems of political power. Far from creating "a system that has no necessary place and makes no provision for men of the founding kind," Federalists expected the machinery of government to work most safely and reliably when it was operated by properly-motivated personnel.[17]

The Presidential Perspective on Space and Time

Public virtue was a key term in the vocabulary of eighteenth-century political debate, but some of the most influential works of moral and political philosophy had taught that the self-sacrificing qualities associated with republicanism were not only rare but also unnatural. Popular writers from Montaigne to Mandeville raised questions about the possibility and even the desirability of those austere and heroic virtues associated with the martial character of ancient republics.[18] Even the Third Earl of Shaftesbury, a pupil of Locke and the celebrated founder of the "moral sense" school of philosophy, who held that public virtue was natural to rational creatures, admitted that "those publick Affections" were extremely demanding and had to be reinforced by private interests.[19] It was contrary to human nature to expect the selfless virtues celebrated in antiquity and privileged in republican discourse to motivate the bulk of citizens, who are governed by self-love and preoccupied with "their present and immediate interest." But as even Hume, the premier eighteenth-century theorist of the passions and interests, had acknowledged, there were noteworthy exceptions to the general rule that reason "can never pretend to any other office than to serve and obey" the passions.[20] Since Hume's philosophical writings demonstrated the relative permanence and resilience of character traits over time, the empirical and historical confirmation contained in the *Histories* that disinterestedness and patriotism were indeed possible if uncommon heartened those whose republican sensibilities were offended and challenged by the crass selfishness of politics in the states. But proving just the limited existence of such virtue still left the formidable task of identifying individuals with these attributes. The framers designed the Electoral College, their most original contribution to representative government, with this task in mind.

Gouverneur Morris's injunction to his fellow delegates "to extend their views beyond the present moment of time; beyond the narrow limits of place from which they derived their political origin" (Farrand I, 529) was a guiding principle in the creation of the presidency. The *Federalist* articulated the rationale for this and other features of the presidency by formulating a theory of the presidency that sought to reconcile the ideals of classical republicanism with the insights of modern social and political psychology developed by Locke and Hume. Accordingly, the essays on the presidency contain both descriptive and normative elements defined in terms of the unique spatio-temporal situation of the president.

Hamilton's account of executive power suggests that the president ideally operates in a spatio-temporal framework that gives him a uniquely far-ranging perspective, both in historical and in geographical terms. Hamilton and other Federalists suggested that a unique combination of personal and institutional factors could explain the president's expansive orientation. On the one hand, there are a variety of institutionally determined external elements conducive to the adoption of a political perspective that is extensive in both spatial and temporal terms. For instance, the president's mode of election establishes a truly national constituency, while a lengthy duration in office and the prospect of reelection provide an incentive to look ahead into the distant future. Madison noted approvingly that the president "will be the choice of the people at large," which will incline him to take a wider view of matters than the provincial officers in the states or even in Congress.[21] Unlike legislators, who are preoccupied with smaller and more immediate affairs, the president's temporal and spatial horizons would be expansive. On the other hand, it is necessary that the president be internally, or habitually, disposed and motivated to assume the perspective required by these institutional imperatives in the first place. Thus, a demonstrated ability to place general concerns over particular ones, and long-term objectives before short-term ones, is essential. The Electoral College was the institutional mechanism that would identify individuals with a reputation for such qualities.[22] These traits were defined both negatively, in contradistinction to the partisan demagoguery and self-serving behavior rampant in the states, and positively, in light of the moral example of "that great patriot chief" George Washington, whose "character, in short, is A TISSUE OF VIRTUES."[23]

Hamilton's extensive use of temporal language in his discussions of the presidency illustrates the characteristics unique to the executive.[24] There are two aspects to the distinct temporal orientation of the president, one short-term, the other long-term. The first aspect involves the ability to respond immediately and expeditiously to pressing emergencies, foreign and domestic. The presidency was designed to address one of the most contemptible defects of government under the Articles of Confederation, namely its tendency to produce "tedious delays" (XXII, 180). Political imperatives frequently demand immediate action and leave little or no time for extensive reflection or deliberation of the kind rightly expected and required from the legislature and the judiciary. Expediency, decisiveness, and dispatch—the hallmarks of executive power—are central to this aspect of the president's time frame. The executive is often confronted with political importunities that require temporary expedients, which nevertheless have far-reaching consequences, both politically and historically.

The second aspect of the president's temporal orientation involves the ability, based on experience, prudence, and wisdom, to foresee the long-term consequences of present actions and to plan for the future accordingly. This quality is most relevant in the routine, day-to-day, detail-oriented administration of government, which requires a long-term perspective because it has such "long-lasting" consequences for the nation.[25] The most important consequences concerned the preservation of liberty in the long run. It was not simply a matter of establishing an efficient or energetic government but also a matter of maintaining a free government that protected the rights of all citizens. One way to do this was to take precautions that would prevent an emergency from developing in the first place. Many Federalists warned that it would be necessary to give the government sufficient powers and leeway to act in the best interests of the country now so that it would not be necessary to resort to a dictator later when things spin out of control. A far-sighted leader might have to take unpopular measures in the present to avoid the need for more drastic measures that are harmful to liberty in the future. According to Hamilton, a long duration in office is one of the principal means of ensuring that the president can "withstand the temporary delusion" that might lead the people to sacrifice their long-term interests in favor of short-term whims. It is necessary for sufficient time to elapse before the people can form a "cool and sedate" judgment on the merits of a policy pertaining to the protection of property or the enforcement of the laws (LXXI, 410).

At first blush, this may seem inconsistent with the demand for dispatch and energy. After all, the qualities that enable an executive to recognize and respond to an emergency with the required swiftness and urgency are not necessarily the same qualities that would enable an executive to develop long-term plans with the needed prescience and foresight. But according to the theory of executive power articulated by Hamilton and other Federalists, the broad spatial and temporal horizons expected to inform the president's conduct are exactly what enable the president to deal with the exigencies of politics in a way that does not forfeit future interests for the sake of momentary pressures. Executive power is exercised most distinctively at both temporal extremes. Unlike the legislature, the executive is constituted in a way that enables the president to act with sufficient vigor and dispatch in the immediate present and to make plans with ample foresight and prescience for the distant future. The presidency combines the ability to act with suddenness and dispatch with the disposition to take a long-range perspective. The former is largely a result of institutional design, while the latter is mainly a reflection of personal character, though personal and institutional factors play a role in both time frames.

A long-term perspective is closely related to the spatial field in which the executive operates. Washington indicated the close association in his own mind between executive power and an expansive perspective when he criticized the opponents of "a strong & energetic government" (itself closely related to executive power) as either "narrow minded politicians" or as "under the influence of local views" (Farrand III, 56). Because a single individual is elected to superintend the affairs of the entire nation, the president would be especially concerned with matters of far-reaching importance, both geographically and historically. Pierce Butler argued for a single executive because he would be "most likely to answer the purpose of the remote parts. If one man should be appointed he would be responsible to the whole, and would be impartial to its interests" (Farrand I, 88). That is also why Gouverneur Morris believed the president would be "the general Guardian of the National interests" (Farrand II, 541; see also II, 52). In the case of the presidency, Madison's famous remark in *Federalist* 51 that the "interest of the man must be connected with the constitutional rights of the place" (LI, 319) means that the chief executive must be interested in the welfare of the entire community and not just a particular portion of it. That interest and responsibility imply a special solicitude for the long-term welfare of the nation, not just the satisfaction of fleeting passions ignited in the heat of the moment.

Federalists argued that the institutional structures of the new government would provide the necessary external impulse to adopt an extensive view of the public good. But as discussed in chapter 5, they recognized the limitations of institutional mechanisms. The electoral system, the system of checks and balances, the possibility of criminal punishment, and other external factors would all encourage the president to exercise powers in a broad-minded and far-sighted manner, but external incentives might only go so far when the people themselves are clamoring for actions that might undermine their own interests and liberties in the long run. There was a sense that institutional structures could not engender dispositions that were not already present— they could only reinforce them. As a consequence, it would be best if the president were already disposed by habit and inclination to take a broad view of matters. This would require the classic intellectual virtues of "wisdom" and "prudence," but the virtues that Federalists stressed in their remarks on the presidency were moral in nature. The virtues most conducive to the adoption of an expansive and extensive view of the public good corresponded most closely to the republican virtues of patriotism, disinterestedness, and love of liberty.

Unfortunately, the virtues that were most necessary seemed to be in short supply. Fortunately, though, a deficit among the multitudes did not necessarily mean a total lack of this precious item. Federalists generally had very low expectations of the people and even of most representatives, but in public and in private they expressed very high hopes for the presidency. Based on subtle lessons learned from Hume, their conception of the presidency roundly rejected the modern notion that individuals are governed and motivated by the same passions and interests. The "noblest minds" may be ruled by the same passions (the "love of fame" or the like), but these passions differ markedly from the common passions that rule ordinary individuals.[26] Designed in reaction against the self-serving and amateur politics of the previous decade, the ideal president was to be a throwback to the bygone era of outstanding deeds and selfless devotion to the republic memorialized in Plutarch's *Lives* and other historical accounts of heroic ancient figures.[27] As they understood it, the presidency was to be the consummate expression of a specialized politics of virtue that reserves a place for the patriotic service of dedicated and public-spirited political elites. According to this understanding, which combined those elements of executive power delineated by Locke, Hume, and Blackstone, the president would be the republicanized incarnation of Bolingbroke's "Patriot-King," who would restore virtue and dignity to government in pursuit of the common good of the polity.[28] For most Federalists, it was not enough to preserve the political forms of republicanism without also securing a space for the possibility of distinction and honor "for a patriotic and dignifying President."[29]

During the Convention, Madison expressed doubts that "personal merit alone could be the ground of political exaltation" in a republic committed to the principle of equality (Farrand I, 138), but when the time came to convince the public that the proposed government would be safe, he and others were claiming that the republic could not endure without it. Federalists presented a vision of virtuous executive leadership and patriotism in their repeated insistence on the likelihood that the mode of presidential election and the requirements of the office would attract only the most "fit characters." The exceptional example of George Washington served as a useful reminder that genuine and incorruptible virtue had not been extinguished in the young republic. Impeachment and other checks would serve as necessary safeguards in case suitable individuals were not located, but the suggestion made by leading Federalists and lesser lights alike was that a virtuous president would make those precautions superfluous.

Not everyone agreed this was a good idea, though. Jefferson, for one, thought that the great error committed by the Framers was their "presumption that all succeeding rulers would be as honest as themselves."[30] Even though Anti-Federalists frequently distorted the potential dangers of the proposed

Constitution, many of them offered incisive critiques of the presidency that are still worth examining because they provide useful reminders that it is in many respects an anomalous, monarchical institution. The perceived inconsistency between the animating spirit of the Revolution and the underlying principles of the Constitution was a common theme among many Anti-Federalists, who considered it "preposterous" that "in the moment when we were free to chuse for ourselves we have made use of the privilege to adopt the form of government we had abjured."[31] Many critics complained that the presidency was monarchical in terms of both its powers and its aura. In the memorable words of Patrick Henry, "It squints towards monarchy."[32]

Implicit in the accusations of many Anti-Federalists was the notion that the presidency was antithetical to republican sensibilities. Everyone was concerned about the potential threat to liberty, but several Anti-Federalists also expressed concerns about the principle of equality. At a minimum, republicanism meant nonmonarchical government,[33] and the resurgence of the single executive threatened to undo the republican experiment in America.[34] "Cato" explicitly warned that a single executive would inevitably possess "the splendor of a prince" and produce a "dangerous inequality."[35] Although republicans had always glorified the outstanding accomplishments of great men, lingering fears about the weakness of human nature and the corrupting influence of power made them reluctant to trust even proven heroes with great power for very long, which is why they often insisted upon ostracism and rotation in their political systems.

Even more obnoxious to Anti-Federalists than the suggestion that a single individual could adequately represent the interests of an entire country was the elitist notion that one individual could resist the siren song of power while everyone else succumbed to its deadly lure.[36] For all their intramural differences and disagreements, nearly all Anti-Federalists exhibited a congenital cynicism and a deep-seated distrust of power.[37] They vehemently rejected as Pollyannaish the proposition that "we shall always have good men to govern us."[38] Reassurances that the president (and senators) could be safely trusted with certain powers because they would be "most distinguished by their abilities and virtue" (LXIV, 376) only reinforced fears that the Constitution did not take enough precautions against corruption and abuse of power. The Federalist position that the president would be an individual "preeminent for ability and virtue" was all too redolent of the detestable doctrine that "the king can do no wrong." Some critics even suggested that "the love of domination is generally in proportion to talents, abilities and superior requirements, and that the men of the greatest purity of intention may be made instruments of despotism in the hands of the *artful and designing.*"[39]

Cultural and ideological considerations were just as important as more strictly political and constitutional ones in opposing the president, who, many Anti-Federalists feared, "will be the source, the fountain of honor, profit and power, whose influence like the rays of the sun will diffuse itself far and wide, will exhale all *democratical vapours* and break the *clouds of popular insurrection.*"[40] There were pervasive fears that the president would undermine republican mores and manners because "his political character" would compel him to maintain a court and "appear with the splendor of a prince."[41] In short, the creation of the presidency represented a hostile retreat from the local and popular forms of politics practiced under the Articles of Confederation. For some, this represented the highest fulfillment of the Revolution, but for others it signified its lowest betrayal.

The Single Executive and Responsibility

The idea that the powers of the executive would be concentrated in a single person seems like a foregone conclusion to contemporary Americans, but there was nothing inevitable or natural about the idea of a single executive to Americans in 1787. Vesting executive powers in a single president was such a remarkable feat that Hamilton himself was forced to admit that it is the "first thing which strikes our attention" (LXIX, 396). In response to critics who warned that abuses of power were more likely to occur with a single executive than the alternatives, Hamilton and others borrowed the concept of "responsibility" developed by Swiss political theorist Jean-Louis de Lolme to argue that the singularity of the office was precisely what would allow both external structural checks and internal moral checks to operate. The inability to hide behind or pass blame on to others would induce good behavior even in a bad president, and the inability of others to drag down the president would encourage good individuals to seek the office. As a Virginia Federalist remarked, the unity of the president and the fact that "*he* and *he alone* is responsible for any perversion of power" would constitute "our greatest safety."[42]

From the very beginning of the Constitutional Convention, the delegates agreed that the new government would be divided into three branches of government, but there was no immediate consensus regarding the numerical composition of the executive. Edmund Randolph favored a plural executive consisting of three magistrates chosen from different sections of the country because he believed that "a unity in the Executive magistracy" would form "the foetus of monarchy" (Farrand I, 66). Rejecting the logic of de Lolme, many Anti-Federalists argued that placing so much power in the hands of a single individual "is repugnant to Republican principles" and suggested either a plural executive or an executive constrained by a council as more consistent with the principles of free government.[43] The Anti-Federalists' mistrust of individual judgment expressed their attachment to the Aristotelian notion that the judgment of many is always superior to the judgment of one or few, even if they are experts.[44] Opponents of unity in the executive did not deny the theory that a single executive would exhibit greater energy and dispatch than the alternatives, but the political and social implications of a single executive were intolerable.[45] George Mason, one of the sharpest critics of the presidency, agreed that "Power and Responsibility are two things essential to a good Executive," but he thought that power could not "be safely given," nor responsibility "insured," without an executive council.[46]

Proponents of a single executive stressed the superior energy and vigor of a single executive, but they also advanced the argument that a single executive would be more "responsible." Anticipating the more complex psychological arguments that Federalists would later put forth, John Rutledge insisted at the Philadelphia Convention that a "single man would feel the greatest responsibility and administer the public affairs best" (Farrand I, 65). In a paraphrase of Hume's point, Hamilton explained that "regard to reputation has a less active influence when the infamy of a bad action is to be divided among a number than when it is to fall singly upon one" (XV, 150). A single executive would also be more accountable because it is so much easier to assign blame when responsibility is undivided, in contrast to the legislature, where responsibility was dispersed so widely that it was virtually nonexistent. Wilson expounded the maxim that would become the mantra of single executive advocates: "In order to controul the Legislative authority, you must divide it. In order to controul the Executive you must unite it. One man will be more responsible than three" (Farrand I, 254).[47] Even some of those who were ambivalent about the Constitution accepted the link between singularity and responsibility. In rejecting the idea of a plural executive or an executive council, James Monroe explained that the president "should stand alone unsupported, and unprotected except by the integrity of his heart and the rectitude of his conduct."[48]

The knowledge that a single executive alone would be held accountable for malfeasance or maladministration would be a powerful psychological inducement to good behavior. An executive council was ultimately rejected by the Convention because it could give a president "protection" for "his wrong measures," thereby undermining his responsibility (Farrand II, 542). Wilson argued that the president will have "responsibility" because the "executive power is better to be trusted when it has no *screen*," a point Hamilton reiterated in the *Federalist* (LXX, 408).[49] James Iredell considered the lack of an executive council one of the guarantees that "the President must be *personally responsible* for every thing."[50] Such a system "will in general be thought infinitely more *safe*, as well as more *just*." Furthermore, however fit a council might be "for the purpose of advising, [it] might be very ill-qualified, especially in a critical period, for an active executive department."[51]

A plural executive, in which powers were shared equally by a number of officials, would be even worse than a council.[52] Based on de Lolme's observation that "all multiplication of the executive is rather dangerous than friendly to liberty," Hamilton considered "that maxim of republican jealousy which considers power as safer in the hands of a number of men than of a single man" completely misguided in the case of the executive (LXX, 407). Not only would plurality in the executive "impede or frustrate the most important measures of the government in the most critical emergencies," but it would also "add[] to the difficulty of detection" by enabling any one or all of the power-holders to blame the others for "a pernicious measure, or series of pernicious measures" (LXX, 404, 406). According to Hamilton, responsibility in the executive involves the possibility of "censure" and "punishment." But because actions that rise to the level of criminal liability would be infrequent (and perhaps difficult to prove, given the inevitable secrecy with which certain executive functions would be conducted), less formal sanctions would be even more important in holding the executive accountable. But because "mutual accusations" would be inevitable in cases of wrongdoing by a plural executive, it would be best to have a single executive who would absorb the full brunt of public opprobrium (LXX, 406).

As discussed in chapter 5, the single most important reason offered in favor of unity in the executive was that a single executive would maximize energy in government. Because a single executive would be free from the internal dissensions and divisions that afflict numerous bodies, the executive could act with unparalleled dispatch, vigor, and secrecy. The need for "vigor and expedition" in the executive, especially during domestic emergencies and times of war, means that the executive cannot be judged by the same standards that apply to the legislature, which ought to conduct its business in an open and deliberative manner (LXX, 405). To the extent that secrecy is required to carry out necessary functions related to national security, no matter how many people make up the executive, the personal character of the executive takes on added importance. Although questionable claims of confidentiality under the rubric of "executive privilege" seem to be on the rise, the possibility of abuse was a price that Hamilton, at least, was willing to pay in order to preserve the independence of the executive branch. The requirement of secrecy would make it nearly impossible to make an objective determination of culpability from the outside, in contrast to the remodeled Congress, which would maintain a public journal of its proceedings and occasionally record the votes of its members.

The notion of responsibility was meant to ease the tension between an "energetic" executive and the "genius of republican liberty" (XXXVII, 243), but the rhetoric that some Federalists used to describe the advantages of a single executive was reminiscent of claims frequently made in favor of monarchy.[53] Employing Humean psychology and Blackstonean imagery to support the idea of a single executive, the "Federal Farmer" argued that "there must be a visible point serving as a common centre in the government, towards which to draw their eyes and attachments." An executive council simply would not do because it inevitably divides the people's attentions and affections.[54] Even attempts to reconcile the presidency with the ideals of popular government sometimes invoked monarchical tropes, as when Tench Coxe suggested that the president would embody the majesty and dignity of the people.[55] Perhaps no one stressed the importance of dignity in the executive as much as Hamilton, though.[56] Borrowing heavily from de Lolme and Blackstone during his epic six-hour speech at the Constitutional Convention on June 18, Hamilton argued that an investment of monarchical dignity in the presidency would serve as an important counterweight against "the amazing violence & turbulence of the democratic spirit" (Farrand I, 289). The ultimate purpose of his infamous speech has been the subject of considerable scholarly dispute, but there is no question that Hamilton's explicit and positive invocations of the British monarchy contributed to his (largely undeserved) reputation as a monarchist and tainted many of fellow Federalists for a long time.

That some Federalists continued to employ the vocabulary of monarchy to describe the presidency provides some indication of how difficult it was not only to reconcile the presidency with republican principles but also to describe executive power without reference to monarchy. Nathaniel Gorham pointed to the tension between a single executive and popular government when he suggested that more energy in the general government was needed as a countervailing force against the excesses of democracy.[57] Sentiments like these provoked accusations that Federalists had betrayed the spirit of the Revolution. Richard Henry Lee expressed his absolute "astonish[ment] that the same people who have just emerged from a long & cruel war in defence of liberty, should now agree to fix an elective despotism upon themselves & their posterity!"[58]

In response to criticisms that a single executive was irreconcilable with the spirit of republicanism, Federalists like James Wilson argued vigorously and consistently for the democratic credentials of the presidency. In an argument he would repeat in his *Lectures on Law,* the future Supreme Court justice reassured worried Pennsylvanians in the state's ratifying convention that the president "will be chosen in such a manner that he may be justly styled *the man of the people,*" that he will have no particular attachments "but will watch over the whole with paternal care and affection."[59] That the executive's mode of selection was ultimately grounded on the principle of popular sovereignty also provided some assurance that the person selected would possess the requisite public virtues. Speaking with the benefit of experience and the example of George Washington before him, Wilson stated that there was an "agreeable prospect . . . that the publick choice will fall upon a man, in whom distinguished abilities will be joined and sublimed by distinguished virtues—on a man, who, on the necessary foundation of a private character, decent, respected, and dignified, will build all the great, and honest, and candid qualities, from which an elevated station derives its most beautiful luster, and publick life its most splendid embellishments."[60] Wilson's claims of virtue in the president could be dismissed as the flattering hyperbole of a man who wanted to pay tribute to the extraordinary qualities of the first president, but the arguments put forth by some Federalists during the struggle over ratification indicate that virtue in the presidency was not left to chance. In their view, the system was designed to elevate individuals with a reputation for virtue.

Elections and Elitism

Representative government has come to be closely associated and even identified with democracy since the nineteenth century, but it is important to remember that it was originally conceived as an alternative to democracy. As Bernard Manin demonstrates, the eighteenth-century founders of representative government, including its foremost American theorist James Madison, viewed it "as an essentially different and superior form of government" because its reliance on elections, as opposed to the more egalitarian system of lots and rotation, was expected to lead to the selection of "notables" superior to the people who chose them.[61] The elites they sought were not necessarily to be defined by their wealth or social status, as progressive historians contended, but by their moral character.[62]

Standard accounts of the *Federalist* frequently claim that the Constitution's institutional designs and structural mechanisms were designed to obviate the need for reliance on the personal virtue of rulers. However, Madison and his fellow Federalists argued that the effective operation of these devices simultaneously presupposes the presence of political virtue and guards against its absence, at least in theory. According to the arguments they advanced, the Framers were optimistic enough to preserve a place for virtue in the presidency but clever enough to hedge their bets against disappointment. Institutional and structural checks and balances were expected to work best when they reinforced virtue that an individual already possesses, but they were also designed to operate well enough even without that virtue.

One of the key documents in the development of this position is Madison's *Federalist* 10. Even though the essay is best known for Madison's argument that an extensive republic can successfully solve the problem of factions, which threaten the rights of others and undermine the common good, it also articulates a theory of representation that looks to virtuous elites to "refine and enlarge the public views" (X, 126). In doing so, it lays the foundations for Hamilton's more fully developed argument that the presidency was designed to attract and reward only those characters renowned for their superior virtue and wisdom.[63] Even though much of Madison's argument in this famous essay sounds incredibly naive when one considers the rise of political parties and the dominance of interest group politics today, it expressed the hope that republican virtue could survive a social environment inhospitable to its flourishing.

The primary aim of Madison's essay was to demonstrate that freedom would still be possible in an extended sphere of government. As Hamilton noted in the preceding essay, Anti-Federalists regularly invoked the authority of the celebrated Montesquieu "on the necessity of a contracted territory for a republican government" because of a widespread, but erroneous, belief that an extensive territory always results in monarchical despotism where it does not splinter "into an infinity of little, jealous, clashing, tumultuous commonwealths" (IX, 119, 120). While Hamilton quoted Montesquieu at length to demonstrate that the French thinker supported the possibility of an extensive republic, Madison relied on Hume to demonstrate that "a well-constructed Union" that took in a diverse array of interests and passions would be able "to break and control the violence of faction" by dealing with the effects rather than the causes of this republican disorder (X, 122).[64] Refusing to destroy the liberty that gives rise to factions as a "remedy . . . worse than the disease" and rejecting the idea of giving all citizens the same passions, interests, and opinions as a proposal inconsistent with human nature left Madison with no option but to accept the inevitable proliferation of factions throughout the social body. While the growth of factions could be fatal to a small republic because of the possibility that a single faction becomes so large that it dominates the rest, the growth of factions would actually be beneficial in a large republic. By extending the sphere to "take in a greater variety of parties and interests," it becomes much more difficult for a single faction to achieve a majority that could dominate the rest. Instead, factions in an extended sphere would cancel each other out (X, 127). But in making the argument that the best way to deal with factions was to allow them to multiply, Madison conceded that the people could no longer be expected to live up to those republican ideals of virtue that required citizens to pursue "the permanent and aggregate interests of the community" over the partial interests of their party, sect, profession, or class (X, 123).

But while Madison resigned himself to the idea that ordinary citizens would divide themselves into groups that pursued their narrow self-interests, he argued that extending the sphere of government would promote the election of representatives "who possess the most attractive merit and the most diffusive and established characters." Because it would be "difficult for unworthy candidates" to rely on electoral tactics that appeal to only a small cross-section of the community, as happens so often in the states, an extended republic would result in "the substitution of representatives whose enlightened views and virtuous sentiments render them superior to local prejudices and to schemes of injustice" (X, 127, 128). John Jay anticipated this argument in *Federalist* 3, where he stated confidently that the quality of government would improve considerably under the proposed Constitution because a "more general and extensive reputation for talents and other qualifications will be necessary to recommend men to offices under the national government" (III, 95).[65] The theme sounded by all three coauthors was that an extensive sphere increased the "probability of a fit choice." Accordingly, senators would possess more "wisdom," "patriotism," and "love of justice" than representatives in the House, and the president would surpass senators in these qualities, resulting in a pyramidal structure of virtue among elected officials in the federal government. In short, the more extensive the electoral sphere, the more virtuous the representative was likely to be.[66]

Representatives, including the president, would manifest their virtues not in replicating the character of their constituents but in representing their long-term interests, including the preservation of liberty in the long run. *The key to* Federalist *10 is not so much the refinement of the views of the people, as the refinement of the quality of elected officials.*[67] The electoral system was expected to operate as a filtration system that eliminates the impurities of partiality and factionalism to distill the virtues essential to the public good—as representatives understand it.[68] If the proposed system worked as planned, the partiality and parochialism that tend to undermine the public good in narrower spheres would dissipate as the sphere is extended. Madison explained that the effect of an extended sphere on the system of representation was "to refine and enlarge the public views by passing them through the medium of a chosen body of citizens, whose wisdom may best discern the true interest of their country and whose patriotism and love of justice will be least likely to sacrifice it to temporary or partial considerations" (X, 126). Each enlargement of the electoral sphere—from a single congressional district, on to an entire state, and all the way to the whole country—would expand and elevate the outlook of the representative.[69]

In light of the unfortunate but unavoidable fact that the people divide themselves into factions, each enlargement of the sphere would actually increase the likelihood that the representative's opinion "will be more consonant to the public good than if pronounced by the people themselves" (X, 126). Because the president would have the most comprehensive perspective of all,

Hamilton was able to contend that the president would be justified in resisting the "temporary delusion" of the people whenever a disagreement over the public good arises (LXXI, 410). Though other Federalists did not necessarily go so far as to suggest that the superior virtues of representatives entitled them to ignore the "temporary delusion" of the people, they expressed similar confidence in the ability of such officials to know what would be best. Washington wrote that he had "no doubt" that "those who are first called to act under the proposed Government . . . will have wisdom enough . . . and will have virtue enough to pursue that line of conduct which will most conduce to the happiness of their Country."[70]

In response to Madison's elitist "policy of refining the popular appointments by successive filtrations" (Farrand I, 50), Anti-Federalists generally argued that the purpose of representation is to provide the most faithful reflection of the people's expressed interests. The purpose of representation was not to filter out the impurities in the people's views but to mirror the people as accurately as possible—even, as George Mason put it, in their "Diseases" (Farrand I, 142). As Robert Yates put it in his "Brutus" essays, rulers "must be such, as to possess, be disposed, and consequently qualified to declare the sentiments of the people; for if they do not know, or are not disposed to speak the sentiments of the people, the people do not govern."[71] The mirror theory of representation required not only intimate familiarity with the wants and interests of the people but the zeal to promote them, as well. If virtue were to be found anywhere in the new government, Anti-Federalists argued, it would be in the institution that would be closest to the people: the House of Representatives.[72] Some Federalists replied to these criticisms by reiterating the original point. At the Pennsylvania Convention, Wilson asserted unapologetically that "it is of more consequence to be able to know the true interest of the people, than their faces, and of more consequence still to have virtue enough to pursue the means of carrying that knowledge usefully into effect."[73]

It might be argued that the extended republic and the complex system of direct and indirect elections were designed to reorient or re-channel the selfish interests and passions of politicians who are not altogether different from—that is, no better than—the people. Perhaps the system does not so much identify individuals with the proper dispositions as check and constrain those destructive passions and interests in all of us. That is one of the most common interpretations of the *Federalist,* which famously relies on "ambition to counteract ambition" because "reflection on human nature" does not permit the dangerously naive view that men are or can even behave like "angels" where power is at stake (LI, 319).[74]

There is no doubt that "auxiliary precautions" were taken to make sure that government would be obliged "to control itself" through the operation of "opposite and rival interests" (LI, 320), but the notion that the Constitution's institutional checks and balances made virtue unnecessary simply ignores the unambiguous and unequivocal language used by Federalists like Madison and Hamilton. Both sets of arguments appeared in the public and private writings and statements of Federalists. Even though they discussed the precautions taken against vicious and corrupt politicians, they always returned to the point that the system would elevate individuals who already have a reputation for being virtuous. Institutional arrangements would give representatives an incentive to behave well, but the expectation was that the electoral system would identify individuals superior in virtue and ability. Indeed, this was the way prominent Anti-Federalists understood proponents of the Constitution as well. Patrick Henry decried the "degrading and mortifying" implications of the Federalists' arguments: "It presupposes that the chosen few who go to Congress will have more upright hearts, and more enlightened minds, than those who are members of the individual Legislatures."[75]

The aim of attracting "fit characters" was not fully articulated until the ratification process was underway, but key Federalists had begun thinking about this before the Constitutional Convention met. In a set of notes on the "Vices of the Political System of the United States," Madison concluded his observations by noting, "An auxiliary desideratum for the melioration of the Republican form is such a process of elections as will most certainly extract from the mass of the society the purest and noblest characters which it contains; such as will at once feel most strongly the proper motives to pursue the end of their appointment, and be most capable to devise the proper means of attaining it."[76] When the framers debated the mode of presidential selection, they considered a variety of factors, including the most effective means of avoiding intrigue and cabal, the best method of keeping the executive independent of Congress, and the most reliable way of determining the moral character of the executive to prevent corruption and abuse of power (for example, Farrand II, 29–31, 100–101). Based on the choices the Convention had made, Hamilton insisted that the presidency was very likely to be filled by men of established reputation—those whose patriotism was renowned and unparalleled.[77] The new government was designed to keep dangerous passions in check, but it was not designed to make fundamental changes in human nature, either among the people or among their representatives. Good government ought to regulate the passions by promoting the calmer ones and controlling the bad ones, but it could not hope to instill proper dispositions that were not already there. The "defect of better motives" that makes "auxiliary precautions" (for example, the opposition of "rival interests") necessary to the preservation of liberty (XLI, 320) reaches potentially into every department of government, but it does not preclude the possibility of better motives. Madison, after all, spoke of the *defect,* not the *absence,* of better motives. As Hamilton argued, the president was expected to have the best motives of all. That "stern virtue" which is capable of resisting the temptations of material gain "is the growth of few soils," but Hamilton expressed great confidence that "there are men who could neither be distressed nor won into a sacrifice of their duty" (LXXIII, 417).

Perhaps the most notorious declaration of expected virtue in the proposed government was made at the Pennsylvania Ratifying Convention by that state's Chief Justice, Thomas McKean. In a widely reprinted—and widely reviled—speech, the jurist defended the general powers of the national government as "necessary to its existence and to the political happiness of the people."[78] But in explaining the necessity of these powers, McKean acknowledged the imperfections of the "system" and affirmed that "the wealth, the prosperity, and the freedom of the people must ultimately depend upon the administration of the best government." As he went on to explain, the form of government would ultimately matter less than the virtues of its representatives: "The wisdom, probity, and patriotism of the rulers will ever be the criterion of public prosperity; and hence it is, that despotism, if well administered, is the best form of government invented by human ingenuity. We have seen nations prosperous and happy under monarchies, aristocracies, and governments compounded of these, and to what can we ascribe their felicity but the wise and prudent conduct of those who exercise the powers of government?"[79] McKean's speech gave Anti-Federalists an easy target for their rhetorical arrows. He committed a grave republican sin in concurring with Alexander Pope's opinion that the administration of government was far more important than its form.[80] Even though Federalists who spoke or wrote following McKean's speech were much more circumspect, many of them continued to point to the expected virtue of representatives as security against abuses of power. Despite the furious outcry that McKean's remarks provoked, Hamilton made many of the same points in his discussion of the president's mode of election in the *Federalist* (LXVIII, 395).

Philadelphia merchant Peletiah Webster blithely dismissed the apprehensions of Anti-Federalists by pointing out that excessive restraints on power actually lead to greater mischiefs than "full" powers. The key to good government, he claimed, lies not in formalized checks but in virtue: "But after all, the *grand secret of forming a good government*, is, *to put good men into the administration*: for *wild, vicious, or idle men,* will ever make a bad government, let its principles be ever so good; but *grave, wise, and faithful men,* acting under a good constitution, will afford the best chance of security, peace, and prosperity, to the citizens, which can be derived from civil police, under the present disorders, and uncertainty of all earthly things."[81] Although he focused on Congress, Webster's moralistic arguments applied just as well to the presidency. He was confident that America will have "as strong and safe an *executive power,* as can be obtained under any form of government whatever," thanks in large part to the complex system of federal elections.[82] He insisted that any potential failures under the proposed government would be attributable to the defects of its personnel, not to flaws in its design. It was ultimately up to the people to appoint the right individuals since the "best constitution possible, even a divine one, badly administered, will make a bad government." Webster left it up to others to provide the theoretical justification for the safety of the presidency, but throughout his pamphlet he took it for granted that the "dignity" of government "will forever depend on the *wisdom* and *firmness* of the officers of government."

As occasional references to the "firmness" of the president's character indicate, the crucial assumption for Webster was that character was stable over time. The general stability of character was addressed even more explicitly by Edmund Pendleton, who remarked: "The President is produced still in the Representa[tive] Character, since what the man I elect For the purpose does, is done by me; his term is Short, & going into Office wth. the Confidence of America in his *Integrity,* can't be reasonably supposed in the course of 4 years to loose that Character, & Form dangerous Systems."[83] For these Americans, the "uncertainty of earthly things" justified reliance on character, which was regarded as a reliable predictor of future conduct. Their argument, which sounds as if it were lifted directly out of Locke's discussion of prerogative, was used to defend not just executive power but the foundations of the entire government as well. It is also a strikingly modern and Humean departure from the republican view that character becomes unreliable when mixed with power. The conception of character as reliable and steady over time stood in marked contrast to the classical view expressed by Cicero that even "a king at his best" might become a tyrant because "his character may change."[84] Despite Cicero's own misgivings, he developed a conception of "constancy" that "became something of a cliché in Enlightenment ethics." As Andrew Sabl explains, the notion of "constancy" adopted by Madison and other Federalists included consistency in one's character, consistency in attachments, and consistency in pursuits—all of which would contribute to long-term goals like liberty and justice "when short-term temptations, in the form of pleasure, ambition, or the like make this difficult."[85]

There was a persistent tension—even an inconsistency—in liberal (including Federalist) accounts of executive power. Because these writers generally denied that character fluctuated significantly or would change dramatically once an individual reached a certain level of maturity, it was necessary to identify and select individuals who already possessed the right qualities for political office. However, one of the basic tenets of seventeenth- and eighteenth-century psychology concerned the universality or "similitude" of the human passions. According to this line of reasoning, different individuals act similarly in similar conditions because the structure (if not the object) of the passions is the same in all individuals. Any individual placed in a situation where it is possible to abuse power will do so unless adequate checks are put in place. But if this were actually true, then character would be moot. Neither Locke nor Hume ever resolved the latent tension between liberal individualism, which posits the distinctness of different individuals, and modern psychology, which tends to reduce the dispositions and inclinations of individuals to a common matrix of passions and interests. The Federalists fared no better in resolving this tension, which is why they combined a demand for virtue with "auxiliary precautions." That they appealed to virtue at all was astounding and disturbing to many Anti-Federalists.

Perhaps the best evidence that the Federalists expected virtue to regulate presidential power comes from the reactions of Anti-Federalists. Nearly all Anti-Federalists thought it was ludicrous to depend on virtue or better motives in rulers.[86] Whenever the subject of presidential character and conduct came up, Anti-Federalists would insist that the only effective way to check the threatening ambitions of politicians was to appeal to the base motives of "self-interest" and "self-love." The debates in the Virginia Ratifying Convention are particularly instructive because Anti-Federalists there fixated on the expectation of virtue as one of the most glaring defects of the Constitution. In their remarks on the presidency, William Grayson warned that there was "nothing to prevent his corruption, but his virtue," while Patrick Henry complained that critics always got the same "unsatisfactory answer, that they [presidents] will be virtuous." [87] George Mason scoffed at the notion "that the cure for all evils—the virtue and integrity of our Representatives, will be thought a sufficient security." [88] Henry clearly had remarks like Webster's and McKean's in mind when he questioned whether "a mere patriotic profession will be equally operative and efficacious, as the check of self-love. . . . If you depend on your President's and Senator's patriotism, you are gone." [89]

Many Anti-Federalists were psychological pessimists who questioned any system of government that was not based on a realistic appraisal of human motives. Like other critics of the Constitution, Monroe insisted on the need for something more institutionally concrete than the expectation that the Electoral College would select a virtuous candidate, something that would operate directly on self-interest. But because the Framers ignored the supposed lessons of modern philosophy, Monroe reasoned, there was "nothing to prevent his [the president's] corruption, but his virtue, which is but precarious, [which means] we have not sufficient security." [90] Henry expressed similar sentiments when he complained that "in this great, this essential part of the Constitution, if you are safe, it is not from the Constitution, but from the virtues of the men in Government. If Gentlemen are willing to trust themselves and posterity to so slender and improbable a chance, they have greater strength of nerves than I have." [91] Although Henry's penchant for paranoid hyperbole prompted him to portray the entire Constitution as an engine of oppression devoid of safety devices, the Federalists did confirm his suspicions about the importance of virtue. They deployed their considerable rhetorical and analytical skills to prove that the Constitution was compatible with and conducive to liberty, but they never denied the insinuation that the virtue of representatives was a critical safeguard to liberty. The silence of the Virginia Federalists, who included Madison and Randolph (a latecomer to the cause), was a deafening admission of the Constitution's reliance on virtuous representatives. To the Anti-Federalists, the elitist tendencies of the Constitution signified a betrayal of public confidence and a repudiation of the egalitarian foundations of government.

One of the most important passages in the *Federalist* occurs in the seldom-cited fifty-seventh paper, which responds directly to Anti-Federalist accusations of elitism. Madison dealt with this objection by proclaiming that it is the very *purpose* of government to secure the rule of elites. He stated bluntly that "the aim of every political constitution is, or ought to be, first to obtain for rulers men who possess most wisdom to discern, and most virtue to pursue, the common good of society; and in the next place, to take the most effectual precautions for *keeping them virtuous* whilst they continue to hold their public trust" (LVII, 343, emphasis added). Significantly, Madison did not contend that constitutional government would *make* representatives virtuous or *instill* virtue in them. Instead, *it would locate wise and virtuous individuals and keep them that way.* The expectation was not that "auxiliary precautions" or checks and balances would supplant the need for virtue, but that they would supplement it.[92] The elaborate system of checks and balances that Madison defended in the *Federalist* was designed primarily with the aim not of producing good behavior in bad individuals but of "preventing the[] degeneracy" of good individuals (LVII, 343).

Madison's admission was not meant to be a concession to critics who warned that too much emphasis was placed on virtue. It was meant to be a vindication of the republican character of the Constitution, for the possibility of virtue in government signified confidence in the people themselves. Even if the people lacked the virtue to govern themselves directly, he argued that they had enough virtue to recognize and esteem virtue in candidates for higher office. Madison strenuously objected to the Anti-Federalist portrayal of human nature as irredeemably depraved because "the inference would be that there is not sufficient virtue among men for self-government." In his view, this was an unappealing proposition that would undermine the foundations and prospects of republican government, which "presupposes the existence of these qualities in a higher degree than any other form" (LV, 339). The elaborate system of presidential election was designed to accomplish the related goals of identifying men of virtue and preventing cabal and intrigue, which could undermine the independence of the president. At stake in the mode of presidential election particularly were the viability of republican government and the prospects of virtue in a modern regime.

Establishing the existence of virtue was one thing, but identifying it was another. Anti-Federalists never raised any ontological questions about the existence of such a thing as virtue or any deep epistemological concerns about the possibility of knowing what virtue is, but they did raise concerns that the sheer size of electoral districts would make it difficult to get to know the character of candidates for office. In fact, virtually no one questioned the possibility that a reputation for virtue might be based on false appearances. The principal defect of the proposed constitution, according to Yates, is that it fails to establish the familiarity between the people and their representatives necessary to "give reasonable ground for public trust." Government cannot long remain free if the people are not acquainted with the abilities and character of their representatives. The people, insisted Yates, "should be satisfied that those who represent them are men of integrity, who will pursue the good of the community with fidelity; and will not be turned aside from their duty by private interest, or corrupted by undue influence; and that they will have such a zeal for the good of those whom they represent, as to excite them to be diligent in their service. . . . a great part of them [the people] will, probably, not know the characters of their own members, much less that of a majority of those who will compose the foederal assembly; they will consist of men whose names they have never heard, and whose talents and regard for the public good, they are total strangers to." [93] This was doubly true of the president, who could not possibly hope to represent the diverse interests of the people of so vast a country as the United States. As many Anti-Federalists noted, the president's character would be known to only a few individuals, who would wield a disproportionate influence in government. But where "Brutus" saw an insuperable defect, "Publius" saw a tremendous advantage. Madison and Hamilton would take these very same observations regarding the extent of territory and draw entirely different conclusions. The large extent of territory and mode of election, they argued, would actually ensure that only individuals with the best reputations would ever achieve the presidency.

Whether or not Yates was right about the ability of the people to know the actual characters (as opposed to manufactured images) of their elected officials, he was absolutely correct in identifying scale as the major issue separating Federalists and Anti-Federalists. It was a truism among republican thinkers since antiquity that virtue and civic engagement are difficult if not impossible to sustain in an extensive polity. But the scale that would make it possible, according to Federalists, to find a person virtuous enough for the office of the presidency is also what, according to Anti-Federalists, would ultimately make virtue among the citizenry impossible to maintain. The fact that America was quickly becoming a commercial republic compounded the problem of virtue. Virtue at the pinnacle of government would come only at the expense of virtue in its foundations among the people.

Presidential Selection and a National Perspective

The express qualifications for president contained in Article II of the Constitution seem unremarkable at first, but the underlying rationale for those qualifications is actually quite revealing. The framers restricted eligibility for the other elective offices of the national government by age because it was a convenient proxy indicator of experience and maturity. But there were additional considerations in mandating the age of thirty-five for eligibility to the office of the presidency. The expectation was that a person's character was fixed and defined well enough by that age that presidential electors could make accurate judgments regarding a candidate's personal integrity.[94] Tench Coxe opined that "his character at thirty-five must be fully understood. Wisdom, virtue, and active qualities of mind and body can alone make him the first servant of a free and enlightened people." Coxe also suggested that the age requirement for the presidency addressed one of the main defects of hereditary monarchies, where imbeciles and infants "may wear the crown."[95] In the *Federalist* John Jay argued that the treaty power could safely be entrusted to the President and the Senate because citizens would select "those men only who have become most distinguished by their abilities and virtue, and in whom the people perceive just grounds for confidence." To a greater extent than either of his coauthors, Jay stressed the importance of the age qualification in helping to ensure that the treaty power would be exercised only by those "whose reputation for integrity inspires and merits confidence" (LXIV, 376). He suggested that by the ages of thirty and thirty-five, the characters of prospective senators and presidents, respectively, would be well enough established and known to the public to lodge safely such important powers (LXIV, 380).[96]

The Electoral College was widely recognized as one of the most innovative features of the Constitution. Despite its novelty, it was one of the few features of the Constitution admired even by its most vociferous critics, who usually deplored the Constitution's departures from time-tested practices. It elicited approval largely because it eliminated the "one great evil" most feared by Wilson and others: "cabal & corruption" (Farrand II, 501). Unlike alternatives such as selection by the national legislature, selection by the Electoral College was thought to guarantee the independence of the president. It was inconceivable that a president chosen in such an indirect manner would be beholden to an impermanent body that immediately disbanded after fulfilling its single function. Because the electors would meet for the first and only time on a specified date in their respective states (because of "their transient existence and their detached situation," LXVIII, 394), it was unlikely that any consideration other than the merit of candidates would enter into their deliberations.

It is impossible to judge the sincerity of such claims. After all, Federalists were engaged in a coordinated propaganda campaign to convince wary Americans that the enormous and potentially extraordinary powers of the presidency were compatible with the principles of republicanism and the aims of the Revolution. At the very least, many writers exaggerated the likelihood that future presidents would be paragons of public virtue. But whatever their real beliefs were, their public and private statements established a standard by which to judge the success of the system they were promoting. And even though the picture they presented was quite rosy, it was fairly consistent and coherent.

Hamilton was uncharacteristically cheery and naive in his description of the effects that the Electoral College would have in selecting a virtuous president:

> This process of election affords a moral certainty that the office of President will seldom fall to the lot of any man who is not in an eminent degree endowed with the requisite qualifications. Talents for low intrigue, and the little arts of popularity, may alone suffice to elevate a man to the first honors in a single State; but it will require other talents, and a different kind of merit, to establish him in the esteem and confidence of the whole Union, or of so considerable a portion of it as would be necessary to make him a successful candidate for the distinguished office of President of the United States. *It will not be too strong to say that there will be constant probability of seeing the station filled by characters pre-eminent for ability and virtue.* (LXVIII, 394–95, emphasis added)

Hamilton reiterated this point and reinforced Jay's reassurances concerning the treaty power in a later essay, where he predicted that this sensitive power could be entrusted to the president because "the office will always bid fair to be filled by men of such characters as to render their concurrence in the formation of treaties peculiarly desirable as well on the score of wisdom as on that of integrity" (LXXV, 426). Similarly, James Iredell stressed the "high personal character" of the president as "an additional check" against abuses of the treaty power.[97] The president's mode of selection seemed particularly well-suited to attract candidates renowned for their "disinterestedness."[98] That the president would be chosen by the country at large made it unthinkable that he or she would risk a reputation for patriotic public service by putting partial interests ahead of the interests of the whole.

The reputation of the president would not only be the basis for his or her selection, but it would also serve as a warranty against misconduct in office. The interests of the office and the interests of the person would coincide more completely in the president than in any other official by dint of the president's singularity. Individuals elevated to the office of the presidency would be loath to tarnish reputations carefully cultivated and established over time for the sake of petty gain or partisan politics. Madison predicted that "as a single magistrate too responsible, for the events of his administration, his pride will the more naturally revolt against a measure which might bring on him the reproach not only of partiality, but of a dishonorable surrender of national right."[99] The notion of "honor," which appears in the *Federalist* most often in discussions of the presidency, was the crucial link that connected the self-interest of the executive and the good of the public. Observations on the president's expected reluctance to tarnish his reputation and bring dishonor to the office of the presidency drew upon insights gleaned from the moral psychology of the Scottish school, which emphasized the positive role that the opinion and approval of others plays in promoting virtuous conduct. But an external reward like honor would not provide the proper incentive unless the president had already internalized a concern for the public good. The presidency was thus designed for a man like Washington, who constantly sought the "approval of his fellow-citizens."[100]

Elections were conceived not as referenda on specific policies but as mechanisms for the selection of patriotic statesmen. A common refrain among Federalists was the claim that only a candidate suffused with public virtue could ever gain the approval of the people. This is not to say that either the Framers or the Federalists intended to establish a plebiscitary presidency that would be reflective of or responsive to the momentary will of the people. The democratic idea of a "plebiscitarian president" thrust into "office on the basis of a mandate from the People for sweeping transformation" would not begin to take hold until the hotly contested election of 1800, but the elitist idea of a virtuous president who could be trusted with the enormous powers of the office because he was a "man of the people" who was not beholden to a particular party or interest was widely expressed by Federalists in 1787.[101] "A Native of Virginia" argued that the presidency was safe because "the Convention wisely judged that the President would in all probability be a man of great experience, and abilities, and as far as his powers extend, ought to be considered as representing the Union; and consequently would be well acquainted with the interests of the whole."[102] Because he will be selected by the whole country and not just one part of it, Wilson contended, he "will watch over the whole with paternal care and affection."[103] In a discussion of the ability of the proposed government to represent a variety of interests, Hamilton contrasted "the momentary humors or dispositions which may happen to prevail in particular parts of the society" with the superior dispositions of a "wise administration" of a "man whose situation leads to extensive inquiry and information" (XXXV, 235). If even legislative representatives in the new government were likely to promote policies "conducive to the general interests of the society" (XXXV, 235), it was virtually guaranteed that the president would adopt a general perspective. The complex mode of presidential election would prevent the selection of individuals with reputations for strong sectional or factional attachments and immunize the president from the "evils of party and intrigue."[104] "An Impartial Citizen" argued that the president could safely be entrusted with the veto power because "he will most infallibly object to any partial or oppressive law, unless he be actuated by the same narrow views [as legislators]: *which, from the mode of his election, cannot be supposed.*"[105]

What all of these remarks indicate is that national election was intended not to instill a national orientation but to *reinforce* the expansive perspective that individuals distinguished for their disinterestedness already possessed. George Nicholas's defense of the president's treaty power, for instance, relied on this premise: "The approbation of the President, who had no local views, being elected by no particular State, but by the people at large, was an *additional* security."[106] Because he "is elected by the people at large[,] [h]e will not have the local interests which the members of Congress may have." And because he will be "responsible to his constituents," he will be loath to jeopardize his position at the "summit of honor and esteem" only to be degraded "to the lowest infamy and disgrace."[107]

Notwithstanding widespread arguments that the Constitution created a complex system of structural checks and balances, many Federalists claimed that elections would be not only necessary checks on power but sufficient ones as well. James Kent, the great legal commentator, stated that "our true and only ground of security in this as well as in every other representative republic, consists in the election, the rotation, and the responsibility of those men to whom the administration of that government is committed." [108] Many Federalists seemed satisfied that the indirect form of popular election would elevate only fit characters to the presidency and that additional checks on the president would be supernumerary. Questioning the reliability of juridical checks contained in declarations of rights, Roger Sherman asserted that elections would provide the only real security against abuses of power. He argued that the re-eligibility of both the executive and the upper house in Congress "will be a very great Security for their fidelity in Office, and will likewise give much greater Stability and energy to government than an exclusion by rotation," as called for by many Anti-Federalists. [109]

The upshot of Sherman's argument is that the real security against abuses of power subsists in character. Character, according to this argument, is a more reliable predictor of behavior than external restraints. For the electoral process to work as some Federalists claimed, the president would have to be virtuous enough to seek reelection even in cases of emergency, when the temptation to circumvent the electoral process for the sake of national security concerns runs high. But neither Sherman nor the other Federalists ever proved to the satisfaction of Anti-Federalists that there was no danger from ambitious executives who might exploit a crisis to remain in office indefinitely. The key assumption underlying Sherman's argument is that the electoral process provides an effective means of identifying individuals with the right characters in the first place. The most effectual checks against encroachments on liberty exist in what is brought *to* the institutions of government rather than anything that inheres *in* those institutions.

This understanding of the purpose of elections meant that the electorate would ultimately be the most significant and effective check on presidential power. According to Wilson, the most dependable checks operated in the voting booths before a politician even takes office. "That *one* ticket may *turn* the election. In *battle,* every *soldier* should consider the *public safety* as depending on his *single arm*. At an *election,* every *citizen* should consider the *public happiness* as depending on his *single vote.*"[110] Not only did popular election make the people responsible for the quality of their government, it also made the president responsible to the people. Because the president would be elected by the people (albeit indirectly), Federalists described this officer variously as a "creature of the people," "the man of the people," (Charles Pinckney, Farrand III, 386), and "the Guardian of the people" (Gouverneur Morris, Farrand II, 53). References to the president as a "creature of the people" were intended to allay fears about the powers of the executive, but they also drew upon the idea that the people themselves were repositories of virtue. This was one of the rhetorical concessions a few Federalists were willing to make to classical republican ideals. If creatures reflect the virtues and vices of their creators, then they would ultimately be responsible for the character and conduct of their creature.

The anonymous "Republican" of Connecticut confidently proclaimed that "the people, we may safely presume, would choose men of abilities and integrity who would withstand every attempt to undermine their liberties. The spirit of the people would oppose every attempt to undermine their liberties." Because "he depends upon the people," the president "will be the guardian of the liberties of the people." The idea that the president would be a republican "creature" was a recurring theme in the writings of those Federalists who spoke directly to the question of the viability of virtue in government. To deny the likelihood, or even the possibility, that the executive and other representatives were capable of virtue once endowed with power was to repudiate the very possibility of republican government tout court. After demonstrating that the presidency was both consistent with and essential to the preservation of liberty, "The Republican" explained, "If we reject this Constitution, it must be upon the principle that those who are chosen by the people are not fit to be trusted with the necessary powers of government. If this be a just principle, all our republican governments are but snares to enslave the people; a free government is impracticable; and we must adopt the gloomy idea that anarchy or tyranny is the only alternative for men."[111] These remarks seemed to express great confidence in the ability of the people, but they actually rested on a conception of citizenship that minimized the role of the people. The notion that the people expressed their own virtue primarily by selecting those with superior virtue conflicted with a central tenet of republicanism. As writers from the ancient Greeks and Romans to the eighteenth-century English Commonwealthmen argued, limiting political participation to voting would undermine civic engagement and lead ultimately to corruption. Once the people had others do for them what they should be doing for themselves, their virtue was lost. This was the main point of Machiavelli's critique of mercenaries. Anti-Federalists had difficulty dealing with arguments advanced by propagandists like "The Republican" because they could not bring themselves to admit that they also lacked confidence in the virtues of the American people.

Duration in Office

Perhaps no other institutional safeguards were treasured by republicans as highly as frequent elections. They operated as periodic checks on the representative's commitment to popular liberties, but they had a more important ideological function as well. The prospect of returning to the common ranks of the people served as a reminder that representatives were no better than their constituents. If a term of office was too long, it was feared that representatives would grow out of touch with constituents and forget that they did not hold their office as a matter of right. In general, as Machiavelli had noted, the longer the term of office, the more important the character of the office-holder.[112] The objective of frequent elections was to maintain their attachment to the people and to minimize their independence. Federalists regularly insisted that the president should—and would—be warmly attached to the people, but they flatly denied that the president should be dependent on the people.

Nothing dramatizes this better than the fact that the four-year term of office for president was longer than the term of any state governor.[113] This was a major point of contention for many Anti-Federalists. Grayson denounced a term of such length as an alarming departure from precedent: "There is hardly an instance where a Republic trusted its Executive so long with much power.—Nor is it warranted by modern Republics. The delegation of power is in most of them only for one year."[114] Many Anti-Federalists feared that the length of the president's tenure would give him enough time and opportunity to consolidate power, eliminate rivals, and establish a tyranny. Most Federalists responded simply by asserting that "an election to this office once in every four years, is a sufficient curb upon the President."[115] Some justified the length of the president's term by linking it to the argument against rotation in the legislature: "a member who but comes and goes, is less responsible for bad public measures, and consequently less animated by a sense of duty and honor."[116] Others made the case that sufficient duration was necessary for effective and energetic government.

Madison drew the connection between duration and energy when he contrasted the "genius of republican liberty [which] seems to demand . . . dependence [of representatives] on the people by a short duration of their appointments" with "Stability," which "requires that the hands in which power is lodged should continue for a length of time the same." Stability itself was dependent upon "energy in government [which] requires not only a certain duration of power, but the execution of it by a single hand" (XXXVII, 243–44). Despite this clear endorsement of long duration, especially in the case of the presidency, Madison was never as enthusiastic or singleminded in promoting stability through duration as Hamilton, who repudiated the accepted wisdom on frequent elections. For the New Yorker, liberty was impossible without stability. Hamilton referred to the "principle of human nature that a man will be interested in whatever he possesses, in proportion to the firmness or precariousness of the tenure by which he holds it" to support his contention that a lengthy duration would have more salutary effects than a "momentary or uncertain title" (LXXI, 409). Instead of tightening the link between the president and the people, as a few Federalists endeavored to do, he sought to loosen it in order to distance the president from those momentary passions that sometimes agitate the community. "Firmness," a term which appeared more frequently in essay 71 than in any other essay, comprising a third of its total appearances in the *Federalist,* was the crucial character consideration at stake here. Hamilton emphatically rejected the notion that the executive should exhibit what he derided as a "servile pliancy . . . to a prevailing current." Sufficient duration in office was essential "to the personal firmness of the executive magistrate in the employment of his constitutional powers, and to the stability of the system of administration" (LXXI, 409). In a breathtaking display of indifference to republican sensibilities, Hamilton declared that duration in office would insulate the president from public pressure to adopt ill-advised projects: "The republican principle demands that the deliberate sense of the community should govern the conduct of those to whom they intrust the management of their affairs; but *it does not require an unqualified complaisance to every sudden breeze of passion, or to every transient impulse which the people may receive from the arts of men, who flatter their prejudices to betray their interests.*" (LXXI, 409–10, emphasis added). The long-term preservation of liberty, Hamilton seemed to be saying, might sometimes best be served by ignoring the current will of the people, who "commonly *intend* the PUBLIC GOOD" but "sometimes err" (LXXI, 410).

This was a thoroughly undemocratic solution to a quintessentially democratic problem. Hamilton's vision of presidential statesmanship required the chief executive to *defy* the people for the sake of the public good, in contrast to those demagogues whose incessant pandering actually undermines the public good. Like Madison, Hamilton denied that the public good was identical to the aggregate preferences of discrete individuals. Since "the inclinations of the people" sometimes conflict with their own best interest, the president should exhibit "the desired firmness and independence" enough "to withstand the temporary delusion in order to give them time and opportunity for more cool and sedate reflection" (LXXI, 410, 411).[117] Furthermore, the president would possess the "wisdom and integrity" (LXXI, 411–12) to identify the public good where the people cannot. The president's insulation from momentary impulses would enable him or her to adopt the long-range perspective so necessary for the health and survival of the nation, which in the end always suffers for indulging in enticing but unhealthy political treats (like all those popular but unjust enactments passed in the states).

This conception of leadership bore a close resemblance to Burke's notion of the representative as a trustee appointed to exercise independent judgment even when that means taking an unpopular stand.[118] In light of Hamilton's remarks on Shays' Rebellion and property relations in the states, resisting the irresponsible caprices of the people was just as likely to involve energetic displays of military force to restore order as the protection of endangered individual rights. In other words, saying "no" to the people would not necessarily result in a contraction of civil liberties but might actually involve their expansion in cases where demagogues begin to scapegoat certain groups during an emergency.

Hamilton's discussion presupposed the ability of the executive to differentiate the genuine, long-term interests of the people from those illusory, short-sighted objects that lead them to err. In fact, unless the president was predisposed to take the long view of matters in the first place, there is no reason why the president's judgment would not coincide with "the ill humors, however transient, which may happen to prevail" (LXXI, 409). This was the implication of Hamilton's prediction that the "prospect of annihilation [that is, removal from office at the next election] would be sufficiently remote not to have an improper effect upon the conduct of a *man endowed with a tolerable portion of fortitude*" (LXXI, 411, emphasis added). Even though Hamilton's ostensible purpose in *Federalist* 71 was to demonstrate the *institutional soundness* of the presidency, he actually demonstrated the dependence of that design upon the *personal qualities* of the president.

Re-Eligibility and the Rejection of Rotation

Rotation in office, similar in purpose to what might now be called term limits, was closely linked to arguments about frequent elections. In the Constitutional Convention, the two issues had to be settled together: the longer the term of office, the more imperative the need for rotation. Thus, proposals for a seven-year term or longer were almost always paired with rotation. Because rotation was regarded by so many Americans as a "noble prerogative of liberty,"[119] it was no surprise when Mason launched the Virginia Convention's debate on Article II by proclaiming that "there is no more important article in the Constitution than this. The great fundamental principle of responsibility in republicanism is here sap[p]ed. The President is elected without rotation." "Nothing," he continued, "is so essential to the preservation of a Republican Government, as a periodical rotation."[120] The corrupting influence of power was offered as the chief justification for rotation in office. According to one Anti-Federalist, experience teaches that "power has altered the mildest and most affable characters, into the most abandoned cruelty and savage temper. History abounds with innumerable instances of those who, previous to their being cursed with power, appeared as ornaments to human nature. Power is dangerous in the hands of men. Power alters all things but God."[121] Polemics against the corrupting influence of power were standard fare among politicians steeped in the Commonwealth tradition.

Luther Martin, a leading member of the Constitutional Convention and briefly a prominent Anti-Federalist, maintained that re-eligibility "without any interval of disqualification" was tantamount to instituting a lifetime executive.[122] The underlying premise of Martin's argument was that the formal powers and expected influence of the executive would enable an ambitious president to stay in office on a permanent basis. When Martin postulated that only a superhuman act of "moderation" would prevent the president from instituting himself in office for life, he was suggesting that no one had enough virtue to resist the intoxicating effects of great power. For Martin and others, power conferred inevitably became power abused. The corrupting effects of power was a central motif of Anti-Federalist polemics, but they pursued two incompatible lines of reasoning on this subject. On the one hand, rotation was necessary to curb ambition and restrain the passion for domination. On the other hand, the lust for power was so great that officeholders would do anything to hold onto it as long as possible regardless of external constraints. Far from being an inducement to good behavior, the possibility of removal from office—by impeachment or electoral loss—was actually an invitation to even greater perfidy. "The Impartial Examiner" explained the psychological mechanisms that make the lust for power insatiable:

> Every man has a natural propensity to power; and when one degree of it is obtained, *that* seldom fails to excite a thirst for more:—an higher point being gained, still the soul is impelled to a farther pursuit. Thus step by step, in regular progression, she proceeds onward; until the lust of domination becomes the ruling passion, and absorbs all other desires. When any man puts himself under the influence of such a passion, it is natural for him to seek after every opportunity, and to employ every means within reach, for obtaining his purpose. There is something so exceedingly bewitching in the possession of power that hardly a man can enjoy it, and not be affected after an unusual manner. The pomp of superiority carries with it charms, which operate strongly on the imagination.[123]

Some Anti-Federalists sneered at the nominal checks on presidential power as worthless safeguards. For instance, impeachment was a sham safeguard as "it would be of little consequence whether he was impeached or convicted, since he will be able to set both at defiance."[124]

Federalists countered the second suggestion with reminders that the president would be a creature of the people, that the electors would choose only those individuals of proven integrity and virtue, and so on. They responded to the first, more serious critique by attacking the very idea of rotation head-on as one of the principal defects of government under the Articles.[125] Madison, in particular, was aghast at the pathological effects of rotation, which made it difficult to attract worthy candidates in the first place, only to force them out of office. Oliver Ellsworth and others thought it would be impossible to attract the "most eminent characters . . . if they foresee a necessary degradation at a fixt period" (Farrand II, 101). Most delegates endorsed the principle of re-eligibility as the only sure means of keeping the most "fit" and "useful characters" in government.[126] Others took up the task of reconciling re-eligibility with the spirit of republicanism.

One of Washington's letters to Lafayette relied on two familiar but distinct republican arguments in his defense of presidential re-eligibility. The first was a recapitulation of the republican credo that corruption in government followed corruption in the people. There was no real danger of intrigue or corruption in the presidency, reassured Washington, "but in the last stage of corrupted morals and political depravity: and even then there is as much danger that any other species of domination would prevail." "Though," he added with a touch of resignation, "when a people shall have become incapable of governing themselves and fit for a master, it is of little consequence from what quarter he comes." But because the purpose of the presidency and the Constitution more generally was to promote the longevity and prosperity of the country, it was imperative to keep the office open to anyone who might be able to save the republic in a crisis. Consequently, Washington articulated a defense of re-eligibility based on the rationale typically offered by republicans in support of the temporary dictatorship. "Under an extended view of this part of the subject, I can see no propriety in precluding ourselves from the services of any man, who on some great emergency, shall be deemed, universally, most capable of serving the Public."[127] This is an argument for expediency and flexibility that is not entirely compatible with the case for a long duration in office, which promotes stability through continuity. If anything, a four-year term means that in an emergency the country is stuck with the president it has—good or bad—until the next election. It is difficult to imagine how a four-year term could be compatible with these desiderata unless the stability that comes from a sufficient duration in office is so great that it prevents emergencies from occurring in the first place. Indeed, Hamilton pursued this argument to its logical end and concluded that a president who was effective in maintaining stability would obviate the need for a change in government. In effect, long duration would mean permanency where the country was fortunate enough to have a virtuous and capable president.

Hamilton also suggested that re-eligibility serves the interests of equality better than rotation, which was traditionally used to institutionalize republican notions of equality. Rotation was rooted in the egalitarian conviction that republican society contained enough worthy individuals that offices should remain open to them all. But the rationale underlying Hamilton's argument that the "door ought to be equally open to all" (XXXVI, 236) defied the conventional republican understanding of equality. He relied on the idea of equal opportunity to *exclude* everyone but a single meritorious individual, who would remain in office indefinitely. Rotation was based on the supposition that citizens were equally deserving of political office and that no individual was inherently better than another. Hamilton's conception of equality echoed the Aristotelian concept of proportionate equality, which presupposed politically relevant differences in virtue and ability among citizens. A political practice that had been based on a notion of absolute equality was now replaced by system of reelection grounded in the concept of proportional equality.[128]

Hamilton contended that the re-eligibility of the president was "necessary to enable the people, when they see reason to approve of his conduct, to continue him in the station in order to prolong the utility of his talents and virtues, and to secure to the government the advantage of permanency in a wise system of administration" (LXXII, 413).[129] This remark could hardly have placated Anti-Federalists, who were already worried that unlimited re-eligibility would be the first step on the road to a hereditary monarchy in America. Instead of focusing on the possible punishments that an ambitious president might face for exploiting the prerogatives of the office to remain in power, Hamilton relied on the Lockean proposition that "the desire of reward is one of the strongest incentives of human conduct" to make the case that the president would have an overriding incentive to live up to the people's high expectations (LXXII, 413–14). But the primary reward he had in mind was neither material nor immediate. Indeed, it was not even a reward that would be fully enjoyed in one's lifetime. Hamilton expected the prospect of immortal "fame" to provide all the motivation a president would need to stay faithful to the public trust.[130]

As Adair has shown, many Founders sought to "earn the perpetual remembrance of posterity" by "transforming egotism and self-aggrandizing impulses into public service" that would lead to immortal fame.[131] One of the things that made fame such an inestimable reward was its rarity. In contrast to the animalistic preoccupation with "a few sensible objects which surround" a base creature, Hume explained that there is an elevated type that looks "forward to see the influence of his actions upon posterity, and the judgments which will be formed of his character a thousand years hence."[132] Americans also viewed the love of fame as an uncommon passion that would benefit the public in the long run. In his *Discourses on Davila*, John Adams argued that this passion ought to be "gratified, encouraged, and arranged," in contrast to the other more common passions, which had to be bridled, balanced, and checked.[133]

In *Federalist* 72, which contains one of the only three references to fame in the entire collection of essays, Hamilton extended the logic of Adams's argument to the president.[134] This essay is worth quoting at length because it reveals the distinctive nature of presidential character:

> Even the love of fame, the ruling passion of the noblest minds, which would prompt a man to plan and undertake extensive and arduous enterprises for the public benefit, requiring considerable time to mature and perfect them, if he could flatter himself with the prospect of being allowed to finish what he had begun, would, on the contrary, deter him from the undertaking, when he foresaw that he must quit the scene before he could accomplish the work, and must commit that, together with his own reputation, to hands which might be unequal or unfriendly to the task. (LXXII, 414)

There are several noteworthy ideas in this passage, which contains, expressly or implicitly, many of the themes central to Hamilton's discussion of executive power. For one thing, it is clear that not everyone is animated by the "love of fame." This should come as no surprise considering, in Humean terms, the "distance" or "remoteness" of the object involved. Only a person of uncommon qualities would be likely to postpone or to forego entirely the enjoyment of more definite and immediate rewards like wealth or power for the pleasures of such an uncertain and remote reward like fame.[135]

The lesson for contemporary politics is unmistakable: the president should seek the distant approval of posterity, rather than the instant applause of the present. The pitiable preoccupation of present-day presidents with popular approval and public opinion polls would surely have struck Hamilton as a contemptible debasement of statesmanship. It was precisely because so many representatives under the old system were motivated by the wrong passions that they were all too ready to oblige the pestiferous preferences of factious majorities. The "love of fame" was the Founders' response to the impulsive passions that typically govern politicians. It was a salutary passion distinct from ambition or love of power.[136] Although Adair refuses to dignify this "passion for secular immortality" as a virtue because he thinks it is rooted in "selfish and self-interested" motives,[137] it is important to keep in mind that seventeenth- and eighteenth-century thinkers like Locke and Hume had re-conceptualized virtue in a way that, so they believed, made it compatible with certain types of passion and self-interest.[138] Unlike the "love of domination" that Locke discussed in his educational writings, the love of fame was a passion that could be justified by reason because it promoted the general good of the public and not just the particular good of the individual.[139]

Another remarkable aspect of the passage by Hamilton is related to the distinct temporal concerns of the president. The notion that the president will undertake projects that require "considerable time to mature and reflect" distinguishes the executive from the legislature, which is generally preoccupied with present concerns. Hamilton did not specify the kinds of enterprises the president might undertake, but the implication is that the executive would participate actively in the formulation of long-term administrative policies like those regarding financial and military matters mentioned at the beginning of the essay. Although a role in the "preparatory plans of finance" was nowhere mentioned as part of the administrative duties of the president in Article II, the future secretary of the Treasury revealed just how indeterminate the constitutional powers of the presidency were when he assigned that administrative responsibility to the president along with all the powers relating to foreign affairs and the conduct of war. But because new chief magistrates are wont to "reverse and undo what has been done by a predecessor," Hamilton seemed to advise that a president should remain in office for life as a way to offset that "disgraceful and ruinous mutability in the administration of the government" that attends the election of a new president (LXXII, 413). This was the position he advocated explicitly in his infamous speech on June 18 at the Constitutional Convention.[140] Not only would term limits deprive the country of the valuable experience that a sitting president has gained, but they would also contribute to instability, since it cannot "be expected that men will vary and measures remain uniform" (LXXII, 415). Needless to say, the enactment of the Twenty-Second Amendment removed one of the key advantages of the Constitution over the Articles of Confederation in seeking to prevent any single individual from gaining a lock on the presidency.

Hamilton's essay took a curiously pessimistic turn immediately after the passage cited above. After setting the president apart from the rest of mankind, he ruefully acknowledged that "the generality of men" could not be expected to suppress their avarice or ambition as they neared the expiration of their term in office. This is the only essay in which Hamilton's analysis of the presidency in temporal terms takes such a negative form. Elsewhere he used time to demonstrate the positive aspects of executive power, including the ability to deal with present emergencies and to attend to long-term considerations. Here, however, he mentioned the dangers involved in the approaching end of a president's tenure. Termination in office would apparently usher in the very instability and disorder that a single executive is supposed to prevent. Hamilton speculated that the president's awareness that "a time is fast approaching" when he will have to relinquish "the summit of his country's honors" would elicit the worst tendencies in ambitious and avaricious men should they get into office (LXXII, 416, 414).

But notice the equivocation here. The entire thrust of Hamilton's argument up to this point had been that the presidency would *not* be filled by such men. Quite the opposite. This paper is so puzzling because it simultaneously argues from apparently opposite premises. What seems to be at stake is the prospect of a frequent change in administrations. However, Hamilton used arguments that failed to disarm his opponents and probably gave them even more ammunition in their assault on the presidency. Some of his arguments against mandatory rotation presupposed the very thing he wanted to deny, namely, that the president might be just like anyone else: ambitious, avaricious, or worse. The most plausible interpretation of this paper consistent with the ideas expressed throughout the *Federalist* is that Hamilton was trying to show how certain institutional features of the presidency facilitate the preservation and continuity of the character that warranted a president's election in the first place. The argument seems to be that, if maintaining consistency in the character of the president is a desirable objective—and Hamilton thought it was—it makes sense to keep the prospect of reward (that is, reelection) open lest the dispositions of the president change. In other words, Hamilton did not want to imply that the president might have a bad character, but he offered the possibility that the ingratitude of the republic might make a good executive go bad. But the notion of character that Hamilton had used throughout his discussion of the presidency seemed to rule out these kinds of fundamental and dramatic shifts in the dispositions of officeholders. In the end, Hamilton's defense of the re-eligibility of the president contradicted his general claims about virtue in the presidency and relied on the kinds of scare tactics his opponents were using to discredit the presidency as an elective despotism.

Conclusion

At the time that Federalists were suggesting that the presidency would be the primary repository of republican virtue, there was a general expectation that the first occupant of the office would be George Washington, the illustrious hero of the Revolution who had already proven his virtue by voluntarily relinquishing his power at its very height.[141] That Washington was almost universally revered as a paragon of republican virtue probably did more than any abstract theoretical arguments or historical examples adduced by the Federalists to persuade anxious Americans that the enormous powers of the president—both defined and undefined—could safely be entrusted to a single magistrate. Even though there were no guarantees that future presidents would actually live up to the towering standards set by the general, they believed that his example would establish a model of statesmanship that would guide voters in choosing a president and guide presidents in choosing how to act. With good reason, Federalists hoped that Washington's initial investment of his personal dignity in the office of the presidency would appreciate enough over time so that dignity would survive even when the principal was gone.

But it might be argued that one reason this plan worked, at least in the beginning, was because Americans knew what to look for in the president. Regardless of what one believed about the people's capacity for civic virtue, virtually everyone understood virtue in republican terms. Yet the steady erosion of civic virtue and its neglect by Federalists raises serious questions about the sustainability of a model of statesmanship that presupposes republican virtue: Can it survive long without periodic reinvestments of virtue? Is it even possible to identify individuals with the requisite virtues if the public no longer takes republican virtue seriously? What if the precondition of a virtuous president is a virtuous public? Would neglect toward civic virtue eventually lead to neglect toward virtue in the presidency? Concerns like these were raised during the ratification debates by Patrick Henry: "If you say, that out of this depraved mass, you can collect luminous characters, it will not avail, unless this luminous breed will be propagated from generation to generation; and even then, if the number of vicious characters will preponderate, you are undone."[142] Even though the Federalists' understanding of the scope of republican virtue was a response to the people's demonstrated failure to live up to the ideals of the Revolution, their elitist conception of representation may have consigned citizens to a "state of civic lethargy" that reinforced and perhaps accelerated the decline of civic virtue.[143] By replacing the traditional republican reliance on virtue within the framework of equal and active citizenship with an elitist conception of virtue that would be concentrated in the presidency, Federalists may have jeopardized the very virtues they hoped to preserve in the presidency.

Conclusion

Liberal Constitutionalism and the Inadequacy of Law

L iberal constitutionalism has become so closely identified with the rule of law that any exercise of political power not explicitly sanctioned by law is viewed either as a betrayal of its core principles or as a sign of its inherent shortcomings. But as the preceding discussion indicates, strict adherence to the formal requirements of law was never considered sufficient to the fulfillment of the substantive principles underlying the rule of law for liberal constitutionalists from Locke to the Federalists. They believed that the ends of liberal constitutionalism are normally best promoted by rigorous observance of the rules and procedures laid out in written constitutions and statutes, but they also understood that those very same rules and procedures could undermine the ends they were designed to serve. As Thomas Jefferson explained a few decades after the creation of the Constitution, "to lose our country by a scrupulous adherence to written law, would be to lose the law itself, with life, liberty, property and all those who are enjoying them with us; *thus absurdly sacrificing the end to the means*."[1] For liberal constitutionalists like Jefferson, the validity of an extralegal power like prerogative ultimately depends on substantive considerations that cannot be fully specified in law.

It is because liberal constitutionalism is defined by both its formal and its substantive commitments that it permits the executive to enforce the spirit rather than the letter of the law in extraordinary circumstances. This gives liberalism enough flexibility to adapt to changing conditions and emergency situations without having to venture into the normative vacuum of Schmittian "decisionism." As Stephen Holmes contends, liberals "never conceived 'the rule of law' as the sovereignty of abstract, self-applying rules. They viewed it, instead, as rule by elected and accountable officials *in accord with* publicly promulgated and revisable laws."[2] Even Hume, who marked the progress of a civilization by the regularity of its laws, stated in a passage on discretionary powers that it was "doubtful, whether human society could ever reach that state of perfection, as to support itself with no other controul than the general and rigid maxims of law and equity."[3] Early liberal thinkers—though certainly motivated to minimize the role of individual discretion and make politics more regular and predictable—recognized that the irrepressible contingency of the world would make it impossible to do away with discretionary exercises of power that are fundamentally irreducible to law.

Since the eighteenth century, however, there has been a dramatic shift away from reliance on extralegal exercises of prerogative toward the use of formal grants of legal authority when it comes to dealing with emergencies. The executive still has primary responsibility for dealing with emergencies, but the source of the executive's power now tends to come from statutory delegations of power that aim to give emergency powers a more solid basis in law. The adoption of a more legalistic approach to emergencies—reflected in major legislation like the National Emergencies Act of 1976, the International Emergency Economic Powers Act of 1977, and the Homeland Security Act of 2002 and in landmark court rulings like *Home Building & Loan Assn. v. Blaisdell* (1934) and *United States v. Curtiss-Wright Export Corp.* (1936)—seems to suggest that exercises of prerogative would now be dangerously unnecessary.

Although the increased reliance on law gives the impression that it is no longer necessary to resort to extralegal action, there may still be good reasons not to abandon the idea of executive prerogative. For one thing, much of the statutory and case law that seems to be relevant to the subject of emergencies deals with situations that fall short of the extraordinary events that concerned proponents of prerogative. For another, their conception of emergency indicates that no legal framework can ever be entirely adequate to the problem of extraordinary life-threatening events, particularly when they are sudden and unexpected. In short, the so-called emergency law contained in statutes and judicial opinions might be both over-inclusive and under-inclusive in ways that continue to make prerogative an indispensable option.

The Limitations of Legal Approaches to Emergencies

Within a decade of the ratification of the Constitution, Congress enacted significant pieces of legislation, such as the Enforcement Act of 1795, passed in response to the Whiskey Rebellion in western Pennsylvania, and the Alien and Sedition Acts of 1798, passed during the Quasi-War with France (and part of which is still in effect), that gave the president legal authority to take actions that might be necessary in an emergency.[4] The trend toward the legalization of emergency powers accelerated so rapidly with the passage of legislation like the Emergency Banking Act of 1933, the National Security Act of 1947, the Defense Production Act of 1950, and the Economic Stabilization Act of 1970 that presidents acquired expansive new powers to act in a broad range of areas. Indeed, so much emergency-related legislation had been passed in the United States since the Great Depression that a special congressional committee concluded in 1974 that "emergency government has become the norm."[5]

In 1976 Congress passed the National Emergencies Act (50 U.S.C. 1601–1651) to address abuses associated with the use of emergency powers by standardizing the procedures that the president would have to follow in declaring and continuing a state of emergency.[6] Even though the NEA requires Congress to meet every six months to decide whether a declared state of emergency should be terminated, it "has never done so."[7] Moreover, presidents have been able to circumvent the statute's requirements simply by renewing declarations of emergency relating to protracted problems like the Iran hostage crisis and Colombian drug trafficking.[8]

There are specific reasons why the NEA has failed to rein in executive power, but its major shortcoming can be traced to a problem it shares with other legislation and court cases that deal with emergencies. They tend to use the term *emergency* so loosely that they often end up expanding the conditions that might justify the use of enhanced government powers even when they aim to constrain executive power. Leaving aside the controversial issue of the president's war powers as commander-in-chief (which raises vexing questions well beyond the scope of this book), there are so many "intermestic" and purely domestic situations that now get classified as emergencies that presidents have greater opportunities to expand their powers. But many of the situations that have been described as emergencies in statutes, judicial opinions, and executive orders do not exhibit the characteristics that Locke and his disciples attributed to emergencies. The kinds of situations that have been designated as "national emergencies" both before and after passage of the NEA—from the Korean War and a postal strike in 1970 to the Balkan War and the trade in "blood diamonds" from Sierra Leone—have stretched the meaning of emergency beyond anything contemplated by early liberal constitutionalists. Even the inauguration of President Barack Obama was treated as an emergency in the legislation passed to accommodate the crowds for this historic event.

Many of the statutes and court cases that purport to deal with emergencies pertain to situations that are abnormal and stressful, but they do not necessarily exhibit the characteristics that Locke and his disciples attributed to emergencies. Although their discussions were maddeningly vague and incompletely theorized—which partially reflects the uncertain and unpredictable nature of emergencies themselves—the specific examples that early liberals did provide suggest that only those irregular events that pose urgent threats to life or well-being rise to the level of emergencies that would call for extralegal exercises of power. From Locke's illustration of the burning house to Hamilton's reference to "unexpected invasions" and Jefferson's examples of a military siege and "a ship at sea in distress," emergencies of the kind that justify extralegal action tend to raise existential questions beyond the ordinary competence of the law.[9] Although there was a preoccupation with events of a violent nature, as reflected in the Constitution's specific reference to "Cases of Rebellion or Invasion" (which actually appears in Article I), the kinds of emergencies liberal constitutionalists generally had in mind involved pressing matters of survival that require immediate attention.

According to this conception, no two emergencies are ever the same, but they tend to be extreme events that arise suddenly and unexpectedly. The reason it is so important to distinguish emergencies from other unstable or irregular scenarios is that proponents of prerogative were willing to permit the executive to resort to extralegal powers only in those cases where a strictly legal approach would do more harm than good. Although it is difficult enough to draw precise distinctions between normalcy and emergency, it is nonetheless useful to try to distinguish between the sudden or severe events that trigger an emergency, on the one hand, and the chronic or ongoing problems that might best be characterized as crises, on the other hand.[10]

Crises can create instabilities and disturbances in the economic, social, legal, and political systems, but they are not necessarily sudden or unpredictable, they do not necessarily demand immediate action by the executive, and they do not necessarily (or even usually) involve matters of life and death. In the past few years, scholars, journalists, and politicians have warned of current or impending crises in education, health care, Social Security, and infrastructure, but none of these problems rises to the level of a sudden or unpredictable emergency that demands extralegal action by the executive. Like the crisis in the global financial markets that started in September 2008, crises that develop over a long period of time are probably best handled through cooperation between the political branches of government rather than unilateral executive action of the kind associated with Teddy Roosevelt's expansive "stewardship theory" of the presidency.

However, the possibility—and desirability—of collaboration between the executive and the legislature in dealing with such crises does not altogether preclude the possibility or desirability of unilateral extralegal action by the executive in genuine cases of emergency. In fact, such action is often necessary. Although it is impossible to establish bright-line distinctions between crises and emergencies, an ongoing crisis turns into an emergency when it becomes so severe that it begins to jeopardize the life and well-being of large segments of the population. Emergencies of this sort may not be entirely unexpected, but the uncertainty they provoke concerning the survival of a nation or its way of life may produce much more volatility and disorder than the law is ordinarily equipped to handle. Epistemic claims about the inability to foresee all the "accidents and necessities" that might arise provided a major justification of prerogative for Locke, Blackstone, Hamilton, and others, but there is little reason to doubt that their understanding of prerogative would permit the executive to act unilaterally even in an emergency that might have been anticipated. The failure of the legislature to heed the warning signs of an impending and large-scale economic collapse, medical catastrophe, insurrection, or natural disaster is no reason to prohibit the exercise of prerogative to prevent the emergency from spiraling even further out of control.

Much of the so-called law on emergencies may go much farther than theorists of prerogative would have been willing to permit, but a legal framework is now generally the preferred means of dealing with the possibility of emergency. This reliance on law only seems to intensify during emergencies. Instead of relying exclusively or even primarily on extralegal claims of authority, as proponents of prerogative have suggested, executives frequently seek further expansions of their legal authority in emergencies. As Kim Scheppele demonstrates, emergencies frequently result in "hyper-legal" responses that substitute and multiply the laws already on the books. Contrary to the claim that emergencies provoke extralegal responses that bypass and violate existing law, Scheppele argues that responses to emergencies generally follow a predictable pattern in which governments devise new laws that expand and concentrate power, curtail civil liberties, and authorize the use of military force at home and abroad.[11] Even the Bush administration, which had aggressively defended the inherent powers of the president to exercise extraordinary powers in dealing with threats to national security, immediately sought explicit legal approval to deal with the September 11 attacks through the USA PATRIOT Act of 2001, the Authorization for Use of Military Force Against Terrorists Resolution of 2001, and other congressional measures.[12]

These developments seem to suggest that prerogative has become nothing more than an outmoded relic of an empirically questionable and normatively dangerous theory. As a descriptive matter, the liberal theory of prerogative does fall short in accounting for the way that governments in the United States and elsewhere actually deal with emergencies. But the Lockean theory of prerogative was never simply a descriptive claim; it was also, and more importantly, a prescriptive argument. Theorists of extralegal power argued that prerogative is a superior method of dealing with emergencies because it provides greater flexibility and precision than the law normally affords. Due to the formal requirement of generality built into the very idea of law as a system of rules, the law often turns out to be a rather blunt instrument no matter how many exceptions and qualifications it specifies. Moreover, any legislation that would delegate new powers to the executive would still require considerable exercises of individual discretion to be effective.

Proponents of an extralegal approach to emergencies are skeptical of legalistic approaches because attempts to plan for future emergencies based on past experience inevitably fail to provide for unpredictable contingencies. Despite their overwhelming moral and political differences, early liberal constitutionalists and Carl Schmitt both agree that legal responses based on emergencies that have already happened may not be adequate to emergencies that are yet to occur. Any legal framework for dealing with emergencies—whether developed through constitutional provisions, statutory enactments, or judicial precedents—tends to be problematically retrospective and lag behind events. This is not to say that legislation aimed at preventing, minimizing, or controlling an emergency cannot or should not be taken. But there are so many imponderables that extralegal action may still be necessary to avert an imminent catastrophe, limit its damage, or manage the governmental response. Regardless of any similarities it may have with previous occurrences, an emergency is always a singular event that defies comparison. Responses to emergencies may take predictable shapes, but these responses represent an attempt to impose a single framework on events that simply cannot be patterned or subsumed under existing legal categories without ignoring the unique particularities of each emergency. The flexibility of prerogative allows the executive to develop a response that is likely to be much more adaptive and fine-tuned than any legislation that already exists or could be enacted.

The prescriptive nature of Lockean prerogative is not limited to prudential considerations about the most effective means of dealing with such irrational and unpredictable contingencies. There is a critical normative dimension to these arguments that places significant moral constraints on the executive. Unlike a Schmittian "decision," which occurs in a normative void that permits the sovereign to do absolutely anything deemed necessary, prerogative is supposed to take account of existing moral and constitutional standards even when contemplating a violation of law.[13] Even if liberals reject the idea of a transcendental law of nature that ought to guide executives when ordinary human laws fall short, they can always fall back on the position that the executive ought to adhere to certain norms and principles contained in the constitutional tradition. In fact, many liberal constitutionalists have urged the executive to act in accordance with the spirit of the constitution even when violating the letter of the law.

Locke was most explicit in this regard, expressly subsuming prerogative under natural law standards that aim to promote the public good. Similar normative standards were built into the conceptions of prerogative developed by statesman as different as Hamilton and Jefferson, who invoked the principle of *salus populi*.[14] Even though Locke and Jefferson conceded that property rights might have to yield to the demands of self-preservation, there is no indication that these or any other proponents of prerogative believed that this power permitted the general curtailment or suspension of civil liberties. Because the aim of prerogative is to uphold the substantive principles of the constitutional order when its formal procedures and rules fail, any intrusions on liberty would have to be as temporary and narrow as possible. Neither the mass arrests ordered by Lincoln during the Civil War nor Roosevelt's indiscriminant internment of individuals of Japanese descent during World War II would be appropriate models. There is no reason that an expansion of power must result in a wholesale contraction of liberties. As Richard Posner observes in a discussion of military detentions of suspected terrorists, "The existence of a power need not extinguish all rights with which the power collides." As he explains, the power of Congress to regulate commerce does not permit it to prohibit the shipment of printed material critical of the government.[15] Likewise, there is no reason to believe, as some Office of Legal Counsel attorneys in the Bush administration argued, that the president's prerogative powers authorize him or her to torture individuals or abridge fundamental rights to free speech and a free press.[16]

Much of the recent debate over executive power has focused on the Bush administration's handling of the so-called war on terrorism, including the conduct of the wars in Iraq and Afghanistan. Even though both wars have been justified as reactions to the ongoing threat of terrorism, it is not obvious that the handling of these or similar combat operations would necessarily raise the prospect of presidential prerogative. After all, there are always emerging and continuing threats to national security, but they do not necessarily qualify as emergencies. The possibility of nuclear annihilation during the Cold War posed the greatest direct threat to the survival of the United States in the second half of the twentieth century, but it did not create a state of emergency that justified the use of extraordinary power by the executive. The current threat of a nuclear Iran or an unstable Pakistan pose grave dangers to the national security of the United States, but neither threat has (yet) resulted in the kind of extreme event that rises to the level of an emergency. Nor is it clear that these or other military threats would necessarily require the exercise of extralegal executive powers as opposed to war powers shared by the president and Congress.

Many public officials, scholars, and journalists have argued that the threat of terrorism is singularly unlike the kinds of military threats posed by distant foreign states because a terrorist plot executed on domestic soil directly endangers the lives, property, and psychological well-being of civilians. There is little doubt that a terrorist attack creates an immediate state of emergency. Wars always place great psychological, financial, and personal strains on citizens—especially on those with loved ones serving in the armed forces—but the traumas induced by a successful terrorist attack, it is argued, are different in quality and scale. Besides the obvious devastation wrought by the attack itself, leaders would have to deal with the widespread fear, confusion, and panic that ensues; massive disruptions in transportation, communications, and financial systems; the attenuation of resources and personnel; and, of course, the possibility of yet another attack that would take advantage of the country's vulnerability. The nature of such an event—like the epidemic outbreak of a lethal and highly communicable disease or a catastrophic natural disaster like a category five hurricane that rips through a low-lying coastal region—tends to place enormous strains on government and often exceeds any provisions made in law.

The emergency powers of the executive would be at their height in the midst of such an event. Even in the absence of legislation permitting the executive to impose martial law or take other extraordinary measures, the Lockean theory of prerogative would allow the executive to do what is necessary to provide for the public good. This could include the use of traditionally legislative powers and perhaps even powers that go beyond anything authorized to any branch or level of government. Depending on the nature and magnitude of the emergency, the executive might be justified in imposing a quarantine in an affected area, seizing private industry, canceling commercial flights, destroying private property, and perhaps abridging certain civil liberties—even without legislation that already permits some of these measures. Every one of these possibilities is a legitimate cause for concern, but it is clear that reluctance or refusal to act because of anxieties about the legality of necessary actions could compound an emergency and spell disaster.

But what is less clear is how long the executive could justifiably resort to prerogative. The longer an emergency persists, the greater the opportunities for the executive to consolidate and abuse powers that should be used only in the most extreme and urgent cases. When it comes to the specific threat of terrorism, there is a danger, in the words of Vice President Dick Cheney, that the struggle "may never end."[17] This could have serious long-term consequences for civil liberties and the separation of powers alike. As Bruce Ackerman points out, that terrorism is a technique means that a "war on terror," in contrast to a war against an identifiable enemy, could go on indefinitely because it is probably impossible to eradicate a technique.[18] Furthermore, there is a potential threat to constitutionalism itself because "calling the challenge a war tilts the constitutional scales in favor of unilateral executive action, and against our tradition of checks and balances."[19] And at some point, an emergency that goes on long enough becomes a "new normality."[20]

Even though early liberal constitutionalists gave no precise answer to the question of how long an executive could exercise unilateral emergency powers, Locke suggested that the executive could rely on these powers until it was possible to convene the legislature. One of the only explicit grants of emergency power in the Constitution states that the president "may, on extraordinary Occasions, convene both Houses, or either of them"—a point often noted in passing by Federalists who analyzed the powers of the presidency, though generally overlooked in contemporary debates.[21] It is always important to remember that liberal constitutionalism normally pursues the aim of limited government through the separation of powers under the rule of law. Government by prerogative is supposed to be the exception, not the rule. It is a temporary expedient, not a permanent fixture. Of course, dramatic improvements in transportation, communications, and other technologies now make it easier for the president to consult and convene Congress on short notice. Some of these developments weaken—though by no means do they refute—arguments for extraordinary unilateral executive action in all cases of actual emergency. But they do suggest that Congress may have a more meaningful role to play in these situations than it has in the past. Not only could new technological developments facilitate congressional involvement in decision-making during an emergency, they could also enhance congressional oversight over the executive branch.

There is no precise moment at which the legislature should get involved, but it is possible for it to intervene too soon or too late. It is obviously possible to wait too long if the executive uses an emergency to consolidate power, alter the distribution of power, punish political enemies, dispense favors to friends, abridge rights, or undertake any other action that the separation of powers and the rule of law are designed to prevent or minimize. It is somewhat less obvious how the president might call upon Congress too soon.

There are at least three major problems with resorting to legislative action too quickly. Because the "consensus-generating effect" of emergencies tends to undercut any "epistemic" advantages that "competition among branches of government" ordinarily brings to public deliberation, there is a danger that the legislature will make ill-advised changes to the law.[22] Legislation created in a state of panic tends to be of poor quality. It is more likely to be either over-inclusive or under-inclusive, indeterminate, indiscriminate, or unenforceable. The legislature might abdicate too much of its own power or oversight responsibility, confer too much power on the executive, fail to make necessary exceptions to the law, abridge liberties that actually pose no danger to public order or safety, or do some combination of these things.[23]

Another problem is that even carefully tailored legislation produced to deal with a specific emergency will be applied too broadly. Unlike the temporary and *ad hoc* nature of prerogative, legislation produced in such circumstances tends to outlive its original purposes unless sunset provisions are built into it. As a result, legislation that was designed for use in a particular emergency may end up being used in normal circumstances. As Justice Robert Jackson said in his famous concurrence in the steel seizure case, "emergency powers . . . tend to kindle emergencies."[24] This fear is echoed by Oren Gross and Fionnuala Ní Aoláin, who suggest that "the very existence of such a system of emergency rules and regulations may result in greater and more frequent use of emergency powers by officials, making extraordinary powers part of the ordinary discourse of government."[25]

A third problem is that emergency legislation might make the extraordinary seem all too ordinary. The danger here is that a legislative stamp of approval on actions that run afoul of the constitution might come to achieve a degree of legitimacy merely by virtue of their legality. Formal rule *by* law provides no guarantee that the substantive rule *of* law is actually being upheld. As David Dyzenhaus explains, this is the difference "between, on the one hand, the rule of law, understood as the rule of substantive principles, and, on the other, rule by law, where as long as there is legal warrant for what government does, government will be considered to be in compliance with the rule of law."[26] The consequence of legislative authorization in many cases is to accustom the public to the exercise of unprecedented powers, create dangerous consolidations of power, or provide a fig leaf that conceals a shameful and unwarranted infringement of individual liberties.

There are serious dangers and drawbacks inherent in any approach, but unlike approaches that seek legalistic answers to political problems, an extralegal approach might be less likely to have long-lasting deleterious effects on political institutions. Some legislation that has been enacted with the salutary intention of constraining the executive in order to prevent concentrations of power or infringements on civil liberties (for instance, the National

Emergencies Act of 1976, the International Emergency Economic Powers Act of 1977, the Foreign Intelligence Surveillance Act of 1978) has actually led in some instances to an increase in the powers of the executive and the gradual normalization of emergencies.[27] One of the purported advantages of emergency action based on prerogative rather than statutory delegations of authority is that it avoids the tendency of emergency legislation enacted in the middle of a crisis to spill over into other areas and times. Although both responses to emergencies threaten to normalize a state of emergency, the understanding that prerogative is an extraordinary but temporary expedient that stands outside—though not necessarily against—the rule of law means that it is less likely to get entrenched as a part of the regular legal order.[28]

Because prerogative lacks the cover of law, any executive who resorts to this extraordinary power is compelled to provide a justification limited to the specific conditions at hand. Hamilton feared that this might have the unfortunate effect of inhibiting or deterring necessary action out of a concern that the people or their representatives would not approve, whereas Jefferson suggested that a virtuous executive would not have to worry about the people's ability to distinguish good from bad intentions.[29] In practice, a president with a reputation for virtue does enjoy more latitude than one who seems to lack the requisite virtue. No president in American history faced greater challenges or exercised more extralegal powers than Abraham Lincoln. To preserve the Union, he blockaded southern ports, suspended the writ of habeas corpus, enlarged the size of the military, diverted federal funds to private individuals, and emancipated slaves in rebellious states—all without explicit congressional or constitutional authorization.[30]

Though Lincoln faced bitter opposition to virtually every aspect of his handling of the Civil War from a variety of quarters, his perceived virtue did make it easier for some to accept his extraordinary actions. The fifth resolution of the Republican Party Platform of 1864 indicates that his character provided part of the justification for his actions. It reads in part:

> RESOLVED: That we approve and applaud the practical wisdom, the unselfish patriotism and the unswerving fidelity to the Constitution and the principles of American liberty, with which ABRAHAM LINCOLN has discharged, under circumstances of unparalled [sic] difficulty, the great duties and responsibilities of the Presidential Office; that we approve and indorse, as demanded by the emergency and essential to the preservation of the nation and as within the

provisions of the Constitution, the measures and acts which he has adopted to defend the nation.[31]

But even this encomium on Lincoln's virtue points to an obvious disparity from the kind of acclaim that Washington received. Lincoln's virtues were viewed through the prism of partisan politics, which has radically transformed the way that Americans evaluate the characters of their leaders and judge their actions.

The Constitution of Virtue in the Age of Party Politics

For the past several decades, political pundits, academics, and politicians across the political spectrum have incessantly bewailed the shallowness and pettiness of presidential politics. To the extent that ordinary citizens are even paying attention, charge critics, they tend to focus on personalities instead of issues and style instead of substance. Press coverage has been filled with reports on the preferred undergarments of candidates, schmaltzy testimonials from their children and spouses, and video montages of them frolicking with pets, all of which are supposed to help the public get to "know the candidates as a person." This often means figuring out which candidate a voter would rather "hang out with," have over for dinner, or "drink a beer with."

Although these are disheartening distractions from substantive political issues, it would be wrong to conclude from these examples alone that attention to personality in presidential politics is unnecessary or superficial. If the Founders' notions of character are any guide, the problem is not that citizens are interested in the personal qualities of presidential contenders. All too often, the problem is that voters fail to consider the right qualities. The right question is not whether the president "feels our pain," as Bill Clinton intoned, or is a "hard-hearted person," as George W. Bush proposed, but whether the president places the interests of the public above competing interests of self, family, sect, or party.

If American voters have abandoned the criteria used by the Founders, that is probably due in large part to the fact that the rise of the party system has changed the way voters evaluate the character of the president and the way they conceive of virtue itself. The rise of partisan politics—and the president's role as presumptive leader of his or her party—has played a significant role in shaping Americans' understanding of the way that executive power is exercised and of the sort of character that the president ought to possess. Because the party system has become such an entrenched part of the political process ever since Jefferson's break with Hamilton over the Treasury Secretary's Anglophilic funding scheme and response to the French Revolution, any aspirant to the presidency is compelled to seek the approval of one segment of the political community before reaching out to voters on the other side of the political spectrum.[32]

Despite lamentations that contemporary campaigns are not substantive enough, there is a greater expectation that candidates advocate particular policy positions now than there was in the eighteenth century, when "men put themselves forward on their social position and character and manners" and "it was rare for a man to run on issues or policies."[33] But candidates' stands on the issues now are filtered through their membership in political parties. To get to the point where an individual can even be considered as a viable candidate, he or she must prove his or her loyalty to the party, endorse its platform, and support party leaders. This makes it nearly impossible for any presidential candidate to make a plausible claim of disinterestedness or bipartisanship. The American political system does provide more opportunities for success to entrepreneurial candidates who are relatively independent from their parties than does a parliamentary system, but it is still quite difficult for any politician who has not worked his or her way through the party structure to get the financial backing, organizational support, and name recognition necessary to run a national campaign.

Perhaps as important as party politics is the fact that presidential candidates must now campaign directly for themselves. The days when George Washington and Thomas Jefferson could pretend that they were not seeking higher office and rely almost entirely on supporters to make the case on their behalf are long gone. No candidate can conceal his or her ambition. No candidate can avoid the grubbiness of asking wealthy donors for money. No candidate can avoid the unseemliness of pandering to narrow interest groups. No matter how much time a candidate spends shaking hands on rope lines, listening to the concerns of voters at town hall meetings, or answering questions at campaign stops in factories, shopping malls, or industrial parks, it is difficult to maintain meaningful interactions with individuals who are not well-connected insiders. This serves to reinforce the popular impression that politicians are not only out of touch with the concerns of ordinary voters but that they are also beholden to special interests and large donors whose interests usually conflict with the interests of the people.

This is not to say that contemporary Americans have completely lost the moral framework of the Founders. Indeed, there is an expectation on the part of voters that the president will "change the tone of politics in Washington," be "a uniter, not a divider," and rise above partisan politics. In recent presidential elections, Republican and Democratic candidates for the presidency have endeavored to distance themselves from hardliners within their own parties in efforts to come across as less partisan or ideological. From Bill Clinton and Al Gore, who ran as "New Democrats" open to welfare reform and other causes identified with the Right, to George W. Bush, who campaigned as a "compassionate conservative" willing to spend money on education and certain programs associated with the Left, candidates' attempts to dissociate themselves from their own parties signify more than general election strategies designed to win over voters in the center. The rhetoric employed by recent presidential candidates contains an implicit acknowledgment that there is something fundamentally wrong with strict partisanship.

Yet even these apparent illustrations of conformity with the values of the Founders reveal sharp differences in contemporary understandings of presidential character. Despite these attempts to rise above party politics, presidential candidates are still expected to be the leaders of their parties. Even though presidents build up their own constituencies and run quasi-independent electoral campaigns, they still coordinate their electoral strategies and policy programs with their parties.[34] As a result, they often end up reinforcing an "us versus them" mentality that divides the country along partisan, ideological, religious, economic, and racial lines. The 2008 election might prove to be a turning point, but it, too, exhibited some of the worst tendencies of partisan politics. The imperatives of partisanship often led to overblown claims that the opposing candidate was beholden to "special interests" (for example, assertions that John McCain's campaign was run by corporate lobbyists who would dominate his administration) or to spurious and sometimes outrageous insinuations that the other candidate was "unpatriotic" (suggestions that Barack Obama's tenuous links to a radical from the 1960s was equivalent to "palling around with terrorists").

These questions concerning character have meaningful and significant implications for the power of the president. Character is a much more significant determinant of power in the presidency than it is in the legislature. Periodic attempts at congressional reform are motivated, at least in part, by an awareness that public outrage directed at a few dirty politicians often turns into public disapproval of the entire institution, which reflects badly on "clean" members of Congress. A sense of responsibility for the integrity of the institution—not to mention an overwhelming desire for reelection—promotes the kind of self-policing that the Founders hoped to encourage through a complex system of checks and balances. But no matter how low the congressional approval rating ever gets, no matter how badly the body's prestige suffers, it almost never endures a loss of power as a consequence. To be sure, it becomes exceedingly difficult when its public approval reaches a low point to enact legislation that directly benefits members of Congress (for example, pertaining to pay raises and honoraria for speaking engagements), but public disapproval of individual members seldom hinders Congress from exercising its constitutional powers. The same, however, is not necessarily true when either an individual president or the presidency as an institution loses the trust and confidence of the public. When presidents fail to police themselves, their power tends to diminish. The history of the American presidency vindicates Locke's claim that the scope of executive power depends on formal as well as personal factors. As the most highly personalized institution in American government, the character of the person who becomes president affects the dignity and prestige of the office in an unparalleled way.

The sense that virtue enhances dignity, and that dignity enhances power, seems to be at the heart of many criticisms directed at presidents of questionable character. For many early liberals, the notion of dignity was what connected virtue to executive power, because an executive who lacks dignity lacks the respect necessary to act effectively. For Federalists, maintaining the dignity of the office was crucial because it would be downright dangerous to have an undignified president in office in a time of genuine national emergency. Without the leeway that virtue earns the executive, the president would be unduly hampered in carrying out important responsibilities. If the motives behind every exercise of executive power are questioned because the president's character is questionable, then there is a real danger that government will not be effective enough to deal with the unexpected. A virtuous executive is a more powerful executive, whereas a vicious executive is likely to be an embattled, hence a weaker, executive. Of course, particular policies and proposals should be judged on their merits, but merit alone is often insufficient in politics. A president who has little or no moral authority eventually becomes a serious liability to his or her own agenda, no matter what its intrinsic merits might be.[35]

Presidents beset by controversy will often find themselves incapable of acting as aggressively as certain situations demand. They usually have to overcome doubts about their intentions and justify their plans before they can act. Unlike the "wisest and best Princes," who can easily act "without or contrary to the Letter of the Law" because they enjoy such widespread public support, vicious executives have to seek prior approval from the public.[36] As important as it is in liberal-democratic societies to have an informed, vigilant, and engaged public, the need to justify extraordinary uses of power undermines the two distinctive advantages that a single executive has over deliberative bodies: secrecy and dispatch. These are the qualities that give the executive department its characteristic energy. As Hamilton often stated, a government with a shortage of energy is a feeble government. Thus, when a genuine crisis erupts, a president who has to address suspicions about his or her motivations deprives the nation of those qualities that a good executive brings to government. A situation in which a president is unable to take extraordinary measures in genuine emergencies because of character concerns can be almost as frightening and dangerous to liberty as one in which a president is able to stretch the limits of his or her powers because of public indifference to considerations of character or acquiescence by the other branches of government.

Despite the rancor that sometimes marred the 2008 presidential election, the predominant rhetoric of the two major party campaigns suggests that the electorate would take the prospects of an emergency very seriously in considering the character of the candidates. Voters seemed to understand that the crises confronting the country—which at any moment could turn into full-blown emergencies—would require the leadership of a president with the right kind of intelligence, ideas, experience, temperament, and virtue. The positive response of many voters to McCain's campaign slogan "Country First" and his continual appeals to patriotism and service suggest that some of the ideals of the Founding still resonate strongly with Americans. Whenever the Republican presidential nominee linked these ideas to his career as a "maverick" who regularly stood up to his own party and the special interests that support it, he harkened back to the republican ideal of a statesman who rises above partisan and sectional interests. Likewise, the enthusiasm that greeted

Obama's promise to move beyond the bitterly divisive "politics as usual" indicates that much of the electorate was eager for a postpartisan politics. These efforts to transcend partisan divisions probably reflected the personal dispositions of the candidates, but they also reflected an understanding that times of uncertainty call for something better. In a sense, the election represented a partial restoration of republican ideals of virtue.

Questions of Character in Contemporary Debates

Discussions of presidential character prior to the 2008 race tend to confirm some of these insights regarding the link between executive virtue and executive power. However, they also demonstrate how much the public understanding of the kinds of virtues that matter in politics had changed.

President Clinton's presidency suggests that even personal vices can have serious effects on the performance of public duties. Clinton had been dogged by questions about his honesty and marital fidelity even before he became president, but revelations of a sexual affair with White House intern Monica Lewinsky and his subsequent lies about the relationship cast even greater doubt on his trustworthiness. Due to his persistent deception and obfuscation about the matter, he soon found himself facing perjury and obstruction of justice charges that led to his impeachment. Although he was eventually acquitted by the Senate, the impeachment proceedings and the surrounding controversy were such a constant distraction that his political agenda suffered, leading many supporters to complain bitterly that he had wasted their efforts for a few tawdry moments of self-gratification.[37] After all, the persuasive power of the president depends not just on rhetorical skills, poll numbers, and the inherent appeal of the policies being promoted. It also depends on perceptions about the president's character.[38]

Clinton's entanglement in the Lewinsky sex scandal may have affected his job performance in an even more serious way that has not received as much attention. It is possible that Clinton's sexual imbroglio negatively impacted his ability to respond to the terrorist bombings of American embassies in Kenya and Tanzania on August 7, 1998. There is no way of knowing how vigorously he would have pursued the groups responsible for the embassy attacks if he had not been embroiled in this sex scandal, but the hostility he provoked made it difficult for him to act with much vigor and dispatch. Accusations that he ordered the retaliatory bombing of alleged terrorist facilities to distract the public from his impending impeachment hampered his ability to pursue more aggressive and sustained antiterrorist policies.[39] A president does not have to be a saint to garner public support for a legislative agenda that brings obvious benefits to ordinary Americans, but if his character is morally questionable, it is difficult to convince the public that he has no ulterior motives in seeking an expansion of ordinary executive powers because of an alleged threat to national security.

Moral deficits in presidents have effects that go beyond particular episodes. Jeremiads about the diminishing moral authority and dignity of the presidency as an institution were greatly exaggerated by partisan critics of Clinton, but concerns about the long-term prestige of the institution were not necessarily illegitimate. Both Clinton's critics and supporters of a strong presidency feared that the ignominy of the person would adhere to the office. What was so unseemly about Clinton was that his apparent lack of respect for the dignity of the office and his apparent disregard for his own reputation would bring the presidency itself as an institution into disrepute.

Much like his predecessor, President Bush developed a reputation for dishonesty that impaired his ability to govern effectively. But unlike Clinton, whose misdeeds were perhaps "more sordid than sinister," Bush suffered a loss of credibility due to his *public* vices.[40] As is now well known, Bush's primary justification for war against Iraq was based on fabricated claims about Iraqi dictator Saddam Hussein's weapons capabilities. Indications that the administration pressured analysts to manipulate intelligence reports so that they would support the case for war raised further doubts about the president's actual motives in launching the invasion. Baseless administration insinuations that Iraq was somehow linked to the September 11 attacks only reinforced these suspicions.

The Bush presidency underscores the differences between public and private vices in a more interesting way. Dispositions that might qualify as virtues in a private context sometimes constitute vices in a public context. For instance, Bush's unflinching loyalty to his friends and supporters would normally be considered an admirable virtue that ought to be encouraged in private life. But that same quality can become a vice when it manifests itself in public life. Persistent loyalty is sometimes squarely at odds with the public interest. This is the case with many of those officials who backed the president's claims that Iraq constituted a grave threat to the national interest. Instead of dismissing those who supplied him with faulty intelligence estimates or mishandled the war in Iraq, Bush rewarded many of them. Former director of central intelligence George Tenet was awarded the Presidential Medal of Freedom in spite his agency's intelligence failures in failing to anticipate the attacks of September 11 and in miscalculating Iraq's weapons capabilities; former national security advisor Condoleezza Rice was promoted to secretary of state despite her inattention to the August 6, 2001, President's Daily Brief warning "Bin Ladin Determined To Strike in U.S."; and Secretary of Defense Donald Rumsfeld was kept on in his position for several years despite underestimating the resistance from insurgents that U.S. forces would encounter in Iraq and failing to provide American soldiers with necessary equipment. And in the midst of one of the most catastrophic natural disasters in the country's history, Bush publicly commended Michael Brown, the director of the Federal Emergency Management Agency, for "doing a heck of a job" in handling the response to Hurricane Katrina even though Brown had neglected to make adequate preparations for the storm and failed to provide effective assistance to citizens in distress.

Other actions taken by President Bush raised questions about his character in terms of those political virtues prized by the Founders. For instance, many officials critical of the president and his policies have been penalized and vilified for their apparent disloyalty. In a perversion of the eighteenth-century meaning of patriotism, which signified loyalty to the ideals of the constitution over the government in power, the word came to be identified with unquestioned loyalty to the administration. Former head of the Office of Legal Counsel Jack Goldsmith has noted that the enforcement of the law "had taken a backseat to politics" in an administration that aggressively monitored the partisan loyalties of its officials.[41] Perhaps even more disturbing was the administration's apparent politicization of national security to gain an electoral advantage. In the months preceding the 2004 presidential election, the terror alert was raised more than half a dozen times—often in apparent response to sagging poll numbers—while it was raised only once after Bush's reelection (following the bombings in London's transportation system in July 2005).[42] After leaving his post as secretary of homeland security, Tom Ridge admitted that the White House often raised the color-coded threat level despite objections from his department.[43]

Despite the questions that have been raised about Bush's character and motives, his administration was able to push the limits of executive power to unprecedented heights. Not only did the administration authorize the National Security Agency to conduct warrantless surveillance that bypassed the FISA system, assert the power to classify and indefinitely detain suspected terrorists as enemy combatants, and condone the use of "harsh interrogation techniques" that have been likened to torture; it consistently thwarted congressional efforts to curb these and other practices. All of this may suggest that executive powers—emergency or otherwise—are unrelated to the real or perceived character of the president. After all, there is a well-documented tendency for the public and the other branches of government to rally around the president during a national crisis regardless of previous approval ratings or political opposition. In fact, even the courts tend to "go to war." [44]

However, the administration's aggressive and uncompromising approach to the "war on terror" prompted criticisms that the frightening possibility of a second attack was used as a pretext to expand presidential power for its own sake. As Jack Goldsmith has suggested, the Bush administration may have left the presidency weaker than it found it. Goldsmith argues that the Bush administration was able to achieve many short-term victories only at the long-term expense of both the institutional standing of the presidency and the health of constitutional democracy. Ironically, the administration's adamant insistence that it did not have to resort to extralegal action or seek legislative approval to carry out controversial counterterrorism polices because it already possessed all the inherent legal authority it needed may actually have hampered its ability to combat the threat of terrorism as effectively as possible. [45] The reason for this, Goldsmith explains, is that the administration's legalistic "go-it-alone" strategy, which was based on "an unquestioned commitment to a peculiar conception of executive power," eventually alienated many members of Congress and forced the Supreme Court's hand. [46] As a result, when the administration did seek a legislative framework for its detention policies in 2006, it got much less than it "could have gotten from a more cooperative Congress in 2002–2003." [47] And when suits were brought against the administration, it suffered at least partial rebukes in cases like *Rasul v. Bush* (2004), *Hamdi v. Rumsfeld* (2004), and especially *Hamdan v. Rumsfeld* (2006) and *Boumediene v. Bush* (2008).

By the time Democrats regained control of Congress, persistent questions about Bush's character—not to mention his judgment and competence—made it difficult for any but the most loyal supporters to endorse further expansions of presidential power. It had also become clear that the administration had used the war on terrorism to implement a controversial vision of executive power and consolidate its party's hold on political power. Members of the administration felt an overwhelming moral and political responsibility to avert a second deadly attack, but its apparent disregard for legal and constitutional limits, its seemingly cavalier attitude toward individual rights, and its avowed indifference to public opinion in fighting the war on terrorism have called into question the president's commitment to the principles of liberal constitutionalism.[48]

Virtue and Equality in Liberal Democracy

One of the many paradoxes of liberal democracy is that it may not be able to recognize what is necessary for its own preservation. It is not, as Carl Schmitt had argued, that liberal democracies are incapable of acknowledging the "exception" or taking the action necessary to confront it.[49] The recognition that there are inherent limitations in any legal approach to the problem of contingency and the corresponding willingness of liberal constitutionalists from Locke and Hume to Blackstone and Madison to resort to extralegal action in cases of emergency demonstrate that Schmitt's criticism of liberal constitutionalism is wrong. However, the liberal democratic commitment to the principle of equality may obstruct its ability to recognize or accept the need for extraordinary virtue in its leaders.

It is not easy to square the notion of virtue with equality because any meaningful conception of virtue necessarily implies substantive differences—hence inequalities—among individuals. To describe one individual as virtuous implies that another either is not or is less so. This introduces the kinds of qualitative moral distinctions among individuals that liberals have generally been reluctant to make.[50] Without a doubt, comparative estimates of moral worth are fraught with peril, but in electoral politics they are unavoidable. However, a reluctance to make claims of moral superiority is not simply a reflection of the low moral quality of politicians. It is also a reflection of an egalitarian ethos that sometimes makes a virtue out of the lowest common denominator. Alexis de Tocqueville and John Stuart Mill recognized that liberal democracy's commitment to equality sometimes exhibits a homogenizing, leveling tendency that stifles the intellectual and moral development of the individual. Even worse, in their view, was the possibility that egalitarian sensibilities would hinder democratic peoples from appreciating—let alone rewarding—intellectual or moral greatness.[51] This does not mean that citizens should ignore the inevitable fallibility of their leaders, but it does mean that they should take notice of leaders, in Hamilton's words, "pre-eminent for ability and virtue."[52] The ideal would be someone the people can look up to but who does not look down on the people.

Even though the Federalists may have triumphed in their quest to establish a strong and independent national executive, the Anti-Federalists seem to have prevailed in their attempt to establish a mirror theory of representation. Nowadays, the virtue of a politician is frequently measured by his or her resemblance to the electorate, warts and all. As a result, candidates are now expected to reveal intimate secrets about their sex lives; openly confess to bygone days of debauchery; prodigality, and substance abuse; share their innermost spiritual and religious convictions; and tell us about their dietary habits, exercise routines, and recreational interests. Many candidates wisely resist the pressure to tell all, but they all work hard now to convey the impression that they are no different from ordinary voters. Even the admiration that voters have for the accomplishments and talents of presidential candidates is often tinged with mistrust of personal qualities that set them apart from the tastes, habits, and background of the general public. Compared to the descriptions of virtuous statesmen in the eighteenth century, the adjectives sometimes used to describe apparent paragons of virtue today can be rather prosaic and uninspiring: "respectful, moderate, commonsensical, courteous."[53] The perception that a presidential candidate is "out of touch" with either the social values and mores of ordinary Americans or the accusation that he or she is an intellectual or cultural "elitist" can seriously damage, if not destroy, a presidential bid. The president is now expected to be a pal, a confidant, a chum, an ordinary "guy" or "gal."

There is a sobering possibility that Americans "get the leaders they deserve." As Joseph Nye remarks, "bad followers help produce bad leaders and constrain good ones."[54] This suggests that improvements in the quality of leaders ultimately depend on improvements in the quality of followers. Federalists and Anti-Federalists alike believed that the ultimate guarantee of liberty and good government is a virtuous citizenry. For liberal theorists more generally, virtue was not regarded as an ultimate ideal or end in itself but as a vital means of promoting the common good. Like many eighteenth-century thinkers, liberals endorsed certain virtues because they produced good societies, not simply because they produced good individuals.[55]

Without improvements in the quality of civic education (not to mention public education more broadly), it is difficult for citizens to fulfill their duty to pursue the common good. Unless citizens develop those critical faculties and intellectual powers that liberals have always prized, they will be incapable of governing themselves and preserving their liberties. Jefferson spent much of his retirement promoting a system of wards modeled after the New England townships because he believed that direct civic participation in these "little republics" was the most effective way to train citizens for the demands of civic life and perpetuate the revolutionary ideal of self-government in such a large country.[56] Even though he badly underestimated the positive educational effects of the Constitution's institutional arrangements (and contradicted his own claims about the educational value of a Bill of Rights), he was correct in pointing out the inadequacy of formal institutions to the preservation of liberty when he observed that republicanism is to be found "in the spirit of our people," which "would oblige even a despot to govern us republicanly."[57]

In the final analysis, the fate of free government depends on the virtue of its citizens. Not only is a virtuous citizenry better equipped to assess the virtues that leaders need to govern well in normal and abnormal times, it is also better equipped to challenge abuses of the power they entrust to their leaders in ordinary and extraordinary circumstances. The institutional machinery of liberal constitutionalism was designed to minimize the need for extraordinary virtue, but it could never entirely eliminate the need for it. The ultimate paradox may be that only virtue can make up for the failures of institutions that have been specifically designed to compensate for the fallibility of virtue.

Notes

INTRODUCTION

1. See the indispensable Oren Gross and Fionnuala Ní Aoláin, *Law in Times of Crisis: Emergency Powers in Theory and Practice* (Cambridge: Cambridge University Press, 2006), pp. 5–6. The difficulty in defining emergencies through law also means that it is difficult to draw "bright-line demarcations between normalcy and emergency," p. 12.

2. See A. V. Dicey, *Introduction to the Study of the Law of the Constitution*, 10th ed. (New York: St. Martin's Press, 1961), especially pp. 183–205, 394–95.

3. Max Weber, *Politics as a Vocation*, in *The Vocation Lectures*, trans. Rodney Livingstone (Indianapolis: Hackett, 2004), p. 34.

4. Carl Schmitt, *Political Theology: Four Chapters on the Concept of Sovereignty*, trans. George Schwab (Chicago: University of Chicago Press, 2005), p. 6. See also Carl Schmitt, *Legality and Legitimacy*, trans. and ed. Jeffrey Seitzer (Durham, NC: Duke University Press, 2004). For summaries of Schmitt's own response to the exception, see Gross and Aoláin, *Law in Times of Crisis*, pp. 162–70; John P. McCormick, "The Dilemmas of Dictatorship: Carl Schmitt and Constitutional Emergency Powers," in *Law as Politics: Carl Schmitt's Critique of Liberalism*, ed. David Dyzenhaus (Durham, NC: Duke University Press, 1998), pp. 217–51.

5. On the multifarious meanings of "normativism" in Schmitt's critique of liberalism, see William E. Scheuerman, *Carl Schmitt: The End of Law* (Lanham, MD: Rowman and Littlefield, 1999), pp. 62–82, especially p. 75.

6. Carl Schmitt, *Constitutional Theory*, trans. Jeffrey Seitzer (Durham, NC: Duke University Press, 2008), p. 174.

7. For an overview of Schmitt's critique of liberalism that seeks to defend a substantive conception of the rule of law as superior to procedural conceptions of the rule of law that focus on formal questions of legality, see David Dyzenhaus, *The Constitution of Law: Legality in a Time of Emergency* (Cambridge: Cambridge University Press, 2006), pp. 34–40, 60.

8. John Locke, *Two Treatises of Government*, ed. Peter Laslett (Cambridge: Cambridge University Press, 1988), § 160.

9. On the distinctions between ex ante, interim, and ex post mechanisms of control, see John Ferejohn and Pasquale Pasquino, "The Law of Exception: A Typology of Emergency Powers," *International Journal of Constitutional Law*, Vol. 2, No. 2 (2004), p. 227.

10. Contrary to those studies that stress the inherently tyrannical tendencies of executive power, my account suggests that early liberals recognized these dangers and looked to personal character as an internal constraint. See, e.g., See Harvey C. Mansfield Jr., *Taming the Prince: The Ambivalence of Modern Executive Power* (Baltimore: Johns Hopkins University Press, 1993); Harvey C. Mansfield Jr., "Machiavelli and the Modern Executive," in *Machiavelli's Virtue* (Chicago: University of Chicago Press, 1998); and Michael A. Genovese, "Democratic Theory and the Emergency Powers of the President," *Presidential Studies Quarterly*, Vol. 9, No. 3 (1979).

11. Kenneth R. Mayer, *With the Stroke of a Pen: Executive Orders and Presidential Power* (Princeton: Princeton University Press, 2001), p. 11; Phillip J. Cooper, *By Order of the President: The Use and Abuse of Executive Direct Action* (Lawrence: University Press of Kansas, 2002), pp. 12, 71; Gross and Aoláin, *Law in Times of Crisis*, pp. 64–65.

12. For an overview of some of the most unusual and controversial claims advanced by the Bush administration, see James P. Pfiffner, "Constraining Executive Power: George W. Bush and the Constitution," *Presidential Studies Quarterly*, Vol. 38, No. 1 (2007); and Scott M. Matheson Jr., *Presidential Constitutionalism in Perilous Times* (Cambridge: Harvard University Press, 2009), pp. 85–148.

13. Substantiating this considerable litany of charges are Noam Scheiber, "Friends," *New Republic*, September 26, 2005, p. 6; Frank Rich, "Bring Back Warren Harding," *New York Times*, September 25, 2005; Ron Suskind, *The One Percent Doctrine: Deep inside America's Pursuit of Its Enemies since 9/11* (New York: Simon and Schuster, 2007), pp. 17, 173–74, 326–28, 334, 340–41, 346, 351; Naomi Klein, *The Shock Doctrine: The Rise of Disaster Capitalism* (New York: Henry Holt, 2007); Ryan Lizza, "He Ain't Heavy," *New Republic*, July 29, 2002, pp. 20–24; Paul Krugman, "Point Those Fingers," *New York Times*, September 9, 2005; Molly Ivins, "Follow the Money for the Real Story," *Chicago Tribune*, September 15, 2005; Paul Krugman, "Find the Brownie," *New York Times*, September 26, 2005; Eric Lipton and Ron Nixon, "Many Contracts for Storm Work Raise Questions," *New York Times*, September 26, 2005; Jack Goldsmith, *The Terror Presidency: Law and Judgment inside the Bush Administration* (New York: W.W. Norton, 2007); John Yoo, *The Powers of War and Peace: The Constitution and Foreign Affairs after 9/11* (Chicago: University of Chicago Press, 2005) and *War by Other Means: An Insider's Account of the War on Terror* (New York: Atlantic Monthly Press, 2006); and Tom Baldwin, "Bush v. Bush: An Oedipal Battle between Men of Rigid Beliefs," *The Times* (November 11, 2006), p. 44.

14. John McCain, Campaign Speech in Racine, Wisconsin, July 31, 2008. Transcript available at http://transcripts.cnn.com/TRANSCRIPTS/0807/31/cnr.04.html, accessed August 1, 2008.

15. Richard E. Neustadt, *Presidential Power: The Politics of Leadership from FDR to Carter* (New York: Macmillan, 1986).

16. The first camp includes Richard M. Pious, *The American Presidency* (New York: Basic Books, 1979); Stephen Skowronek, *The Politics Presidents Make: Leadership from John Adams to George Bush* (Cambridge: Belknap Press, 1993); Mayer, *With*

the Stroke of a Pen; Cooper, *By Order of the President*; and Yoo, *Powers of War and Peace*; the second camp includes James David Barber, *The Presidential Character: Predicting Performance in the White House*, 2d ed. (Englewood Cliffs, NJ: Prentice-Hall, 1977); Alexander L. George and Juliette L. George, *Presidential Personality and Performance* (Boulder, CO: Westview Press, 1998); Ethan M. Fishman, *The Prudential Presidency: An Aristotelian Approach to Presidential Leadership* (Westport, CT: Praeger, 2001); and James P. Pfiffner, *The Character Factor: How We Judge America's Presidents* (College Station: Texas A&M University Press, 2004).

17. See Theodore J. Lowi, *The Personal President: Power Invested, Promise Unfulfilled* (Ithaca, NY: Cornell University Press, 1985); Richard Rose, *The Postmodern President: George Bush Meets the World* (Chatham, NJ: Chatham House, 1991); and Skowronek, *The Politics Presidents Make*. However, it is important to note that toward the end of the Clinton presidency, a number of studies dealing with the personal integrity and morality of the president began to appear, but these issues were not necessarily linked to questions of executive power. See, for example, J. Patrick Dobel, "Judging the Private Lives of Public Officials," *Administration and Society*, Vol. 30, No. 2 (1998); James P. Pfiffner, "Sexual Probity and Presidential Character," *Presidential Studies Quarterly*, Vol. 28, No. 4 (1998); Richard A. Posner, *An Affair of State* (Cambridge: Harvard University Press, 1999), ch. 4; and James P. Pfiffner, "Presidential Lies," *Presidential Studies Quarterly*, Vol. 29, No. 4 (1999).

18. Jeffrey Tulis, "On Presidential Character," in *The Presidency in the Constitutional Order*, ed. Joseph M. Bessette and Jeffrey Tulis (Baton Rouge: Louisiana State University Press, 1981), p. 283.

19. For an example of this critique, see Carnes Lord, *The Modern Prince: What Leaders Need to Know Now* (New Haven: Yale University Press, 2003), p. 1.

20. A noteworthy exception and attempt to correct this narrowly jurisprudential interpretation of constitutional development is Keith E. Whittington, *Constitutional Construction: Divided Powers and Constitutional Meaning* (Cambridge: Harvard University Press, 1999).

21. The case was *Youngstown Sheet & Tube Co. v. Sawyer* 343 U.S. 579 (1952). For such arguments, see, for example, Arthur M. Schlesinger, *The Imperial Presidency* (Boston: Houghton Mifflin, 1973); Jules Lobel, "Emergency Power and the Decline of Liberalism," *Yale Law Journal*, Vol. 98, No. 7 (1989); Lawrence Lessig and Cass R. Sunstein, "The President and the Administration," *Columbia Law Review*, Vol. 94 (1994); Louis Fisher, *Presidential War Power* (Lawrence: University Press of Kansas, 2004); and Louis Fisher, *Constitutional Conflicts between Congress and the President*, 5th ed. (Lawrence: University Press of Kansas, 2007).

22. See Steven G. Calabresi and Saikrishna B. Prakash, "The President's Power to Execute the Laws," *Yale Law Journal*, Vol. 104, No. 6 (1994); Steven G. Calabresi, "Some Normative Arguments for the Unitary Executive," *Arkansas Law Review*, Vol. 48, No. 1 (1995); Yoo, *Powers of War and Peace*; and Steven G. Calabresi and Christopher S. Yoo, *Unitary Executive: Presidential Power from Washington to Bush* (New Haven: Yale University Press, 2008).

23. Martin S. Flaherty, "The Most Dangerous Branch," *Yale Law Journal,* Vol. 105, No. 7 (1996), pp. 1725–1839.

24. Goldsmith, *Terror Presidency.*

CHAPTER 1: "So Many Unexpected Things"

Epigraph. Niccolò Machiavelli, *Discourses on Livy,* trans. and ed. Harvey C. Mansfield and Nathan Tarcov (Chicago: University of Chicago Press, 1996), p. 197.

1. Niccolò Machiavelli, *The Prince,* ed. Quentin Skinner and Russell Price (Cambridge: Cambridge University Press, 1988), p. 85.

2. On Machiavelli's use of *accidenti* and its distinction from *fortuna,* see John P. McCormick, "Addressing the Political Exception: Machiavelli's 'Accidents' and the Mixed Regime," *American Political Science Review,* Vol. 87, No. 4 (1993), pp. 888–900.

3. Niccolò Machiavelli, *Discourses on Livy,* trans. and ed. Harvey C. Mansfield and Nathan Tarcov (Chicago: University of Chicago Press, 1996), p. 197.

4. Contrary to the argument that Machiavelli looked to the executive to deal with the contingencies of politics, McCormick argues that Machiavelli proposed the "mixed regime as the most effective antidote to those irregular forces" described as *accidenti.* See "Addressing the Political Exception," p. 888.

5. See Harvey C. Mansfield Jr., *Taming the Prince: The Ambivalence of Modern Executive Power* (Baltimore: Johns Hopkins University Press, 1993) and "Machiavelli and the Modern Executive," in *Machiavelli's Virtue* (Chicago: University of Chicago Press, 1998).

6. Machiavelli, *The Prince,* p. 39.

7. Ibid., pp. 33–34, 54–58. On Machiavelli's use of the paradiastolic re-description in *The Prince,* see Quentin Skinner, *Visions of Politics,* Vol. 3, *Hobbes and Civil Science* (Cambridge: Cambridge University Press, 2002), pp. 107–10.

8. According to Hannah Arendt, the excellence of Machiavellian virtue is displayed in the action itself relative to circumstances, not in an end state that conforms to absolute standards derived from Platonic Forms or other transcendental ideals. Arendt, *Between Past and Future: Eight Exercises in Political Thought* (New York: Penguin, 1977), p. 153.

9. J. G. A. Pocock, *The Machiavellian Moment: Florentine Political Thought and the Atlantic Republican Tradition* (Princeton: Princeton University Press, 1975), p. 38.

10. On the advice-books, or mirror-for-princes literature, see Quentin Skinner, *The Foundations of Modern Political Thought: Volume One: The Renaissance* (Cambridge: Cambridge University Press, 1978), especially pp. 113–38.

11. Aquinas' discussion of the legitimacy of theft in cases of dire need is a prominent example. St. Thomas Aquinas, *Political Writings,* ed. and trans. R. W. Tyson (Cambridge: Cambridge University Press, 2002), pp. 216–17. See also William of Ockham, *A Short Discourse on Tyrannical Government,* ed. Arthur Stephen McGrade (Cambridge: Cambridge University Press, 1992), pp. 91–92.

12. Skinner, *The Foundations of Modern Political Thought*, Vol. 1, pp. 125–27. On the "old-fashioned and simple opinion" that "Machiavelli was a teacher of evil," see Leo Strauss, *Thoughts on Machiavelli* (Chicago: University of Chicago Press, 1958), quotation at p. 9. Cf. Hannah Arendt, who argued that Machiavelli's insistence that princes must learn how not to be good was not an endorsement of evil but a rejection of otherworldly moral absolutes associated with Christian and classical notions of goodness. See Arendt, *Between Past and Future*, p. 137. It is worth noting that Machiavelli toned down his apparent enthusiasm for unfettered executive power in the *Discourses*, where he stated that the best princes are constrained by law, for "a prince unshackled from the laws will be more ungrateful, varying, and imprudent than a people." Machiavelli, *Discourses on Livy*, p. 117.

13. Machiavelli, *The Prince*, pp. 32–34, quotation at p. 55.

14. See, for instance, ibid,, pp. 38–39, 63–72. For a revisionist interpretation of Machiavelli that identifies certain quasi-democratic forms of accountability recommended in *Discourses on Livy*, see John McCormick, "Machiavelli against Republicanism: On the Cambridge School's 'Guicciardinian Moments,'" *Political Theory*, Vol. 31, No. 5 (2003).

15. It might be objected that the ancient theory of mixed or balanced government belies the suggestion that executive power is a constitutional aberration in this tradition. However, this theory did not distinguish the constituent parts of government according to function. Rather, they were identified with separate estates (king, nobility, commons) that shared a portion of sovereignty. The separation of powers doctrine was a much later historical development that distinguished the three parts of government (legislative, executive, and judicial) according to their legal functions, not the socioeconomic status of their agents. On these important distinctions, see M. J. C. Vile, *Constitutionalism and the Separation of Powers*, 2d ed. (Indianapolis: Liberty Fund, 1998).

16. "Introduction," *Two Republican Tracts*, ed. Caroline Robbins (Cambridge: Cambridge University Press, 1969), p. 45.

17. John Milton, *Defence of the People of England*, in *Areopagitica and Other Political Writings of John Milton*, ed. John Alvis (Indianapolis: Liberty Fund, 1999), p. 259; see also pp. 265, 275.

18. See G. M. Trevelyan, *The English Revolution: 1688–1689* (Oxford: Oxford University Press, 1938), especially pp. 87–88, 105–6.

19. See Clinton Rossiter, *Constitutional Dictatorship: Crisis Government in the Modern Democracies* (New Brunswick, NJ: Transaction Publishers, 2002), pp. 15–28; and Claude Nicolet, "Dictatorship in Rome," in *Dictatorship in History and Theory: Bonapartism, Caesarism, and Totalitarianism*, ed. Peter Baehr and Melvin Richter (Cambridge: Cambridge University Press, 2004), pp. 263–78.

20. John Ferejohn and Pasquale Pasquino, "The Law of Exception: A Typology of Emergency Powers," *International Journal of Constitutional Law*, Vol. 2, No. 2 (2004), pp. 213, 219–20.

21. See Pocock's magisterial *The Machiavellian Moment*, from which this account of political contingency and secular time borrows.

22. My argument is not that early liberals explicitly or consciously traced their understanding of contingency in politics directly back to Machiavelli, though his works were quite familiar to them, as judged by their library holdings and generally positive citations to his works. My argument is rather that their own (sometimes incompletely theorized) ideas about the unpredictable, irregular, and often irrational quality of politics can best be understood in Machiavellian terms. On Locke's extensive collection of Machiavelli's writings, see John Harrison and Peter Laslett, *The Library of John Locke*, 2d ed. (Oxford: Clarendon Press, 1971), p. 181. On the frequency of citations to Machiavelli in the documents of the American Founding, see Donald S. Lutz, *The Origins of American Constitutionalism* (Baton Rouge: Louisiana State University Press, 1988), pp. 139–47.

23. John Lamberton Harper, *American Machiavelli: Alexander Hamilton and the Origins of U.S. Foreign Policy* (Cambridge: Cambridge University Press, 2004), p. 15; and Ron Chernow, *Alexander Hamilton* (New York: Penguin, 2004), p. 24.

24. See Carl Schmitt, *Political Theology: Four Chapters on the Concept of Sovereignty*, trans. George Schwab (Chicago: University of Chicago Press, 2005), especially ch. 3.

25. James Madison, Alexander Hamilton, and John Jay, *The Federalist Papers*, ed. Isaac Kramnick (New York: Penguin, 1987), p. 87.

26. See Georg Wilhelm Friedrich Hegel, *Introduction to the Philosophy of History*, ed. and trans. Leo Rauch (Indianapolis: Hackett, 1988).

27. John Locke, *Two Treatises of Government*, ed. Peter Laslett (Cambridge: Cambridge University Press, 1988), § 160.

28. Machiavelli, *The Prince*, p. 85.

29. For a powerful defense of the view that classical liberals favored a strong but controlled government, see Stephen Holmes, *Passions and Constraint: On the Theory of Liberal Democracy* (Chicago: University of Chicago Press, 1995).

30. Machiavelli, *The Prince*, p. 62.

31. On Locke's pessimism regarding the vigilance of the people in times of emergency, see Benjamin A. Kleinerman, "Can the Prince Really Be Tamed? Executive Prerogative, Popular Apathy, and the Constitutional Frame in Locke's *Second Treatise*," *American Political Science Review*, Vol. 101, No. 2 (2007), pp. 209–22.

32. David Hume, "Of the Middle Station of Life," *Essays: Moral, Political, and Literary*, ed. Eugene F. Miller (Indianapolis: Liberty Fund, 1985), p. 549.

33. These references to republican virtue—which was unintelligible to most republican thinkers outside the context of an engaged and equal citizenry dedicated to the selfless pursuit of the public good—do not mean that all mentions of virtue by liberals implied republican, or even public, ideals. The word *virtue* was used in a variety of conflicting senses—sometimes by the same writer—to refer to superior mental abilities, agreeable social skills, and exemplary moral qualities. Samuel Johnson's *Dictionary of the English Language* defined virtue variously as: "moral goodness," "medicinal quality," "efficacy," "acting power," and "excellence," to give just a few examples. Samuel Johnson, *A Dictionary of the English Language: In Which the Words Are Deduced from Their Originals, and Illustrated in Their Different Significations by Exam-*

ples from the Best Writers, To Which Are Prefixed, A History of the Language, and an English Grammar (London: W. Strahan, 1755). Revolutionary-era Americans, in particular, would often qualify the virtues they believed were essential to a healthy republic as either public or private. Sometimes there was some overlap between the qualities a citizen was expected to exhibit in different arenas of life—honesty and frugality, for example—but context and usage usually make it clear that their conceptions of public virtue correspond to republican ideals.

34. Charles Louis de Secondat Montesquieu, *The Spirit of the Laws*, ed. Anne M. Cohler, Basia Carolyn Miller, and Harold Samuel Stone (Cambridge: Cambridge University Press, 1989), p. 36.

35. Maurizio Viroli insists that there is a significant difference between conceptions of political virtue articulated by eighteenth-century writers like Montesquieu and the *philosophes* and those formulated by "classical" republicans such as Machiavelli. The latter, he claims, "did not think of civic virtue as a renunciation and sacrifice" but instead stressed the compatibility of public and private interests. Viroli, *Republicanism* (New York: Hill and Wang, 2002), p. 71. Viroli's discussion offers a useful reminder that republican conceptions of virtue were not limited to heroic ideals of self-sacrifice, but it goes too far in denying these understandings when public and private interest *do* conflict.

36. Ibid., pp. 79–87; and Mary G. Dietz, "Patriotism," in *Political Innovation and Conceptual Change*, ed. Terence Ball, James Farr, and Russell L. Hanson (Cambridge: Cambridge University Press, 1989), pp. 177–93.

37. Gordon Wood, "Interests and Disinterestedness in the Making of the Constitution," in *Beyond Confederation: Origins of the Constitution and American National Identity*, ed. Richard Beeman, Stephen Botein, and Edward C. Carter II (Chapel Hill: University of North Carolina Press, 1987).

38. John Trenchard and Thomas Gordon, *Cato's Letters, or Essays on Liberty, Civil and Religious, and Other Important Subjects*, ed. Ronald Hamowy (Indianapolis: Liberty Fund, 1995), Vol. 2, p. 279.

39. Montesquieu, *Spirit of the Laws*, p. 35.

40. J. G. A. Pocock, *Politics, Language, and Time: Essays on Political Thought and History* (Chicago: University of Chicago Press, 1989), pp. 123–35, quotation at p. 131; and *Virtue, Commerce, and History* (Cambridge: Cambridge University Press, 1985), pp. 75–80.

41. For instance, Aristotle claimed that "no function of man has so much permanence as virtuous activities." Aristotle, *The Nicomachean Ethics*, ed. and trans. David Ross (Oxford: Oxford University Press, 1925). Cary J. Nederman argues that Western thought from Aristotle to Machiavelli was dominated by the belief that "human action arises from a fixed character" in "Machiavelli and Moral Character: Principality, Republic and the Psychology of Virtù," *History of Political Thought*, Vol. 21, No. 3 (2000), quotation at p. 355.

42. Nancy Sherman, *The Fabric of Character: Aristotle's Theory of Virtue* (Oxford: Clarendon Press, 1989), p. 1.

43. The justification behind the law banning seditious libel in this period was the notion that a good opinion of government and its officers was a prerequisite of effective government. Leonard W. Levy, *Emergence of a Free Press* (New York: Oxford University Press, 1985).

44. See Scott Gordon, *Controlling the State: Constitutionalism from Ancient Athens to Today* (Cambridge: Harvard University Press, 1999).

45. It should be remembered that "citizens" were conceptually and politically distinct from the mass of the "people" in republican thought.

46. J. G. A. Pocock, "Civic Humanism and Its Role in Anglo-American Thought," *Politics, Language, and Time,* pp. 85, 87. As Viroli explains, participation by a virtuous citizenry was not an end in itself but a means of preserving freedom. Viroli, *Republicanism,* p. 66.

47. Pocock, *Machiavellian Moment,* p. 76.

48. Madison, Hamilton, and Jay, *The Federalist Papers,* X, pp. 123, 128.

49. Ibid., VI, p. 108. The first appearance of the term in the second essay referred to the "patriotism, virtue, and wisdom" of the delegates to the Convention; ibid., II, 92. All references to the frequency and use of particular terms in the *Federalist* are corroborated by the comprehensive analyses contained in Tomas S. Engeman, Edward J. Erler, and Thomas B. Hofeller, eds., *The* Federalist *Concordance* (Middletown, CT: Wesleyan University Press, 1980).

50. See Hannah Arendt, *The Human Condition* (Chicago: University of Chicago Press, 1958).

51. This has obvious parallels to John Rawls's idea of an "overlapping consensus." See his *Political Liberalism* (New York: Columbia University Press, 2005).

52. A good, if surprising, example of this modern bifurcation of public and private virtues appears in Alexander Hamilton's "Reynolds Pamphlet," where he confessed to an adulterous relationship with a married woman, and therefore acknowledged his private vices and personal failings, in order to salvage his reputation as an honest and upright public servant. The most comprehensive account of the affair and its aftermath is Ron Chernow, *Alexander Hamilton* (New York: Penguin, 2004), pp. 364–70, 409–18, 528–45.

53. Ernst H. Kantorowicz, *The King's Two Bodies: A Study in Medieval Political Theology* (Princeton: Princeton University Press, 1957), p. 58. The discussion here is based largely on Kantorowicz's excellent study.

54. See the title essay by Douglass Adair in *Fame and the Founding Fathers,* ed. Trevor Colbourn (Indianapolis: Liberty Fund, 1998) and all of the essays in *The Noblest Minds: Fame, Honor, and the American Founding,* ed. Peter McNamara (Lanham, MD: Rowman and Littlefield, 1999).

55. See Stephen Holmes, "The Liberal Idea," *The American Prospect,* No. 7 (1991), pp. 88–89.

56. The views of Locke and Hume on this point are discussed in chapters 2 and 3, respectively. Adam Smith's famous notion of the "impartial spectator" is the most

powerful expression of the normative role that the opinion of others plays in encouraging moral conduct. See Adam Smith, *The Theory of Moral Sentiments,* ed. D. D. Raphael and A. L. Macfie (Indianapolis: Liberty Classics, 1982).

57. See Arendt, *Human Condition,* p. 74.

58. Of course, not all scholars who acknowledge the continuing importance of virtue in the constitutional system necessarily define these virtues in republican terms. See, for example, Alan Gibson, "Impartial Representation and the Extended Republic: Towards a Comprehensive and Balanced Reading of the Tenth *Federalist* Paper," *History of Political Thought,* Vol. 12, No. 2 (Summer 1991); Charles R. Kesler, "Introduction," *The Federalist Papers,* ed. Clinton Rossiter (New York: Mentor, 1999), pp. xxi, xxxi; and James P. Pfiffner, "Presidential Character in Perspective," paper presented at the Annual Meeting of the American Political Science Association, August 30–September 2, 2001, pp. 17–18. Two notable exceptions include Jean Yarbrough, "Republicanism Reconsidered: Some Thoughts on the Foundation and Preservation of the American Republic," *Review of Politics,* Vol. 41, No. 1 (1979), pp. 61–95; and Wood, "Interests and Disinterestedness," pp. 69–109.

59. Good reviews of this literature include Robert E. Shalhope, "Toward a Republican Synthesis: The Emergence of an Understanding of Republicanism in American Historiography," *William and Mary Quarterly,* 3rd Series, Vol. 29, No. 1 (1972); and Daniel T. Rodgers, "Republicanism: the Career of a Concept," *Journal of American History,* Vol. 79, No. 1 (1992). See also John Zvesper, "The American Founders and Classical Political Thought," *History of Political Thought,* Vol. 10, No. 4 (1989). The shortcomings of this literature are dissected in Isaac Kramnick, "Republican Revisionism Revisited," in *Republicanism and Bourgeois Radicalism: Political Ideology in Late Eighteenth-Century England and America* (Ithaca: Cornell University Press, 1990).

60. Bernard Bailyn, *To Begin the World Anew: The Genius and Ambiguities of the American Founders* (New York: Vintage Books, 2003), p. 123.

61. Martin Diamond, "Democracy and *The Federalist*: A Reconsideration of the Framers' Intent," *American Political Science Review,* Vol. 53, No. 1 (1959), p. 68.

62. Robert A. Dahl, *A Preface to Democratic Theory* (Chicago: University of Chicago Press, 1956), pp. 22, 83.

63. Rahe, *Republics Ancient and Modern,* Vol. 3, *Inventions of Prudence: Constituting the American Regime* (Chapel Hill: University of North Carolina Press, 1994), p. xxx.

64. Beer, *To Make a Nation: The Rediscovery of American Federalism* (Cambridge: Belknap Press, 1993), pp. 281–82. See also Richard K. Matthews, *If Men Were Angels: James Madison and the Heartless Empire of Reason* (Lawrence: University Press of Kansas, 1995), pp. 77–82, 207; and Michael P. Zuckert, "The Political Science of James Madison," *History of American Political Thought,* ed. Bryan-Paul Frost and Jeffrey Sikkenga (Lanham, MD: Lexington Books, 2003), p. 163.

65. John P. Diggins, *The Lost Soul of American Politics: Virtue, Self-Interest, and the Foundations of Liberalism* (New York: Basic Books, 1984), p. 24.

66. Shklar, "A New Constitution for a New Nation," in *Redeeming American Political Thought,* ed. Stanley Hoffman and Dennis F. Thompson (Chicago: University of Chicago Press, 1998), p. 164.

67. On the mechanical metaphors of eighteenth- and early nineteenth-century constitutionalism, see Michael Kammen, *A Machine That Would Go of Itself: The Constitution in American Culture* (New York: Vintage Books, 1987).

68. Alexander Hamilton to William Heth, June 23[-24], 1791, *The Papers of Alexander Hamilton,* Vol. 8, p. 500. In another letter he explained that he returned to politics in 1787 because he felt "an obligation to lend my aid towards putting the machine in some regular motion." *Alexander Hamilton: Writings,* ed. Joanne B. Freeman (New York: Library of America, 2001), p. 880.

69. Carl J. Richard, *The Founders and the Classics: Greece, Rome, and the American Enlightenment* (Cambridge: Harvard University Press, 1994).

70. Shklar, "New Constitution," p. 164.

71. On the frequency of citation of different European writers, see Lutz, *Origins of American Constitutionalism,* pp. 139–47. Subsequent remarks regarding the popularity of different writers are based on Lutz's tabulations.

72. See Adair's title essay and "Hamiltonian Sidelights: A Note on Certain of Hamilton's Pseudonyms" in *Fame and the Founding Fathers.*

73. There are interesting allusions to this idea in Jonathan Swift, *Gulliver's Travels,* ed. Peter Dixon and John Chalker (New York: Penguin, 1967), especially Part II, ch. 7, pp. 175–76; Part III, ch. 6, p. 232; and Part IV, ch. 12, pp. 343–44.

74. Frederic M. Litto, "Addison's *Cato* in the Colonies," *William and Mary Quarterly,* 3rd Series, Vol. 23, No. 3 (1966).

75. On the various "modes of discourse" engaged in by Americans, see Kramnick, "The Great National Discussion," in *Republicanism and Bourgeois Radicalism.*

76. The idea of limited government is very often regarded as the very essence of constitutionalism, but the tendency to equate the two ideas ignores all of the constitutional theories from Bodin to Schmitt that stress the concept of sovereignty over that of individual or natural rights.

77. See A. V. Dicey, *Introduction to the Study of the Law of the Constitution,* 10th ed. (New York: St. Martin's Press, 1961), especially pp. 183–205, 394–95.

78. A notable exception to this legalistic tendency is Harvey C. Mansfield Jr., "Constitutionalism and the Rule of Law," *Harvard Journal of Law and Public Policy,* Vol. 8, No. 2 (1985).

79. See, for example, Jürgen Habermas, *Between Facts and Norms: Contributions to a Discourse Theory of Law and Democracy,* trans. William Rehg (Cambridge: MIT Press, 1998); and Sheldon S. Wolin, *The Presence of the Past: Essays on the State and the Constitution* (Baltimore: Johns Hopkins University Press, 1989). See also Larry Alexander, ed., *Constitutionalism: Philosophical Foundations* (Cambridge: Cambridge University Press, 1998), where executive power receives only passing notice. However, it has received a little more theoretical attention of late due to growing scholarly interest in the political thought of Carl Schmitt and in response to the current "war on

terror." See, for example, Giorgio Agamben, *State of Exception*, trans. Kevin Attell (Chicago: University of Chicago Press, 2005).

80. See Timothy A. O. Endicott, "The Impossibility of the Rule of Law," *Oxford Journal of Legal Studies*, Vol. 19, No. 1 (1999).

81. Cass R. Sunstein, *Legal Reasoning and Political Conflict* (Oxford: Oxford University Press, 1996), pp. 21–32; and H. L. A. Hart, *The Concept of Law* (Oxford: Oxford University Press, 1961), pp. 121–32.

82. See Clement Fatovic, "Constitutionalism and Presidential Prerogative: Jeffersonian and Hamiltonian Perspectives," *American Journal of Political Science*, Vol. 48, No. 3 (2004), pp. 429–44.

83. James Madison to Thomas Jefferson, January 18, 1800, *The Writings of James Madison*, ed. Gaillard Hunt (New York: J. P. Putnam's Sons, 1901), Vol. 6, p. 370.

84. For an elaboration, see Keith Whittington, *Constitutional Construction: Divided Powers and Constitutional Meaning* (Cambridge: Harvard University Press, 1999), pp. 1–19, 207–28.

85. Harvey C. Mansfield and Nathan Tarcov, "Introduction," *Discourses on Livy*, p. xxx.

86. See Phillip J. Cooper, *By Order of the President: The Use and Abuse of Executive Direct Action* (Lawrence: University Press of Kansas, 2002).

87. Mansfield, "Machiavelli's New Regime," in *Machiavelli's Virtue*, p. 256.

88. On the use of principles to resolve hard cases, see Ronald Dworkin, *Taking Rights Seriously* (Cambridge: Harvard University Press, 1978) and *Law's Empire* (Cambridge: Belknap Press, 1986).

89. Thomas Jefferson to Doctor James Brown, October 27, 1808, *The Writings of Thomas Jefferson*, ed. Paul Leicester Ford (New York: G. P. Putnam's Sons, 1905), Vol. 11, p. 211. As one interpreter explains, Jefferson believed that an executive must "look to the principle of the law to set aside its details." Jeremy David Bailey, "Executive Prerogative and the 'Good Officer' in Thomas Jefferson's Letter to John B. Colvin," *Presidential Studies Quarterly*, Vol. 34, No. 4 (2004), p. 750.

90. Even Jefferson, the premier exponent of strict constructionism, argued that express constitutional limits should not deter government from achieving vital objectives: "Congress must legalize all *means* which may be necessary to obtain it's [sic] *end*." Thomas Jefferson to Albert Gallatin, August 11, 1808, *The Writings of Thomas Jefferson*, Vol. 11, p. 41.

91. David Hume, "Of Passive Obedience," *Essays*, p. 489.

CHAPTER 2: "Without the Prescription of the Law"

Epigraph. John Locke, *Two Treatises of Government*, ed. Peter Laslett (Cambridge: Cambridge University Press, 1988), II, § 160. An earlier version of portions of this chapter has been published as Clement Fatovic, "Constitutionalism and Contingency: Locke's Theory of Prerogative," *History of Political Thought*, Vol. XXV, No. 2 (2004).

1. For an elaboration of this "antityrannical strand" in liberal thought, see Stephen Holmes, *Passions and Constraint: On the Theory of Liberal Democracy* (Chicago: University of Chicago Press, 1995), pp. 13–23.

2. Henceforth references to *Two Treatises* will appear in the body of the text, with the number of the treatise followed by the section number. Unless otherwise noted, italics in quotations appear in the original.

3. Ronald Dworkin labels this notion the "'rule-book' conception" of the rule of law, which "insists that, so far as is possible, the power of the state should never be exercised against individual citizens except in accordance with rules explicitly set out in a public rule book available to all." Dworkin, *A Matter of Principle* (Cambridge: Harvard University Press, 1985), p. 11.

4. Carl Schmitt, *Political Theology*, trans. George Schwab (Chicago: University of Chicago Press, 1985), p. 13.

5. Edward Corwin argued that this feature of Locke's politics, "in view both of the immediate occasion for which he wrote and of his 'constitutionalism,' [is] not a little astonishing." *The "Higher Law" Background of American Constitutional Law* (Ithaca: Cornell University Press, 1955), p. 71. See also Robert Scigliano, "The President's 'Prerogative Power,'" in Thomas E. Cronin, *Inventing the American Presidency* (Lawrence: University Press of Kansas, 1989), p. 242.

6. The best study of Locke's involvement in these political events is Richard Ashcraft, *Revolutionary Politics and Locke's "Two Treatises of Government"* (Princeton: Princeton University Press, 1986). See also Richard Ashcraft, "The *Two Treatises* and the Exclusion Crisis: The Problem of Lockean Political Theory as Bourgeois Ideology," in *John Locke: Papers Read at a Clark Library Seminar, 10 December 1977* (Los Angeles: William Andrews Clark Memorial Library, 1980); Lois G. Schwoerer, "Locke, Lockean Ideas, and the Glorious Revolution," *Journal of the History of Ideas,* Vol. 51, No. 4 (1990); and John Marshall, *John Locke: Resistance, Religion, and Responsibility* (Cambridge: Cambridge University Press, 1994), pp. 205–91.

7. See Gordon J. Schochet, *Patriarchalism in Political Thought: The Authoritarian Family and Political Speculation and Attitudes Especially in Seventeenth-Century England* (New York: Basic Books, 1975).

8. See, for example, Edward S. Corwin, *The President: Office and Powers, 1787–1957,* 4th rev. ed. (New York: New York University Press, 1957), pp. 5–10; Richard M. Pious, *The American Presidency* (New York: Basic Books, 1979); Larry Arnhart, "'The God-Like Prince': John Locke, Executive Prerogative, and the American Presidency," *Presidential Studies Quarterly,* Vol. 9, No. 2 (1979); John Yoo, *The Powers of War and Peace: The Constitution and Foreign Affairs after 9/11* (Chicago: University of Chicago Press, 2005), pp. 36–39, 44–45. See also Thomas S. Langston and Michael E. Lind, "John Locke and the Limits of Presidential Prerogative," *Polity,* Vol. 24, No. 1 (1991); and Phillip J. Cooper, *By Order of the President: The Use and Abuse of Executive Direct Action* (Lawrence: University Press of Kansas, 2002).

9. John Gray, *Enlightenment's Wake: Politics and Culture at the Close of the Modern Age* (London: Routledge, 1995), p. 6. One of the few works that actually distinguishes

Locke's constitutionalism from the rationalistic constitutionalism of thinkers like Kant and Condorcet is Pasquale Pasquino, "Locke on King's Prerogative," *Political Theory*, Vol. 26, No. 2 (1998).

10. See Jeremy Waldron, *The Dignity of Legislation* (Cambridge: Cambridge University Press, 1999), p. 84, which also makes the case that Lockean liberalism looks beyond "formal declarations or other institutional arrangements" to protect individual rights.

11. The most relevant scholarship in the voluminous secondary literature on Locke's theory of natural law can be found in the first five footnotes of Francis Oakley, "Locke, Natural Law, and God—Again," *History of Political Thought*, Vol. 18, No. 4 (1997), pp. 624–26.

12. See A. John Simmons, *The Lockean Theory of Rights* (Princeton: Princeton University Press, 1992). For a good analysis of Locke's "conception of the common good and a conception of civil society as more than an aggregate of atomistic individuals," see Nathan Tarcov, "A 'Non-Lockean' Locke and the Character of Liberalism," *Liberalism Reconsidered*, ed. Douglas MacLean and Claudia Mills (Totowa, NJ: Rowman and Allanheld, 1983), quotation at p. 131.

13. Although *salus populi suprema lex* has a different meaning and developmental history than the modern doctrine of natural law, Locke does not envision any scenario in which the two might come into conflict.

14. Arnhart, "The God-Like Prince," p. 124.

15. John Locke, *An Essay concerning Human Understanding*, ed. Peter H. Nidditch (Oxford: Clarendon Press, 1975), Book II, ch. 28, § 11.

16. See Corwin, *"Higher Law" Background*, pp. 39–40; and Charles Howard McIlwain, *Constitutionalism Ancient and Modern* (Indianapolis: Liberty Fund, 2008), pp. 61–83.

17. On this point, see the discussion of John of Salisbury in Ernst H. Kantorowicz, *The King's Two Bodies: A Study in Medieval Political Theology* (Princeton: Princeton University Press, 1957), pp. 94–97, as well as passages in John of Salisbury, *Policraticus: Of the Frivolities of Courtiers and the Footprints of Philosophers*, ed. Cary J. Nederman (Cambridge: Cambridge University Press, 1990), pp. 28–31, 190–91. John of Salisbury admonished his readers that "he who directs the laws, while he is subject to none of them, is more strictly prohibited from illegal acts," p. 223.

18. See Paul Birdsall, "Non Obstante," in *Essays in History and Political Theory in Honor of Charles Howard McIlwain*, ed. Carl Wittke (New York: Russell and Russell, 1936).

19. Max Adams Shepard, "The Political and Constitutional Theory of Sir John Fortescue," in ibid., p. 289. See also R. W. K. Hinton, "English Constitutional Doctrines from the Fifteenth Century to the Seventeenth: English Constitutional Theories from Sir John Fortescue to Sir John Eliot," *English Historical Review*, Vol. 75 (1960); and Sir John Fortescue, *On the Laws and Governance of England*, ed. Shelley Lockwood (Cambridge: Cambridge University Press, 1997).

20. Goldwin Smith, *A Constitutional and Legal History of England* (New York: Charles Scribner's Sons, 1955), p. 253.

21. Quoted in Conrad Russell, *The Crisis of Parliaments: English History, 1509–1660* (Oxford: Oxford University Press, 1974), p. 196. On the historical transformations of this maxim, see Greenberg, "Our Grand Maxim of State." Sir Edward Coke put the point in no uncertain terms: as God's lieutenant on earth, the king "must do no wrong." Quoted in Russell, p. 202. Coke was the most outspoken critic of royal prerogative in this period and sought to limit its reach under the common law. In 1616 he was dismissed as Chief Justice of the King's Bench for his recalcitrance but continued to oppose the Stuarts as a member of Parliament.

22. King James VI and I, *Political Writings*, ed. Johann P. Sommerville (Cambridge: Cambridge University Press, 1994). On early seventeenth-century constitutional theory generally, see Smith, *Constitutional and Legal History of England*, pp. 302–31.

23. On this "duplex" understanding of prerogative, see Glenn Burgess, *The Politics of the Ancient Constitution: An Introduction to English Political Thought, 1603–1642* (University Park: Pennsylvania State University Press, 1992), pp. 139–78.

24. Clement Fatovic, "The Anti-Catholic Roots of Liberal and Republican Conceptions of Freedom in English Political Thought," *Journal of the History of Ideas*, Vol. 66, No. 1 (2005).

25. Ashcraft, *Revolutionary Politics*, p. 35.

26. Ibid., pp. 111–12.

27. Ibid., p. 119.

28. Quoted in ibid., p. 313.

29. Ibid., p. 314.

30. Ibid., p. 495.

31. Lois G. Schwoerer, *The Declaration of Rights, 1689* (Baltimore: Johns Hopkins University Press, 1972).

32. John Dunn argues that Whigs sought the abolition of many royal prerogatives on constitutional grounds but harbored no personal animosity toward the king himself. John Dunn, *The Political Thought of John Locke: An Historical Account of the Argument of the "Two Treatises of Government"* (Cambridge: Cambridge University Press, 1969), p. 46. Locke himself took exactly the opposite position, namely, that prerogative was a useful and even necessary instrument, but that unscrupulous executives who abused it deserved to be hated by their subjects.

33. See Schochet, *Patriarchalism in Political Thought*, passim; and Dunn, *Political Thought of John Locke*, pp. 73–74. In fact, Locke claims that the origin of prerogative lies "in the Infancy of Governments, when Commonwealths differ'd little from Families in number of People" (II, § 162).

34. Due to the peculiar nature of the federative power, it would not have the benefit of guidance by positive law or be amenable to the kinds of institutional strictures imposed on the legislative. As a result, Locke argued that it must be entrusted "to the Prudence and Wisdom of those whose hands it is in, to be managed for the publick good" (II, § 147). But like the legislative, it is duty-bound to fulfill the end for

which political society is established: the preservation of its members. In other words, the exercise of federative power beyond the letter of positive law does not subvert constitutional government as long as it seeks to fulfill the reason, or purpose, behind the people's consent. For an analysis of the relation between extralegal activities and popular consent, see John Dunn, "Consent in the Political Theory of John Locke," in *Life, Liberty, and Property: Essays on Locke's Political Ideas,* ed. Gordon J. Schochet (Belmont, CA: Wadsworth, 1971), pp. 156–58.

35. Waldron, *Dignity of Legislation,* p. 66.

36. As Schwoerer writes, "Locke is among the few political theorists in late Stuart England who, like earlier royalists, understood the possibility of legislative tyranny." Schwoerer, "Locke, Lockean Ideas, and the Glorious Revolution," p. 542.

37. Niccolò Machiavelli, *Discourses on Livy,* trans. Harvey C. Mansfield and Nathan Tarcov (Chicago: University of Chicago Press, 1996), pp. 209–12.

38. Grant proposes that this act of prerogative is an instance of constitutional "maintenance" rather than alteration. Grant, *John Locke's Liberalism,* pp. 144–45.

39. Note the apparent annoyance with which Locke observes that "People are not so easily got out of their old Forms" (II, § 223).

40. Nor were they limited to the realm of politics. The "unsteady fleeting conditions of our bodys and spirits" also makes it "impossible to set a standing rule" when it comes to recreation or other matters relating to physical and mental well-being. John Locke to Dr. Denis Grenville [9/19–11/21 March 1677], *The Correspondence of John Locke,* ed. E. S. De Beer (Oxford: Clarendon Press, 1976), Vol. I, p. 473.

41. Laslett charges Locke with being the most unhistorical of the canonical political theorists: "Neither Machiavelli, nor Hobbes, nor Rousseau succeeded in making the discussion of politics so completely independent of historical example, so entirely autonomous an area of discourse." "Introduction," *Two Treatises,* p. 78. There is truth in this statement, but it misleadingly suggests that Locke was an ahistorical thinker who neglected historical changes. Locke's historical sensibility manifests itself in the logic of his argument and in his anthropological claims, though not in any references to specific events. What distinguishes him from these other thinkers was his reluctance to make his system depend on the contingencies of particular historical events. On Locke's studious avoidance of some of the most pressing historical controversies of his day, see J. G. A. Pocock, "The Myth of John Locke and the Obsession with Liberalism," in *John Locke: Papers Read at a Clark Library Seminar, 10 December 1977* (Los Angeles: William Andrews Clark Memorial Library, 1980), pp. 3–7; and *The Ancient Constitution and the Feudal Law: A Study in English Historical Thought in the Seventeenth Century: A Reissue with a Retrospect* (Cambridge: Cambridge University Press, 1987), pp. 235–36.

42. Jonathan Scott, *England's Troubles: Seventeenth-Century English Political Instability in European Context* (Cambridge: Cambridge University Press, 2000), pp. 33–37.

43. Christopher Anderson is one of the only commentators to note this Machiavellian strain in Locke's thought. Anderson, "Safe Enough in His Honesty and Prudence," p. 623. A more typical reading of Locke is in the claim that "no literary debt

to Machiavelli shows upon the surface for all [Locke's] pains to collect editions of that author." John Harrison and Peter Laslett, *The Library of John Locke*, 2d ed. (Oxford: Clarendon Press, 1971), p. 22. That remark is clearly belied by Locke's description of the contingency of politics in connection with his presentation of prerogative power. By the end of his life Locke owned at least ten volumes of Machiavelli's writings, including three different versions of *The Prince*. Harrison and Laslett, *Library of John Locke*, p. 21. One can only speculate when Locke acquired each of the volumes of Machiavelli he owned, but there is no indication that he bought any of the copies in his library later in his life, when he adopted the practice of annotating new acquisitions with a letter code. On Locke's cataloguing system in his later years, see Harrison and Laslett, *Library of John Locke*, p. 35. Although it is uncertain if Locke had ready access to all of Machiavelli's texts while he was exiled in Holland, he purchased several works by Machiavelli, including *The Prince* and the *Discourses*, before his departure and acquired "the corrected Latin version of the *Prince*" in Holland. For a list of the volumes by Machiavelli contained in Locke's library, see Harrison and Laslett, *Library of John Locke*, p. 181.

44. J. G. A. Pocock, *The Machiavellian Moment: Florentine Political Thought and the Atlantic Republican Tradition* (Princeton: Princeton University Press, 1975), p. 117. Locke participated actively in bringing about the changes eventually ushered in by the Glorious Revolution through his involvement in radical Whig politics and revolutionary intrigue. Locke's life in this period reads like a story of Machiavellian political intrigue. Ashcraft points out that Locke began to take a keen interest in political conspiracies between 1681 and 1683, as reflected in his journal notes, which indicated that he was reading both *The Prince* and the *Discourses* very carefully at an extremely tense moment in his involvement in radical politics. Ashcraft, *Revolutionary Politics*, pp. 382–83.

45. Anthony Ashley Cooper, Earl of Shaftesbury, "A Letter from a Person of Quality, to His Friend in the Country," in *The Struggle for Sovereignty: Seventeenth-Century English Political Tracts*, ed. Joyce Lee Malcolm (Indianapolis: Liberty Fund, 1999), p. 638.

46. Harvey C. Mansfield Jr., *Taming the Prince: The Ambivalence of Modern Executive Power* (Baltimore: Johns Hopkins University Press, 1989).

47. Arnhart, "The God-Like Prince," p. 125.

48. Richard H. Cox reaches a similar conclusion, but takes a far more circuitous path that relies on convoluted numerical formulas to make the case that Locke's theory of prerogative signifies "a turning to Machiavelli's teaching on 'princely government.'" Cox, "Executive and Prerogative: A Problem for Adherents of Constitutional Government," in *E Pluribus Unum: Constitutional Principles and the Institutions of Government*, ed. Sarah Baumgartner Thurow (Lanham, MD: University Press of America, 1988), pp. 111–18.

49. Laslett, "Introduction," *Two Treatises*, pp. 87–88.

50. On the humanist advice-books that appeared in thirteenth-century Italy, see Quentin Skinner, *The Foundations of Modern Political Thought: Volume One: The Renaissance* (Cambridge: Cambridge University Press, 1978), pp. 33–35.

51. The Lockean executive does not seek to "innovate" in the Machiavellian sense of dispensing with or overthrowing a legitimate system of government that has become obsolete in the face of unprecedented change. (On the concept of innovation in Machiavelli's thought, see Pocock, *Machiavellian Moment*, pp. 160–69.) Instead of initiating wholesale changes, Locke's executive seeks piecemeal solutions to problems as they arise. Finally, although Locke's executive must be as ready as Machiavelli's prince to deal with emergencies, the former is not as aggressive as the latter in controlling the course of events, and is expected to react to, rather than initiate, change.

52. This language also appears in many of Locke's earlier writings. See, for example, *First Tract on Government*, in *Political Essays*, pp. 32–33; and *An Essay on Toleration*, in *Political Essays*, p. 142.

53. Richard Tuck attributes the emergence of this vocabulary in England to the spread of the "new humanism, that constitutional and legal forms should be overridden in the *interests* of a people or a prince." Tuck, *Philosophy and Government: 1572–1651* (Cambridge: Cambridge University Press, 1993), p. 223.

54. Ibid., p. 56, emphasis in original. For instance, Locke does not allow his executive to violate the natural law in responding to necessity. In contrast, Richelieu and the French Lipsians permitted the king to commit certain acts of oppression if warranted by necessity, pp. 88–89.

55. It is worth bearing in mind that natural law is not identical to the public good. It is conceivable that a civil law or government policy that ostensibly promotes the welfare of a particular community violates natural law, as in the cases of imperialism and colonialism.

56. Thomas S. Langston and Michael E. Lind contend that prerogative comes in two main varieties: the "specific," which includes those enumerated powers that supplement or correct the legislative, and the "general," which consists of the "prelegal," the "antilegal," and the "alegal" prerogatives to act before, against, or in the absence of legislative enactments. They deny that Locke upheld alegal prerogative, but this denial stems from a misunderstanding of the relation between executive power and natural law, which I discuss below. They define law strictly in terms of legislative enactments, overlooking the primacy of natural law in Locke's political theory. Langston and Lind, "John Locke and the Limits of Presidential Prerogative," *Polity*, Vol. 24, No. 1 (1991).

57. Burgess, *Politics of the Ancient Constitution*, pp. 139–78.

58. Ross J. Corbett, "The Extraconstitutionality of Lockean Prerogative," *Review of Politics*, Vol. 68, No. 3 (2006), p. 436.

59. Despite Locke's unambiguous words to the contrary, Robert Scigliano argues that Lockean prerogative does not allow the executive to act against the law. Scigliano contends that Locke is so confusing on this point because he "wished to disguise his meaning regarding prerogative in order to protect himself"—a very strange thing for a man explicitly advocating rebellion and regicide to do. Scigliano, "President's 'Prerogative Power,'" p. 243.

60. Grant, *John Locke's Liberalism*, p. 84.

61. Locke concluded this discussion with a brief and general historical excursus that confirms the prevalence of such acquiescence in English history: "The People therefore finding reason to be satisfied with these Princes, whenever they acted without or contrary to the Letter of the Law, acquiesced in what they did, and, without the least complaint, let them inlarge their *Prerogative* as they pleased, judging rightly, that they did nothing herein to the prejudice of their Laws, since they acted conformable to the Foundation and End of all Laws, the publick good" (II, § 165).

62. The legitimacy of government for Locke is not determined solely or even primarily in terms of its consensual basis but depends to a large degree on its effectiveness in actually realizing the instructions of the laws of nature, just as the security of the people in the broadest sense depends on more than merely formal observance of the rule of law. In fact, the validity of consent itself is delimited by the laws of nature. Locke relied on the indifference of the people, who "are far from examining *Prerogative*" (II, § 161), to buttress its stability. On the apathy of the people in this context, see Benjamin A. Kleinerman, "Can the Prince Really be Tamed? Executive Prerogative, Popular Apathy, and the Constitutional Frame in Locke's *Second Treatise*," *American Political Science Review*, Vol. 101, No. 2 (2007), pp. 209–22.

63. On the distinction between arbitrary power and discretionary power, see Grant, *John Locke's Liberalism*, pp. 72–73.

64. Quoted in Margaret Atwood Judson, *The Crisis of the Constitution: An Essay in Constitutional and Political Thought in England, 1602–1645* (New York: Octagon Books, 1964), p. 233.

65. See ibid., pp. 232–34, 237, 242.

66. Ibid., p. 355.

67. Quoted in Skinner, *Liberty Before Liberalism*, p. 1.

68. Quoted in Pocock, *Ancient Constitution and the Feudal Law*, p. 176; on Hale's denial that individual reason was equal to the reason and experience embodied in the common law, see pp. 170–81.

69. For a comparison of Locke's and Sidney's views, see James Conniff, "Reason and History in Early Whig Thought: The Case of Algernon Sidney," *Journal of the History of Ideas*, Vol. 43 (1982), pp. 397–416. Sidney's treatise is fairly representative of ideas shared by many other seventeenth-century English republicans, including John Milton and Henry Neville, so the following presentation draws out the main differences between two alternative schools of thought on executive power and constitutional government.

70. Algernon Sidney, *Discourses concerning Government*, ed. Thomas G. West (Indianapolis: Liberty Fund, 1996), pp. 222, 284; on Sidney's meritocratic tendencies, see pp. 38, 44, 50, 80–86, and 135. Although Neville acknowledged the validity of certain exercises of prerogative, he limited prerogative to what was defined in law— which is, in effect, an almost entirely different notion of prerogative from Locke's. See Henry Neville, *Plato Redivivus*, in *Two English Republican Tracts*, ed. Caroline Robbins (Cambridge: Cambridge University Press, 1969), pp. 126, 131.

71. Sidney, *Discourses concerning Government,* p. 376.

72. Ibid., p. 310.

73. Ibid., p. 403.

74. Ibid., p. 86.

75. Ibid., p. 381.

76. Ibid., p. 364. He also noted that, "the end which was ever proposed, being the good of the publick, they only performed their duty, who procured it according to the laws of the society, which were equally valid as to their own magistrates, whether they were few or many," p. 99.

77. John Milton, *The Tenure of Kings and Magistrates,* in *Areopagitica and Other Political Writings of John Milton,* ed. John Alvis (Indianapolis: Liberty Fund, 1999), p. 59.

78. Neville, *Plato Redivivus,* pp. 130–31, quotation at p. 130.

79. Sidney, *Discourses concerning Government,* p. 109.

80. On this indifference, see ibid., p. 386. Recognizing the imperfection of human laws, Sidney did permit judges to exercise discretion, but that is only because of a circumstance peculiar to England: namely, the confusion resulting from voluminous, contradictory laws; see pp. 465–68.

81. Ibid., p. 451. Sidney's reservations about the pardon power stem from a preference for strict executions of justice that is reminiscent of Machiavelli's position; see p. 556.

82. Ibid., p. 401.

83. Ibid., p. 572.

84. Ibid., pp. 151, 152.

85. Ibid., p. 121.

86. Ibid., p. 301.

87. Quoted in Judson, *Crisis of the Constitution,* p. 113, emphasis added. On the general welfare powers of the king, see pp. 111–16.

88. Ibid., pp. 136, 140–47.

89. Dunn, *Political Thought of John Locke,* pp. 149, 151.

90. Ibid., pp. 150–51.

91. Pocock claims that of all the great seventeenth-century political writers, Locke exhibited the least interest in the concept of the ancient constitution and the origins of the English constitution. But as discussed above, Locke's main interest in history was really in the historicity and contingency of political and social life, not in the events of the past per se. If, as Pocock alleges, "Locke's whole cast of mind led him towards a non-historical theory of politics," that was only because Locke rejected the idea that antiquity validates present political practices, not because he did not appreciate historical change. For Locke, the legitimacy of a political arrangement is independent of its historical pedigree, which is of paramount importance to republicans. Pocock, *Ancient Constitution and the Feudal Law,* p. 46, quotation at p. 236.

92. Dunn, *Political Thought of John Locke,* p. 151.

93. On nature as the source of right, see Grant, *John Locke's Liberalism,* pp. 64–72.

94. John Locke, *Essays on the Law of Nature*, in *Political Essays*, ed. Mark Goldie (Cambridge: Cambridge University Press, 1997), pp. 87–88.

95. Mansfield, *Taming the Prince*, pp. 184, 187.

96. Ibid., p. 194.

97. Ibid., p. 196.

98. Locke, *Essays on the Law of Nature*, p. 88. Locke admitted that individuals will seek self-serving interpretations of the natural law, saying that "men being biassed by their Interest, as well as ignorant for want of study of it, are not apt to allow of it as a Law binding to them in the application of it to their particular Case" (II, § 124). But in response to critics who deny the existence of the law of nature by pointing to pervasive ignorance of its contents, he contended that knowledge of the laws of nature is not automatic but requires effort, so "they do not present themselves to idle and listless people." Locke, *Essays on the Law of Nature*, p. 95.

99. Locke reiterated this idea in the *Essay concerning Human Understanding*, where he claimed that enforcement is axiomatic of any law. A "Power to inforce it," Locke asserts, is "so necessary, and essential to a Law," that without an adequate enforcement mechanism, individuals may not be motivated to adhere to moral rules. (Book II, ch. XXVIII, § 12.) Locke held this position as early as the *Essays on the Law of Nature*, where he noted that "law is to no purpose without punishment," which is why the law of nature presupposes the notions of hell and the immortality of the soul. *Essays on the Law of Nature*, p. 113.

100. Locke, *Essays on the Law of Nature*, pp. 86, 92–96.

101. Kantorowicz, *King's Two Bodies*. While the Crown was a permanent and impersonal institution, symbolizing the inalienability of the polity, the king was a mortal, corporeal being, who represented, or personified, the office. According to this doctrine, the Crown remained incorruptible regardless of the fallibility of the particular individual who happened to occupy the office. The medieval distinction between the person of the king and the appurtenances of the crown continued to form an important part of English political discourse right up until the eve of Civil War, when the Parliamentary opposition still insisted its resistance was not directed against Charles I himself. See Judson, *Crisis of the Constitution*. Locke would have been familiar with this distinction from the "Puritan cry of 'fighting the king [individual] to defend the King [office],'" which drew on this tradition. Kantorowicz, *King's Two Bodies*, p. 23.

102. In this regard, Locke followed those seventeenth-century parliamentarians who separated the personal and the political capacities of the king. See Janelle Greenberg, "Our Grand Maxim of State, 'The King Can Do No Wrong,'" *History of Political Thought*, Vol. 12, No. 2 (1991), pp. 219–21.

103. The phrase belongs to Richard Ashcraft, who uses it in a different sense and context. See Ashcraft, *Locke's Two Treatises of Government* (London: Unwin Hyman, 1987), p. 184.

104. Christopher Anderson explains that "Locke's conception of prudence revolved around the accommodation of an individual's actions to the facts of the world.

It is always a knowledge concerned with finding the most advantageous action in a particular situation." Anderson, "'Safe Enough in His Honesty and Prudence': The Ordinary Conduct of Government in the Thought of John Locke," *History of Political Thought,* Vol. 13, No. 4 (1992), p. 619.

105. Of course, such acquiescence may signify an abdication of the people's moral and intellectual responsibility to judge the claims of power for themselves. See Clement Fatovic, "Emergency Action as Jurisprudential Miracle: Liberalism's Political Theology of Prerogative," *Perspectives on Politics,* Vol. 6, No. 3 (2008), pp. 487–501.

106. It is important to note that, upon the dissolution of government, power reverts to the community as a whole, not to individuals.

107. This was not always the avowed position of either Locke or Shaftesbury, who sidestepped the delicate question about the justifiability of taking up arms against a king in their coauthored "Letter from a Person of Quality," pp. 626–27.

108. Grant, *John Locke's Liberalism,* p. 55.

109. For a full analysis of the conditions under which the people are justified in resisting government, see Ashcraft, *Locke's Two Treatises,* pp. 196–228.

110. Ashcraft actually confirmed this interpretation elsewhere. He admitted that conflicts between the executive and the legislative, or between either of these and the people, constitute "a crisis of constitutional government. This is because there is no means for resolving this conflict within the framework of the original constitution." Ashcraft, *Locke's Two Treatises,* p. 196. Julian H. Franklin concurs as well: "Locke's answer in effect is that there is a final judgment, but it is a constituent power outside of, or underneath, the constitution, rather than internal to it." Franklin, *John Locke and the Theory of Sovereignty: Mixed Monarchy and the Right of Resistance in the Political Thought of the English Revolution* (Cambridge: Cambridge University Press, 1978), p. 95.

111. A similar point is made in Pasquino, "Locke on King's Prerogative," p. 205.

112. Holmes, *Passions and Constraint,* p. 4.

113. Ibid., p. 5.

114. J. G. A. Pocock, "The Myth of John Locke and the Obsession with Liberalism," in *John Locke: Papers Read at a Clark Library Seminar, 10 December 1977* (Los Angeles: William Andrews Clark Memorial Library, 1980), pp. 18, 20.

115. John Locke, *Of the Conduct of the Understanding,* in *Some Thoughts concerning Education and Of the Conduct of the Understanding,* ed. Ruth W. Grant and Nathan Tarcov (Indianapolis: Hackett Publishing, 1996), p. 174.

116. Ibid., p. 10.

117. Locke, "Justitia," in *Political Essays,* p. 273.

118. The force of habits is so powerful, according to Locke, that even "*going to stool regularly*" can become a habitual activity! *Some Thoughts concerning Education,* p. 22, emphasis in original. Additional passages on the habits—especially as regards their superiority to strict rules and "cautions"—can be found at pp. 14–15, 19–24, 32, 40. For a detailed discussion of Locke's views on this subject, see Nathan Tarcov, *Locke's Education for Liberty* (Chicago: University of Chicago Press, 1984), pp. 84–93.

119. John Locke, *Some Thoughts concerning Education*, p. 139. See also pp. 73, 85. Locke reiterated his opposition to the use of rules and precepts throughout his educational writings, which indicates how thoroughly he repudiated legalistic approaches in any area of social life. He elaborated, "Nobody is made anything by hearing rules, or laying them up in his memory; practice must settle the habit of doing without reflecting on the rule." *Of the Conduct of the Understanding*, p. 175.

120. Alasdair MacIntyre, *After Virtue*, 2d ed. (Notre Dame: Notre Dame University Press, 1984), p. 118. As compelling as MacIntyre's interpretation of Aristotle is, his presentation of the "modern moralities" tends to be monolithic, lumping together thinkers with such radically divergent views as Locke, Kant, and Nietzsche. MacIntyre's assertion that liberal moralities are preoccupied with what rules we ought to follow is especially problematic. This is mistaken with respect to Locke, who railed against the use of precepts and rules in the moral upbringing of children and refused to reduce ethics to rigid moral codes.

121. On Aristotle's theory of character, see Nancy Sherman, *The Fabric of Character: Aristotle's Theory of Virtue* (Oxford: Clarendon Press, 1989).

122. Locke, *Essay concerning Human Understanding*, Book I, ch. 3, § 6, p. 69.

123. Locke, *Some Thoughts concerning Education*, p. 8.

124. Ibid., p. 8.

125. Ibid., p. 7.

126. Ibid., p. 139.

127. Tarcov draws a similar conclusion in " 'Non-Lockean' Locke," p. 137.

128. Locke elaborated this point further on where he avers that "it seems plain to me that the principle of all virtue and excellency lies in a power of denying ourselves the satisfaction of our own desires where reason does not authorize them." *Some Thoughts concerning Education*, pp. 25, 29, emphasis in original.

129. John Locke to Edward Clark [January 29, 1686], *Correspondence of John Locke*, Vol. II, p. 777.

130. Locke, *Some Thoughts concerning Education*, p. 152.

131. Ibid., p. 76.

132. Ibid., p. 32.

133. This dichotomy between tyranny and virtue is very similar to Milton's usage. In fact, Milton defined a tyrant as "one who regards his own welfare and profit only, and not that of the people," and praised Cromwell precisely because he was "a commander first over himself." John Milton, *Defence of the People of England*, in *Areopagitica*, pp. 297, 398.

134. Locke, *Some Thoughts concerning Education*, pp. 76, 32.

135. Locke, *Essay concerning Human Understanding*, Book II, ch. 21, § 70. Locke also expressed his disappointment that the "infinitely greatest confessed good [is] often neglected, to satisfy the successive *uneasiness* of our desires pursuing trifles," Book II, ch. 21, § 68.

136. *Of the Conduct of the Understanding*, p. 169.

137. Locke, *Some Thoughts concerning Education*, p. 38.

138. See Waldron, *Dignity of Legislation*, pp. 74–75.

139. Locke, *Of the Conduct of the Understanding*, pp. 185, 179.

140. *Essays on the Law of Nature*, p. 89. See the second essay for Locke's arguments concerning the knowability of natural law.

141. Locke, *Essay concerning Human Understanding*, Book II, ch. 21, § 69.

142. Ibid., emphasis added.

143. *Some Thoughts concerning Education*, p. 102. There are similarities to Aristotle's theory of the relation between virtue and happiness; see *The Nicomachean Ethics*, trans. and ed. David Ross (Oxford: Oxford University Press, 1980), Book I. MacIntyre explicates Aristotle's position and argues that virtue and happiness were "indissolubly linked" for the Greeks in *After Virtue*, pp. 140, 148–50.

144. Locke, "Reputation," in *Political Essays*, p. 271. He made a related point elsewhere: "I think, I may say, that he, who imagines Commendation and Disgrace, not to be strong Motives on Men, to accommodate themselves to the Opinions and Rules of those, with whom they converse, seems little skill'd in the Nature, or History of Mankind: the greatest part whereof he shall find to govern themselves chiefly, if not solely, by this Law of Fashion." *Essay concerning Human Understanding*, Book II, ch. 28, § 12, pp. 356–57.

145. Shaftesbury, "Letter from a Person of Quality," p. 642.

146. See Tarcov's discussion in *Locke's Education for Liberty*, pp. 96–107. Tarcov cites a passage from the *Thoughts* that suggests that "reputation is the proper provisional standard for children, while adults are to be guided by their own reason," p. 106. Of course, the passages cited above from the *Treatises* indicate that reason is not the exclusive standard even for adults.

147. *Some Thoughts concerning Education*, p. 36.

148. Shaftesbury, "Letter from a Person of Quality," p. 642. This sentiment is reminiscent of the remark by James I that even a legitimate king should seek the "loue of his people" as well as "the affections of the people." *Political Writings*, p. 248. Contrast Machiavelli's thoughts on the question "whether it is better to be loved than feared, or vice versa." He thought "it is desirable to be both loved and feared; but it is difficult to achieve both and, if one of them has to be lacking, it is much safer to be feared than loved." *The Prince*, p. 59. He went on to argue, though, that "the best fortress a ruler can have is not to be hated by the people," p. 75.

149. "Things then are Good or Evil, only in reference to Pleasure or Pain. That we call *Good*, which *is apt to cause or increase Pleasure, or diminish Pain in us; or else to procure or preserve us the possession of any other Good, or absence of any Evil*. And on the contrary we name that *Evil*, which *is apt to produce or increase any Pain, or diminish any Pleasure in us; or else to procure us any Evil, or deprive us of any Good*." Locke, *Essay concerning Human Understanding*, Book II, ch. 20, § 2. Lest Locke be mistaken for a pure hedonist, it is worthwhile to point out the central role he assigned to reason. Uday Singh Mehta argues that the notion of reason Locke "has in mind is quite

specific": "It is reason informed by a particular substantive content and one deeply invested in and extremely sensitive to conventional norms of acceptability." Mehta, *Anxiety of Freedom: Imagination and Individuality in Locke's Political Thought* (Ithaca, NY: Cornell University Press, 1992), pp. 116–17.

150. As Tarcov explains, Locke approved of fear as a kind of uneasiness that is useful in promoting rational behavior. See Tarcov, *Locke's Education for Liberty*, p. 154.

151. See Anderson, who focuses on virtue, prudence, wisdom, and rationality as the qualities necessary for good rulers. Anderson, "Safe Enough in His Honesty and Prudence."

152. *Some Thoughts concerning Education*, p. 83.

153. Locke, *Essay concerning Human Understanding*, Book II, ch. 20, § 14.

154. John Locke, *The Reasonableness of Christianity* (Washington, D.C.: Regnery, 1965), p. 148.

155. Locke, *Essay concerning Human Understanding*, Book II, ch. 21, § 29. Later he notes that even the prospect of a greater good "though apprehended and acknowledged to be so, does not determine the *will*, until our desire, raised proportionally to it, makes us *uneasy* in the want of it," Book II, ch. 21, § 35.

156. Even though Locke refers to legislative power here, his argument applies with equal force to executive power. Although corruption or abuse of power by the executive may not always call for revolution and the dissolution of government, it certainly justifies removal from office. In either case, revolution or removal, the result is the same: the recalcitrant holder of power is divested of authority and power and treated as an enemy of the people.

157. Locke, *Essay concerning Human Understanding*, Book II, ch. 28, § 6.

158. See Judith N. Shklar, "Political Theory and the Rule of Law," in *The Rule of Law: Ideal or Ideology*, ed. Allan C. Hutchinson and Patrick Monahan (Toronto: Carswell, 1987).

159. In many respects, this describes the practice of "constitutional politics" in the United States, where the frequent conjunction of those terms indicates the flexibility of constitutional law. American constitutional law is more often than not guided by abstract principles than by determinate legal rules. See, for example, Ronald Dworkin, *Taking Rights Seriously* (Cambridge: Harvard University Press, 1978), pp. 22–28, and *Law's Empire* (Cambridge: Belknap Press, 1986).

CHAPTER 3: "All Was Confusion and Disorder"

Epigraph. David Hume, *The History of England from the Invasion of Julius Caesar to the Revolution in 1688*, ed. William B. Todd (Indianapolis: Liberty Fund, 1983), Vol. V, p. 329.

1. David Hume, "That Politics May Be Reduced to a Science," in *Essays: Moral, Political, and Literary*, rev. ed., ed. Eugene F. Miller (Indianapolis: Liberty Fund, 1985), pp. 16, 15.

2. Ibid., p. 18.

3. On the political uses of Newtonian methods in Hume's political thought, see James Farr, "Political Science and the Enlightenment on Enthusiasm," *American Political Science Review,* Vol. 82, No. 1 (1988).

4. Duncan Forbes, *Hume's Philosophical Politics* (Cambridge: Cambridge University Press, 1975), p. 227.

5. David Hume, *An Enquiry concerning Human Understanding,* in *Enquiries concerning Human Understanding and concerning the Principles of Morals,* 3d ed., ed. P. H. Nidditch (Oxford: Clarendon Press, 1975), p. 90.

6. John Gray suggests that "we find the most powerful defense of the liberal system of limited government" in Hume. Gray, *Liberalism* (Minneapolis: University of Minnesota Press, 1986), p. 24.

7. See Douglass Adair, "'That Politics May Be Reduced to a Science': David Hume, James Madison, and the Tenth Federalist," in *Fame and the Founding Fathers: Essays by Douglass Adair,* ed. Trevor Colbourn (Indianapolis: Liberty Fund, 1998); Garry Wills: *Inventing America: Jefferson's Declaration of Independence* (New York: Vintage Books, 1978); Garry Wills, *Explaining America: The Federalist* (Garden City, NY: Doubleday, 1981); and Mark G. Spencer, *David Hume and Eighteenth-Century America: The Reception of Hume's Political Thought in America, 1740–1830* (Rochester, NY: University of Rochester Press, 2005). A notable exception to this trend is James Conniff, who argues that scholarly focus on Madison's supposed reliance on Humean institutionalism is based on a fundamental misunderstanding of Hume's skepticism toward the science of politics. See Conniff, "The Enlightenment and American Political Thought: A Study of the Origins of Madison's *Federalist Number 10,*" *Political Theory,* Vol. 8, No. 3 (1980). Although I agree with Conniff's characterization of Hume as a skeptic, I disagree with his interpretation of *Federalist* 10, which overstates Madison's own confidence in the science of politics. As I discuss in chapter 5, Madison also "had serious doubts about the applicability of the scientific method to politics." Conniff, p. 382.

8. As Knud Haakonssen explains, institutional stability played such an important role for Hume precisely because it was so likely to lead to such predictability. Haakonssen, "The Structure of Hume's Political Theory," in *The Cambridge Companion to Hume,* ed. David Fate Norton (Cambridge: Cambridge University Press, 1993), p. 196.

9. On this (somewhat overdrawn) contrast, see Quentin Skinner, *The Foundations of Modern Political Thought,* Volume One, *The Renaissance* (Cambridge: Cambridge University Press, 1978), pp. 44–45.

10. As Hume notes, "There is a degree of doubt, and caution, and modesty, which, in all kinds of scrutiny and decision, ought for ever to accompany a just reasoner." *Enquiry concerning Human Understanding,* pp. 161–62.

11. See, for example, Hume's discussion of necessity in *Enquiry concerning the Principles of Morals,* pp. 186–87.

12. Hume was quite critical of the abstract, rationalistic approach that he associated with Thomas Hobbes, John Locke, and other natural law and Enlightenment figures. He expressed a clear preference for the more empirically grounded work of

Montesquieu, who helped to establish comparative politics as a serious intellectual practice. For a nuanced study of Hume's method as "based on experience and observation," see Forbes, *Hume's Philosophical Politics,* p. 59.

13. Hume, "Of the Middle Station of Life," in *Essays,* p. 549.

14. For a standard account of this reading of Hume, see Forbes, *Hume's Philosophical Politics,* pp. 222–30.

15. Ibid., p. x.

16. See Henry St. John, Viscount Bolingbroke, *Political Writings,* ed. David Armitage (Cambridge: Cambridge University Press, 1997). On the nature of this debate and the participants involved, see Isaac Kramnick, *Bolingbroke and His Circle: The Politics of Nostalgia in the Age of Walpole* (Ithaca, NY: Cornell University Press, 1992), pp. 111–87.

17. Despite his efforts to remain above party politics, he usually came out on the ministerial side because he believed such "corruption" was unavoidable and "necessary to the preservation of our mixed government." Hume, "Of the Independency of Parliament," in *Essays,* p. 45.

18. Forrest McDonald, *Novus Ordo Seclorum: The Intellectual Origins of the Constitution* (Lawrence: University Press of Kansas, 1985), p. 247.

19. J. G. A. Pocock, *Barbarism and Religion,* Volume Two, *Narratives of Civil Government* (Cambridge: Cambridge University Press, 1999), p. 201.

20. See Trevor Colbourn, *The Lamp of Experience: Whig History and the Intellectual Origins of the American Revolution* (Indianapolis: Liberty Fund, 1998), especially Appendix II; and Spencer, *David Hume and Eighteenth-Century America.*

21. See Jefferson's August 12, 1810, letter to William Duane in *Thomas Jefferson: Writings,* ed. Merrill D. Peterson (New York: Library of America, 1984), pp. 1228–29; and Douglas L. Wilson, "Jefferson vs. Hume," *William and Mary Quarterly,* 3rd Series, Vol. 46 (1989). On Madison and Hamilton, see Wills, *Explaining America.*

22. On the role of historical conditions in limiting human action in Hume's historical writings, see Pocock, *Barbarism and Religion,* pp. 201–8.

23. Robert A. Manzer has noted that Hume's constitutionalism preserves "a place for virtue in the private sphere of honor and character," but he does not consider the role of virtue or character in the public sphere in Hume's thought. "Hume on Pride and Love of Fame," *Polity,* Vol. 18, No. 3 (1996).

24. Hume, "Of the Study of History," *Essays,* p. 567.

25. David Hume, *History of England,* Vol. I, pp. 361–62. As Richard H. Dees notes, there were times when "even 'regular' government was a matter of personality: during these times, laws could only be strictly enforced by kings who were themselves strong and who had the inclination to follow a rule of law." Dees, "Hume and the Contexts of Politics," *Journal of the History of Philosophy,* Vol. 30, No. 2, (1992), p. 239.

26. "Of the Coalition of Parties," *Essays,* pp. 494–95.

27. Ibid., p. 495.

28. On Hume's philosophical aversion to thought experiments and hypotheticals, see Annette C. Baier, *A Progress of Sentiments: Reflections on Hume's* Treatise (Cambridge: Harvard University Press, 1991), pp. 154–55, quotation at p. 155.

29. Hume's awareness of the limitations of political science is evident in "Of Civil Liberty," where he noted that "the world is still too young to fix many general truths in politics, which will remain true to the latest posterity." *Essays*, p. 87.

30. "Of the Rise and Progress of the Arts and Sciences," *Essays*, p. 111. In this essay Hume delineated some of the methodological precepts one ought to observe in conducting social scientific inquiries.

31. "Of Simplicity and Refinement in Writing," *Essays*, p. 194.

32. Hume, *Enquiry concerning Human Understanding*, p. 83. Pocock's argument that the act of locating the causes of political change in malleable social structures as opposed to a fixed human nature makes James Harrington's political theory more scientific than Machiavelli's is also applicable to Hume, who emphasized the importance of institutions in forming national character and shaping the course of political and social events. See J. G. A. Pocock, *The Ancient Constitution and the Feudal Law: A Study in English Historical Thought in the Seventeenth Century: A Reissue with a Retrospect* (Cambridge: Cambridge University Press, 1987), p. 146.

33. Hume discussed some of the features of his methodology at the beginning of his essay, "Of the Rise and Progress of the Arts and Sciences," *Essays*, pp. 111–13. For an incisive interpretation of Hume as a "contextualist" whose "political thought is more dependent on his judgments about particular situations than on his general pronouncements about abstract possibilities," see Dees, "Hume and the Contexts of Politics," p. 220.

34. Hume, "Of the Original Contract," *Essays*, p. 476.

35. Hume, *Enquiry concerning Human Understanding*, p. 174. "The science of man," Hume notes in his philosophical masterpiece, which "is the only solid foundation for the other sciences . . . itself must be laid on *experience and observation*." "Introduction," *A Treatise of Human Nature*, ed. Ernest C. Mossner (New York: Penguin, 1969), p. 43, emphasis added.

36. On history as the philosophical equivalent of "laboratory research" for Hume, see Franklin A. Kalinowski, "David Hume on the Philosophic Underpinnings of Interest Group Politics," *Polity*, Vol. 25, No. 3 (1993), p. 368.

37. Hume, "Of the Populousness of Ancient Nations," *Essays*, p. 400.

38. Hume, "That Politics May Be Reduced to a Science," p. 14.

39. Ibid., p. 15.

40. Ibid., p. 16.

41. James Conniff, "Hume's Political Methodology: A Reconsideration of 'That Politics May be Reduced to a Science,'" *Review of Politics*, Vol. 38, No. 1 (1976), p. 97.

42. James Conniff, "The Enlightenment and American Political Thought: A Study of the Origins of Madison's *Federalist Number 10*," *Political Theory*, Vol. 8, No. 3 (1980), p. 382.

43. Hume, "Of Civil Liberty," *Essays*, p. 89.

44. Hume, "Of the Standard of Taste," *Essays*, p. 242.

45. Hume, "That Politics May Be Reduced to a Science," p. 29.

46. Ibid., p. 27n20; and Hume, "A Character of Sir Robert Walpole," *Essays*, p. 576.

47. Hume, "Whether the British Government Inclines More to Absolute Monarchy or to a Republic," *Essays*, p. 47.

48. Jean-Louis de Lolme, *The Constitution of England; or, An Account of the English Government; in Which It Is Compared Both with the Republican Form of Government, and the Other Monarchies in Europe* (London: 1822), p. xiv. It is instructive to look at de Lolme for two related reasons. First, in presenting a comprehensive interpretation of the stability and liberty of the English system of government, he often borrowed from and synthesized the ideas of eighteenth-century political writers, most notably Hume and Blackstone. Second, his account was very popular in the United States during the 1780s when Americans were trying to figure out how to improve their own system of national government.

49. Garry Wills argues that Alexander Hamilton shared this characteristic with Hume. Wills, *Explaining America*, p. 90.

50. Hume, "Idea of a Perfect Commonwealth," *Essays*, pp. 513–14.

51. See Forbes, *Hume's Philosophical Politics*, p. 121; Farr, "Political Science and the Enlightenment of Enthusiasm"; and Conniff, "Hume's Political Methodology."

52. Hume declared, "For my own part, I shall always be more fond of promoting moderation than zeal; though perhaps the surest way of producing moderation in every party is to increase our zeal for the public. . . . every individual is bound to pursue the good of his country," which Hume often defined in minimalist terms as peace, order, and security. "That Politics May Be Reduced to a Science," p. 27.

53. Ibid., p. 31.

54. Ibid., p. 15.

55. Hume, "Of the Protestant Succession," *Essays*, p. 508.

56. Hume, "Idea of a Perfect Commonwealth," *Essays*, p. 527.

57. Ibid., pp. 516–17.

58. Hume, *Treatise of Human Nature*, p. 609.

59. Ibid., p. 319.

60. Ibid., p. 320.

61. Robert A. Manzer, for instance, claims that constitutionalists like Hume "encourage us to revere the constitution as law because in the name of freedom it demands the rule of laws rather than of individuals." Manzer, "Hume's Constitutionalism and the Identity of Constitutional Democracy," *American Political Science Review*, Vol. 90, No. 3 (1996), p. 49.

62. Hume, "Of the Origin of Government," *Essays*, pp. 40, 41. Constant Noble Stockton characterizes Hume's understanding of this historical dialectic as "an eternal and irrepressible conflict between liberty and authority." Stockton, "Hume: Historian of the English Constitution," *Eighteenth-Century Studies*, Vol. 4 (1970–1971), p. 292.

63. Hume, Variant Reading of "Of the Protestant Succession," *Essays*, p. 646.

64. See, for example, "Of the Original Contract," *Essays*, p. 480. Elsewhere, Hume wrote that "the heart of man naturally delights in liberty, and hates every thing to which it is confined." "Of Polygamy and Divorces," *Essays*, p. 188. On the relation

between liberty and historical progress, see Forbes, *Hume's Philosophical Politics,* pp. 296–300.

65. On Hume's conception of liberty and its contributions to order and authority, see John Valdimir Price, "Hume's Concept of Liberty and *The History of England,*" *Studies in Romanticism,* Vol. 5 (1966). As Forbes points out, Hume made an implicit distinction between personal and political liberty. Hume was more concerned with the former, which is present to some degree even in absolute governments, than with the latter, which was uncommon even in the freest governments of his day. Forbes, *Hume's Philosophical Politics,* p. 160.

66. Hume, "Of the Original Contract," *Essays,* pp. 480, 481. Hume reiterated this essential point in *Enquiry concerning the Principles of Morals,* p. 206, where he supplied a utilitarian justification for obedience to civil magistrates.

67. Hume, *History of England,* Vol. VI, p. 533.

68. Hume, "Of the Origin of Government," *Essays,* p. 40.

69. One of the few rays of light to gleam out of the dark age of feudal ignorance and depravity, according to Hume, was the discovery of Justinian's *Pandects* in the twelfth century, which contributed to the development of jurisprudence and the gradual rise of law over violence. *History of England,* Vol. II, p. 520.

70. Hume, *Treatise of Human Nature,* p. 566. Hume, whose discussion of justice contains his most comprehensive treatment of general rules, continues: "The rules of justice seek some medium betwixt a rigid stability, and this changeable and uncertain adjustment."

71. Hume, "Of the Rise and Progress of the Arts and Sciences," *Essays,* p. 124.

72. Hume, *History of England,* Vol. II, p. 458

73. "Of Some Remarkable Customs," *Essays,* p. 374.

74. Like formal theories of the rule of law, Hume's notion of regularity promotes the values of predictability and certainty. In contrast to these theories, though, Hume's theory of regularity encompasses much more than formal rules and includes a variety of informal and habitual practices. For examples of formal, rule-oriented conceptions of the rule of law, see Robert S. Summers, "A Formal Theory of the Rule of Law," *Ratio Juris,* Vol. 6, No. 2 (1993); and Antonin Scalia, "The Rule of Law as a Law of Rules," *University of Chicago Law Review,* Vol. 56, No. 4 (1989).

75. Hume, *History of England,* Vol. I, p. 362. See the extract on page 87.

76. Duncan Forbes, "Politics and History in David Hume," *Historical Journal,* Vol. 6, No. 2 (1963), p. 283.

77. Hume, *Enquiry concerning the Principles of Morals,* pp. 305–6.

78. Hume, *History of England,* Vol. I, p. 324.

79. "Of the Rise and Progress of the Arts and Sciences," *Essays,* p. 116. On the need for constitutional flexibility that only the executive can provide, see the discussion of Hume in Forrest McDonald, *The American Presidency: An Intellectual History* (Lawrence: University Press of Kansas, 1994), pp. 95–96.

80. He cited the dreadful example of Turkey, where "the judges are not restrained by any methods, forms or laws," where the "barbarous monarch" exercises

an "altogether ruinous and intolerable" arbitrary power." "Of the Rise and Progress of the Arts and Sciences," *Essays,* p. 116.

81. Hume, "Of the Rise and Progress of the Arts and Sciences," *Essays,* p. 118.

82. Hume, *History of England,* Vol. VI, p. 95.

83. Hume quoted Pope in "That Politics May Be Reduced to a Science," p. 14.

84. Adair, " 'That Politics May Be Reduced to a Science': David Hume, James Madison, and the Tenth Federalist," p. 139.

85. Hume, "Idea of a Perfect Commonwealth," *Essays,* p. 513.

86. Ibid., p. 527.

87. Ibid., p. 512.

88. Ibid., p. 529.

89. Ibid., p. 528.

90. Hume, "That Politics May Be Reduced to a Science," p. 15.

91. Hume, "Idea of a Perfect Commonwealth," *Essays,* p. 527.

92. For an example of the contrary and more conventional interpretation, see James Moore, "Hume's Political Science and the Classical Republican Tradition," *Canadian Journal of Political Science,* Vol. 10, No. 4 (1977).

93. Hume, "Idea of a Perfect Commonwealth," *Essays,* p. 515.

94. Hume, "Of the Protestant Succession," *Essays,* p. 503.

95. Hume, *Treatise of Human Nature,* pp. 392, 395.

96. Ibid., p. 406.

97. Ibid., p. 395.

98. Ibid., p. 481.

99. The classic statement of this interpretation is Albert O. Hirschman, *The Passions and the Interests: Political Arguments for Capitalism before Its Triumph* (Princeton: Princeton University Press, 1977).

100. Hume, *Treatise of Human Nature,* p. 573.

101. Ibid., pp. 585–86. "If we consider the ordinary course of human actions, we shall find, that the mind restrains not itself by any general and universal rules; but acts on most occasions as it is determin'd by its present motives and inclinations," p. 583.

102. Ibid., pp. 588–89, emphasis added.

103. Hume, "That Politics May Be Reduced to a Science," p. 16.

104. Hume, *Treatise of Human Nature,* p. 581.

105. Ibid., p. 603.

106. Ibid., p. 586.

107. Hume, "A Character of Sir Robert Walpole," *Essays,* p. 576.

108. Hume, *Enquiry concerning the Principles of Morals,* p. 178.

109. Duncan Forbes, "Hume and the Scottish Enlightenment," in *Philosophers of the Enlightenment,* ed. S. C. Brown (Sussex: Harvester Press of the Royal Institute of Philosophy, 1979), p. 106.

110. Wills, *Explaining America,* p. 39.

111. Forbes, *Hume's Philosophical Politics,* p. 225.

112. Hume, *History of England,* Vol. II, p. 262.

113. On the modern break with the understanding of human nature in terms of its ends and potentials rather than its lowest common denominators, see the classic discussion in Hirschman, *Passions and the Interests,* especially pp. 12–14.

114. Hume, *Treatise of Human Nature,* p. 573.

115. Ibid., p. 466. See also his initial division of the passions, p. 328.

116. Ibid., p. 465.

117. Quoted in John P. Wright, "Butler and Hume on Habit and Moral Character," in *Hume and Hume's Connexions,* ed. M. A. Stewart and John P. Wright (University Park: Pennsylvania State University Press, 1995), p. 109. As Wright explains, both the violent and the calm passions can be either strong or weak in their intensity.

118. Hume, *Treatise of Human Nature,* pp. 602, 586–87.

119. On the effects of custom and habit on the passions, see Wright, "Butler and Hume."

120. Hume, *Treatise of Human Nature,* pp. 538–41.

121. Ibid., p. 521.

122. On the hedonism of Hume's moral psychology, see Baier, *Progress of Sentiments,* especially pp. 198–205; on his favorable revaluation of pride, see pp. 206–10.

123. Hume, *History of England,* Vol. I, p. 74. Conversely, he piled scorn on Henry VIII, whose "arbitrary administration" is attributable to his wicked passions: "A catalogue of his vices would comprehend many of the worst qualities incident to human nature: Violence, cruelty, profusion, rapacity, injustice, obstinacy, arrogance, bigotry, presumption, caprice," Vol. III, p. 322.

124. For a general discussion of Hume's "consistent determinist" views on character as the object of moral evaluation, see Baier, *Progress of Sentiments,* pp. 152–97. Since my interpretation of Hume's theory of character is consistent with Baier's, I focus mainly on the political implications and refer the reader to Baier's discussion for elaboration on some of the finer philosophical points.

125. Hume's theory of character has some affinities with Aristotelian psychology, particularly the notions of *hexis* and *habitus,* which are explored in the context of Henry Bracton's thought in Cary C. Nederman, "Bracton on Kingship Revisited," *History of Political Thought,* Vol. 5, No. 1 (1984). Nederman argues that belief in the constancy of character was an enduring theme of political thought from Aristotle to Machiavelli; see Nederman, "Machiavelli and Moral Character: Principality, Republic and the Psychology of Virtù," *History of Political Thought,* Vol. 21, No. 3 (2000).

126. Hume, *Treatise of Human Nature,* p. 626.

127. On this process of habituation, see Wright, "Butler and Hume."

128. Hume, *Treatise of Human Nature,* pp. 458–59. Hume notes that "it may be establish'd as an undoubted maxim, *that no action can be virtuous, or morally good, unless there be in human nature some motive to produce it, distinct from the sense of its morality,*" pp. 530–31, emphasis in original.

129. Hume, *Treatise of Human Nature,* p. 626. He continues: "'Tis therefore from the influence of characters and qualities, upon those who have an intercourse with any person, that we blame or praise him," p. 633.

130. Ibid., p. 459.

131. As Baier notes, Hume drew an important distinction between emotions, which he denigrated for causing violent disturbances in the mind, and passions, which varied in their effects on the mind. See Baier, *Progress of Sentiments*, pp. 164–67.

132. As Nederman shows in "Machiavelli and Moral Character," Machiavelli's advice conflicted sharply with his own views on the fixity of character.

133. A. J. Beitzinger argues that Hume's preference for such leaders suggests a preference for an aristocratic government. See Beitzinger, "Hume's Aristocratic Preference," *Review of Politics*, Vol. 28, No. 2 (1966).

134. On the psychological and moral predispositions proper to politicians, see Kalinowski, "David Hume on the Philosophic Underpinnings."

135. Baier, *Progress of Sentiments*, p. 187.

136. Quoted in Beitzinger, "Hume's Aristocratic Preference," p. 170.

137. Hume, "A Character of Sir Robert Walpole," *Essays*, p. 576.

138. The reason for this is that the "critical Times" that demand extraordinary capacity or exceptional qualities in governors are relatively uncommon. Ordinarily, those qualities that prevail in the "middle stations of life" are sufficient in politics. Hume, "Of the Middle Station of Life," *Essays*, p. 549. Unfortunately, Hume did not specify which nonmoral qualities would be most relevant during "critical Times."

139. See Baier, *Progress of Sentiments*, p. 219. As Hume put it, "Virtue is consider'd as means to an end. Means to an end are only valued so far as the end is valued." *Treatise of Human Nature*, p. 668.

140. Hume, "Of Refinement in the Arts," *Essays*, pp. 273–74.

141. Hume, *History of England*, Vol. II, p. 64.

142. Ibid., Vol. II, p. 75.

143. Ibid., Vol. II, p. 355. Prior to Henry's reformation, he indulged in excesses that deeply disturbed the people: "The active spirit of young Henry, restrained from its proper exercise, broke out in extravagancies of every kind; and the riot of pleasure, the frolic of debauchery, the outrage of wine, filled the vacancies of a mind, better adapted to the pursuits of ambition, and the cares of government," Vol. II, p. 352.

144. Ibid., Vol. II, pp. 380, 381.

145. Ibid., Vol. VI, p. 539.

146. Ibid., Vol. VI, pp. 157, 447.

147. Ibid., Vol. II, pp. 171–72.

148. Ibid., Vol. I, p. 414. In a great historical irony, this heinous crime actually contributed indirectly to the erection of liberty in the nation, since John's weakened position forced him to accede to Magna Carta.

149. Ibid., Vol. II, pp. 15, 64, 35.

150. Ibid., Vol. II, p. 29.

151. Ibid., Vol. II, p. 38.

152. Ibid., Vol. II, p. 141.

153. See de Lolme, *Constitution of England*, p. 103.

154. Hume, *Treatise of Human Nature*, p. 462.

155. Ibid., p. 463.

156. Ibid., p. 465.

157. Hume, "Of the Dignity or Meanness of Human Nature," *Essays*, p. 81.

158. Hume, *Treatise of Human Nature*, p. 354. For a discussion of these interpersonal forces, see Manzer, "Hume on Pride and Love of Fame."

159. Hume, *Treatise of Human Nature*, p. 381.

160. James Madison, Alexander Hamilton, and John Jay, *The Federalist Papers*, ed. Isaac Kramnick (New York: Penguin, 1987), No. 72, p. 414. Hamilton made a similar point in *Federalist 70*, where he wrote of the "restraints of public opinion," p. 406. Hume, *Enquiry concerning the Principles of Morals*, p. 265.

161. Ibid., p. 276.

162. See Adam Smith, *The Theory of Moral Sentiments*, ed. D. D. Raphael and A. L. Macfie (Indianapolis: Liberty Fund, 1982).

163. Hume, "Of the Dependency of Parliament," *Essays*, pp. 42–43, emphasis in original.

164. Hume, "Of the First Principles of Government," *Essays*, p. 34, emphasis added.

165. Hume, *Essays*, p. 647.

166. Hume, "Of the First Principles of Government," *Essays*, p. 34.

167. De Lolme went even farther than Hume in his assessment of the English Constitution, arguing that "it was the excessive power of the king which made England free." De Lolme, *Constitution of England*, p. 17.

168. Another of Hume's political aims in undertaking his ambitious historical project was the refutation of the erroneous Whig orthodoxies—most notably, a belief in the immemorial libertarian heritage epitomized by the ancient constitution—contained in the writings of Whig historians like Paul de Rapin-Thoyras, whose static theory of constitutional continuity Hume countered with a more dynamic view of historical change, disruption, and accident. On Hume's avowed purpose in refuting the myth of the ancient constitution, see Stockton, "Hume: Historian of the English Constitution." On his vindication as a historian, see Quentin Skinner, "History and Ideology in the English Revolution," *Historical Journal*, Vol. 8, No. 2 (1965). On Hume's critique of Rapin's thesis, methodology, and style, see Hugh Trevor-Roper, "Our First Whig Historian," in *From Counter-Reformation to Glorious Revolution* (London: Pimlico, 1992), pp. 264–65. Hume carried his conviction about the mutability and flux of things into his discussions of the soul and the afterlife, where he suggested that change is perhaps the only constant in the universe. See "Of the Immortality of the Soul," *Essays*, p. 597.

169. Hume, *History of England*, Vol. I, p. 167. For Hume's most sustained critique of this myth, see Vol. II, pp. 524–25.

170. Ibid., Vol. II, p. 521.

171. "It must indeed be confessed," observed Hume, "that such a state of the country required great discretionary power in the sovereign; nor will the same maxims of

government suit such a rude people, that may be proper in a more advanced stage of society. The establishment of the Star-chamber or the enlargement of its power in the reign of Henry VII. might have been as wise as the abolition of it in that of Charles I." *History of England,* Vol. III, p. 469. Interestingly, Hume did not make the converse claim with anything approaching the same emphasis, suggesting that what suited ruder ages might not be totally inappropriate in more advanced states.

172. Hume, *History of England,* Vol. I, pp. 488, 487.

173. Ibid., Vol. II, p. 102.

174. Ibid., Vol. V, p. 557.

175. Hume, *History of England,* Vol. I, p. 484.

176. Among the uncivilized and rude multitudes, Hume suggested, it is appropriate to exercise a degree of discretionary power that might be unwarranted in a polite nation. Thus, Hume criticized the Long Parliament for, among other things, "despoiling all succeeding governors of that power [discretionary authority], by which alone the Irish [backward bigots, in Hume's view] could be retained in subjection." *History of England,* Vol. V, p. 336.

177. Ibid., Vol. V, p. 126.

178. Hume, *Enquiry concerning the Principles of Morals,* p. 206.

179. Thus, Hume recognized a right of resistance in "extraordinary emergencies." See "Of Passive Obedience," *Essays,* p. 490.

180. See Hume's discussion of justice in Section III of *Enquiry concerning the Principles of Morals.*

181. Hume, *History of England,* Vol. V, p. 329.

182. Hume, *Enquiry concerning the Principles of Morals,* p. 196.

183. Ibid., p. 126. Ordinary individuals follow rules because it is natural for them to do so: "We naturally suppose ourselves born to submission; and imagine, that such particular persons have a right to command, as we on our part are bound to obey." *Treatise of Human Nature,* p. 606.

184. Hume, *History of England,* Vol. V, p. 128, emphasis added.

185. Ibid., Vol. II, p. 21

186. Ibid., Vol. V, p. 543.

187. Ibid., Vol. IV, pp. 145, 361, 286–87.

188. Ibid., Vol. IV, p. 145. Furthermore, according to prevailing constitutional doctrines, "prerogative in general, especially the supremacy [of the crown], was supposed in that age to involve powers, which no law, precedent, or reason could limit and determine," Vol. IV, p. 208.

189. Hume maintained that "the great popularity, which she enjoyed, proves, that she did not infringe any *established* liberties of the people." Ibid., Vol. IV, p. 355, emphasis in original.

190. Ibid., Vol. IV, p. 354, emphasis added.

191. Ibid., Vol. I, p. 484.

192. Ibid., Vol. VI, p. 367.

193. Ibid., Vol. V, p. 129. Hume notes that the English monarchy was the most powerful in Europe after the Norman Conquest because of the introduction of feudalism and the "necessity also of entrusting great power in the hands of a prince, who was to maintain military dominion over a vanquished nation," Vol. I, p. 437.

194. Ibid., Vol. III, p. 266.

195. Ibid., Vol. III, pp. 266, 267; Vol. IV, pp. 363, 374. As a consequence of Parliament's pliancy, Henry VIII was able to compel any man to serve in any office, imprison anyone at pleasure, and extort loans from his subjects with impunity. Vol. III, p. 305.

196. Ibid., Vol. IV, p. 366.

197. Ibid., Vol. III, p. 310.

198. Ibid., Vol. III, pp. 266–67, 264.

199. Ibid., Vol. III, p. 267.

200. Hume, "Of the Origin of Government," *Essays*, pp. 38–39.

201. Hume, *History of England*, Vol. IV, p. 354.

202. It should be noted that the statute making royal proclamations equivalent to legislative enactments was finally repealed with the assent of the protector during the regency of young Edward VI. Ibid., Vol. III, p. 354.

203. Robert A. Manzer suggests that Hume's theory "is an important landmark on the road to modern constitutional democracy" in part because of the importance he attaches to public opinion. Manzer, "Hume's Constitutionalism," p. 49.

204. Hume, "Of the First Principles of Government," *Essays*, p. 32, emphasis added.

205. See Richard E. Flathman, *The Practice of Political Authority: Authority and the Authoritative* (Chicago: University of Chicago Press, 1980), a thoroughly Humean work that makes no mention of Hume.

206. See Pocock, *Barbarism and Religion*, pp. 186–87.

CHAPTER 4: "The King Can Do No Wrong"

Epigraph. William Blackstone, *Commentaries on the Laws of England* (Chicago: University of Chicago Press, 1979), Vol. I, p. 234.

1. See H. T. Dickinson, "The Eighteenth-Century Debate on the Sovereignty of Parliament," *Transactions of the Royal Historical Society*, Fifth Series, Vol. 26 (1976), p. 190.

2. William Blackstone, *Commentaries on the Laws of England* (Chicago: University of Chicago Press, 1979). Citations to Blackstone's *Commentaries* will appear directly in the text by volume and page number. The best analysis of Blackstone's influences and aims in writing the *Commentaries* is Alan Watson, "The Structure of Blackstone's Commentaries," *Yale Law Journal*, Vol. 97, No. 5 (1988).

3. On the ostensible primacy of the legislature in Blackstone's constitutional theory, see Stanley N. Katz, "Introduction," *Commentaries*, Vol. I, p. ix.

4. See Albert Venn Dicey, *Lectures on the Relation between Law and Public Opinion in England during the Nineteenth Century* (New Brunswick, NJ: Transaction Books, 1981), p. 72. The most vigorous critic of Blackstone as a liberal is Duncan Kennedy, whose article, "The Structure of Blackstone's Commentaries," *Buffalo Law Review*, Vol. 28, No. 2 (1979), argues that Blackstone's thought is characteristic of the contradictions and reifications inherent in liberalism.

5. Daniel J. Boorstin claims that "in the history of American Institutions, no other book—except the Bible—has played so great a role as Blackstone's *Commentaries on the Laws of England.*" Boorstin, *The Mysterious Science of the Law* (Boston: Beacon Hill Press, 1958). Dicey called the late eighteenth century the "age of Blackstone." Dicey, *Lectures on the Relation Between Law and Public Opinion*, p. 70. For a general survey of Blackstone's contribution to American law and the extent of his influence among members of the Founding generation, see Dennis R. Nolan, "Sir William Blackstone and the New American Republic: A Study of Intellectual Impact," *New York University Law Review*, Vol. 51, No. 5 (1976), especially pp. 738–52. On the publication history and impact of the *Commentaries* in America, see Albert W. Alschuler, "Rediscovering Blackstone," *University of Pennsylvania Law Review*, Vol. 145, No. 1 (1996). On the ubiquity of Blackstone's work in colonial and Revolutionary-era libraries, see Trevor Colbourn, *The Lamp of Experience: Whig History and the Intellectual Origins of the American Revolution* (Indianapolis: Liberty Fund, 1998), Appendix II. Blackstone's influence was felt so widely that in his speech on "Conciliation with the Colonies," Edmund Burke remarked, "I hear that they have sold nearly as many of Blackstone's Commentaries in America as in England."

6. On the varieties of Whiggism in eighteenth-century political thought, see the last essay in J. G. A. Pocock, *Virtue, Commerce, and History: Essays on Political Thought and History, Chiefly in the Eighteenth Century* (Cambridge: Cambridge University Press, 1985).

7. Forrest McDonald, *Novus Ordo Seclorum: The Intellectual Origins of the Constitution* (Lawrence: University Press of Kansas, 1985), p. 247.

8. See Donald S. Lutz, *The Origins of American Constitutionalism* (Baton Rouge: Louisiana State University Press, 1988), pp. 142–46.

9. James Burgh, *Political Disquisitions: An Enquiry into Public Errors, Defects, and Abuses* (London: 1774), Vol. III, p. 285.

10. Harold J. Laski, *Political Thought in England: From Locke to Bentham* (Oxford: Oxford University Press, 1920), p. 119.

11. Gerald Stourzh claims that Blackstone was used by the revolutionaries to justify their resistance against England because he was such a widely respectable figure that his name carried great weight even with George III. See Stourzh, "William Blackstone: Teacher of Revolution," *Jahrbuch für Amerikastudien*, Vol. 15 (1970).

12. On his apologetics, see Kennedy, "Structure of Blackstone's Commentaries," pp. 218, 234, 353–54.

13. On the relation between Blackstone's optimistic outlook on the law and his conservative appeals to legislative inactivity, see Dicey, *Lectures on the Relation be-*

tween Law and Public Opinion, pp. 70–84. Richard A. Cosgrove accuses Blackstone of "encouraging a complacency with contemporary society that discouraged reform." Cosgrove, *Scholars of the Law: English Jurisprudence from Blackstone to Hart* (New York: New York University Press, 1996), p. 37.

14. On Blackstone's attitude toward legislatures, see David Lieberman, "Blackstone's Science of Legislation," *Journal of British Studies,* Vol. 27, No. 2 (1988), pp. 142–49.

15. "His [Blackstone's] conclusions and even more the insular self-congratulation of the account all seem to epitomize that unreflective and complacent attitude that Bentham lampooned as 'everything is as it should be' Blackstone." Lieberman, "Blackstone's Science of Legislation," p. 136. On the view that Blackstone was "cautious" and "diffident" but not conservative, see I. G. Doolittle, "Sir William Blackstone and his *Commentaries on the Laws of England* (1765–9): A Biographical Approach," *Oxford Journal of Legal Studies,* Vol. 3, No. 1 (1983), pp. 104–8.

16. It might be wondered how a "perfect" system could be improved upon, but such questions did not perturb Blackstone. As he put it, "The obsolete doctrines of our laws are frequently the foundation, upon which what remains is erected" (II, 44). Legal additions are acceptable as long as they conform to the principles contained in these foundations, which are themselves perfect.

17. See, for example, Jeremy Bentham, *A Fragment on Government* (Cambridge: Cambridge University Press, 1988). On the captiousness of some of Bentham's criticisms, see Rupert Cross, "Blackstone v. Bentham," *Law Quarterly Review,* Vol. 92 (1976).

18. On the development of this doctrine in English constitutional thought, see Janelle Greenberg, "Our Grand Maxim of State: 'The King Can Do No Wrong,'" *History of Political Thought,* Vol. 12, No. 2 (1991).

19. A review of the *Commentaries* in the *Annual Register* for 1767 thought to be written by Edmund Burke praised Blackstone for having removed "any part of the obscurity in which our system of laws is involved." The review continued: "These obligations we owe to Mr. Blackstone, who has entirely cleared the law of England from the rubbish in which it was buried; and now shows it to the public, in a clear, concise, and intelligible form." Quoted in A. V. Dicey, "Blackstone's Commentaries," *Cambridge Law Journal,* Vol. 4, No. 3 (1932), p. 286. Edward Gibbon explained that "this excellent work . . . may be considered as a rational System of the English Jurisprudence, digested into a natural method, and cleared of the pedantry, the obscurity, and the superfluities which rendered it the unknown horror of all men of taste." Quoted in W. S. Holdsworth, "Some Aspects of Blackstone and his *Commentaries,*" *Cambridge Law Journal,* Vol. 4, No. 3 (1932), p. 48.

20. Carl Schmitt, *Political Theology: Four Chapters on the Concept of Sovereignty,* trans. George Schwab (Chicago: University of Chicago Press, 2005), pp. 36–52.

21. For an overview of the critical, and sometimes abusive, responses to the *Commentaries* beginning with Bentham, see J. E. G. de Montmorency, "Sir William Blackstone," *Journal of the Society of Comparative Legislation,* New Series, Vol. 17, No. ½ (1917).

22. On Blackstone's preference for an "experiential," as opposed to a "deductive," understanding of reason, see Cosgrove, *Scholars of the Law*, p. 33.

23. Jeremy Bentham, *A Comment on the Commentaries* (London: Athlone Press, 1977), pp. 180, 202. On the unfairness of Bentham's vicious attacks on his former teacher, see Richard A. Posner, "Blackstone and Bentham," *Journal of Law and Economics*, Vol. 19, No. 3 (1976). H. L. A. Hart argues that Blackstone made "insidious" use of the natural law to "stifle criticism" of existing legal institutions. Hart, "Blackstone's Use of the Law of Nature," *Butterworths South African Law Review* (1956), p. 170.

24. It is noteworthy that Blackstone's admonition that "it is the duty of every good Englishman to understand, to revere, to defend" the constitution concludes his chapter on the king's title to rule (I, 211), another indication of the special status of the executive.

25. On the distinction (which Blackstone often blurred) between the separation of powers, which refers to a functional division of powers allocated among distinct and more or less independent branches of government, and mixed government, which refers to a system in which sovereignty is shared by political groups differentiated by their particular socioeconomic or ethico-political qualities, see M. J. C. Vile, *Constitutionalism and the Separation of Powers*, 2d ed. (Indianapolis: Liberty Fund, 1998).

26. Consistent with his common law approach, Blackstone did not consider constitutional law a separate system of law. John W. Cairns notes that, at that time, "The common law was, in a sense, the constitution." Cairns, "Blackstone, an English Institutist: Legal Literature and the Rise of the Nation State," *Oxford Journal of Legal Studies*, Vol. 4, No. 3 (1984), p. 347.

27. Boorstin, *Mysterious Science of the Law*, p. 70.

28. William Blackstone, "Note," *Harvard Law Review*, Vol. 32, No. 7 (1919), pp. 975–76. Even though Blackstone preferred the orderly and rational structure of law "as it stood in Littleton's Days" to the distorted state of law in his own day, he did not attribute the orderly structure of the former to deliberate planning or engineering on the part of any single architect, as Schmitt had claimed of other eighteenth-century writers. See Schmitt, *Political Theology*, pp. 47–48.

29. In the fourth volume of the *Commentaries*, Blackstone insisted that gentlemen have a duty to serve their country in a legal capacity or else the burden will fall to inferiors, who are "but the mere tools of office" (IV, 279).

30. On Blackstone's attempt to systematize the common law, see Michael Lobban, "Blackstone and the Science of Law," *Historical Journal*, Vol. 30, No. 2 (1987).

31. Dicey, "Blackstone's *Commentaries*," p. 298.

32. On Newton's influence on eighteenth-century ideas, see the excellent study by Richard Striner, "Political Newtonianism: The Cosmic Model of Politics in Europe and America," *William and Mary Quarterly*, 3d Series, Vol. 52, No. 4 (1995), in which political Newtonianism is characterized as a pervasive "*mentalité*." See also Carl L. Becker, *The Declaration of Independence: A Study in the History of Political Ideas* (New York: Vintage Books, 1958), pp. 40–53.

33. On the numerous "assumptions of eighteenth-century England enlisted" by Blackstone, see Boorstin, *Mysterious Science of the Law*, p. 8. Although Boorstin observes that Blackstone modeled his own project on the accomplishments of Newton (and Locke), he does not draw attention to the specifically Newtonian echoes of Blackstone's metaphors regarding the appropriate role of the executive. Blackstone's Newtonian pretensions have recently been noticed by Alschuler, who points out some of the scientific imagery in "Rediscovering Blackstone," pp. 20–21.

34. Enlightenment thinkers did not necessarily see a fundamental contradiction between science and theology, so Blackstone's own blend of these elements is not all that unusual. See Striner, "Political Newtonianism."

35. Schmitt, *Political Theology*, p. 48.

36. James Wilson, *Collected Works of James Wilson*, ed. Kermit Hall and Mark David Hall (Indianapolis: Liberty Fund, 2008), Vol. II, p. 883.

37. On the "pure" version of the separation of powers and Blackstone's deviations from it, see Vile, *Constitutionalism and the Separation of Powers*.

38. On the king's prerogatives with regards to foreign relations and enforcing the law of nations, see Blackstone, *Commentaries* (I, 245–53).

39. Striner, "Political Newtonianism," pp. 584, 588.

40. Blackstone called the king "the fountain of honour, of office, and of privilege," as well (I, 261).

41. Blackstone was careful here not to claim that the king is the original source of all justice because that would undermine his avowals of natural law. Nonetheless, he does assert that justice *emanates* from the king.

42. On the depiction of God in rationalist scientific discourse as a "first cause," see Barbara J. Shapiro, "Law and Science in Seventeenth-Century England," *Stanford Law Review*, Vol. 21, No. 4 (1969), p. 736. On the intellectual sources of Blackstone's conception of God's attributes, see J. M. Finnis, "Blackstone's Theoretical Intentions," *Natural Law Forum*, Vol. 12 (1967), p. 171.

43. For a trenchant critique of Blackstone's theory of sovereignty and executive power, particularly the notion that the king is a special being, see Bentham, *A Fragment on Government*, chs. 2–3.

44. On the medieval notion that the king was limited yet absolute within his sphere, see Charles Howard McIlwain, *Constitutionalism: Ancient and Modern*, rev. ed. (Ithaca: Cornell University Press, 1947), chs. 4–5; and Paul Birdsall, "Non Obstante," in *Essays in Honor of Charles Howard McIlwain*, ed. Carl Wittke (New York: Russell and Russell, 1936). On the development of the Whig theory of sovereignty, see Julian H. Franklin, *John Locke and the Theory of Sovereignty: Mixed Monarchy and the Right of Resistance in the Political Thought of the English Revolution* (Cambridge: Cambridge University Press, 1978); and Charles Howard McIlwain, "Whig Sovereignty and Real Sovereignty," in *Constitutionalism and the Changing World* (Cambridge: Cambridge University Press, 1938), ch. 4.

45. See C. B. Macpherson's classic study *The Political Theory of Possessive Individualism: Hobbes to Locke* (Oxford: Oxford University Press, 1962).

46. Jean-Louis de Lolme, *The Constitution of England; or, An Account of the English Government* (London: 1822), p. 356.

47. De Lolme's account of the English constitution establishes another link between Blackstone and constitutional thinkers in America. Like Montesquieu's *Spirit of the Laws*, de Lolme's *Constitution of England* relied on native sources in interpreting the English system of government. These works helped popularize the constitutional writings of Bolingbroke and Blackstone, respectively, in America. See Robert Shackleton, "Montesquieu, Bolingbroke, and the Separation of Powers," *French Studies*, Vol. III, No. 1 (1949).

48. De Lolme, *Constitution of England*, p. 167. De Lolme summarized his own argument this way: "The remarkable liberty enjoyed by the English nation is essentially owing to the impossibility under which their leaders, or in general all men of power among them, are placed, of invading and transferring to themselves any branch of the governing executive authority; which authority is exclusively vested, and firmly secured in the crown," p. 327.

49. Ibid., p. 312.

50. Ibid., quotations at pp. 347, 173. References to the general stability that arises from a stable executive appear throughout de Lolme's text.

51. Ibid., p. 447.

52. De Lolme attacked republicanism on a variety of grounds. On his treatment of republican virtue, see ibid., pp. 206–7, 356. Cf. Forrest McDonald, *The American Presidency: An Intellectual History* (Lawrence: University Press of Kansas, 1994), p. 61. On de Lolme's aspirations to advance the science of politics, see Mark Francis with John Morrow, "After the Ancient Constitution: Political Theory and English Constitutional Writings, 1765–1832," *History of Political Thought*, Vol. 9, No. 2 (1988).

53. On the development of an American conception of popular sovereignty as an alternative to Blackstone's conception of parliamentary sovereignty, see John V. Jezierski, "Parliament or People: James Wilson and Blackstone on the Nature and Location of Sovereignty," *Journal of the History of Ideas*, Vol. 32, No. 1 (1971).

54. On the political, moral, and epistemological implications of this theological imagery, see Clement Fatovic, "Emergency Action as Jurisprudential Miracle: Liberalism's Political Theology of Prerogative," *Perspectives on Politics*, Vol. 6, No. 3 (2008).

55. That majestic aura can be diminished by negative character traits. For instance, the vanity of James I, who was "easily taught by the flatterers of the times to believe there was something divine in [his hereditary] right" undermined the authority and title that incontestably belonged to him (I, 202).

56. There is some sloppiness in Blackstone's use of the term *prerogative*. It refers both to the specific powers belonging to the Crown and to the general discretionary powers of the executive. Some of the king's specific powers include "the right of erecting courts of judicature" (I, 257); the right to "prosecute for all public offences and breaches of the peace" (I, 259); the power to pardon; the power to issue proclamations; the power to create and dispense offices and the related "prerogative of conferring privileges upon private persons" (I, 261–63); the power to make treaties

and make war; the right to arbitrate commerce, including the power to coin money; and the governance of the national church. All these powers show "how regularly connected all the links are in this vast chain of prerogative" (I, 259).

57. Blackstone even approvingly cited two separate cases in which members of Parliament were sent to the tower for making impolitic remarks about the king (I, 240).

58. Among the qualities of the "heart . . . necessary to form a truly valuable English lawyer," Blackstone listed not only "a zeal for liberty and the constitution" but also "affectionate loyalty to the king" (I, 34).

59. If the amount of space devoted to a particular topic is any indication of its importance to Blackstone, then his chapter on prerogative qualifies as one of the most significant in the *Commentaries*. Chapter 7 on prerogative and the next and related one on royal revenue are two of the lengthiest chapters in the entire work. Together they occupy over one-fifth of the first volume. The chapter on Parliament is about as long as the one on prerogative, while the section on revenue exceeds all others.

60. On the "striking modernity" of Blackstone's anti-literal theory of statutory interpretation, see Cross, "Blackstone v. Bentham," pp. 520–22.

61. Algernon Sidney, *Discourses concerning Government*, ed. Thomas G. West (Indianapolis: Liberty Fund, 1996), p. 400.

62. It was important to Blackstone to prove that the law had not changed in any fundamental sense, since evidence of significant change would undermine his claim that the English system had long ago achieved a state of perfection. In one of his more memorable metaphors, he likened the legal changes that have occurred to "the changes of the bed of a river, which varies it's shores by continual decreases and alluvions." The laws themselves, "which, being accommodated to the exigencies of the times, suffer by degrees insensible variations . . . yet it is impossible to define the precise period in which that alteration accrued" (IV, 402).

63. Boorstin attacks Blackstone for the inconsistency of his values and questions his commitment to liberty as little more than a shibboleth. See Boorstin, *Mysterious Science of the Law*, 139–66.

64. He mentioned this limitation once more, and again only in the most cursory—and almost rueful—way: "It is true it was formerly held, that the king might in many cases dispense with penal statutes: but now by statute . . . it is declared, that the suspending or dispensing with laws by regal authority, without consent of parliament, is illegal" (I, 178–79). Then he moved on to a discussion of the king's power to convene and adjourn Parliament, which concludes his chapter on that body.

65. For Blackstone's views on influence and his contribution to American debates on this subject, see Gordon S. Wood, *The Creation of the American Republic: 1776–1787* (Chapel Hill: University of North Carolina Press, 1998), pp. 144–45.

66. On the changes in the monarchy since the Glorious Revolution, see Robert Blake, "Constitutional Monarchy: The Prerogative Powers," in *The Law, Politics, and the Constitution: Essays in Honour of Geoffrey Marshall*, ed. David Butler, Vernon Bogdanor, and Robert Summers (Oxford: Oxford University Press, 2000).

67. On the bitterness of politics in "the age of Walpole," see Isaac Kramnick, *Bolingbroke and His Circle: The Politics of Nostalgia in the Age of Walpole* (Ithaca, NY: Cornell University Press, 1992).

68. For the text of Hamilton's infamous June 18 speech, see Max Farrand, ed., *The Records of the Federal Convention of 1787* (New Haven: Yale University Press, 1966), Vol. I, pp. 282–93.

69. On John Adams's conception of executive power, see Bruce Miroff, "John Adams and the Presidency," in *Inventing the American Presidency*, ed. Thomas E. Cronin (Lawrence: University Press of Kansas, 1989).

CHAPTER 5: "It Squints towards Monarchy"

Epigraph. John P. Kaminski, Gaspare J. Saladino, Richard Leffler, Charles H. Schoenleber, and Margaret A. Hogan, eds., *The Documentary History of the Ratification of the Constitution* (Madison: State Historical Society of Wisconsin, 1976–2000), Vol. IX, p. 963.

1. On common attitudes toward executive power, see Jack P. Greene, *Negotiated Authorities: Essays in Colonial Political and Constitutional History* (Charlottesville: University Press of Virginia, 1994), pp. 202–14, quotation at p. 204.

2. See Willi Paul Adams, *The First American Constitutions: Republican Ideology and the Making of the State Constitutions in the Revolutionary Era* (Chapel Hill: University of North Carolina Press, 1980); and Gordon S. Wood, *The Creation of the American Republic: 1776–1787* (Chapel Hill: University of North Carolina Press, 1998), pp. 135–50.

3. Alexander Hamilton, "The Farmer Refuted," in *The Papers of Alexander Hamilton*, ed. Harold C. Syrett and Jacob E. Cooke (New York: Columbia University Press, 1962), Vol. I, p. 92.

4. Alexander Hamilton, "New York Ratifying Convention Speech, June 21, 1788," in ibid., Vol. V, p. 36.

5. Gouverneur Morris, the most active participant at the Convention and a major force in the creation of the presidency, observed that "it is [the] most difficult of all rightly to balance the Executive." See Max Farrand, ed., *The Records of the Federal Convention of 1787* (New Haven: Yale University Press, 1937), Vol. II, p. 105. Subsequent references to this collection will be given in the text as "Farrand" along with volume and page number.

6. Even James Madison, the so-called father of the Constitution, did not "attempt a systematic rationalization of the summer's work" until he began his collaboration with Hamilton on the *Federalist*. See Lance Banning, *The Sacred Fire of Liberty: James Madison and the Founding of the Federal Republic* (Ithaca, NY: Cornell University Press, 1995), pp. 8, 171–72.

7. On the "Pre-Constitution Presidencies," see Richard B. Morris, "The Origins of the Presidency," *Presidential Studies Quarterly*, Vol. 17, No. 4 (1987), pp. 673–78. The appellation was also familiar to subscribers of various libraries and social clubs,

which had their own presidents. The Anti-Federalist "Centinel" charged the Federalists with trying to dupe the people by a clever subterfuge recommended by the "corrupt politician Machiavel, who advises any one who would change the constitution of a state, to keep as much as possible to the old forms." Quoted in John P. Kaminski, Gaspare J. Saladino, Richard Leffler, Charles H. Schoenleber, and Margaret A. Hogan, eds., *The Documentary History of the Ratification of the Constitution* (Madison: State Historical Society of Wisconsin, 1976–2000), Vol. XIV, p. 58. Subsequent references to these volumes will be abbreviated as *DHRC* and will refer to volume and page number(s).

8. See Greene, *Negotiated Authorities*, p. 203. The monarchical qualities of the presidency were implicitly acknowledged even by Convention delegates and Federalists like Charles Cotesworth Pinckney, who in the South Carolina ratifying convention often compared and contrasted the president's powers with those of the English king (Farrand III, 251).

9. A few words on the Federalists and Anti-Federalists are in order at this point. The superior organization of the Federalists helped them stay "on message" in their support for the Constitution, resulting in arguments that were much more consistent than those of their opponents. Despite important differences in emphasis, there were few significant substantive disagreements over executive power among the Federalists. In contrast, Anti-Federalist opinions on the presidency differed "irreconcilably" from each other. As Madison observed, they were "little agreed with one another," especially "on the Constitution of the Executive" (*DHRC*, XVI, 169; VIII, 253–54). Many Anti-Federalists feared that the powers of the president were too great, but some actually argued that the president was not strong enough to resist encroachments by the legislature.

10. One of the few scholars to have noted this sub rosa incorporation of prerogative into the Constitution is Daniel Franklin, *Extraordinary Measures: The Exercise of Prerogative Powers in the United States* (Pittsburgh: University of Pittsburgh Press, 1991), pp. 19–20.

11. On the idea that the president would be a disinterested statesman who would stand "above party," see Ralph Ketcham, *Presidents above Party: The First American Presidency, 1789–1829* (Chapel Hill: University of North Carolina Press, 1984).

12. On the Anti-Federalists' insistence on "more explicit limitations written into the Constitution" and "detailed explicitness" to curb the discretion of the national government, see Cecilia M. Kenyon, "Men of Little Faith: The Anti-Federalists on the Nature of Representative Government," *William and Mary Quarterly*, Vol. 12, No. 1 (1955), especially pp. 21–22.

13. On the conflicting tendencies between "the empirical or pragmatic, and the doctrinaire or ideological" in American political thought during the Founding, see Cecilia Kenyon, ed., *The Antifederalists* (Boston: Northeastern University Press, 1985), pp. xxxiii–xxxiv; quotation at p. xxxiii.

14. James H. Hutson, ed., *The Supplement to Max Farrand's The Records of the Federal Convention of 1787* (New Haven: Yale University Press, 1987), p. 183.

15. James Madison, Alexander Hamilton, and John Jay, *The Federalist Papers,* ed. Isaac Kramnick (New York: Penguin, 1987), Vol. I, p. 87. Subsequent references to the *Federalist* providing essay and page information appear parenthetically in the text.

16. Hamilton, "The New York Ratifying Convention," *The Papers of Alexander Hamilton,* Vol. 5, p. 125. On the upheavals in Hamilton's early life, see Ron Chernow, *Alexander Hamilton* (New York: Penguin, 2004), pp. 7–40. On the Machiavellian background of Hamilton's youth, see John Lamberton Harper, *American Machiavelli: Alexander Hamilton and the Origins of U.S. Foreign Policy* (Cambridge: Cambridge University Press, 2004), pp. 13–15.

17. Quoted in Louis Fisher, *Presidential War Power* (Lawrence: University Press of Kansas, 2004), p. 14.

18. See Wood, *Creation of the American Republic,* ch. 4.

19. Isaac Kramnick, "Skepticism in English Political Thought: From Temple to Burke," *Studies in Burke and His Time,* Vol. 12, No. 1 (1970), pp. 1629, 1630.

20. A notable exception is Morton White, *Philosophy,* The Federalist, *and the Constitution* (Oxford: Oxford University Press, 1987).

21. In fairness to Kant, it should be pointed out that he recognized the need for a "middle term" like judgment to mediate between theory and practice in his essay "On the Common Saying: 'This May Be True in Theory, but it Does Not Apply in Practice,'" but he still qualifies as a representative of the rationalist tradition that privileges the dictates of abstract reason over practical experience due to his confidence in the ability of institutional arrangements to regulate even "a nation of devils." Immanuel Kant, "Perpetual Peace," *Political Writings,* ed. Hans Reiss (Cambridge: Cambridge University Press, 1970), p. 112.

22. For critiques of rationalism in politics from a variety of intellectual perspectives and political positions, see Michael Oakeshott, *Rationalism in Politics and Other Essays,* new and expanded edition (Indianapolis: Liberty Press, 1991), pp. 5–42; Friedrich A. Hayek, *The Counter-Revolution of Science: Studies on the Abuse of Reason* (Indianapolis: Liberty Press, 1980), pp. 185–211; Isaiah Berlin, "Two Concepts of Liberty," in *Four Essays on Liberty* (Oxford: Oxford University Press, 1969), pp. 145–54; Michel Foucault, *Language, Counter-Memory, Practice: Selected Essays and Interviews,* ed. Donald F. Bouchard (Ithaca, NY: Cornell University Press, 1977), part III; and Bonnie Honig, *Political Theory and the Displacement of Politics* (Ithaca, NY: Cornell University Press, 1993).

23. James Iredell, "Marcus I" (*DHRC,* XVI, 168, 165).

24. James Madison, "Letter to Thomas Jefferson," October 24, November 1, 1787 (*DHRC,* XIII, 446). Madison also noted ruefully that the distinction between regulation of trade and revenue that was so critical and apparently obvious to Americans in their dispute with the imperial government "was found on fair discussion, to be absolutely undefinable."

25. James Iredell, "Marcus II" (*DHRC,* XVI, 243).

26. James Wilson, Speech at the Pennsylvania Convention, November 24, 1787, in *Friends of the Constitution,* p. 78.

27. James Iredell, "Marcus IV" (*DHRC*, XVI, 379).

28. "Denatus," *Virginia Independent Chronicle*, June 11, 1788 (*DHRC*, X, 1605).

29. William Grayson, The Virginia Convention, June 23, 1788 (*DHRC*, X, 1469).

30. Caleb Wallace to William Fleming, May 3, 1788 (*DHRC*, XVII, 377).

31. Mercy Otis Warren, "A Columbian Patriot: Observations on the Constitution," February 1788 (*DHRC*, IX, 276), emphasis in original.

32. "Denatus," *Virginia Independent Chronicle*, June 11, 1788 (*DHRC*, X, 1600).

33. Luther Martin, "Genuine Information II," *Baltimore Maryland Gazette*, January 1, 1788 (*DHRC*, XV, 206), emphasis in original.

34. "Cato V," *New York Journal*, November 22, 1787 (*DHRC*, XIV, 182), emphasis in original.

35. "A Georgian," *Gazette of the State of Georgia*, November 15, 1787 (*DHRC*, III, 236).

36. Lance Banning, "Republican Ideology and the Triumph of the Constitution, 1789 to 1793," *William and Mary Quarterly*, 3rd Series, Vol. 31, No. 2 (1974), p. 179.

37. The Articles of Confederation differ in many ways from the document that replaced it, but the most significant difference in this context might be that so many provisions are negative—that is, they spell out what the states shall not do, thus affirming the principle that the states possess ultimate sovereignty in the confederation. The Articles of Confederation stipulated so many explicit exceptions to Congress's powers that the document eliminated a major source of uncertainty, and therefore controversy, that has come to plague debates about the proper powers of Congress under the Constitution.

38. See Patrick Henry, The Virginia Convention, June 7, 1788 (*DHRC*, IX, 1046).

39. On the difficulties of defining executive power at the Constitutional Convention, see Charles C. Thach, *The Creation of the Presidency, 1775–1789: A Study in Constitutional History* (Indianapolis: Liberty Fund, 2007), pp. 69–78, 103–6. The aversion to defining executive power in the Constitution was matched only by the Framers' reluctance to define the law of nations, an undertaking that struck many of them as preposterous and hubristic.

40. Federalists reminded the uncommitted that formal amendments could resolve some of the Constitution's more glaring defects, although they hoped that this would be kept to a minimum. The ambivalent Federalist Edmund Randolph hoped that future amendments to the Constitution would have "all ambiguities of expression to be precisely explained." See "The Publication of Edmund Randolph's Reasons for Not Signing the Constitution," December 27, 1787 (*DHRC*, VIII, 273). James Iredell simply dismissed concerns about the indeterminacy of certain constitutional clauses by pointing out that "it is impracticable to define every thing." Future Congresses would correct these deficiencies (*DHRC*, XVI, 243).

41. Edmund Randolph, The Virginia Convention, June 17, 1788 (*DHRC*, X, 1347).

42. James Madison, The Virginia Convention, June 20, 1788 (*DHRC*, X, 1412, 1413).

43. See Wood's exemplary discussion of the "legislative arrogation" and "popular despotism" of this period. Wood, *The Creation of the American Republic*, ch. 10.

44. Much of the following account of national politics is based on Rakove, *Beginnings of National Politics*.

45. James Madison, *Madison: Writings*, ed. Jack N. Rakove (New York: Library of America, 1999), p. 77.

46. The institutional dynamics of popular assemblies were so distressing that Madison was forced to conclude, "had every Athenian citizen been a Socrates, every Athenian assembly would still have been a mob" (LV, 336).

47. James Madison, Virginia Ratifying Convention, June 18, 1788 (*DHRC*, X, 1379–80).

48. Madison's diagnosis of the pathologies of legislatures in the *Federalist* was anticipated in "Vices of the Political System of the United States," a set of notes he prepared before attending the Constitutional Convention. See the quoted passages in *Madison: Writings*, p. 75.

49. Hamilton reiterated his criticisms of the "unaccommodating spirit of party" that infects state legislatures in his June 21, 1788, Speech to the New York Ratifying Convention. See *The Papers of Alexander Hamilton*, Vol. 5, p. 56.

50. The adoption of the Northwest Ordinance is a notable exception.

51. Rakove, *Beginnings of National Politics*, p. 291.

52. Forrest McDonald, *E Pluribus Unum: The Formation of the American Republic 1776–1790* (Indianapolis: Liberty Fund, 1979), pp. 248–57.

53. For a discussion of the concept of energy in the *Federalist*, see David F. Epstein, *The Political Theory of the Federalist* (Chicago: University of Chicago Press, 1984), pp. 35–37, 171–76.

54. George Washington, "Circular to the States," June 14, 1783, in *Friends of the Constitution: Writings of the "Other" Federalists 1787–1788*, ed. Colleen A. Sheehan and Gary L. McDowell (Indianapolis: Liberty Fund, 1998), p. 21.

55. Later Hamilton explained that energy is essential to the discharge of the "principal purposes" served by government: "common defense," "the preservation of the public peace," "regulation of commerce," and the "superintendence" of foreign relations (XXIII, 184). At least three of these four functions are the exclusive province of the executive.

56. On the link between state-building and liberty in Hamilton's political thought, see Karl-Friedrich Walling, *Republican Empire: Alexander Hamilton on War and Free Government* (Lawrence: University Press of Kansas, 1999).

57. George Washington, "Letter to Sir Edward Newenham," August 29, 1788 (*DHRC*, XVIII, 359).

58. James Wilson, Speech in the Pennsylvania Convention, November 24, 1787, in *Friends of the Constitution*, p. 81.

59. Thomas Paine, *Common Sense*, in *The Thomas Paine Reader*, ed. Isaac Kramnick (New York: Penguin, 1987), p. 68, emphasis in original.

60. Hamilton identified the four ingredients that make up energy in the executive as "unity; duration; an adequate provision for its support; and competent powers" (LXX, 403).

61. "A Federalist," in *Friends of the Constitution: Writings of the "Other" Federalists, 1787–1788*, ed. Colleen A. Sheehan and Gary L. McDowell (Indianapolis: Liberty Fund, 1998), p. 41.

62. Thomas Jefferson, *Notes on the State of Virginia*, ed. William Peden (New York: W.W. Norton, 1954), p. 214.

63. On the state constitutions and the subordination of the executive to state legislatures, see Wood, *Creation of the American Republic*, pp. 132–50; and Thach, *Creation of the Presidency*, pp. 13–44.

64. Jean-Louis de Lolme, *The Constitution of England: Or, an Account of the English Government* (London: 1822), pp. 381–82.

65. See Thach, *Creation of the Presidency*, ch. 2. On the state constitutions generally, see Adams, *First American Constitutions*.

66. Madison to George Washington, April 16, 1787, *Madison: Writings*, pp. 82–83. On the curious incoherence of Madison's thought on executive power, see Jack N. Rakove and Susan Zlomke, "James Madison and the Independent Executive," *Presidential Studies Quarterly*, Vol. 17, No. 2 (1987). On the view that Madison had a clear conception of executive power, which is not well supported, see Ruth Weissbourd Grant and Stephen Grant, "The Madisonian Presidency," in *The Presidency in the Constitutional Order*, ed. Joseph M. Bessette and Jeffrey Tulis (Baton Rouge: Louisiana State University Press, 1981), p. 44.

67. On Madison's (relative lack of) participation in debates on the executive at the Philadelphia Convention, see Jeffrey Leigh Sedgwick, "James Madison and the Problem of Executive Character," *Polity*, Vol. 21, No. 1 (1988).

68. Alexander Hamilton, "Letter to James Duane," September 3, 1780, *Hamilton: Writings*, ed. Joanne B. Freeman (New York: Library of America, 2001), p. 71.

69. Some of the uncertainty, even mystery, surrounding executive power is suggested in Madison's "Notes on Confederacies," drafted in preparation for the Convention. Madison wrote that the executive magistrate of the Netherlands "has a general and secret influence on the great machine [of government] which cannot be defined." See James Madison, *The Writings of James Madison*, ed. Gaillard Hunt (New York: J. P. Putnam's Sons, 1901), Vol. II, p. 384.

70. This dual strategy paid off handsomely a few years later in his debate with Madison over the president's authority to interpret treaties and other laws and issue a proclamation of neutrality. See Alexander Hamilton and James Madison, *The Pacificus-Helvidius Debates of 1793–1794: Toward the Completion of the American Founding*, ed. Morton J. Frisch (Indianapolis: Liberty Fund, 2007).

71. Alexander Hamilton to William Heth, June 23[-24], 1791, *Papers of Alexander Hamilton*, Vol. VIII, p. 499.

72. Hamilton to James Duane, September 3, 1780, *Hamilton: Writings*, p. 71.

73. Hamilton, "Opinion on the Constitutionality of a National Bank," *Hamilton: Writings*, p. 613.

74. See Walling, *Republican Empire*, pp. 80–83.

75. The classic study on this subject is Edward S. Corwin, The "Higher Law" Background of American Constitutional Law (Ithaca, NY: Cornell University Press, 1955).

76. Harvey C. Mansfield Jr., "Republicanizing the Executive," in Saving the Revolution: The Federalist Papers and the American Founding, ed. Charles R. Kesler (New York: Free Press, 1987), pp. 174–75.

77. My account differs slightly from, but is consistent with, the argument in Leonard R. Sorenson, "The Federalist Papers on the Constitutionality of Executive Prerogative," Presidential Studies Quarterly, Vol. 19, No. 2 (1989). This is the best analysis of the relation between executive prerogative and the "doctrine of proportionate means," that is, the doctrine that proper ends are "paramount" to and authorize means, which are subordinate.

78. Sheldon S. Wolin, "Norm and Form: The Constitutionalizing of Democracy," in Athenian Political Thought and the Reconstruction of American Democracy, ed. J. Peter Euben, John R. Wallach, and Josiah Ober (Ithaca, NY: Cornell University Press, 1994), p. 47.

79. On the dogmatic, legalistic, and doctrinaire thinking of Anti-Federalists, see the introduction to The Antifederalists, ed. Cecilia Kenyon (Boston: Northeastern University Press, 1985), pp. xcix–ci, cxiv.

80. Cf. Banning, Sacred Fire of Liberty, p. 8.

81. William Symmes Jr., "Letter to Peter Osgood, Jr.," November 15, 1787 (DHRC, XIV, 114).

82. Hutson, Supplement to Max Farrand, p. 87.

83. See Jefferson's objections to the Constitution in his letter to Madison, December 20, 1787, in which he acknowledged that he was "not a friend to a very energetic government. It is always oppressive." Thomas Jefferson: Writings, ed. Merrill D. Peterson (New York: Library of America, 1984), pp. 917–18.

84. Niccolò Machiavelli, Discourses on Livy, trans. and eds. Harvey C. Mansfield and Nathan Tarcov (Chicago: University of Chicago Press, 1996), pp. 10–14.

85. Harvey C. Mansfield Jr., Taming the Prince: The Ambivalence of Modern Executive Power (Baltimore: Johns Hopkins University Press, 1993), pp. 255–59, quotation at p. 259.

86. Edmund Pendleton, "Letter to James Madison," October 8, 1787 (DHRC, VIII, 46).

87. James Madison, The Virginia Ratifying Convention, June 14, 1788 (DHRC, X, 1282).

88. James Iredell, "Marcus III" (DHRC, XVI, 323).

89. Quoted in Robert E. DiClerico, "James Wilson's Presidency," Presidential Studies Quarterly, Vol. 17, No. 2 (1987), p. 305.

90. John Marshall, The Virginia Convention, June 10, 1788 (DHRC, IX, 1120).

91. George Nicholas, The Virginia Convention, June 16, 1788 (DHRC, X, 1333).

92. Patrick Henry, The Virginia Convention, June 14, 1788 (DHRC, X, 1275).

93. Mansfield develops this theme in "Republicanizing the Executive," pp. 171–74.

94. A Freeholder," Virginia Independent Chronicle, April 9, 1788 (DHRC, IX, 722).

95. William Grayson, The Virginia Convention, June 11, 1788 (*DHRC*, IX, 1169).

96. James Madison, The Virginia Ratifying Convention, June 14, 1788 (*DHRC*, X, 1274). Without a doubt, emergency powers are dictatorial in the Roman sense, but it is wrong to suggest that they are "authoritarian," as suggested by Michael A. Genovese, "Democratic Theory and the Emergency Powers of the President," *Presidential Studies Quarterly*, Vol. 9, No. 3 (1979). Though they are always open to abuse, emergency powers do not necessarily entail the repression of dissent, nor are they necessarily exercised for the sake of authority. None of the liberal writers discussed here would justify the use of emergency powers for illiberal ends.

97. A Native of Virginia: Observations on the Proposed Plan of Federal Government, April 2, 1788 (*DHRC*, IX, 681).

98. "An Impartial Citizen," *Petersburg Virginia Gazette*, February 28, 1788 (*DHRC*, VIII, 428).

99. Roger Sherman, "A Countryman III," November 29, 1787 (*DHRC*, XIV, 296).

100. James Iredell, "Marcus III," March 5, 1788 (*DHRC*, XVI, 322).

101. On the qualities that Hamilton thought were necessary for "administrative efficacy," see Harvey Flaumenhaft, *The Effective Republic: Administration and Constitution in the Thought of Alexander Hamilton* (Durham, NC: Duke University Press, 1992), pp. 69–81.

102. James Iredell, "Marcus II" (*DHRC*, XVI, 247).

103. Gouverneur Morris, "Letter to George Washington," October 30, 1787 (*DHRC*, XIII, 514).

104. Ibid.

105. The metaphor of the Constitution as a machine appears in a letter by Madison in which he suggests that "advocates" in Congress are needed to set the machine in motion, so the executive's responsibility is not an exclusive one. James Madison, "Letter to George Nicholas," April 8, 1788 (*DHRC*, XVII, 35).

106. Marquis de Lafayette, "Letter to George Washington," January 1, 1788 (*DHRC*, XIV, 492).

107. White, *Philosophy*, The Federalist, *and the Constitution*, p. 4.

108. Thomas Jefferson, "Letter to William Carmichael," August 12, 1788 (*DHRC*, XVIII, 325).

109. Thomas Jefferson, "Letter to Edward Carrington," May 27, 1788 (*DHRC*, XVIII, 81), emphasis added.

110. Anthony Wayne, "Letter to Marquis de Lafayette," July 4, 1788 (*DHRC*, XVIII, 221).

111. Jeremy Rabkin draws a contrast between the ideas of administration and modern bureaucracy, though not quite sharply enough to indicate just how much administration was identified with personal rule in the *Federalist*. See Rabkin, "Bureaucratic Idealism and Executive Power: A Perspective on *The Federalist's* View of Public Administration," in *Saving the Revolution*, ed. Kesler.

112. Alexander Hamilton, "Conjectures About the Constitution," September 1787 (*DHRC*, XIII, 278).

113. On the different applications that Hamilton and Jefferson made of Lockean prerogative, see Clement Fatovic, "Constitutionalism and Presidential Prerogative: Jeffersonian and Hamiltonian Perspectives," *American Journal of Political Science,* Vol. 48, No. 3 (2004).

114. Hamilton, *Pacificus-Helvidius Debates,* p. 16.

115. Ibid., p. 14.

116. Alexander Hamilton to William Heth, June 23[-24], 1791, *Papers of Alexander Hamilton,* Vol. VIII, pp. 499–500.

117. Hamilton, *Pacificus-Helvidius Debates,* p. 12.

118. Ibid., p. 13.

119. Madison, *Pacificus-Helvidius Debates,* p. 56.

120. Hamilton, in particular, shamelessly pandered to the public's warm affection for Washington to defend the neutrality proclamation.

121. Madison, *Pacificus-Helvidius Debates,* p. 64.

122. Although Hamilton had asserted in the *Federalist* that the power to make treaties was not, strictly speaking, an executive power, he was just as emphatic in asserting that it was not a legislative power and that the "qualities elsewhere detailed as indispensable in the management of foreign negotiations point out the executive as the most fit agent in those transactions" (LXXV, 425).

123. Madison, *Pacific-Helvidius Debates,* p. 59.

124. Ibid., p. 58.

125. Ibid. Madison's footnote on Locke is even more severe toward the English philosopher: "The chapter on prerogative shows how much the reason of the philosopher was clouded by the royalism of the Englishman."

126. Ibid., p. 59.

127. Ibid., p. 61.

128. Thomas Jefferson to Doctor James Brown, October 27, 1808, *The Writings of Thomas Jefferson,* ed. Paul Leicester Ford (New York: G. P. Putnam's Sons, 1898), Vol. IX, p. 211.

129. On the background and significance of this letter, see Jeremy David Bailey, "Executive Prerogative and the 'Good Officer' in Thomas Jefferson's Letter to John B. Colvin," *Presidential Studies Quarterly,* Vol. 34, No. 4 (2004).

130. Jefferson to John B. Colvin, September 20, 1810, *Writings of Thomas Jefferson,* Vol. IX, pp. 280, 281.

131. The following discussion is taken from Fatovic, "Constitutionalism and Presidential Prerogative."

132. On Jefferson's disagreement with Hamilton and the differences in their interpretive methodologies, see H. Jefferson Powell, "The Original Understanding of Original Intent," *Harvard Law Review,* Vol. 98, No. 5 (1985), pp. 914–17.

133. Jefferson to John B. Colvin, *Writings of Thomas Jefferson,* pp. 279–82.

134. On the need for an indemnity to legitimize the risk that an executive takes in exceeding the law, see Richard J. Dougherty, "Thomas Jefferson and the Rule of Law: Executive Power and American Constitutionalism," *Northern Kentucky Law Re-*

view, Vol. 28, No. 3 (2001), pp. 527–28; David Gray Adler, "The Steel Seizure Case and Inherent Presidential Power," *Constitutional Commentary,* Vol. 19, No. 1 (2002), pp. 174–78; and Bailey, "Executive Prerogative."

135. In a letter addressed to "Elias Shipman and Others," July 12, 1801, Jefferson wrote: "Of the various executive duties, no one excites more anxious concern than that of placing the interests of our fellow citizens in the hands of *honest men,* with understandings sufficient for their station. No duty, at the same time, is more diffi-cult to fulfill. The knolege [*sic*] of *characters* possessed by a single individual is, of necessity, limited. To seek out *the best* through the whole Union, we must resort to other information, which, from *the best of men,* acting *disinterestedly* and with *the purest motives,* is sometimes incorrect." See *Jefferson: Writings,* p. 497.

CHAPTER 6: A "Patriotic and Dignifying President"

Epigraph. Tench Coxe, "An American Citizen," in *Friends of the Constitution: Writ-ings of the "Other" Federalists, 1787–1788,* ed. Colleen A. Sheehan and Gary L. McDow-ell (Indianapolis: Liberty Fund, 1998), pp. 462–63.

1. On the classical education and reading habits of the Founders, see Carl J. Rich-ard, *The Founders and the Classics: Greece, Rome, and the American Enlightenment* (Cam-bridge: Harvard University Press, 1994).

2. John Adams to Mercy Otis Warren, April 16, 1776, *Papers of John Adams,* ed. Robert J. Taylor (Cambridge: Belknap Press, 1977), Vol. IV, pp. 124–25.

3. Gordon S. Wood, *The Creation of the American Republic: 1776–1787* (Chapel Hill: University of North Carolina Press, 1998), pp. 65–70, 118–24.

4. See, for instance, Thomas Paine's complaint about the "summer soldier and the sunshine patriot" in the first installment of *The American Crisis,* in *The Thomas Paine Reader,* ed. Isaac Kramnick (New York: Penguin, 1987), p. 116. See also David McCullough, *1776* (New York: Simon and Schuster, 2005), pp. 64, 90–91, 204–5.

5. Gordon S. Wood, "Interests and Disinterestedness in the Making of the Con-stitution," in *Beyond Confederation: Origins of the Constitution and American National Identity,* ed. Richard Beeman, Stephen Botein, and Edward C. Carter II (Chapel Hill: University of North Carolina Press, 1987), pp. 69–109; and Forrest McDonald, *Novus Ordo Seclorum: The Intellectual Origins of the Constitution* (Lawrence: University Press of Kansas, 1985), pp. 143–83.

6. James Madison, "Vices of the Political System of the United States," in *Madi-son: Writings,* ed. Jack N. Rakove (New York: Library of America, 1999), p. 75.

7. Wood, *The Radicalism of the American Revolution* (New York: Vintage Books, 1991), pp. 253, 254.

8. This is not to say that arguments offered in defense of the presidency during the constitutional ratification debates expressed or presupposed a single rational de-sign contrived at the Philadelphia Convention. As David Brian Robertson has argued, the work of the Convention proceeded along a highly contingent and "path-dependent sequence of political compromise" that left everyone, including Madison, unsatisfied

with certain aspects of the Constitution. Robertson, "Madison's Opponents and Constitutional Design," *American Political Science Review*, Vol. 99, No. 2 (2005), p. 240. Even though many arguments about the need for virtue in the executive were developed only after the final draft of the Constitution was unveiled, claims made during the ratification debates were more important than speeches made at the Constitutional Convention in establishing public expectations for the presidency.

9. Alexander Hamilton, "Speech at the Philadelphia Convention," June 22, 1787, in *The Records of the Federal Convention of 1787*, ed. Max Farrand (New Haven: Yale University Press, 1966), Vol. I, p. 381. Subsequent references to this collection will be given in the text as "Farrand" along with volume and page number. Hamilton invoked "Hume's opinion of the British constitution" to support his contention that "there is always a body of firm patriots, who often shake a corrupt administration," even though the mass of mankind is governed by vicious passions. Ibid.

10. On the schemes to improve the people, see Lorraine Smith Pangle and Thomas L. Pangle, *The Learning of Liberty: The Educational Ideas of the American Founders* (Lawrence: University Press of Kansas, 1993). It would be easy to dismiss the rhetoric of virtue in this context as insincere propaganda designed to rationalize the powers of the presidency to a skeptical public, rather than sincere expressions of theoretical aims. However, the sincerity of these references to virtue is supported by their frequent appearance in private correspondence. In any case, it may not be such "a profitable task to attempt to judge the sincere and insincere uses of a theory." As Glenn Burgess explains, "The political world is at least as much a world of rhetoric as a world of philosophy." Burgess, *The Politics of the Ancient Constitution: An Introduction to English Political Thought, 1603–1642* (University Park: Pennsylvania State University Press, 1992), p. 169. And once those ideas, sincere or not, are out in circulation, there is nothing to prevent anyone, including the initial critics, from using them to hold political actors up to the standards they set.

11. Alexander Hamilton, Speech to the New York Ratifying Convention, *The Papers of Alexander Hamilton,* ed. Harold C. Syrett (New York: Columbia University Press, 1976), Vol. V, p. 95.

12. John Brown Cutting to William Short, November 3, 1787, in John P. Kaminski, Gaspare J. Saladino, Richard Leffler, Charles H. Schoenleber, and Margaret A. Hogan, eds., *The Documentary History of the Ratification of the Constitution* (Madison: State Historical Society of Wisconsin, 1976–2000), Vol. XIV, p. 461. Subsequent references to items in this collection will appear as *DHRC*, followed by volume and page numbers.

13. Simeon Baldwin, "Oration in New Haven," July 4, 1788 (*DHRC*, XVIII, 241–42).

14. Harvey C. Mansfield Jr., *Taming the Prince: The Ambivalence of Modern Executive Power* (Baltimore: Johns Hopkins University Press, 1993), p. 247.

15. I owe a special debt of gratitude to Jeffery Tulis for helping me to clarify these three different ways of thinking about the way virtue works in the Constitution: (1) as a floor used to establish a bare minimum, (2) as a practical standard used to design

institutions that would elicit good behavior, and (3) as an ideal standard used to guide the selection of worthy candidates.

16. James Madison, "Speech in the Virginia Ratifying Convention on the Judicial Power," June 20, 1788, in *Madison: Writings*, p. 398. The populist claim that the people could and should be trusted to elevate individuals of virtue was a common rhetorical strategy employed by Federalists of all stripes. See Bernard Bailyn, *The Ideological Origins of the American Revolution*, enlarged edition (Cambridge: Belknap Press, 1990), pp. 369–71.

17. Martin Diamond, "Democracy and *The Federalist*: A Reconsideration of the Framers' Intent," *American Political Science Review*, Vol. 53, No. 1 (1959), p. 68. Similarly, Robert A. Dahl argues that the Madisonian system places all its confidence in institutional-constitutional checks and none in social ones. See Dahl, *A Preface to Democratic Theory* (Chicago: University of Chicago Press, 1956), especially pp. 22, 83. Hamilton's remark concerning the formation of confederate governments ("there is no absolute rule on the subject") is apropos of the entire Constitution and consistent with Federalist skepticism regarding institutional design. James Madison, Alexander Hamilton, and John Jay, *The Federalist Papers*, ed. Isaac Kramnick (New York: Penguin, 1987), Vol. IX, p. 242. Subsequent references to the *Federalist* according to essay and page number will appear in parentheses in the text.

18. For an overview of these criticisms, see Paul A. Rahe, "Fame, Founders, and the Idea of Founding in the Eighteenth Century," in *The Noblest Minds: Fame, Honor, and the American Founding*, ed. Peter McNamara (Lanham, MD: Rowman and Littlefield, 1999), pp. 14–23.

19. Anthony Ashley Cooper, the Third Earl of Shaftesbury, *An Inquiry concerning Virtue, or Merit*, in *Characteristicks of Men, Manners, Opinions, Times* (Indianapolis: Liberty Fund, 2001), Vol. II, p. 46.

20. David Hume, *A Treatise of Human Nature*, ed. Ernest C. Mossner (New York: Penguin, 1969), pp. 602, 462.

21. James Madison, The Virginia Convention, June 17, 1788 (*DHRC*, X, 1368).

22. James W. Ceaser demonstrates the institutional purposes of the Electoral College in selecting individuals with the right reputation "as determined largely by previous public experience," but he does not specify the type of character except to say that the president should be "non-partisan." See Ceaser, *Presidential Selection: Theory and Development* (Princeton: Princeton University Press, 1979), p. 29.

23. "Caesar I," October 1, 1787 (*DHRC*, XIII, 288); "Federalist," *Massachusetts Centinel*, March 26, 1788 (*DHRC*, XVI, 538). Encomiums to Washington's unparalleled virtue and unmatched qualifications for the presidency were as common in this period as attacks on the institution itself. For example, Enos Hitchcock gushed, "Here again rises to view, from the placid shades of domestic life, the great AMERICAN CINCINNATUS, whose virtues in the field can be equalled only by his wisdom in the senate!" (*DHRC*, XVIII, 233–34). On the perception of Washington as the virtuous Catonian statesman, see Ketcham, pp. 89–93.

24. Bernard Bailyn states that Hamilton considered "breadth of vision" a requirement for *all* representatives. See Bailyn, *To Begin the World Anew: The Genius and Ambiguities of the American Founders* (New York: Vintage, 2003), p. 118.

25. On the foresight needed in the administration of government, see Harvey Flaumenhaft, *The Effective Republic: Administration and Constitution in the Thought of Alexander Hamilton* (Durham: Duke University Press, 1992), pp. 75–81, quotation at p. 78.

26. On the "love of fame" as a spur to virtuous conduct, see the essays in *The Noblest Minds*.

27. On the unprofessional and self-interested nature of politics in America following the Revolution, see Rakove, *Beginnings of National Politics*; and Gordon S. Wood, *The Radicalism of the American Revolution* (New York: Vintage, 1991).

28. Henry St. John, Viscount Bolingbroke, "The Idea of a Patriot King," in *Political Writings,* ed. David Armitage (Cambridge: Cambridge University Press, 1997).

29. John Brown Cutting, "Letter to William Short," November 3, 1787 (*DHRC,* XIV, 461).

30. Thomas Jefferson, "Letter to Uriah Forrest," December 31, 1787 (*DHRC,* XIV, 488).

31. Thomas Lee Shippen to William Shippen Jr., November 20, 1787 (*DHRC,* XIV, 469).

32. Patrick Henry, The Virginia Convention, June 5, 1788 (*DHRC,* IX, 963).

33. As J. G. A. Pocock points out, one of the core senses of republican government was simply that of a kingless state. Pocock, "States, Republics, and Empires: The American Founding in Early Modern Perspective," in *Conceptual Change and the Constitution,* ed. Terence Ball and J. G. A. Pocock (Lawrence: University Press of Kansas, 1988), p. 61. Pocock distinguishes the concept of "kinship" from "monarchy," only the latter of which, he suggests, was compatible with the idea of republican government, as evidenced by references to mixed governments as republics. That is why Pocock considers the president a monarch, "in the sense in which that term was used in the old vocabulary of mixed government: a single person who is ultimately responsible for the exercise of executive authority in a republic of separated powers," p. 73. That is the sense in which I refer to the president as a monarch, too, although I disagree with the suggestion that Americans would have considered a monarchical institution compatible with the republican form of government. Even if we grant the traditional compatibility of monarchy with a republic as part of a mixed system, that arrangement was predicated on a recognition and division of distinct and permanent classes in society, a proposition that was anathema to most Americans in this period.

34. Pauline Maier writes that "disillusionment with monarchy was the major component of the new republicanism." Maier, *From Resistance to Revolution: Colonial Radicals and the Development of American Opposition to Britain, 1765–1776* (New York: Vintage, 1974), pp. 287–96, quotation at p. 288. See also Zera S. Fink, *The Classical Republicans: An Essay in the Recovery of a Pattern of Thought in Seventeenth-Century England,* 2d ed. (Chicago: Northwestern University Press, 1962); and Pocock, *The*

Machiavellian Moment: Florentine Political Thought and the Atlantic Republican Tradition (Princeton: Princeton University Press, 1975).

35. "Cato IV," *New York Journal*, November 8, 1787 (*DHRC*, XIV, 10). Like others, "Cato" thought that the president was virtually indistinguishable from the British monarch, for "wherein does this president, invested with his powers and prerogatives, essentially differ from the king of Great-Britain" (*DHRC*, XIV, 10). In his next essay, "Cato" reiterated his belief "that the president possessed of the power, given him by this frame of government differs but very immaterially from the establishment of monarchy in Great-Britain" (*DHRC*, XIV, 182).

36. See the introduction to *The Antifederalists*, ed. Cecilia Kenyon (Boston: Northeastern University Press, 1985), p. cii.

37. George Clinton approvingly cited the advice of Demosthenes: "Distrust. Of this be mindful; to this adhere; preserve this carefully, and no calamity can affect you." "Cato," VII, *The Antifederalists*, p. 321. On this theme, see the classic study by Cecilia Kenyon, "Men of Little Faith: The Anti-Federalists on the Nature of Representative Government," *William and Mary Quarterly*, Vol. 12, No. 1 (1955).

38. James Winthrop, "Agrippa," XVII, *The Antifederalists*, p. 151.

39. Samuel Bryan, "Centinel," I, *The Antifederalists*, p. 4.

40. "Montezuma," *The Antifederalists*, p. 64, emphasis in original.

41. George Clinton, "Cato," IV, *The Antifederalists*, pp. 305, 306.

42. "Americanus II," *Virginia Independent Chronicle*, December 19, 1787 (*DHRC*, VIII, 245).

43. Francis Corbin, The Virginia Convention, June 19, 1788 (*DHRC*, X, 1391). It should be noted that a small handful of Anti-Federalists did accept de Lolme's logic and approved the unity of the chief executive. For an example, see "Cincinnatus IV," November 22, 1787 (*DHRC*, XIV, 191).

44. The *locus classicus* for the idea that collective judgment is superior to the judgment of a single expert appears in Aristotle, *The Politics*, rev. ed., trans. Ernest Barker (Oxford: Oxford University Press, 1995), pp. 108–11, 124–25.

45. Hamilton asseverated that "decision, activity, secrecy, and dispatch will generally characterize the proceedings of one man in a much more eminent degree than the proceedings of any greater number." Reason, good sense, and "historical research" all demonstrate the propriety of vesting the executive power in a single person (LXX, 403, 404).

46. George Mason, "Letter to John Lamb," June 9, 1788 (*DHRC*, IX, 818).

47. Wilson reiterated this point in the Pennsylvania Ratifying Convention and throughout his *Lectures on Law*. See also James Wilson, *Collected Works of James Wilson*, ed. Kermit Hall and Mark David Hall (Indianapolis: Liberty Fund, 2008), pp. 236.

48. James Monroe, "Some Observations on the Constitution" (*DHRC*, IX, p. 865).

49. James Wilson, Remarks in the Pennsylvania Convention, December 4, 1787, *Collected Works of James Wilson*, Vol. I, p. 236.

50. James Iredell, "Marcus II," February 27, 1788 (*DHRC*, XVI, 246).

51. Ibid., pp. 246, 247.

52. On the preferences of English republicans like John Milton and Henry Neville for a plural executive, see Fink, *Classical Republicans*.

53. Prior to the Constitutional Convention, some eventual Federalists began flirting with the idea of monarchy in America. Noah Webster indicated the differences between a republic and a monarchy in terms of their respective defects when he wrote in 1786, "I should infinitely prefer a limited monarchy, for I would sooner be subject to the caprice of one man, than to the ignorance and passions of a multitude" (*DHRC*, XIII, 169). Those Federalists at least nominally committed to republicanism admitted the tension between a single executive and republican ideals. For instance, in his notorious speech of June 18, in which he proposed an upper legislative branch and a single executive for life, Hamilton admitted the difficulty of reconciling executive power of any sort with "Republican principles" (Farrand I, 289).

54. "Federal Farmer: An Additional Number of Letters to the Republican," Letter XIV, January 17, 1788 (*DHRC*, XVII, 328).

55. Tench Coxe, "Letter to James Madison," September 27, 1787 (*DHRC*, XIII, 251).

56. On Hamilton's appropriation of monarchical rhetoric in theorizing executive power, see William E. Scheuerman, "American Kingship? Monarchical Origins of Modern Presidentialism," *Polity*, Vol. 37, No. 1 (2005), pp. 34–46.

57. James H. Hutson, ed., *The Supplement to Max Farrand's The Records of the Federal Convention of 1787* (New Haven: Yale University Press, 1987), p. 109.

58. Richard Henry Lee, "Letter to John Lamb," June 27, 1788 (*DHRC*, IX, 826).

59. Wilson, Remarks in the Pennsylvania Convention, December 1, 1787, *Collected Works of James Wilson*, Vol. I, p. 205.

60. Ibid., Vol. I, p. 703.

61. Bernard Manin, *The Principles of Representative Government* (Cambridge: Cambridge University Press, 1997), pp. 1–7, 42–93; quotation at p. 2. On the use of lot and rotation in democracy, see pp. 27–31.

62. The classic account of this thesis is Charles A. Beard, *An Economic Interpretation of the Constitution of the United States* (New York: Free Press, 1986).

63. Cf. Diamond, who argues that "the Founding Fathers' belief that they had created a system of institutions and an arrangement of the passions and interests, that would be durable and self-perpetuating, helps explain their failure to make provision for men of their own kind to come after them" in "Democracy and *The Federalist*," p. 68. For a useful corrective to this reading of the *Federalist* 10, see Alan Gibson, "Impartial Representation and the Extended Republic: Towards a Comprehensive and Balanced Reading of the Tenth *Federalist* Paper," *History of Political Thought*, Vol. 12, No. 2 (1991), which gives more attention to the selection of legislative representatives rather than the president, but supports the general point made here.

64. Douglass Adair established the intellectual link between *Federalist* 10 and Hume's political philosophy in "'That Politics May Be Reduced to a Science': David

Hume, James Madison and the Tenth Federalist," in *Fame and the Founding Fathers: Essays by Douglass Adair,* ed. Trevor Colbourn (Indianapolis: Liberty Fund, 1998). Adair's essay is still the starting point for any study of the connection between these thinkers, but, as argued in chapter 4, it does overstate somewhat the predictive purposes of the "science of politics."

65. Jay reiterated this point in the next paper: "One government can collect and avail itself of the talents and experience of the ablest men" (IV, 99).

66. Hamilton echoed these sentiments in the New York Ratifying Convention. See his speech of June 21, 1788, in *The Papers of Alexander Hamilton,* ed. Harold C. Syrett (New York: Columbia University Press, 1962), Vol. V, p. 38.

67. Some of these themes are discussed more fully in David F. Epstein, *The Political Theory of the Federalist* (Chicago: University of Chicago Press, 1984).

68. Hamilton favored what he called "a tertiary election" of the president that was even more indirect than the system finally adopted, which he considered as only a "secondary" mode (Farrand III, 617). It is worth noting that Hamilton had expressed an interest in an indirect mode of elections for executives as early as 1777. See his letter to Gouverneur Morris, May 19, 1777, *Papers of Alexander Hamilton,* Vol. I, p. 255.

69. On enlargement as one of the primary purposes of representation, see Garry Wills, *Explaining America: The Federalist* (Garden City, NY: Doubleday, 1981), pp. 231–37. James Wilson implied a linkage between the representative character of the presidency and "the qualities of freedom, wisdom and energy" in his critique of "the executive power of Great Britain." See his Remarks in the Pennsylvania Convention, *Collected Works of James Wilson,* Vol. I, p. 183.

70. George Washington, "Letter to John Armstrong, Sr.," April 25, 1788 (*DHRC*, XVII, 214).

71. Robert Yates, "Brutus," in Herbert Storing, *The Anti-Federalist: Writings by the Opponents of the Constitution,* abridged by Murray Dry (Chicago: University of Chicago Press, 1981), p. 114. On the predominant Anti-Federalist theory of representation, see Cecilia Kenyon, *The Antifederalists,* pp. li–lvi.

72. William Findley, "Hampden," February 16, 1788 (*DHRC*, II, 666).

73. Wilson, Remarks in the Pennsylvania Convention, *Collected Works of James Wilson,* Vol. I, p. 231.

74. See Diamond, "Democracy and *The Federalist*," and "The Federalist," in *History of Political Philosophy,* ed. Leo Strauss and Joseph Cropsey (Chicago: Rand McNally, 1963); Pocock, *Machiavellian Moment,* ch. 15; Daniel Walker Howe, "The Language of Faculty Psychology in *The Federalist Papers*," in *Conceptual Change and the Constitution,* ed. Ball and Pocock; and Charles R. Kesler, who downplays, but does not deny entirely the role of virtue in statesmen in "*Federalist* 10 and American Republicanism," in *Saving the Revolution: The Federalist Papers and The American Founding* (New York: Free Press, 1987). Richard Loss contrasts Washington's commitment to virtue with what he calls the "institutionalism and moral skepticism" of "Publius" in "The Political Thought of President George Washington," *Presidential Studies Quarterly,*

Vol. 19, No. 3 (1989), p. 483. Although James Ceasar notes that the system of presidential selection was expected to rely on virtue, he places the greatest emphasis on institutional mechanisms that channel the president's ambition in positive directions. See his "Presidential Selection" in *The Presidency in the Constitutional Order,* ed. Joseph M. Bessette and Jeffrey Tulis (Baton Rouge: Louisiana State University Press, 1981), pp. 238, 242–43, 251.

75. The Virginia Convention, June 9, 1788 (*DHRC,* IX, 1064). Not a single Federalist in any of the ratifying conventions refuted the accusation of moral elitism, but they vigorously denied the charge that personal character was the only check on representatives.

76. Madison, *Madison: Writings,* pp. 79–80.

77. The anonymous "State Soldier" stated that, of the "many accomplishments which are necessary to entitle men to the presidency," a "general reputation throughout the continent, both military and political . . . will be sufficient recommendations." See Essay II in *Friends of the Constitution,* pp. 122, 123.

78. On the circulation and criticism of McKean's remarks, see *DHRC,* II, 421.

79. Thomas McKean, Speech at the Pennsylvania Convention, November 28, 1787 (*DHRC,* II, 418).

80. See criticisms in "Poplicola," *Boston Gazette,* December 24, 1787, and in "Centinel XIII," *Philadelphia Independent Gazetteer,* January 3, 1788 (*DHRC,* XV, 72, 507).

81. Peletiah Webster, "A Citizen of Philadelphia" (*DHRC,* XIV, 74), emphasis in original. Compare this passage to Madison's explication of the "aim of every political constitution" in *Federalist* 57, quoted two paragraphs below.

82. Ibid., pp. 193, 187, 194.

83. Edmund Pendleton, "Letter to Richard Henry Lee," June 14, 1788 (*DHRC,* XVIII, 182).

84. Marcus Tullius Cicero, *On the Commonwealth,* trans. George Holland Sabine and Stanley Barney Smith (New York: Macmillan, 1976), p. 133.

85. Andrew Sabl, *Ruling Passions: Political Offices and Democratic Ethics* (Princeton: Princeton University Press, 2002), p. 46.

86. On the Anti-Federalists' political suspicions and distrust of power generally, see Kenyon, "Men of Little Faith."

87. William Grayson, The Virginia Convention, June 18, 1788 (*DHRC,* X, 1372); and Patrick Henry, The Virginia Convention, June 14, 1788 (*DHRC,* X, 1277).

88. George Mason, The Virginia Convention, June 18, 1788 (*DHRC,* X, 1376).

89. Patrick Henry, The Virginia Convention, June 9, 1788 (*DHRC,* IX, 1062).

90. James Monroe, The Virginia Convention, June 18, 1788 (*DHRC,* X, 1371, 1372).

91. Patrick Henry, The Virginia Convention, June 14, 1788 (*DHRC,* X, 1277).

92. Decades later, Jefferson endorsed the view that the Constitution provided a system whereby citizens could separate "the wheat from the chaff" so that "they will elect the real good and wise" rather than the "psuedo-aristoi" of wealth and birth. Thomas Jefferson, Letter to John Adams, October 28, 1813, *Jefferson: Writings,* ed. Merrill D. Peterson (New York: Library of America, 1984), p. 1306. Jefferson also

confirmed Madison's theory about the aim of government. "May we not even say that that form of government is the best which provides the most effectually for a pure selection of these natural aristoi into the offices of government?" p. 1306.

93. "Brutus IV," in *Anti-Federalists*, pp. 129–30.

94. Thomas Paine singled out this fact in making the case for the superiority of the presidency compared to monarchy in *The Rights of Man*. See *Thomas Paine Reader*, p. 283.

95. Tench Coxe, "An American Citizen I: On the Federal Government," September 26, 1787 (*DHRC*, XIII, 250).

96. In a draft of an essay that never became part of the *Federalist* series, Jay praised the framers for establishing an age requirement for the president, which would help identify those "men who had become eminently distinguished by their vertue and Talents," as opposed to "those brilliant appearances of Genius and Patriotism which like transient Meteors sometimes mislead as well as dazzle" (*DHRC*, XVI, 315).

97. James Iredell, "Marcus III," March 5, 1788 (*DHRC*, XVI, 325).

98. On the concept of disinterestedness as an important eighteenth-century prerequisite for leadership, see Gordon Wood, "Interests and Disinterestedness in the Making of the Constitution." In contrast to Wood's account, which emphasizes the continuity of Federalist thought with classical republicanism, I would highlight the postrepublican quality of Federalist thought inasmuch as it abandons hope for genuine disinterestedness among any but the elite.

99. James Madison, Letter to George Nicholas, May 17, 1788 (*DHRC*, XVIII, 27).

100. Forrest McDonald, *The Presidency of George Washington* (New York: W.W. Norton, 1974), p. 25.

101. Bruce Ackerman, *The Failure of the Founding Fathers: Jefferson, Marshall, and the Rise of Presidential Democracy* (Cambridge: Belknap Press, 2005), p. 5.

102. "A Native of Virginia: Observations upon the Proposed Plan of Federal Government," April 2, 1788 (*DHRC*, IX, 668).

103. Wilson, The Pennsylvania Convention, December 1, 1787 (*DHRC*, II, 452).

104. Wilson, The Pennsylvania Convention, December 11, 1787 (*DHRC*, II, 567).

105. "An Impartial Citizen V," February 28, 1788 (*DHRC*, VIII, 432), emphasis added. In the North Carolina Convention Davie explained that because the president would be "elected by the people of the United States at large, [he] will have their general interest at heart" (Farrand III, 348).

106. George Nicholas, The Virginia Convention, June 18, 1788 (*DHRC*, X, 1381), emphasis added.

107. George Nicholas, The Virginia Convention, June 10, 1788 (*DHRC*, IX, 1130–31).

108. *Philadelphia Freeman's Journal*, October 3, 1787 (*DHRC*, XIII, 309).

109. Roger Sherman, Unaddressed Letter, December 8, 1787 (*DHRC*, XIV, 387).

110. James Wilson, "Oration in Philadelphia," July 4, 1788 (*DHRC*, XVIII, 245–46). On Wilson's view of voting as a constitutive exercise of civic patriotism, see

Daniel J. McCarthy, "James Wilson and the Creation of the Presidency," *Presidential Studies Quarterly*, Vol. 17, No. 4 (1987).

111. "The Republican: To the People," *Connecticut Courant*, January 7, 1788 (*DHRC*, III, 531, 532).

112. "If a free authority [Machiavelli's term for discretionary power] is given for a long time—calling a long time one year or more—it will always be dangerous and will have either good or bad effects according as those to whom it is given are bad or good." Niccolò Machiavelli, *Discourses on Livy*, ed. Harvey C. Mansfield and Nathan Tarcov (Chicago: University of Chicago Press, 1996), p. 76.

113. The governors of New York and Massachusetts were elected to three-year terms, but most state constitutions established terms of only two years. On the terms of office of governors at the time of the Constitutional Convention, see Thach, *Creation of the Presidency*, p. 28.

114. William Grayson, The Virginia Convention, June 18, 1788 (*DHRC*, X, 1374).

115. "A Native of Virginia: Observations upon the Proposed Plan of Federal Government," April 2, 1788 (*DHRC*, IX, 679).

116. Nicholas Collin, "A Foreign Spectator XXV," in *Friends of the Constitution*, pp. 49–50.

117. Even though the paper in which Hamilton made these arguments does not so much as mention the veto power, the implication is clear enough: the veto power should not be reserved only for unconstitutional acts.

118. On Burke's theory of statesmanship, see Harvey C. Mansfield Jr., *Statesmanship and Party Government: A Study of Burke and Bolingbroke* (Chicago: University of Chicago Press, 1965).

119. "An Officer of the Late Continental Army," *Independent Gazetteer*, November 6, 1787 (*DHRC*, II, 212).

120. George Mason, The Virginia Convention, June 17, 1788 (*DHRC*, X, 1365, 1366).

121. *Winchester Virginia Gazette*, March 7, 1788 (*DHRC*, VIII, 471–72).

122. Luther Martin, "Genuine Information IX," *Baltimore Maryland Gazette*, January 29, 1788 (*DHRC*, XV, 494).

123. "The Impartial Examiner I," *Virginia Independent Chronicle*, March 5, 1788 (*DHRC*, VIII, 464).

124. Luther Martin, "Genuine Information IX," *Baltimore Maryland Gazette*, January 29, 1788 (*DHRC*, XV, 496, 497).

125. In an "Address to the People of the United States" in January 1787, Benjamin Rush listed the frequency of rotation as one of the four major defects of the Articles. Reprinted in *Friends of the Constitution*, p. 2.

126. See especially the debate that took place on June 23 (Farrand I, 84–96).

127. George Washington to Marquis de Lafayette, Mount Vernon, April 28 and May 1, 1788 (*DHRC*, XVII, 235). On the Roman recourse to dictators as a fine republican remedy for "urgent dangers," see Machiavelli, *Discourses on Livy*, pp. 73–75. On the superiority of a republic because "it can accommodate itself better than one prince can to the diversity of times through the diversity of the citizens that are in it," see p. 240.

128. The classic discussion of the differences between these competing conceptions of equality is in Aristotle, *The Nicomachean Ethics,* and *The Politics,* Book III, ch. XII.

129. Madison reminded Jefferson that without the prospect of reelection, it would be very difficult to entice "the most distinguished characters from aspiring to the office" (*DHRC,* XIII, 444). Charles Cotesworth Pinckney, in contrast, favored the possibility of reelection for the more democratic reason that it would be "imprudent" to remove "a man whose talents, abilities, and integrity, were such as to render him the object of the general choice of his country" (Farrand III, 256).

130. It is noteworthy that Hamilton used almost exactly the same language that Gouverneur Morris did at the Convention to describe the motivations of the executive: "The love of fame is the great spring to noble & illustrious actions" (Farrand II, 53).

131. Adair, *Fame and the Founding Fathers,* p. 10. Adair points out that the pursuit of fame, like the related goals of honor and glory, was "both the goal of character formation and an instrument of social control, building into the heart and mind of an individual a powerful sense of socially expected conduct," p. 13. On "The Love of Fame as an Inspiration to Virtue," see Rahe, "Fame, Founders," pp. 5–10.

132. David Hume, *Essays: Moral, Political, and Literary,* rev. ed., ed. Eugene F. Miller (Indianapolis: Liberty Fund, 1985), p. 82.

133. On Adams's views of the salutary "passion for distinction," see Bruce Miroff, "John Adams and the Presidency," in *Inventing the American Presidency,* ed. Thomas E. Cronin (Lawrence: University Press of Kansas, 1989), quotation at p. 306.

134. The first was in conjunction with the "valor" of the militia during the Revolutionary War (XXV, 195), and the other appeared in the context of presidential impeachment (LXV, 382). Hamilton was responsible for each of the references, which are in one way or another related to some aspect of matters pertaining to executive power.

135. At the Convention, Franklin optimistically expressed the related idea that honor alone would be the greatest inducement to the office (Farrand I, 84).

136. Martin Diamond conflates these divergent passions when he refers to "love of power or fame" as if they were the same thing. See "The Federalist," p. 586.

137. Adair, *Fame and the Founding Fathers,* pp. 34, 33.

138. Rahe, "Fame, Founders," pp. 16–29.

139. Even though Howe detects a sharp distinction between reason and passion in the *Federalist,* he notes that the authors sometimes used the term "self-interest" to refer to a "partial, short-term, and passionate" motive and sometimes to refer to "collective, long-range, and rational." Howe, "The Language of Faculty Psychology in *The Federalist Papers,*" in *Conceptual Change and the Constitution,* ed. Ball and Pocock, p. 111.

140. Madison recorded Hamilton as saying that "we ought to go as far in order to attain stability and permanency, as republican principles will admit," so one branch of the legislature and the executive should "be for life" (Farrand I, 289).

141. On Washington's reputation as the "embodiment" of republican virtue, see Gordon S. Wood, *Revolutionary Characters: What Made the Founders Different* (New York: Penguin, 2006), pp. 31–63.

142. Patrick Henry, Virginia Ratifying Convention, June 9, 1788 (*DHRC*, IX, 1062).

143. Russell L. Hanson, "Democracy," in *Political Innovation and Conceptual Change*, ed. Terence Ball, James Farr, and Russell L. Hanson (Cambridge: Cambridge University Press, 1989), p. 77.

CHAPTER 7: Conclusion

1. Thomas Jefferson to John B. Colvin, September 20, 1810, *Jefferson: Writings*, ed. Merrill D. Peterson (New York: Library of America, 1984), p. 1231, emphasis added.

2. Stephen Holmes, *The Anatomy of Antiliberalism* (Cambridge: Harvard University Press, 1993), p. 59, emphasis in original.

3. David Hume, *The History of England* (Indianapolis: Liberty Fund, 1983), Vol. V, p. 329.

4. On the context in which these acts were passed, see Stanley Elkins and Eric McKitrick, *The Age of Federalism: The Early American Republic, 1788–1800* (Oxford: Oxford University Press, 1993).

5. Frank Church and Charles Mathias, *A Brief History of Emergency Powers in the United States: A Working Paper Prepared for the Special Committee on National Emergencies and Delegated Emergency Powers United States Senate*, 93d Cong. 2d Sess. (1974), p. v.

6. For an overview of the background to and subsequent history of the National Emergencies Act, see Harold C. Relyea, "National Emergency Powers," Congressional Research Service Report for Congress (updated August 30, 2001). Available at www.fas.org/sgp/crs/natsec/98–505.pdf.

7. David Cole, "The Priority of Morality: The Emergency Constitution's Blind Spot," *Yale Law Journal*, Vol. 113, No. 8 (2004), p. 1765.

8. Bruce Ackerman, *Before the Next Attack: Preserving Civil Liberties in an Age of Terrorism* (New Haven: Yale University Press, 2006), pp. 124–25, 196–98.

9. Alexander Hamilton, Speech in the New York Ratifying Convention, *Hamilton: Writings*, ed. Joanne B. Freeman (New York: Library of America, 2001), p. 505; and Jefferson to John B. Colvin, *Jefferson: Writings*, p. 1231.

10. Contrary to the account developed here, Scott M. Matheson Jr. treats the concept of emergency as a "continuum" that ranges "from discrete and apparently temporary to chronic and seemingly unending." See *Presidential Constitutionalism in Perilous Times* (Cambridge: Harvard University Press, 2009), p. 9.

11. Kim Lane Scheppele, *The International State of Emergency: Challenges to Constitutionalism after September 11* (forthcoming).

12. The single best overview and critique of this strategy is Jack Goldsmith, *The Terror Presidency: Law and Judgment inside the Bush Administration* (New York: W. W.

Norton, 2007). See also Office of Legal Counsel statement justifying the president's use of the National Security Agency to intercept international communications involving persons with suspected links to terrorist organizations in U.S. Department of Justice, "Legal Authorities Supporting the Activities of the National Security Agency Described by the President," January 19, 2006, available at www.usdoj.gov/opa/whitepaperonnsalegalauthorities.pdf.

13. See Carl Schmitt, *On the Three Types of Juristic Thought*, trans. Joseph Bendersky (Westport, CT: Praeger, 2004); Carl Schmitt, *Political Theology*, trans. George Schwab (Chicago: University of Chicago Press, 2005); Andrew Norris, "Carl Schmitt's Political Metaphysics: On the Secularization of 'the Outermost Sphere,'" *Theory and Event*, Vol. 4, No. 1 (2000); and Paul Hirst, "Carl Schmitt's Decisionism," in *The Challenge of Carl Schmitt*, ed. Chantal Mouffe (New York: Verso, 1999).

14. Jefferson to John B. Colvin, *Jefferson: Writings*, p. 1233.

15. Richard A. Posner, *Not a Suicide Pact: The Constitution in a Time of National Emergency* (Oxford: Oxford University Press, 2006), p. 68.

16. On the secret legal memos arguing that the president's national security powers could trump the limitations specified in the First Amendment, the Fourth Amendment, the Posse Comitatus Act, and other laws, see Neil A. Lewis, "Memos Reveal Scope of the Power Bush Sought," *New York Times*, March 2, 2009.

17. Quoted in Cole, "Priority of Morality," p. 1773.

18. Ackerman, *Before the Next Attack*, pp. 13–38.

19. Ibid., p. 5.

20. Oren Gross, "What 'Emergency' Regime?" *Constellations*, Vol. 13, No. 1 (2006), p. 74.

21. See, for example, Alexander Hamilton, *The Federalist Papers*, ed. Isaac Kramnick (New York: Penguin Books, 1987), LXXVII, p. 435.

22. See Gross, "What 'Emergency' Regime?" p. 78; Gross and Aoláin, *Law in Times of Crisis*, p. 64; and Posner, *Not a Suicide Pact*, p. 5.

23. Some of these problems are discussed in Cole, "Priority of Morality," pp. 1768–73.

24. *Youngstown Sheet & Tube Co. v. Sawyer*, 343 U.S. 579 (1952), p. 650.

25. Gross and Aoláin, *Law in Times of Crisis*, p. 82.

26. David Dyzenhaus, *The Constitution of Law: Legality in a Time of Emergency* (Cambridge: Cambridge University Press, 2006), p. 42.

27. Jules Lobel, "Emergency Power and the Decline of Liberalism," *Yale Law Journal*, Vol. 98, No. 7 (1989), pp. 1412–18.

28. On the tendency of emergency legislation to spill over and establish a "new normalcy," see Giorgio Agamben, *State of Exception*, trans. Kevin Attell (Chicago: University of Chicago Press, 2005); Dyzenhaus, *The Constitution of Law*; Cole, "Priority of Morality," pp. 1769–75; and Gross and Aoláin, *Law in Times of Crisis*, pp. 174–80.

29. On the different concerns of these two Founders, see Clement Fatovic, "Constitutionalism and Presidential Prerogative: Jeffersonian and Hamiltonian Perspectives," *American Journal of Political Science*, Vol. 48, No. 3 (2004).

30. On Lincoln's emergency actions and his invocation of necessity as a justification, see Clinton Rossiter, *Constitutional Dictatorship: Crisis Government in the Modern Democracies* (New Brunswick, NJ: Transaction Publishers, 2002), pp. 223–39; Daniel Farber, *Lincoln's Constitution* (Chicago: University of Chicago Press, 2003); and Benjamin A. Kleinerman, "Lincoln's Example: Executive Power and the Survival of Constitutionalism," *Perspectives on Politics*, Vol. 3, No. 4 (2005).

31. Quoted in Richard M. Pious, *The American Presidency* (New York: Basic Books, 1979), p. 59.

32. On the development of the party system within the first decade of government under the Constitution, see Richard Hofstadter, *The Rise of a Party System: The Rise of Legitimate Opposition in the United States, 1780–1840* (Berkeley: University of California Press, 1969), pp. 40–121; and Elkins and McKitrick, *Age of Federalism*.

33. Hofstadter, *Rise of a Party System*, p. 48.

34. On the need to govern "without parties," see Theodore J. Lowi, *The Personal President: Power Invested, Promise Unfulfilled* (Ithaca: Cornell University Press, 1985), pp. 67–96.

35. Perception—or misperception, as the case may be—obviously plays an important part in politics, but the important point to bear in mind is that perceptions of moral turpitude or deficiencies in virtue will often have some basis in fact now that investigative journalism and media interest in politicians' personal lives have become staples of contemporary politics. Deliberate distortions and misrepresentations are always possible, but presidential candidates with skeletons in their closets open themselves up to vigorous and sustained attacks on their character that are typically much more difficult to rebut than fabricated or exaggerated reports of vice.

36. Locke, *Two Treatises of Government* (II, § 165).

37. See James P. Pfiffner, "Sexual Probity and Presidential Character," *Presidential Studies Quarterly*, Vol. 28, No. 4 (1998), p. 885.

38. Erwin Hargrove, *The President as Leader: Appealing to the Better Angels of Our Nature* (Lawrence: University Press of Kansas, 1998), p. 186.

39. In light of the way Clinton responded to the June 25, 1996, bombing of the Khobar Towers in Saudi Arabia, which occurred before the impeachment crisis, it is possible that he might not have taken aggressive action in response to the subsequent attacks. Nevertheless, the point of this discussion is that pervasive distrust of Clinton hampered his ability to wield the full powers at his disposal as Commander-in-Chief. On Clinton's antiterrorist policies, see Barton Gellman, "Terrorism Wasn't a Top Priority," *Washington Post National Weekly Edition*, January 14–20, 2002, pp. 9–11.

40. Pfiffner, "Sexual Probity and Presidential Character," p. 885.

41. Jack Goldsmith, *Terror Presidency*, pp. 19, 26.

42. Even when there were credible threats, it appears that the administration exploited some of those threats for political gain. See Ron Suskind, *The One Percent Doctrine: Deep Inside America's Pursuit of Its Enemies since 9/11* (New York: Simon and Schuster, 2006), pp. 326–28, 336, 340–41.

43. Mimi Hall, "Ridge Reveals Clashes on Alerts," *USA Today*, May 10, 2005.

44. Gross and Aoláin, *Law in Times of Crisis*, p. 265–89.

45. Goldsmith, *Terror Presidency*, pp. 80–82; 102.

46. Ibid., p. 123. This expansive notion of executive power is perhaps best exemplified by former deputy assistant attorney general in the Office of Legal Counsel John Yoo in books such as *The Powers of War and Peace: The Constitution and Foreign Affairs after 9/11* (Chicago: University of Chicago Press, 2005) and *War by Other Means: An Insider's Account of the War on Terror* (New York: Atlantic Monthly Press, 2006).

47. Goldsmith, *Terror Presidency*, p. 139.

48. See Suskind, *One Percent Doctrine*; and Goldsmith, *Terror Presidency*, pp. 11–13, 71–76. John Yoo has protested that "many people have an exaggerated view of the role of law" and erroneously believe that the administration should "bend" to public pressure. Yoo, *War by Other Means*, pp. xii, 182.

49. Schmitt, *Political Theology*, pp. 11–15, 36–37.

50. This explains why liberals have been much more open to distinctions supposedly based on industry and effort, which are often externally measurable in economic terms. Wealth provides an ostensibly objective and uniform standard of measure that moral valuations (which are extremely difficult to reduce to a single measure) do not.

51. See John Stuart Mill, *On Liberty*, in *On Liberty and Other Essays*, ed. John Gray (Oxford: Oxford University Press, 1991); and Alexis de Tocqueville, *Democracy in America*, ed. and trans. Harvey C. Mansfield and Delba Winthrop (Chicago: University of Chicago Press, 2000).

52. Hamilton, *Federalist Papers*, LXVIII, p. 395.

53. See the discussion of conservative hagiography of George W. Bush in Jonathan Chait, "Right Reverent," *New Republic*, March 25, 2002, p. 14.

54. Joseph S. Nye Jr., *The Powers to Lead* (Oxford: Oxford University Press, 2008), p. 135.

55. This understanding of virtue as an instrument is what links the liberalism of virtue theorists like Locke to the liberalism of duty theorists like Kant. The historical irony is that the modern instrumentalization of virtue connected it even more closely to the good of the community than classical conceptions of virtue did.

56. On the importance of the ward system to Jefferson's political thought, see Hannah Arendt, *On Revolution* (New York: Penguin Books, 1963), pp. 248–55.

57. Thomas Jefferson to Samuel Kercheval, July 12, 1816, *Jefferson: Writings*, p. 1397.

Index

on executive, 155, 159, 170–72, 176, 179–81,
182–83, 191, 193, 194–95, 203, 219–21, 222,
238, 249; influences on, 30, 113, 125, 222; on
law, 161, 186; on rotation in office, 244, 249;
and science of politics, 163, 166, 167
constitutionalism: and Blackstone, 127, 129,
133–37, 140, 151; and Federalists, 160, 163,
196–97, 201, 210–11, 212, 216, 224; and
Hume, 83–84, 98, 122; and Locke, 41;
machinery of, 8, 23, 27–31, 276
Contarini, Gasparo, 23
Continental Congress, 162; defects of, 158,
160–61, 172, 174; powers of, 182
contingency: Blackstone on, 4, 16, 125, 127,
139, 146, 150–51, 257, 274; and executive, 2,
9, 13, 16–18, 35–36, 49, 50–52, 63, 119, 139,
186–87, 190–95, 258–59; Founders on,
162–64, 167, 178, 183, 185–95, 206, 215;
Hume on, 4, 85–86, 88–90, 98, 115–18, 119;
and law, 2, 3–4, 9, 12, 35–36, 41, 50–51, 63,
116, 119, 162, 192, 258–59, 274; in liberal
constitutionalism, 3–4, 10, 15–18, 122, 154,
254, 258–59, 274; Locke on, 15–16, 18, 41,
49–52, 56, 63, 68–69, 81, 85, 93, 259, 274,
291–92n43; Machiavelli on, 10, 11–13, 15–18,
50, 51–52, 85, 188, 192. *See also* emergency
Cooper, Anthony Ashley. *See* Shaftesbury,
First Earl of
courts: Blackstone on, 137; and deference to
executive, 6, 273; and emergencies, 2, 9, 10,
255–56; rulings of, 9, 254–55, 258, 273
Coxe, Tench, 208, 222, 235
crisis, distinguished from emergency, 256–57
Cromwell, Oliver, 86, 97, 111

Declaration of Indulgence, 44
de Lolme, Jean-Louis, 91, 140–41, 179, 219–22,
304n48, 316n47, 316n48
democracy: Blackstone on, 130, 152; and
emergency, 269, 273, 274; equality in,
274–76; executive as check on, 223, 242–43;
Founders on, 170, 223, 224, 237–38, 242–43;
and rule of law, 38
Dicey, A. V., 31, 134
Dickinson, John, 187
dictators, Roman, 15, 53, 58–59, 191, 192

dictatorship, proposed in America, 36, 174,
191–92, 204, 246
Diggins, John P., 28
dignity: presidential, 155, 196, 217, 222, 251,
268, 271; royal, 128–29, 141–46, 154–55, 222
disinterestedness, 20, 22, 24, 30, 73, 102, 104,
111, 195, 210–11, 213, 216, 237, 238, 266. *See
also* character; liberty: love of; patriotism;
virtue
Dissenters, 44–45
Dunn, John, 60
Dyzenhaus, David, 263

Edward I, 110
Edward II, 110
Electoral College, 213–14, 232, 235–40
elitism: in liberalism, 24–27, 29; of presidency,
198, 209, 217–18, 224, 226–27, 230–32,
234–35, 238, 252, 275–76; in representative
government, 224–35, 251–52
Elizabeth I, 109, 118–19
Ellsworth, Oliver, 245
emergency: Blackstone on, 125, 127, 146,
150–151; and character, 5–9, 17–19, 22,
72–73, 82, 122, 194–95, 214–15, 239, 243,
246, 250, 264–65, 268–69, 273; in common
law, 56; and Constitution, U.S., 9–10, 160,
186–94, 199, 246, 256, 262; distinguished
from crisis, 256–57; and executive, 2, 4–6,
16–19, 36, 39, 53–56, 82, 86, 150–51, 177,
186–95, 214–15, 221–22, 239, 243, 246, 250,
254–56, 257–65, 268–69, 273, 325n96;
Federalists on, 160, 186–95, 214–15, 221–22,
239, 246, 262, 268; Fortescue on, 42–43;
Founders on, 4, 160, 162, 186–95, 214–15,
246; Hume on, 4, 86, 115–18, 121, 122, 274;
and law, 2–6, 22, 33, 36, 41, 53–54, 86,
116–18, 121, 150–51, 160, 188–89, 192,
254–60, 262–64, 274; in liberal constitutionalism, 2–6, 8, 16–18, 33, 254, 274;
Locke on, 4–5, 36, 39, 41, 50, 52–56, 60, 65,
82, 86, 127, 256, 257, 261, 274; Machiavelli
on, 12, 17–18, 52; normalization of, 121,
261–64; parliamentarians on, 56; royalists
on, 43, 59; Sidney on, 58–59. *See also*
contingency